A Practical Introduction
to Software Design
with C++

WORLDWIDE
SERIES IN
COMPUTER
SCIENCE

SERIES EDITORS   **Professor Peter Wegner,** *Brown University, USA*

Professor David Barron, *Southampton University, UK*

The Worldwide Series in Computer Science has been created to publish textbooks which both address and anticipate the needs of an ever-evolving curriculum, thereby shaping its future. It is designed for undergraduates majoring in Computer Science and practitioners who need to reskill. Its philosophy derives from the conviction that the discipline of computing needs to produce technically skilled engineers who will inevitably face, and possibly invent, radically new technologies throughout their future careers. New media will be used innovatively to support high-quality texts written by leaders in the field.

Books in Series

Winder, *Developing Java Software*

Kotonya & Sommerville, *Requirements Engineering*

Goodrich & Tamassia, *Data Structures and Algorithms in Java*

Reiss, *A Practical Introduction to Software Design with C++*

Preiss, *Data Structures and Algorithms with Object-Oriented Design Patterns in C++*

Ammeraal, *Computer Graphics for Java Programmers*

Ercegovac, *Introduction to Digital Systems*

A Practical Introduction to Software Design with C++

Steven P. Reiss

Brown University
Providence, RI

JOHN WILEY & SONS, INC.

New York • Chichester • Weinheim • Brisbane • Toronto • Singapore

ACQUISITIONS EDITOR	Regina Brooks
MARKETING MANAGER	Katherine Hepburn
PRODUCTION EDITOR	Ken Santor
COVER DESIGNER	Harry Nolan

This book was set in New Century Schoolbook by the author and printed and bound by Quebecor - Fairfield, Inc. The cover was printed by Phoenix Color Corporation.

Recognizing the importance of preserving what has been written, it is a policy of John Wiley & Sons, Inc. to have books of enduring value published in the United States printed on acid-free paper, and we exert our best efforts to that end.

The paper in this book was manufactured by a mill whose forest management programs include sustained yield harvesting of its timberlands. Sustained yield harvesting principles ensure that the numbers of trees cut each year does not exceed the amount of new growth.

ISBN 0-471-24213-6

Printed in the United States of America

10 9 8 7 6 5 4 3 2 1

Dedicated to the many students and TAs who have worked with me in CS 32 so I could get this right, and to my family for putting up with my frustrations and foibles while writing.

Preface

The advanced programming course I have taught at Brown for about ten years is designed to follow an introductory programming sequence and to provide the background needed by the students in order to undertake serious programming projects in advanced courses, research, or actual jobs. It teaches the essential topics that are needed for serious programming but not generally covered in the earlier courses such as small-scale and large-scale object-oriented design, the ability to use a modern object-oriented programming language effectively (in this case C++), advanced programming concepts, user interface construction, debugging and testing, and basic software engineering. The course has a strong practical side, and the students actually design and implement significant projects during the semester. While there are individual books on each of the topics in the course, I have not found a single book that provided the right level of information on each subject with a strong practical bent. Thus I eventually broke down and undertook to write this one.

I designed this text to fit an intermediate-level programming course such as that described above. The text assumes the students have had a reasonable introductory programming sequence that includes basic programming and algorithms and data structures. At Brown, we teach Java in the introductory courses, but the text should be suitable for students with a C++ or procedural background as well. The book uses C++ rather than Java since C++ is still the language of choice for writing large systems and is still the basis for most advanced programming courses at Brown and elsewhere.

The text provides students with the tools and techniques that will enable them to be comfortable designing and implementing moderate-sized software systems alone or in a team, preparing them for more directed systems courses in specific areas such as databases, compilers, computer graphics, and software engineering, as well as for summer and full-time programming jobs.

The text assumes that the students have access to and familiarity with other books or manuals on the basic concepts of C++, a user interface framework such as Motif or Microsoft Foundation Classes, and a good suite of programming tools. If students have no C++ background, then a C++ text should probably accompany the first few chapters. Even with a C++ background, the students should have access to a language reference manual. A text, manual, or appropriate handouts are also needed to provide the details on the target interface for graphical user interfaces and the relevant programming environment. These additional works provide the raw materials that this text attempts to organize, integrate, and prescribe for the students.

OVERVIEW OF THE TEXT

The material is organized into sections, each concentrating on a particular topic, with some overlap. The basic topics include:

- *Object-Oriented Design* (Chapters 1, 2, 5, 6, 10, 13, 16): This is the primary focus of the text and in fact pervades most other chapters as well. The first two chapters provide an overview of object-oriented design and a detailed look at small-scale design. Chapter 5 extends this with issues related to class design, while Chapter 6 explores various notations used to express design. Chapter 11 covers the design issues related to user interfaces and Chapter 13 provides an overview to design patterns. Chapter 16 concludes the text by discussing issues in the design of larger systems.

- *Effective Use of C*++ (Chapters 3, 4, 7, 12): A secondary focus in teaching students to be good programmers is to make effective use of the language. Chapter 3 covers the implementation of an object-oriented design and Chapter 4 provides guidelines for using and not abusing C++. Chapter 7 covers the standard C++ libraries and the use of libraries in general, while Chapter 12 goes over building libraries and the use of C++ templates.

- *User Interfaces* (Chapters 9, 10, 11): Since most modern applications use a graphical user interface, it is essential that an advanced programming course cover enough material to enable the students to design and implement their own interfaces. Chapter 9 covers the basic concepts of graphical user interfaces. Chapter 10 covers the design and implementation issues related to building an actual interface. Chapter 11 then provides a set of guidelines for thinking about and evaluating user interfaces.

- *Advanced Programming Topics* (Chapters 10, 12, 14): Today's programmers need to be aware of new features and methodologies. Chapter 10 covers user-interface programming and Chapter 12 covers building libraries, including template libraries. Chapter 14 discusses multiple-process and multithreaded programming and the various interprocess communication and synchronization mechanisms needed for their support.

- *Software Engineering* (Chapters 8, 15, 16): This part of the text covers the material students need in order to use programming tools effectively and to plan and implement a group project. Chapter 8 describes the essentials of debugging and testing, providing practical suggestions to help the students with their own programs. Chapter 15 covers the basics of software engineering, emphasizing requirements and specifications. Finally, Chapter 16 discusses the design and management of larger software projects.

Each of these topics is treated in a practical, hands-on manner. Most chapters work through an example relevant to the material, using its concreteness to give the abstract principles a solid and understandable basis. The text is peppered with guidelines giving my best advice on how to build reasonable software systems. Complete code for the example of Chapters 2 and 3 and that of Chapter 7 is included in Appendices B and C, offering additional details to supplement the material in these chapters.

USE OF THE TEXT

This text was designed for an advanced programming/introductory software engineering course at Brown. The organization of the chapters in the text is essentially the one I use in class. The basic concepts of object-oriented design and implementation are taught early to give students the tools to implement actual programs. The first assignment is a simple program designed to familiarize the students with C++. Then, having gone through the material in Chapters 1 through 5, I assign a moderate-sized individual programming project (currently the control logic for a 3D pinball program). As the students work on this, I go through the material on design, libraries, debugging, and user interfaces. The next programming project involves developing a user interface and accompanying back end for a two-person project. While this project is under way, I cover most of the material in Chapters 12 through 14. The fourth programming project gives the students additional experience with user interfaces and an introduction to multiple-process programming. The last month of the course is occupied by a larger, four-person team project that the students select themselves and then specify and implement, which generally turns out to be a multiplayer game program. I cover the material in Chapters 15 and 16 while they are finishing up the previous program and starting to think about this project. Once this is done, the students give two in-class presentations, the first briefly describing what their project will do and the second describing its top-level design.

The material in the text can be used in other ways as well. Most of the chapters can, with only minor additions, be considered in a different order. The material on debugging, for example, can be easily moved either earlier or later in the course. Chapter 11 on user interface principles can be read earlier or omitted entirely, as can Chapters 12 and 14. Chapters 4 and 5 can be used before Chapters 2 and 3, but this makes it more difficult to start the students on a serious programming problem early in the course.

To provide supplementary material to this text, we have established a web site at:

http://www.cs.brown.edu/people/spr/designbook

We will be updating this site with corrections, suggestions, code, problems, etc., as appropriate. Contributions are encouraged.

ACKNOWLEDGMENTS

I would like to thank the many people who have read and commented on the material in this text. Notable among these is Scott Lewandowski, who suffered through the first draft of the whole text and offered helpful comments and suggestions throughout. Others who have given helpful comments include Henrik Christensen and Andrew Schulak. I am also very appreciative for the many suggestions I received from outside reviewers including Owen Astrachan, Duke University; Sallie Henry, Virginia Tech; Ronald McCarty, Pennsylvania State University at Erie; James Purtillo, University of Maryland at College Park; Edna Reiter, California State University at Hayward; and David Stotts, University of North Carolina at Chapel Hill. Finally I would like to thank Trina Avery for making the prose more readable.

Contents

Figures

Chapter 1

What Is Object-Oriented Design?

Design is a wondrous thing. Converting a vague concept into a working program is both challenging and rewarding. The challenge comes from the puzzles posed by the myriad details. The reward comes when you see something you produced being using by others. The wonder arises when you look back and question how you ever built it.

Today's software systems are some of the most complex items ever built. Designing such software is both difficult and fun. After analyzing and understanding a problem, you design the overall software system framework. You then break the system down into a variety of interacting components. In turn you break these down into classes, procedures and data structures. You then code these, debug them, test them, and debug them again. After lots of work and even more decisions, a final product emerges.

Learning to do software design takes these steps in the opposite order. You first learn to write code, algorithms, and data structures, the basic programming skills you are already comfortable with. This text takes you through the next steps. It starts with software design in the small, looking at techniques for building small packages or systems. From there, it steps up, using additional techniques to combine packages into larger packages and systems with features such as graphical user interfaces. Finally, it introduces yet more techniques for combining these systems into even larger ones. It does all this in an object-oriented framework using C++.

In this chapter we discuss what we mean by design and then describe the object-oriented approach to design and how it differs from other approaches. This description illustrates the basic techniques of object-oriented design and the basic principles of software design. The chapter concludes with an overview of the remainder of the text.

WHAT IS DESIGN?

Design in the most general sense is an abstract description of how something is built. The process of design is the process of making decisions on how the thing is built. It involves making tradeoffs between various alternatives, each of which have their strengths and weaknesses. Design involves finding the set

1

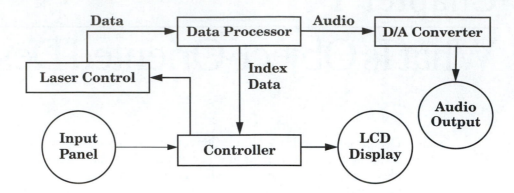

Figure 1-1 Block diagram of a CD player.

of alternatives most relevant to the problem, analyzing that set, and then choosing a subset of the alternatives that cooperatively solves the problem at hand in the "best" manner.

To consider what is involved in design, we look at descriptions given by three different people of how an audio CD player works. The first description looked at information encodings:

> A compact disk consists of a mirrored surface in a transparent plastic covering. The surface is divided into circular tracks and each track consists of a series of dots. Each dot can be either left as is or etched into a pit. In a CD player, this disk is spun at a relatively high rate and a low-powered laser is shone at a particular track. As each dot comes under the laser, the light is either reflected if the surface had been left mirrored or scattered if a pit had been etched. The CD player detects the presence or absence of the reflection and translates this into a one or a zero. By composing multiple bits into 16-bit words and treating the words as samples 44,000 times a second, the player can generate audio.

The second person gave a more functional description:

> A CD player works by reading a compact disk inserted into its drive bay. It converts digital audio information on the CD into an analog signal that is then sent to an amplifier. The player also reads an index off the disk to build an internal table of contents of the various tracks. This table is used to let the user control the order of play and to set up a digital display showing what the player is currently doing.

The third person went to the whiteboard and drew a diagram similar to Figure 1-1 with the following explanation:

> The center of the CD player is a controller. It takes commands from an input panel and shows its current state and other information through an LCD display. The actual compact disk is read by a laser control unit, which handles positioning the laser and determining what is currently being read. Data read by the laser is sent to a processor that separates index information for the con-

troller from audio data. Audio data is converted from digital form into an analog signal by a digital-to-analog converter.

Each of these three design descriptions has its uses. If you want to understand the details of how CDs are read and how information is stored on them, the first description is preferable. If you are more interested in using a CD player and want a top-level description of what it does, the second description is the most appropriate. And if you actually want to build a CD player, the third description is the most helpful. To understand why this is so, let's consider the notions of *abstraction* and *hierarchy* in design.

Abstraction and Hierarchy in Design

Any design, by necessity, starts with *abstraction*, the process of hiding details about an object while still describing its functionality. The first description above gives details about CDs and how information is stored on them, but abstracts or hides the details about everything else the CD player does. Even where it goes into detail, it omits information on the size of the pits, how the laser light is reflected or scattered, how the laser is positioned and detected, timing issues, etc. The second description essentially views the CD player as a black box that takes certain inputs and provides certain outputs: it offers a single abstraction that is the CD player itself. The third description is preferable as a general picture because it provides a more balanced set of abstractions. The various blocks in the diagram can be understood as performing specific functions that together create a working CD player. At the same time, one can go into more detail about how each of these components actually works.

Taking a problem and breaking it down into appropriate components is a central issue in design. The breakdown must let the programmer understand how the overall solution arises from the interaction of the various components. The components represent abstractions and can each be further described in terms of other, smaller components, which in turn can be described in terms of other components. This description of a system in terms of components and each component in terms of smaller components is called a *design hierarchy*.

Three factors affect the quality of the design in this process: the relative level of detail, the number of components at each level, and the final level of detail.

First, in a high-quality design the level of detail or granularity of the various components should be about the same. One reason the first description is not appropriate for building a CD player is that part of it is given at a much finer level of detail than the remainder. While all the details will eventually be necessary for building a CD player, they are not relevant to a top-level understanding. Moreover, as in the second example, few if any details are given about the remaining parts of the CD player and the reader gets little understanding of how the CD player actually works.

Second, the number of components should be reasonable. A problem with the second description is that it views the CD player as a single component and gives little new information. A description that separates a CD player into its 200 or so physical components would be similarly inappropriate: this is too much detail to give an overall understanding. The ideal number of components varies from problem to problem, but should in general be in the range of five to ten.

Third, the hierarchy of components should be terminated at an appropriate level. What this level is depends not on the problem, but rather on the audience for the design. A physicist might want to ignore the details of the CD player's software and instead focus on the physical operations of the laser. A mechanical engineer would worry about the circuitry for the controller and the mechanisms for positioning the laser, but would ignore the software and the physics behind the laser. A programmer would ignore most of the mechanical issues and instead focus on the inputs and outputs the controller has available. Similar situations arise when looking solely at a software system. Some components of the system might be already existing libraries or subsystems to be developed by others. These need only be viewed at a high level of abstraction. Components that actually will be implemented by the reader need to be examined at a finer level of detail. But even here, there is a limit. If the intended readers are competent programmers, there is no need to view components down to the statement level of a programming language. Instead, a reasonable stopping point would be the level at which the reader would feel comfortable implementing the design without further details.

Another design issue highlighted by the simple CD-player example is the form in which the design is presented. The first two explanations relied solely on textual descriptions; the third profited from using a diagram along with a description. Most designs are best understood from some sort of design diagram. While its exact form does not matter, it must be understandable by both the original author and any subsequent readers. This means that the diagram should be consistent and should be annotated. As we get more into design, we will cover standard forms of design diagrams including data-flow diagrams similar to Figure 1-1, class diagrams showing the static structure of a system, message-trace diagrams illustrating the dynamic behavior, and state diagrams showing control information.

Procedural and Data-Oriented Design

There are several different ways of using abstraction to break a problem into components in order to create a design. The earliest approach to software design, one still widely used, focuses on how the system works. This is *procedural* or *functional* design.

In procedural design one takes a problem and looks at what the system does and in what order it does it. Take the design of a screen editor. The editor operates by reading from the input terminal, translating the input into a com-

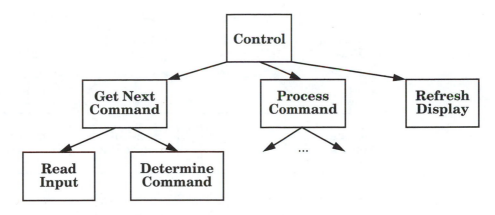

Figure 1-2 Top-level procedural design of a screen editor.

mand, processing the command, and then updating the display to reflect the results of the command. Figure 1-2 shows a corresponding procedural design. Here the node labeled `Control` represents the main loop of the editor and has three components underneath it. The first, `Get Next Command`, is responsible for reading and decoding input from the user to determine the proper command. The next component, which processes that input, would have lots of subcomponents, essentially one for each possible command. Finally, once the command has been processed, the `Refresh Display` component updates the display.

Procedural design works in terms of modules and procedures. The high-level components in Figure 1-2 would actually be implemented as a *module*, a related set of procedures and data. Each component would have one primary procedure. For example, the `Refresh Display` component would provide a top-level function to update the display. This function would call other functions in turn within that module to keep track of the current contents of the display, compare it to the new contents, and perform an intelligent update.

Procedural design works well for control-oriented applications: problems in which there is some specific order to what needs to be done and in which control, what the application is doing at any point, is more important than data. Such applications include command-driven systems and device controllers. However, most real-world problems do not have this form. Most problems addressed by today's software, including game programs, business applications, programming tools, and simulations, are more data-oriented than control-oriented: the input and output data and the transformations used to map the input to the output are more important in these problems than the actual control flow. Designs for these problems are best viewed in terms of data.

Data-oriented design breaks the problem into components by looking at the data flow implicit in the problem. To do this, one typically starts with a data-flow diagram describing the inputs and outputs of a system and how the data

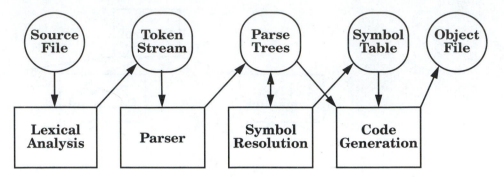

Figure 1-3 Simplified data-flow diagram of a compiler.

will be manipulated. For example, Figure 1-3 shows a data-flow diagram for a compiler. The starting point for the compiler is the source file. This is processed by the lexical analyzer, which converts the stream of characters from the file into a stream of *tokens*, logical units such as numbers, keywords, variables, or punctuation. This token stream is then processed by a parser, which identifies the various syntactic constructs such as statements, routines, or expressions. It generates a parse tree that represents the logical underlying structure of the program and is the basis for the later phases of the compiler. The first thing the compiler does after the parse tree is created is to analyze this tree in order to define all names created by the source and resolve all references to their appropriate definition. This is done in a symbol-resolution module, which creates a symbol table to store the definitions and modifies the parse trees to indicate which definition goes with each name. The final pass uses the modified parse trees and the symbol table to generate the resultant code and stores the result in an object file.

This data-flow diagram can be used directly to yield the components of a data-oriented design. Components are created for each transformation indicated in the diagram as well as for any specified data structures. In the case of Figure 1-3, there would be components for the four transformations and additional components for the token stream, parse trees, and symbol table. To refine this data-oriented design further, one could either use procedural analysis for the various components or create second-level data-flow diagrams to construct a more detailed data-oriented design.

OBJECT-ORIENTED DESIGN

Data-oriented design is preferable to procedure-oriented design for many problems because it lets one model the problem better and thus get a better understanding of the solution. However, it is limited to problems dealing with "real" data. The data in a data-oriented design is passive: it consists of numbers or strings or simple structures created by one box in the data-flow diagram and used by another. Data in real-world problems is often more complex than this.

For example, suppose we want to design an orrery, a program to simulate a solar system. We can start by describing the problem and how such a simulation should work:

> You are to write a program that simulates a solar system. The program will accept as input the initial location, mass, and velocity of the sun, each of the planets and their moons, and some set of asteroids and comets. The program should then simulate the specified solar system in action by repeatedly computing the next position of each of the specified bodies over a period ranging from hundreds to millions of years. The only force you need consider is the gravitational attraction between bodies. Do not worry about collisions.

> A solar system can be comprised of about one hundred bodies. The simulation of these bodies will proceed in discrete time steps. At each time step the total gravitational force on each body is computed by summing the gravitational attraction between that body and all other bodies. Then, using the current position, velocity, and this accumulated force, the next position is found. To make the computation more tractable given the large number of bodies, the bodies are grouped hierarchically into subsystems. This sharply reduces the number of necessary gravity computations at a small cost in accuracy. For example, in our solar system Jupiter and all its moons are considered as a single subsystem when computing its attraction with the distant Earth.

While this problem can be attacked either procedurally or using data flow, a more intuitive approach is to view it in terms of *active data*. In this case, each of the planetary bodies, the overall solar system, and each of the subsystems is a data element. These data elements maintain information about themselves and undertake actions. In this case there is one action, updating the positions and velocities for the next time step of all the planetary bodies corresponding to the data element. This action, applied to the solar system element, updates everything in the solar system by performing some magic computation and calling the same action on each constituent element to update the element in turn. At the lowest level, applying this action to an element representing a planetary body actually updates the data associated with that body.

Thinking of this problem in these terms, with objects that "know" how to do things, makes describing and understanding the potential solution much easier by making the solution more intuitive. This is the basis for object-oriented design.

Object-oriented design describes a solution to a problem in terms of active data elements called *objects*. Objects are a composition of data and actions. The data represents the state of the object. In the case of the solar system, the various planetary bodies are represented by objects containing the bodies' position, velocity and mass. The actions use the objects themselves as the basis for describing how the solution will work. This way an object is seen as a

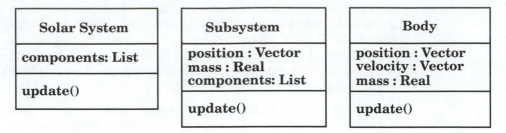

Figure 1-4 Simple object-oriented design for a solar-system simulation.

wrapper providing functionality to its data. In the solar system, each object has an associated action that updates its position for the next time increment and the design is defined in terms of these actions applied recursively.

A program built using object-oriented design generally includes a large number of objects. Many of these objects, however, are essentially the same. For example, in the solar system all objects representing planets will be treated in basically the same way. It is sufficient for design purposes to describe the behavior of sets of similar objects as a whole. A group of objects with the same data and actions is called a *class*. In object-oriented design we actually define the data and actions of classes rather than individual objects. The terminology used in the field, however, uses the word "object" to denote both classes and individual objects when such use is unambiguous.

An object-oriented design thus consists of a set of classes, the data associated with these classes, and the set of actions the classes can be asked to undertake. A simple view of the solar system design in this form is shown in Figure 1-4. Three classes of objects are noted here, the **Solar System** itself, each **Subsystem**, and each individual planetary **Body**. **Subsystem** and **Body** objects both have a mass and current position; **Body** objects additionally have a velocity. **Solar System** and **Subsystem** objects have a list of their immediate components. All three classes of objects have an associated action updating their data and any constituents for the next time step.

One key to constructing an object-oriented design like this is to understand what an object of each given class can be and do. The most intuitive way of approaching this is to view objects anthropomorphically, i.e. as if they were people. Objects should be seen as living, intelligent entities of various types. They are living in that their properties can change over time. This lets them more closely model entities in real-world problems by conforming to those entities as they change within the problem. For example, in the solar system example, a planetary system should be able to add or subtract components as new planetoids are captured as moons or as moons collide with each other or the planet. Objects are intelligent in that they can undertake actions and somehow "know" how to perform these actions. An object's intelligence actually represents a form of abstraction: by assuming an object can handle an action, one can hide the details of how this action is actually performed. Hierarchy in the design then comes into play in defining how the actions are performed, i.e. providing this level of intelligence, and in defining the secondary objects needed for the action. Finally, objects have a variety of types. The objects we used above represented physical entities, but we will also see objects representing algorithms, relationships, or whole subsystems. In a complete solar system implementation, for example, there could be a control object managing the time-step size and how many time steps are taken, as well as gravity objects whose sole purpose is to compute the gravitational attraction between two components.

The second key to constructing an object-oriented design is to understand the interaction of the different classes. Classes interact by providing actions that can be invoked by other classes and by invoking other classes' actions in order to perform their own. In building an object-oriented design, one is first concerned with finding the right set of classes, then with defining what these classes are in terms of data and actions, and finally with delineating how the actions of the various classes rely on one another. The right set of classes covers all aspects of the problem without duplication and provides a sound basis for describing the solution. The actions and data associated with these classes let the designer and eventually the programmer fully understand what they are and what they can do. The interactions among the classes form the procedural portion of the overall solution in that they describe how the problem is actually solved using the given set of classes. It is the combination of these design aspects that lets object-oriented design describe complex systems in a natural way.

Object-oriented design provides abstraction by isolating information inside classes and then viewing these classes in terms of interfaces. A class *interface* is the set of actions and data the class makes available to other classes. It provides a separation between what the class does and how the class does it. The interface specifies what the class can do. In an actual design it provides a set of operations other classes can invoke to obtain the desired behavior. It does not, however, specify how this behavior is achieved. The implementation can involve many additional methods, data, and even other classes and their operations and data. When we do object-oriented design, we first view each class in terms of its interface. This lets us hide the implementation details and concentrate on the high-level structure of the system. It is only after this structure is understood that we work on the implementation by providing the details behind the interface. Working in terms of interfaces is central to object-oriented design.

Object-Oriented Design Methodology

Object-oriented design centers on finding an appropriate set of classes and defining their contents and behavior. It involves determining the proper set of classes and then filling in the details of their implementation. While there is some magic to this process, overall it is quite simple and straightforward.

Object-oriented design is fundamentally a three-step process: identifying the classes, characterizing them, and then defining the associated actions. In a large-scale design these operations occur repeatedly at different levels of detail.

Identifying the Classes.   The first step in object-oriented design involves determining what aspects of the problem objects will represent. This is done by first identifying a larger set of candidate classes and then finding a subset of this set that provides a meaningful solution to the problem at an appropriate level of abstraction.

The first part of this, finding a set of potential classes, is fairly mechanical. It involves finding everything in the problem description or idealized solution that could possibly be implemented as an object. This can be done by looking for frequently used nouns in a problem statement or by creating a scenario of the solution and looking in it for active elements. For example, in the solar system description on page 7, the following nouns occur two or more times and hence are one set of potential classes: **Attraction**, **Body**, **Force**, **Moon**, **Number**, **Position**, **Program**, **Solar System**, **Subsystem**, and **Velocity**.

The second part, determining which of these potential classes should appear in the eventual solution, is much harder. Here, as we show in the next and subsequent chapters, one needs to classify the classes, note the level of abstraction of each, and understand their relationships. Then one can determine what subset of the classes is sufficient to describe a solution. For example, we can reduce the set of potential solar system classes we identified above. **Program** and **Number** are used as generic terms and can be ignored. We can eliminate **Moon** as being an instance of **Body**. At a finer level of detail in the design, we might actually want to have separate classes representing planets, moons, asteroids, comets, and the sun, but at the top level, in determining how the overall system works, they can all be considered instances of the same type of class. We can also eliminate **Attraction**, **Force**, **Position**, and **Velocity** as physical entities that have a value but no associated behavior and are thus too detailed to be top-level classes. This leaves **Body**, **Solar System**, and **Subsystem**, which indeed were the three classes in our earlier solution.

Characterizing the Classes.   The second step in object-oriented design is to explain the role of each of the classes selected as part of the design. This is typically done by providing a verbal description of each object and defining the data associated with it.

This stage of object-oriented design is relatively straightforward. Primarily, one needs to understand each class name and then specify what data might go with objects of that class. For example, in the solar system example, we know that each **Body** object has an associated mass, velocity and position, that **Solar**

Body	A planetary body (sun, planet, moon, comet, asteroid,...)
Mass	mass of the body in kg
Velocity	current velocity of the body in km/s^2
Position	position of the body in three-space (km from origin)
Solar System	The overall solar system
Components	list of top-level bodies or subsystems
Subsystem	A coherent subset of the solar system for gravity computation, for example a planet and its moons
Components	list of top-level bodies or subsystems
Mass	combined mass of the components of the subsystem (kg)
Position	center of gravity of the subsystem (km/s^2)

Figure 1-5 A characterization of the objects in the solar-system simulation.

System and **Subsystem** objects have a list of components, and that each **Subsystem** object has an overall or average position (its center of gravity) and mass. This gives us object descriptions similar to those in Figure 1-5.

The major difficulty at this stage of object-oriented design is avoiding too much detail. The classes are intended to be viewed as abstractions. When providing a verbal description of each class, one must be careful to describe the abstraction and not a particular instance of the abstraction. Similarly, when associating properties with classes, one must be careful to add only properties essential to the definition of the class. For example, in specifying that the **Solar System** and **Subsystem** classes have a list of components, we do not specify whether this is stored as a linked list, a vector, a tree, or in some implicit representation.

Defining the Implementation. The last step in object-oriented design involves describing how each of the classes in the solution works. This means defining the actions each of the objects of the class needs to provide. This again is a difficult process requiring creativity and design expertise.

One typically starts to define the implementation at a known point. This means finding an action that is certain to be part of the final implementation, such as the main program or top-level method. In the solar system example, where we did not include the top-level actions in the design, the starting point should be the need to update the position of each object in the solar system for the next time step, a requirement imposed by the problem and its solution.

This stage of object-oriented design defines the intelligence associated with each object. This involves outlining how each selected action will be implemented, utilizing other objects by invoking actions on those objects. As new actions are specified as part of the solution, they should be added to the appro-

```
System::update()
    For each component: clear its accumulated force
    For each pair of components:
        Accumulate gravitational force between components
    For each component: update()

Subsystem::update()
    For each component: clear its accumulated force
    For each component:
        Allocate accumulated force to component by mass
    For each pair of components
        Accumulate gravitational force between components
    For each component: update()

Body::update()
    Update velocity and position using accumulated force
    Clear accumulated force
```

Figure 1-6 Pseudocode for the update methods in the solar-system simulation.

priate classes. Similarly, as new data elements are required by the action out-lines, they too should be added.

The outline can be given in a variety of ways, ranging from formal logic to informal natural language. A typical description, however, involves *pseudocode*, natural-language text written in a program format. The overall process of defining the implementation then proceeds by specifying the actions identified as necessary a priori and then selecting some other action that is required by one of these actions and specifying it. This process is repeated until all actions are specified or understood.

Figure 1-6 shows the pseudocode for the update methods of the various classes in the solar system example. Updating the solar system first computes the gravitational attraction between each pair of components and then requests each of these components to update themselves. Leaving the compu-tation of gravity to a further level of abstraction (i.e., assuming we can do this relatively easily), this description adds new actions for updating both a sub-system and a body. It also adds new data components to both **Body** and **Sub-system** classes to hold the accumulated gravitational force. Updating a body involves a simple numerical computation that can be ignored at this level of detail. Updating a subsystem involves computing the gravitational forces on each of its components. This is done in essentially the same way as with the solar system, except that the overall attraction imposed on the subsystem must be distributed among the components. The result of defining these three actions is an understandable solution to the problem.

Figure 1-7 provides an alternative view of the update process by showing the dynamics of a specific instance of the design. In this case, we are consider-ing only the solar system itself, the earth, and the moon. The arrows going to

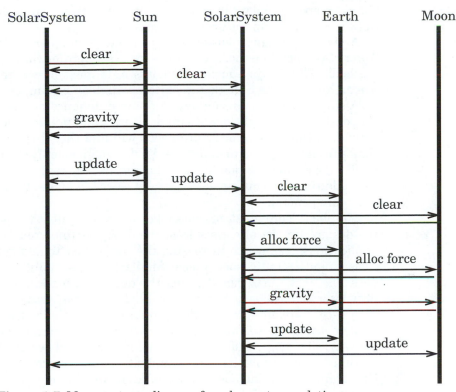

Figure 1-7 Message-trace diagram for solar-system updating.

the right represent action invocations on the targeted objects; the arrows going to the left indicate when the action has been completed. This type of diagram is covered in more detail in Chapter 6.

Design Simplicity

The difficult parts of object-oriented design require creativity and good judgment. Generally there is no one correct design for a given problem. Rather, there is a wide range of appropriate solutions, each with its own strengths and weaknesses. Programmers learn, generally through studying designs of others, which designs work and which don't. While there is no substitute for this experience, a few basic principles can help one to understand what makes one design good and another design bad.

The first goal of the designer should be *simplicity*. Simplicity helps create better designs in a variety of ways. A simpler design is generally easier to understand. A design that is not easy to understand is more likely to be misinterpreted, and its eventual implementation is more likely to be incorrect. Since one of the goals of design is to convey instructions from the designer to the developer on how the software is to be written, an easier-to-understand design can only help the overall process.

A simpler design is easier to implement. A simpler design generally has fewer classes and methods as well as more straightforward code in each of the methods. This in turn means that less code must be written to achieve the design and that the code that is written will itself be simpler.

A simple design is also a key to the maintenance of a software system. If the design is straightforward and clear, then programmers modifying or extending the system for future needs will find their task easier. Part of this comes from being able to understand a design given only the code. (Most original design documentation tends to disappear.) The rest will come from the fact that additions or changes are generally easier to make if the design is simple and more general.

Simplicity here must, of course, be balanced against the other demands on the design. If a set of classes from the design is to be reused in this or other applications, it is worth increasing the complexity to add generality to those classes and simplify such reuse. Similarly, if portability or extensibility is desirable, it is worth complicating the design with additional classes to simplify later extensions or future attempts to port the system.

A second, related design goal should be to minimize the risk inherent in implementing the software system. Software has a tendency to be late, over budget, full of bugs, and difficult to maintain. A good design should attempt to minimize these problems, and simplicity is one approach that often works. Other approaches include the use of known techniques versus experimental ones, borrowing design ideas from similar systems, using standard design patterns, and testing or prototyping high-risk portions of the design.

Finally, we note that design is not a one-shot process: a good design is not created in one step the first time. Instead, software designs evolve over time, changing when the design is being created, when it is being implemented, and as the software is being maintained. Good designers are always asking questions about their designs, aiming continually to improve them. You should never be satisfied with a second-best design if a better one is available.

OUTLINE OF THE TEXT

In the following chapters we consider a wide variety of design examples, going over the overall design process several times. We emphasize throughout the basic steps used to create an object-oriented design and the basic design principles outlined above.

Chapters 2 through 5, 12 and 14 all deal with small-scale object-oriented design. Chapter 2 focuses on defining classes and methods to solve a particular problem, covering how to do class design using the above methodology and principles and providing some standards for what makes a good or bad design.

This is followed in Chapter 3 by a detailed consideration of implementing a class design and, in Chapter 4, of using C++ as a powerful and effective programming language. Chapter 5 looks at the broader issues of designing class hierarchies and more complex sets of classes. Chapter 12 covers the design of object libraries and the use of templates. Finally, Chapter 14 considers small-scale design issues in multiple-process and multithreaded programming.

Chapter 6 deals with design notations and presents a simplification of the standard notations used today to express object-oriented designs. As we noted, graphical notations are generally easier to understand and more satisfying than purely textual descriptions. However, unless the graphical notation conforms to a set of standards that is well-known to both the creator and the reader, it can be more confusing than helpful. We introduce a simplified form of today's standard representation, the Unified Modeling Language, that is suitable for intermediate programmers to describe both the static structure and the dynamics inherent in a design.

Issues of library design and reuse are considered in Chapters 7, 12, and 13. The first two cover respectively using and constructing object-oriented libraries. Here the focus is on code reuse, i.e. either using an off-the-shelf library to simplify the implementation or creating new libraries for use in a variety of applications. Chapter 13 covers patterns at all levels of design, with emphasis on reusing designs and design concepts. Design patterns or object patterns provide such reuse at the class level; architectural patterns provide such reuse at the system level. Many of the patterns covered in this chapter are illustrated in examples earlier in the text.

Chapter 8 provides an overview of the important topics of testing and debugging. It covers the generation of test cases, defensive programming, and a variety of debugging methodologies. It also contains many hints and suggestions for minimizing and simplifying debugging.

Another topic covered in some depth is user-interface design. Most applications developed today involve a graphical user interface. Chapters 9 and 10 cover issues in designing and implementing such interfaces. Chapter 11 goes over some of the basic principles of human-computer interaction governing the whole area of user-interface design.

Finally, the remainder of the text, Chapters 15 and 16, cover the design and implementation of larger software systems. Here we discuss what happens when the problem to be solved is too large for a single person to understand, design, or implement. We cover how to design larger projects using design hierarchies with well-defined interfaces, and describe design and coding techniques aimed at simplifying and coordinating multiple-person projects. All this comes under the rubric of software engineering, a field devoted to developing the methodologies, techniques, and tools needed for large-scale software development.

EXERCISES

1.1   Write an explanation of how a computer works. Assume your target audience is a friend who is interested in a good overview of the inner workings but is not a computer major.

1.2   Use objects and an object-oriented design to model how the telephone system works. Use a message-trace diagram to show what happens when one person attempts to call another.

1.3   You are asked to design a program to do roommate matching. The input is a set of questionnaires filled out by the applicants in which each question is answered on a 1-5 scale. The input also gives a priority value for each question that specifies its importance. Your program should generate a list of pairs of applicants such that all applicants are paired and the overall pairing exhibits a high degree of compatibility.
a)   Do a simple design using control- or data-oriented techniques.
b)   Do a simple object-oriented design.

1.4   Design a program that simulates activities in a sprocket factory. Here the five different parts making up a sprocket need to be ordered, delivered, and shipped, sprockets have to be assembled, orders for sprockets need to be taken, and sprockets need to be shipped. The program will be used by the factory managers to implement just-in-time parts delivery.
a)   Explain how the program might work and what it might do, using both text and diagrams.
b)   Identify a set of candidate objects, explain what each does, and show how they interact.

1.5   Consider a system that manages library books, letting them be indexed, checked in and out, and so on.
a)   List a set of candidate objects.
b)   Identify an appropriate subset of these objects to make up a top-level design.
c)   Write pseudocode to explain what happens when a book is checked out.
d)   Use a message-trace diagram to explain what happens when a book is checked out.

Chapter 2

A Simple Example of Object-Oriented Design

This chapter uses a relatively simple problem to illustrate object-oriented design. It starts with a description of knight's tour, a classic search problem. Then it goes through the three phases of object-oriented design introduced in the previous chapter, first identifying the candidate classes and choosing the correct set of top-level classes, then providing detailed information about each class, and finally defining their implementations. Along the way, it discusses the different categories of classes, how to represent object-oriented designs, and ways of analyzing the quality of the resultant design.

THE KNIGHT'S-TOUR PROBLEM

The first step in designing a software solution to a problem is to understand the problem. This means having a statement of the problem that is as complete as possible. The problem here is the classic search problem called knight's tour. Here one starts with a chess board and a knight. The task is to find a sequence of legal moves for the knight covering the whole board and bringing the knight back to where it started.

We start with a detailed description of what we want our program to do:

Consider a k by k board of squares and a chess piece called a knight. A knight in chess makes a move consisting either of two squares in a horizontal direction followed by one in a vertical direction or two squares in a vertical direction followed by one in a horizontal, as seen in Figure 2-1. A move in this sense conveys the knight from one square on the board to another. A "knight's tour" is a sequence of moves such that each square on the board is visited by the knight exactly once and the knight ends up in the square where it started, as in Figure 2-2. That is, the knight must visit each square of the board as part of its tour and must not visit any square (other than its starting one) more than once. Your task is to write a program inputting k, the size of the board, and outputting a valid tour if there is one or a message if there is not. The tour should be output by showing a view of the board with each square

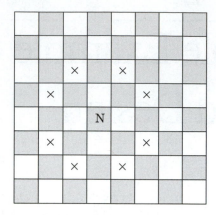

Figure 2-1 The legal moves of the knight in chess.

35	8	19	22	1	10
20	23	0	9	18	29
7	34	21	30	11	2
24	31	6	15	28	17
5	14	33	26	3	12
32	25	4	13	16	27

```
fred$ knight 6
   35    8   19   22    1   10
   20   23    0    9   18   29
    7   34   21   30   11    2
   24   31    6   15   28   17
    5   14   33   26    3   12
   32   25    4   13   16   27
fred$
```

Figure 2-2 Sample knight's tour on a 6×6 board and the desired program output.

labeled with the index of that move on a valid tour. An example of possible output is shown in Figure 2-2.

There are several things to note about this description. First, it specifies the inputs and the outputs in enough detail that the implementor will have no difficulty understanding what is provided or required. Second, it defines precisely what is meant by a valid solution, providing the details of what moves a knight can make and what a valid tour is. Third, it uses diagrams and examples to make the statement as clear as possible. The description is also noteworthy for what it does not say. It defines the problem and not the solution: it provides no details on how the problem is to be solved or what the solution should look like. These are left to the program designer.

The first step in developing a design for this problem is outlining the solution. Knight's tour is a search problem. The knight starts in some square. It then has its choice of moves to a second square. Then it has a choice of moves to a third square, and so forth. At each point there are between two and eight legal knight moves, which are then limited by the constraint that no square can be visited more than once. A brute-force search (considering all possibilities), especially for a moderately large to large board, will not yield a practical solution. (Even for an 8×8 board, with 64 squares and assuming only four alternatives per move, the number of possible solutions is about 4^{64}, which would take forever to consider.) Thus to make the program practical, the solution must embody some intelligence in the form of heuristics that let us look at a much smaller number of moves. We might want to experiment with several different heuristics to see which works best as part of our solution.

Heuristics are experimental approaches to solving a given problem. They provide a set of guidelines that, while not guaranteed to be the best, is likely to yield a good solution. Search heuristics such as we use here are guidelines on how best to perform the search. They provide a set of rules specifying what to look at next. The order specified by the rules is not necessarily the fastest or the best, but we hope it is good enough and fast enough for our purposes. Note that heuristics are needed here because it is difficult or impossible to determine an algorithm to find a tour without doing any searching. This is characteristic of many complex problems.

The need to use some unspecified heuristics is not unique to the knight's-tour problem. Most real-world problems have one or more components that are not well understood in advance. Part of the process of design involves studying the problem from various points of view to determine what will or will not work. Often this is not enough and experimentation is required to determine a viable solution. In this case, the system design must allow easy experimentation and take into account the fact that the relevant sections of the program are likely to change as the system is developed.

A second step in developing a design for a system involves establishing some criteria for correctness that will tell us if the program is working when it is actually built and give us a basis for checking the design. In this case, there are two things to consider. First, the program should find a valid knight's tour if one exists on a board, and second, it should output a message if no tour exists for a given board size. Here the designer must attempt to understand the problem. For the knight's tour, it is known that no solution exists if the board is smaller than 4×4 (the corners on a 4×4 cannot be on a tour, it is impossible to reach the center of a 3×3 board, and there are no moves on a smaller board), or if the board size is odd (a tour alternates black and white squares so it would be impossible to end up at the starting square after an odd number of moves).[1] Thus, once the solution is implemented, we should expect it to output a message indicating no solution is found for these cases, and to output a valid solution for other board sizes.

---

1. For a good overview of the problem see Ian Stewart, "Knight's Tours," *Scientific American*, 276(4), April 1997, pp. 102-104.

IDENTIFYING CANDIDATE CLASSES

Once a problem is understood and there is some sense of how it should be solved, object-oriented design can commence. The first stage in object-oriented design involves identifying a set of classes to describe the solution. This is generally done by enumerating a large list of potential classes. This set is then narrowed to a reasonably sized set of classes, all at about the same level of abstraction sufficient for understanding the overall solution. The goal of this stage of design is to describe the solution in terms of a small set of interacting classes each of which is significantly simpler and easier to understand than the problem as a whole.

Candidate classes can be found in various ways. A straightforward approach used in the previous chapter is to look for potential classes in the problem statement. Since objects are things, nouns are generally used to represent them. Moreover, potential classes are those that are central to the problem and thus generally appear several times in the problem statement. This analysis is complicated by the vagaries of natural language. A single noun can have multiple forms and synonyms that should all be considered instances of the same item; pronouns can refer to different nouns without the noun explicitly appearing; different writers use different writing styles and vocabulary. Still, given its simplicity, it is an easy and worthwhile first step in developing an object-oriented design.

A part-of-speech analysis for the problem description at the beginning of this chapter is shown in Figure 2-3. Here nouns are printed in bold and doubly underlined and verbs are singly underlined. When looking for nouns as potential classes, it can also be worthwhile to look at the verbs and adjectives relating to these nouns. Verbs can represent potential actions either taken by or applied to the noun, and thus provide a set of candidate methods for the potential classes. Adjectives provide further descriptions of the nouns and can suggest properties or characteristics of the potential classes relevant to the task. The analysis shown here was derived automatically by a tool in the Desert environment.[1] The tool can go a step further and produce the simple table of potential classes and their methods shown in Figure 2-4. Tools are not a necessity here, however; doing the analysis by hand can be just as effective.

Where the problem description contains diagrams, these too should be used to augment the set of candidate classes. Although this cannot be done mechanically, it is fairly simple to look at each diagram and, if it is essential to the problem, add potential classes corresponding to the various components of the diagram. For example, the components of Figure 2-1 would include **Knight**,

---

1. See Steven P. Reiss, "Simplifying data integration: The design of the Desert software development environment," *Proc. 18th Int'l Conf. on Software Engineering*, pp. 398-407, March 1996, and the web site http://www.cs.brown.edu/software/desert.

Consider a k by k **board** of **squares** and a **chess piece called** a **knight**. A **knight** in **chess makes** a **move** that **consists** either of two **squares** in a horizontal **direction followed** by one in a vertical **direction** or two **squares** in a vertical **direction followed** by one in a horizontal as **seen** in **Figure** 7. A **move** in this **sense conveys** the **knight** from one **square** on the **board** to another. A "**knight's tour**" **consists** of a **sequence** of **moves** such that each **square** on the **board** is **visited** by the **knight** exactly once and the **knight ends** up in the **square** where it **started** as in **Figure** 2-2. That is, the **knight** must **visit** each **square** of the **board** as **part** of its **tour** and **must** not **visit** any **square** (other that its starting one) more than once. Your **task** is to **write** a **program** that **inputs** k, the **size** of the **board**, and that **outputs** a valid **tour** if there is one or a **message** if there is not. The **tour** should be **output** by showing a **view** of the **board** with each **square labeled** with the **index** of that **move** on a valid **tour**.

Figure 2-3 A part-of-speech analysis of the knight's-tour problem description.

Move and **Square**, while the components of Figure 2-2 would include **Tour**, **Square**, and **Move**.

Another approach to developing a set of potential classes involves restating the problem in one's own terms. This statement, which should also include any information deduced about the potential solution through problem analysis, can then be used either in addition to or in place of the original problem description for finding potential classes. Rewriting the problem description in one's own terms is generally beneficial not only because it lets the designer incorporate any additional details, but also because it forces the designer really to understand the problem.

A third technique for finding classes is to analyze how a potential solution might work and identify the items used in this solution that could qualify as classes. Here the designer looks at *scenarios*, concrete cases of what the system would do for particular problems, rather than attempting to describe the general solution. In the knight's-tour example we would look at how the program might construct a tour. We would show the knight on the starting square, labeling it 1, and would highlight the squares reachable from this square. Then the program would choose one of these squares, mark that as 2, and then look at the valid moves from this point. This procedure would continue until either a tour was found or a square was reached with no valid moves and the tour was incomplete. In this latter case, the program would backtrack, i.e., would go back to the last point at which there was more than one valid move and try an alternative not tried before. This process would continue until either a tour was found or all alternatives at each juncture had been tried. For example, the full search for a 3×3 board is shown in Figure 2-5.

Class Name	Method	Description
Square	Description of class Square (9)	
	visit	
	labeled	
	started	
Knight	Description of class Knight (7)	
	assume	
	called	
	convey	
	end	
	start	
	visit	
	visited	
Board	Description of class Board (6)	
	visited	
Tour	Description of class Tour (5)	
	consist	
	outputs	
Move	Description of class Move (4)	
	consist	
	make	
Direction	Description of class Direction (3)	
	followed	

Figure 2-4 Classes and methods from part-of-speech analysis.

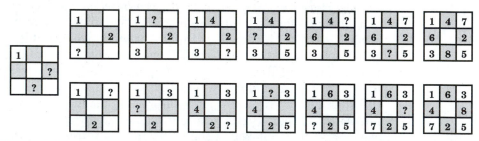

Figure 2-5 Searching over a 3-by-3 board.

A full analysis would consider several alternatives, although not necessarily with complete examples. The set of classes involved in the scenario can be determined either by attempting to explain the scenario textually and extracting nouns and verbs from that text, or by simply listing the basic components of the solution. In this case, the basic components are **Knight**, **Board**, **Tour**, **Solution**, **Square**, and **Move**.

Categories of Classes

The various analyses considered above deal mainly with physical or virtual entities. For example, the board, the knight, and squares are all physical parts of the problem, while a move sequence or the set of legal moves from a square is a virtual aspect of the problem or its solution. While these constitute the most obvious set of potential classes and can readily be found using the techniques cited, there are also other forms of classes the designer should be looking for.

The first of these are placeholders. *Placeholder classes* are abstract interfaces to components of the solution, and are especially useful for representing portions of the target system that are not completely specified. For example, in the knight's-tour problem, we have not specified exactly what the user interface is to look like. We might want to build a textual interface initially and then, if the system is to be used for demonstration purposes later, add a graphical interface to let the user specify the board size and then show the knight's tour as it evolves. To accommodate such future change, we could create a class representing the user interface to the system that would serve as a placeholder for either a textual or a graphical interface. We would implement it first using a simple textual front end. Then, as the system evolved, we could replace it with another implementation supporting a graphical front end. Little if any change would be required in the remainder of the system.

Potential placeholder classes should also be created for any aspects of the problem where change is anticipated. If portability is a concern, for example, then a placeholder class can be used to represent the underlying operating system or windowing interface. If an external database is required and the database might change over time or there are multiple candidate databases, then a placeholder class can represent the interface to the database. In all these cases, using a placeholder lets the anticipated change occur with minimal effect on the remainder of the system.

A second kind of abstract class represents algorithms. While placeholder classes represent interfaces to system components, either internal or external, *algorithm classes* represent internal aspects of the solution that are complex or not well understood. Here classes are used to represent a potential solution. For example, in the knight's-tour problem, we have noted that appropriate heuristics need to be used in choosing the next move to consider. At this point, we don't know what heuristics are possible or which ones will work well enough to yield a practical solution. Thus we might want to create a **Heuristic** class encapsulating whatever heuristics are to be used. This would let us experiment with and change the heuristics used in the solution without affecting the remainder of the system.

Class	Description
Board	The k by k chess board for which the tour will be found
Direction	The direction in which to move
Heuristics	Heuristics used to determine which move to try next
Knight	The knight that moves around the board
Move	A move the knight can make
Search	The overall search process
Solution	The solution to the problem
Square	A square on the chess board
Tour	The completed tour
User Interface	The input and output for the problem

Figure 2-6 The complete set of potential classes for the knight's-tour problem.

A second possible algorithmic class in the knight's-tour example would represent the overall search process. This class would be in charge of managing the search by finding the next move, detecting success or failure of the search, and backtracking appropriately. In general, when developing a set of potential classes for a problem, one should attempt to identify the key algorithms and note that these might correspond to classes.

Choosing the Top-Level Classes

So far we have covered how to find candidate classes by analyzing the problem and its proposed solution, considering what system components might change, and looking at the essential algorithms in the system. Figure 2-6 shows the resultant set of potential classes for the knight's tour. The next step in identifying the top-level classes of the system is to narrow this initial set into a subset that can be used to describe the problem.

The proposed programming solution to a problem is best understood when described in terms of a small set of classes interacting in well-prescribed ways. The number of classes in this set can vary, but should generally be from five to 10. Using too few classes generally does not provide a detailed enough description that the solution can be understood. At least one of these components will generally be as difficult to specify as the overall solution itself. On the other hand, using too many classes yields a solution too complex to understand easily.

The numbers chosen here are derived from experience, from our goal of simplicity, and from psychology. Psychologists have determined that memory can be viewed as having two parts, short-term memory containing a small set of items that can be recalled very quickly, and long-term memory of almost unlimited capacity that can take significant time to recall items. The number of items that can be retained in short-term memory has been derived experimentally as 7 +/- 2. (You can try a simple experiment by seeing how long a string of random digits you can recall.) This means that a proposed solution with five to 10 components should fit pretty well into short-term memory and be easier to understand.

In choosing the set of top-level classes, care should be taken to make it independent, balanced and interrelated. The classes should be selected so that any particular aspect of the solution fits into one and only one class. This ensures there is no ambiguity as to what each class should be doing and thus makes the design simpler and more understandable. At the same time, the classes should be at about the same level of detail. This ensures that the problem is broken down into pieces of about the same size that are significantly simpler than the original problem. Finally, the set of classes should be chosen so that their interactions are sufficient to describe the solution to the problem.

This last criterion is what makes selecting the proper set of classes difficult: it involves a real understanding of the problem and the potential classes as well as some degree of creativity and ingenuity. Designers must envision each potential solution in terms of the classes. They must ensure the selected classes have meaningful interactions that cover all aspects of the solution. This is the key to this phase of design and is difficult to learn except through experience.

Certain guidelines can be used, however, to simplify this process and provide logical starting points for the actual analysis. The first task is to eliminate as many of the potential classes as possible. One way a potential class can be eliminated is by being completely subsumed by some other class, for example when one class is an instance of a more general class. The solar-system example of the previous chapter had both **Moon** classes and **Body** classes. Since a moon is a type of planetary body, the **Body** class subsumes the **Moon** class and the **Moon** class should not be considered a top-level class. Subsumption can occur less directly. For example, in the knight's-tour problem we have both **Tour** class and **Solution** class. Since the final tour is a solution, we can eliminate a **Solution** class from consideration. A simple analysis of the knight's-tour problem shows we can also eliminate the **Direction** class, since it is included as part of a **Move**.

Once the obvious classes are eliminated, the designer needs to find a balanced set of classes representing the solution. The first step here is to envision how a solution would work and then determine what classes are necessary to that solution. This is done by selecting one or two key class types and using them as a basis for the solution. There are several ways to implement a knight's-tour search. In the alternative we consider, we start with a square on the board and develop a solution around it:

> The program reads in the size of the board, builds the board, finds a valid tour, and then prints the resultant tour. We assume each square maintains the set of valid moves from that square as we build the tour. All legal knight moves

Class	Description
Main	This class represents the main flow of control. It is responsible for handling the user interface (both input and output), for setting up all the other classes as needed, and for finding the tour.
Board	This class provides a container for the overall board, holding all the squares and taking charge of the search. For example, it is responsible for the special handling of the starting square.
Square	This is the main object used in the search algorithm. It represents a square, maintains a list of valid moves (the set of reachable squares), and provides routines for implementing the search.
Heuristic	This is the algorithm class in charge of ordering the list of valid moves for a square so that the most likely candidates come first.
Solution	This is the holder for the solution.

Figure 2-7 The classes to be utilized in the solution.

are added to this set when the square is initialized. Assume we start and end in the upper left corner. There are only two valid moves from this square, and the tours based on these moves are symmetric; we need consider only one of them. We identify the second square on the tour and remove its legal move to the starting corner. (This lets us find a valid tour by simply finding a sequence of moves covering all squares, since there is now only one way of getting to the starting square and hence it must be the last node of such a sequence.) Then we ask that second square to find a sequence of moves containing all unused squares starting at that square. Each square, when asked to find such a sequence, first updates the valid move lists of other squares, then uses some heuristic algorithm to order the list of valid moves so that the most likely to succeed is considered first. Then, for each move in the resultant order, it asks the next square to find the remaining sequence. If a square determines it cannot continue a sequence, it restores the valid move lists and returns failure to its caller. If a square determines it has completed the tour, it returns the solution to its caller, which passes it back up to the top level.

From this description we can select an appropriate set of classes as shown in Figure 2-7.

Once a potential design has been constructed, it must be evaluated and enhanced. If too many classes have been selected, then a logical subset of the classes should be grouped together and a new class inserted in its place. This class is a *facade* class, a class encapsulating a set of classes so that any access to a member of this set from outside the set goes through the facade. Any class that is too large or too small compared to the others should be either decomposed into subclasses or subsumed by another class. Finally, the designer should check that the design is complete. A simple way to do this is to take each of the initial set of potential classes and make sure its presumed functionality is covered by one of the selected classes of the design. For example,

Class	Where the class is defined
Board	Board
Direction	Component of a move
Heuristics	Heuristic
Knight	Current square reflects the knight's position
Move	Set of valid moves contained in current square
Search	Top-level search done by Board
Solution	Solution
Square	Square
Tour	Synonym for solution
User Interface	Main

Figure 2-8 Mapping potential classes into the select set of classes.

Figure 2-8 shows how each of the potential classes is included in one of the five selected classes.

CHARACTERIZING THE CLASSES

So far we have envisioned a potential solution and chosen the set of classes needed for that solution. The two remaining steps in object-oriented design refine the solution to the point that it can be implemented. The first step defines the classes so that each is well understood; the second step defines how the classes operate.

The classes are characterized by attempting to define what each class does. One should already have a brief description of the class such as that in Figure 2-7. The next step is describing each of these classes in terms of data, operations, and relationships, in order to help the designer understand them better. The description of data associated with the class helps make the class concrete. The description of potential operations helps define what the designer thinks the class can do. The description of relationships between this and the other classes in the solution helps to show how this class fits in and clarifies the overall solution.

For the knight's-tour example, we start with the top-level class, **Main**, which represents the overall control process and implements the user interface. Its data elements include the board size input from the user and the actual board. The operations on the class include a process operation that reads the board size, sets up the board, does the search, and prints the result. This information is gleaned from a simple analysis of the description of the class.

The other classes are also relatively simple to define. The **Board** class contains the squares. It provides operations to set up the board and to find the actual tour. The **Square** class contains a square's position (row and column) and the set of legal moves from that square. It provides operations to set up the square by defining the initial set of legal moves and to find the remainder of a tour starting at this square. The **Heuristic** class contains no data and provides methods to order a set of moves. Finally, the **Solution** class contains a sequence of squares and provides an operation to access the solution so it can be output.

The relationships among the classes can be deduced from the descriptions as well. The class **Main** sets up, contains, and requests a path from the **Board** class and gets information from the **Solution** class to output the resultant tour. The **Board** class contains **Square** objects and uses them to find the tour. The **Square** class uses the **Heuristic** class to order the moves. Finally, the **Move** class refers to **Square** objects as part of the solution.

Describing Object-Oriented Designs

The natural-language description of the objects given above is not very satisfactory. Considerable effort is required for the reader or the designer to see exactly what it contains and thus to understand what is there. Moreover, the description will be difficult to modify as the design evolves and we need to add or remove data, operations, or relationships.

A better approach is to draw a picture of the design. This picture should reflect the various components of each of the classes and should also show the relationship between the classes graphically. A number of such diagrams have been developed over the years in an attempt to standardize the representation of object-oriented designs. In Chapter 6 we introduce the static-structure and message-trace diagrams of the Unified Modeling Language (UML). At this point, we want to introduce a simplified form of the static-structure-diagram notation to represent the initial designs.

The basic idea in our notation for object design is to represent a class as a box and the relationships between classes as lines between the boxes. The class box contains the data and operations defined for the class. To accomplish this we use a three-part box similar to that in Figure 2-9. At the top is the name of the class. Below this is a box containing the data elements of the class. At the bottom is a box containing the class operations.

The complete object-oriented design contains such boxes for each of the classes along with arcs expressing relationships among the boxes. These relationships can express containment; for example, a **Board** object contains **Square** objects. They can also express dependencies; here the **Square** class depends on the **Heuristic** class to order the legal moves. Typically, the different relationship lines are labeled to indicate the nature of the relationship.

This textual object design for knight's tour is shown diagrammatically in Figure 2-10. Each of the classes has a box with the appropriate labels, data

Square
row_number
column_number
Legal moves
setup()
finishTour()

Figure 2-9 Simple static structure diagram.

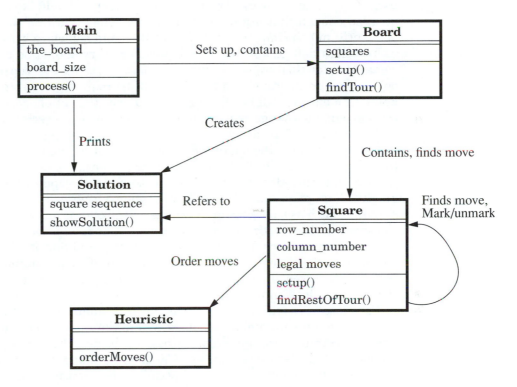

Figure 2-10 Class-design diagram for the knight's-tour problem.

elements, and the proposed methods alluded to in the previous description. The relationships among the classes are shown as labeled arcs.

This diagram serves as the basis for further refinements of the design. It should be accompanied with an annotated description of each of the classes (for example, the table in Figure 2-7). Such annotations could be further expanded to include a one-line description of each data element and operation. The data elements can be further qualified by defining their types. The operations can be further qualified by listing their arguments, the argument types, and the return types. Most of this refinement, however, comes in the next stage of object-oriented design.

DEFINING THE IMPLEMENTATION

The final stage of object-oriented design completes this initial description of the objects by looking at how the various operations are implemented. The designer's task here is to ensure that each object is correct and the whole system can be made to work. The result of this phase should be a design that is detailed enough that a programmer can implement each of the classes independently, put the implementations together, and achieve a working system.

The class definitions done in the previous stage should be taken as provisional during this stage. As the various operations are considered for an object, new or different data members will be required and some of the original data members will be eliminated. Similarly, the set of operations for each class is likely to change as the definitions become more precise. This is all part of the evolution of the design.

Because some of the operations will change, it is important when defining the implementation to find a stable starting point., i.e. an operation guaranteed to be included in the final design. In a simple application such as the knight's-tour program, this can be the top-level method. In a more complex situation, such as a package or library, essential operations must be identified.

Once a stable starting point has been identified, its implementation can be defined. This involves defining both its interface and how it works. The interface defines the return type and the parameters. The description of the operation can be given in natural language or in *pseudocode*, natural language structured to look and act like a program.

Pseudocode is typically written as natural language structured along the lines of some programming language. While the underlying language can be almost anything, programmers are best off basing their pseudocode on the proposed target language, since this makes the mapping from pseudocode to real code a bit simpler. However, especially when writing pseudocode for personal use only, programmers should use whatever they are most comfortable with. Pseudocode has applications beyond design. Some of the pseudocode written for design can be carried over to the final code as comments, while other fragments of pseudocode can act as placeholders while the code is being written. A pseudocode description for design should concentrate on how a class uses the operations provided by it and other related classes, while at the same time ensuring the operation can be done with the information available.

As the pseudocode for an operation is defined, it will need to invoke operations on the same or other classes. At this point, an initial interface for these operations can be defined and the operations can be marked as needed in the design. The remainder of the overall system implementation is then defined one operation at a time by repeatedly specifying pseudocode for one of these marked operations until all such operations have been defined. Any remaining operations are either not needed (and can be eliminated) or can serve as additional stable starting points (and the process can begin again).

In the knight's-tour example, the stable operation is the `process` operation of the class **Main**. This operation should take as input the argument list specified by the user in starting the system. Hence we can define its interface for UNIX:

```
void process(int argc,const char ** argv)
```

The actual implementation needs to set things up, find the tour, and then print the tour. We can express this in pseudocode as:

```
void
Main::process(int argc,const char ** argv)
{
    Determine the board_size
    Create a board
    Set up the board by calling Board::setup(board_size)
    If (tour exists for board size)
        result_tour = Board::findTour()
    Else result_tour = no_tour
    Output the contents of result_tour
}
```

There are several things to note about this code. First, it is both vague and precise. It is precise about its interaction with other classes. When an operation from another class is used, the code provides the full name and the arguments for that operation. This gives the designer the proper starting point for defining the implementation of that method.

It is vague when it refers to the internal implementation of the class **Main**. For example, the first line says to determine the board size. It does not specify whether this should be obtained from the argument list, by reading from the terminal, or from an interactive dialog box. This vagueness provides the flexibility necessary to refine the class further. In a large system, each top-level class generally hides a large number of classes providing its implementation. The details of this implementation need not be revealed to understand the top-level details, and can be developed later. This type of information hiding is essential in the design of larger systems.

The knight's-tour problem, however, is not a large, complex problem. At the lowest levels of the design, it is generally best to be as precise as possible when designing the actual implementation. Here we could either specify exactly how we want to determine the board size within the process operation or we could define a new operation to determine the board type. The advantage of the latter is that if we later decide to improve the program by providing a different interface, the hooks for doing so will already be present. Taking this into account, we can provide more precise pseudocode for `Main::process`:

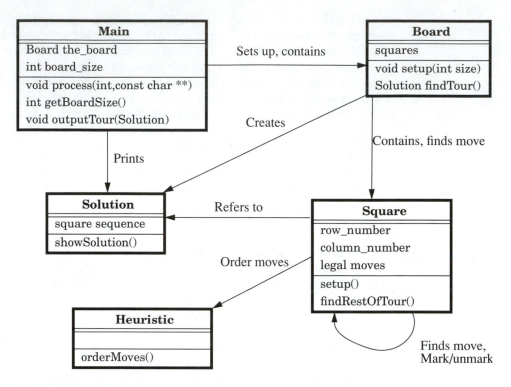

Figure 2-11 Revised static structure diagram.

```
void
Main::process(int argc,const char ** argv)
{
    board_size = Main::getBoardSize(argc,argv)
    the_board = new Board
    Set up board by calling the_board->Board::setup(board_size)
    If (tour exists for board size)
        result_tour = Board::findTour()
    Else result_tour = no_tour
    Main::outputTour(result_tour)
}
```

This definition uses four methods. At this point we should update the class-design diagram in Figure 2-10 to include these. We have also noted the types of the data members of the class **Main** and should put these in the diagram. The resultant diagram is shown in Figure 2-11.

The next step in defining the implementation is to choose another method and provide the pseudocode for it. Where possible, it is generally best to proceed with other methods of the same class first. Assuming we want to simplify the program as much as possible at first, we will get the board size directly from the command line arguments and will output the tour in the form of a board. Thus we can define:

```
int
Main::getBoardSize(int argc,const char ** argv)
{
    Get board size from argv[1]. If not present, use 8
    Return board size
}
```

and

```
void
Main::outputTour(Solution tour)
{
    If ! tour->Solution::isValid() then Output message
    Else
        For row = 0 to board_size-1
            For col = 0 to board_size-1
                i = tour->Solution::findIndex(row,col)
                    Output i using exactly 4 spaces
                Next col
            Output end of line
        Next row
}
```

This definition removes the `showSolution` operation from the **Solution** class and substitutes the `findIndex` operation, returning the move number at which a given square is included in the tour. It also implies that the solution should maintain enough information that the index for a given row and column can be determined. This completes the description of the class **Main**.

We can next define operations for either **Board** or **Solution,** since we have specified methods in both of these classes. In this case, however, we should do **Board** first because all its incoming dependencies have been resolved, while **Solution** has a dependency from **Board**. One should try to define the classes in an order in which as much as possible is known about the class before any of its methods must be defined.

The operation `Board::setup` must define the board. Its responsibilities include setting up the array of squares and initializing the squares:

```
void
Board::setup(int size)
{
    squares = new Square[size][size]
    For row = 0 to size-1
        For col = 0 to size-1
            squares->Square::setup(row,col)
        Next col
    Next row
}
```

The operation `Board::findTour` is more complex. As noted, it must special-case the first move to let the program search for a path that includes all squares. Moreover, it needs to construct the resultant tour. Since the **Solution** object needs to know the board size, it is easiest to build an initial solution object at this point and then let the methods that find the rest of the tour just fill in the solution. Thus:

```
Solution
Board::findTour()
{
    Square start = squares[1][2]
    Square sq0 = squares[0][0]
    start->Square::markUsed(sq0)
    sq0->Square::markUsed(start)
    sol = new Solution
    sol->Solution::setup(board_size)
    start->Square::findRestOfTour(sol)
    Return sol
}
```

The operation `Square::markUsed` is introduced here to remove the square given as the argument from the set of valid moves of the base square. The method `findRestOfTour` is assumed to fill in the solution and return true if a solution exists, false otherwise. A solution that has not been filled in is considered invalid.

We next look at the operations for the class **Square**. Each square must keep track of the remaining legal moves from the square. The initial set is defined by the setup operation. Before we can define this operation, however, we need to determine how we are going to represent the legal moves.

This decision should be based on an analysis of how the set of moves will be used. Here we note several things. First, the set needs to be defined using the rules for how a knight moves. Second, as we go through a tour, we order the moves using the **Heuristic** class and then choose them in order to call `find-RestOfTour` recursively. Third, when a square becomes part of a tour, we want to remove moves to that square from other squares. This last operation must be undone when we backtrack during the search. All these uses imply that a move is best represented as the **Square** object to which the knight can move from the current square. Moreover, because we need to sort the set of moves, it is probably best to keep the moves in an array. Storage is not a problem since the set of legal moves can have at most eight elements.

The next issue is to find the initial set of legal moves for a square given its row and column. Finding the legal rows and columns is not difficult, but these then must be translated into the appropriate squares, which are known only to the **Board** class. Hence we have to introduce a new method `Board::find-Square` to return the square at a given row and column and to return nothing if the row or column position is invalid. This also means that the

`Square::setup` operation requires an additional argument, the board. We modify the code for the board setup operation accordingly:

```
void
Board::setup(int size)
{
    squares = new Square[size][size]
    For row = 0 to size-1
        For col = 0 to size-1
            squares->Square::setup(this,row,col)
        Next col
    Next row
}
```

And then we can define the `Square::setup` method:

```
void
Square::setup(Board board,int row,int col)
{
    row_number = row
    column_number = col
    num_moves = 0
    For (x,y) In (-2,-1),(-2,1),(-1,-2),(-1,2),(1,-2),(1,2),
                 (2,-1), (2,2)
        s = board->Board::findSquare(row+x,col+y)
        If (s is valid)
            legal_moves[num_moves] = s
            num_moves = num_moves+1
        EndIf
    Next (x,y)
}
```

The operation `Board::findSquare` can then be defined. However, to test if the given row and column are valid, it must know the board size. Thus we need to add the data member `board_size` to the **Board** class and set this member in the operation `Board::setup`:

```
void
Board::setup(int size)
{
    board_size = size
    squares = new Square[size][size]
    For row = 0 to size-1
        For col = 0 to size-1
            squares->Square::setup(row,col)
        Next col
    Next row
}
```

Then we get:

```
Square
Board::findSquare(int row,int col)
{
    If (row < 0 || row >= board_size) Return no square
    If (col < 0 || col >= board_size) Return no square
    Return squares[row][col]
}
```

Next we are ready to define the operation `Square::findRestOfTour`. The first step involves checking if we have completed the tour and, if so, returning the solution. Since we are passing the solution as a parameter to this operation, we can let the solution class determine if the tour is complete. To maintain the solution, we need to be able to add the current square to the solution and, if no path is found, to remove the square from the tour. Finally, we have to decide how to incorporate the heuristics. We want to give the heuristic algorithm as much flexibility as possible. It might detect a failure through lookahead or might detect symmetries and want to consider only a subset of the moves. Moreover, as a separate class, it should not change the data within the **Square** class. Thus, we define an interface in which the **Heuristic** object is set up for the given square by passing it the legal moves, and is then called to return the next move to consider. We can now define the operation:

```
Boolean
Square::findRestOfTour(Solution sol)
{
    sol->Solution::addSquare(row_number,column_number)
    If (sol->isValid()) Return True

    Foreach Move m from this square
       m->Square::markUsed(this)
     Next m

    h = new Heuristic
    h->Heuristic::setup(num_moves,legal_moves)
    While ((sq = h->Heuristic::nextMove()) != no square) Do
       If (sq->Square::findRestOfTour(sol)) Return true
     Next i

    Foreach Move m from this square
       m->Square::unmarkUsed(this)
     Next m
    sol->Solution::removeSquare(row_number,column_number)

    Return False
}
```

The first part of this pseudocode adds the square to the solution, checks to see if the solution is complete, and handles it if so. The next part removes moves to this square from the reachable squares. The next section orders the moves and then tries each in turn to find a tour using that move. Finally, if no tour is found, the last section restores moves to this square and removes the square from the solution before returning failure.

The two remaining methods for **Square** handle maintaining the list of valid moves:

```
void
Square::markUsed(Square sq)
{
    Remove sq from the legal_moves and decrement num_moves
}
```

and

```
void
Square::unmarkUsed(Square sq)
{
    legal_moves[num_moves] = sq
    num_moves = num_moves+1
}
```

The class **Heuristic** only has to order the set of moves. While a large range of heuristics could be tried (and the class was created just to do this), we need to select an initial heuristic to use in the design. A simple (and we hope effective) heuristic is to look at the moves from the most to the least restrictive. This means looking at the number of legal moves available at each of the squares and sorting them accordingly. We can improve this somewhat by considering squares with no valid moves and unreachable sequences. Here we can keep track of the number of squares accessible from the current square with either zero or one valid moves. If there is a square with no valid moves and we are not at the end of the tour, then no tour can exist. Similarly, if there is more than one reachable square with only a single successor, no tour can exist. Finally, we note that if there is one square with a single successor it must be tried next.

In order to obtain the necessary information for **Heuristic**, we need to introduce another operation on **Square**:

```
int
Square::numMoves()
{
    return num_moves
}
```

Note that this operation just returns the value of the data element `num_moves`. Both during design and coding it is important that other classes not have access to the data fields of a class. This lets the implementation of the class be changed more easily without affecting the other classes.

Within the **Heuristic** class we keep a list of the valid squares and the move count for each. Rather than actually sorting the moves, we simply find the move with the minimum count that hasn't been tried yet. The `setup` method can then be defined:

```
void
Heuristic::setup(int num,Square moves[])
{
    num_moves = num
    numzero = 0
    numone = 0
    For i = 0 to num-1
        valid_square[i] = moves[i]
        move_count[i]=valid_square[i]->Square::numMoves()
        If (move_count[i] == 1) numone = numone+1
        If (move_count[i] == 0) numzero = numzero+1
      Next i

    If (numzero > 1 || (numzero == 1 && num > 1)) num_moves = 0
    Else If (numone > 2) num_moves = 0
    Else If (numone > 0)
        Eliminate all but the move with move_count = 1
}
```

The first part of this pseudocode sets up the data. The `if` statement at the end checks for cases where the search is guaranteed to fail and sets the count of moves to zero so that nothing is tried. The actual next move is found by:

```
Square
Heuristic::nextMove()
{
    i = index of the remaining move with minimum move_count
    If (there is no such i) Return no_square
    move_count[i] = MAX_MOVES+1
    Return valid_square[i]
}
```

All that remains to be defined at this point is the operations for the class **Solution**. The solution needs to track when each square on the board is used in a tour. One way to do this is to maintain an array containing the number of the move for each square of the board. Its five operations can be defined as:

```
void
Solution::setup(int size)
{
    tour_index = new Integer[size][size]
    num_moves = 0
    board_size = size
}
```

```
void
Solution::addMove(int row,int col)
{
    tour_index[row][col] = num_moves
    num_moves = num_moves + 1
}

void
Solution::removeMove(int row,int col)
{
    tour_index[row][col] = -1
    num_moves = num_moves - 1
}

int
Solution::findIndex(int row,int col)
{
    Return tour_index[row][col]
}

Boolean
Solution::isValid()
{
    Return num_moves == board_size * board_size
}
```

This completes the implementation of all the classes and their operations. Note that, in creating these definitions, we have changed our view of several of the objects, altered the available operations, etc. In some instances, new objects were added and old ones removed. In any case, throughout the process, the static structure diagram with its associated information should be maintained to track the current state of the definition. The final static structure diagram for the knight's-tour example is in Figure 2-12.

EVALUATING A DESIGN

Many implicit decisions were made during the design of the knight's-tour solution. Moreover, as we saw, design is not a one-time process. As the design progresses, previously decided elements will change. As the design is implemented, some aspects of it will probably change as well. The purpose of this section is to attempt to make explicit some of the principles to be used both in building the initial design and in reevaluating and improving an existing design.

The most important criterion, so important that it is almost taken for granted, is that the design must be correct. It must address and solve all

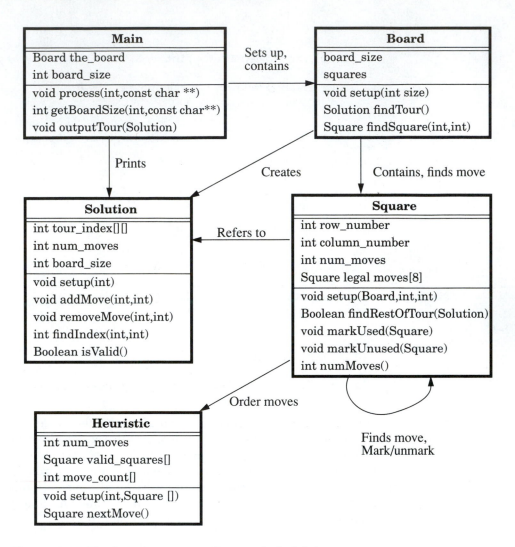

Figure 2-12 Final static structure diagram for knight's tour.

issues brought up in the problem definition, and the solution it presents must actually solve the given problem within the specified constraints. The design must also be complete. Each class and method in the design should be needed and no class or method necessary at the level the design is given should be omitted.

The first step in evaluating a design is thus to make sure the design is correct. There are, however, a wide range of correct designs. The basic design criteria of simplicity and risk minimization discussed briefly in the previous chapter can then be used to choose among these. Simplicity is the overriding principle, since a simple design is generally easier to implement and easier to maintain. Risk minimization also attempts to ensure that the design can be implemented and is robust in the presence of change. While the knight's-tour problem is too simple for large-scale design issues to arise, these same principles were applied at the class level to guide and evaluate the above design.

A number of class properties, some concrete, some abstract, can be used to determine if a design is good or bad. These can guide the design process, help in reevaluating and improving the design, and be used during maintenance to assist in design modifications. These include simplicity itself, coupling and cohesion, information hiding, and error handling.

Simplicity

The first criterion in evaluating a design is simplicity. Classes, methods, and the overall design should all be as simple as possible. Designers should always be asking themselves how they can simplify a design. This is especially true before the design is actually implemented, when changes are relatively inexpensive and any simplification will result in less work down the line.

Simplicity is easiest to achieve at the class level. Some of the questions to ask about each class to help simplify it include:

Can any operations be removed?

Can any data elements be removed?

Can any parameters be removed from the operations?

Can the parameter and return types for any operations be simplified?

Are the operations and their parameter lists logically consistent?

The first two of these questions attempt to minimize the class interface by removing unnecessary operations and data elements. Generally, the fewer the operations to be implemented, the more straightforward the implementation will be. However, operations that are not basically the same should not be combined artificially, since this will actually complicate the resultant code.

The next two attempt to simplify the remaining operations by reducing the number of parameters or simplifying the parameter and return types. Operations with fewer parameters are simpler and more understandable than those with more parameters. Moreover, simple data types, for example built-in ones, are easier to understand and lead to fewer problems than complex data types such as structures, arrays, and objects.

The final question is aimed at ensuring the design is consistent and should be asked of all classes at once. The order in which parameters are passed should be logical and the same throughout. If a buffer and its length are passed (`buffer_pointer, length`) in one operation, they should not be passed (`length, buffer_pointer`) in another. If external libraries such as an I/O library are used, the same library should be used throughout. Similarly, names should be created and used consistently throughout the system.

Simplicity in the design is also reflected in the implementation of the methods. Methods should be relatively simple. The code for any particular method should fit on one page (really one screen). Any method longer than this should be split into separate methods. This length limitation should be considered during the implementation design. If the method definition is too complex, it should be broken down into separate methods that become part of the design and are reflected in the pseudocode.

Another way simplicity is reflected in the method implementations is in how the method code uses methods of this and other classes. Interaction patterns tend to work best when they are kept simple. The *Law of Demeter*, a general guideline for object-oriented design, states that a method should talk only to its friends.[1] "Friends" in this context are methods of its own class, methods of classes that are data fields of its own class, methods of its parameters, and methods of any newly created objects. It should not find objects using these methods and then use these object directly. Following this guideline ensures that each method need only be aware of its local environment and need not be aware of the overall class structure of the implementation of other classes, which could easily change.

Cohesion and Coupling

Simplifying a class design goes beyond just simplifying the set of operations. One must ensure that the proper set of classes has been chosen. Two properties of a class that can help in evaluating this are cohesion and coupling.

A class is *cohesive* if everything in it is directed at a single purpose. Classes serving more than one purpose are generally better split into two simpler classes. Similarly, operations should be cohesive, serving a single purpose. A simple test for cohesion is to attempt to describe what a class or operation does in a single sentence. If the sentence is compound (i.e. includes "and"), then the class probably serves multiple purposes and should be simplified.

While cohesion involves a single class, *coupling* involves the relationship between classes. A class has good coupling if it has minimal dependencies on other classes. Classes should never depend on knowing the internal implementations of other classes. All relationships among classes should be based on operations, not on data elements. The number of operations one class provides for another (and the number of parameters in those operations) should be minimized.

If two classes are too closely related, then the design should be modified. This can be done in a variety of ways. The two classes could be merged into one if the resultant class would still be cohesive. Alternatively, an intermediate class could be created to factor out the common properties of the two

---

1. See Karl Lieberherr, *Adaptive Object-Oriented Software: The Demeter Method with Propagation Patterns*, PWS Publishing Company, 1996.

classes, so the two original classes are each related in lesser ways to the intermediate class.

Information Hiding

A third principle used in evaluating a design is to ensure that it provides a high degree of abstraction or *information hiding*. Information hiding enhances simplicity by concealing implementation details within a particular class or method and separating those details from other classes. It also provides for risk management since any aspects of the system in which change might be required can be hidden inside a particular class or method so that later changes affect only that class and not the remainder of the system.

In general, a good design hides the implementation of any one class from all other classes. This means that the data elements of each class must be local to that class and not accessible elsewhere, and that methods of the class should be separated into those accessible by other classes and those used as part of the implementation. We reflect this in our design by using methods exclusively for communication between different classes and not using data fields. When we code the knight's-tour example in the next chapter, we utilize the C++ protection mechanisms here as well.

A good design will also attempt to identify, as we have with the **Heuristic** class, those portions of the design that are not well understood, that are subject to change, or that are machine- or operating-system-specific in a system where portability may be a concern. All these cases are situations in which new classes should be created to hide the appropriate implementation and form a basis for later change.

Error Handling

The final principle is to ensure that the design can deal with error. Error handling is not generally the first thing on a designer's mind when specifying the system. However, a large percentage of the code of most systems turns out to involve handling special cases and errors. For example, in a typical database system, half the code may involve handling concurrency, integrity, logging, and system and disk recovery. Moreover, this code is typically more complex than the code that handles normal query and data storage. Good error handling is also an essential part of a good user interface and is necessary in any system that deals directly with users.

Error handling, however, is difficult to do because it means anticipating the unanticipated. It is especially hard to add to a system once it has been designed and implemented. Error handling, to be done correctly, must be thought about as part of the initial problem statement and should be an important design criterion in considering alternative designs. Moreover, as we see in the next few chapters, the coding of a design should also emphasize proper error handling, through defensive coding techniques and appropriate interface definitions and in the assumptions made about valid and invalid values.

SUMMARY

In designing a solution to the knight's-tour problem, we followed a series of simple steps. We start by looking at the problem in depth. Here we are trying to:

- Understand the problem.
- Explore potential solutions.
- Establish how success would be defined.

The complete understanding of the problem and the potential solutions that these goals entail is a necessary starting point for a successful design.

Once we understand the problem, we next attempt to identify an appropriate set of classes for describing the solution. Here we:

- Analyze the problem description, diagrams and possible solutions for potential classes.
- Consider placeholder and algorithm classes.
- Select a subset of five to ten classes that is independent, balanced, and covers the problem by analyzing how a solution would work.

The resulting set of classes forms the basis for an object-oriented description of the solution.

The next step in building an object-oriented design is to flesh out these classes with further descriptions of what they are and what they can do. This involves characterizing the classes; here we:

- Use both diagrams and text to define what each class is and does and how the various classes relate.
- Attempt to understand the function and use of each class.

The result of this step is a high-level view of the solution represented in terms of objects and their interaction.

In the final step in object-oriented design, we map this high-level view into a detailed implementation view. Here we:

- Write pseudocode to understand each operation.
- Define the exact interfaces of all operations.
- Keep the diagrams and text describing the classes up-to-date.
- Use operations exclusively without accessing data from other classes.
- Let the design evolve.

The overall result is a complete and annotated object diagram that provides the solution overview along with pseudocode that gives details of how to implement each of the operations. The combination of these is a solid basis for an eventual object-oriented implementation of the design.

Throughout these stages, we used a set of guidelines to help us achieve a simple and workable design:

- Keep the design as simple as possible.
- Ensure that each class is cohesive.
- Ensure that different classes are not tightly coupled.
- Use information hiding so each class's implementation is invisible to other classes.
- Ensure that the design can tolerate errors.

EXERCISES

2.1   Consider a program to play tic-tac-toe.

a) Write a suitable description of the program.
b) Identify a set of objects from this description.
c) Write a scenario illustrating how the program might work.
d) Identify a set of objects from the scenario.
e) Select an appropriate set of top-level objects.
f) Can you identify more than one candidate set?

2.2   Consider another chess-related puzzle, the eight-queens problem. The goal here is to place eight queens on an 8×8 chess board so that no two queens are in the same row, column, or diagonal.
a) Write a suitable description of the program.
b) Identify a set of objects from this description.
c) Write a scenario illustrating how the program might work.
d) Identify a set of objects from the scenario.
e) Select an appropriate set of top-level objects.
f) Can you identify more than one candidate set?

2.3   How would you modify the knight's-tour design if you were asked to find paths rather than tours?

2.4   How would you modify the knight's-tour design if boards could have arbitrary rectangular dimensions rather than being square?

2.5   Another way of thinking about the knight's-tour problem is to concentrate on paths. Here one would build partial paths and connect them together. At each stage, either a move is added to a path or a path is connected to another path. Again, a heuristic such as extending the path with the minimum number of options needs to be used. Design a knight's-tour implementation that follows this approach.

2.6   One way of appreciating your designs is to review other designs for the same problem. Take a design you have done (for one of the above exercises or some other problem) and swap it with another person in the class. Attempt to understand the design that you are given and then evaluate it on the basis of correctness, simplicity, class cohesion and coupling, information hiding, and error handling.

2.7   Design a program that reads in a regular expression and then a sequence of strings and identifies which of the strings is matched by the regular expression.

2.8   Produce an object-oriented design for a program that creates and draws (or prints) a maze.

Chapter 3

Implementing an Object-Oriented Design

Once an object-oriented design has been completed and checked, we can begin implementing it. The implementation should be relatively straightforward. The design is first converted into declarations, and then the code is constructed from the pseudocode written for each operation.

A variety of issues come up during implementation. These include code style, how best to use the language, how to implement classes, and when to reevaluate and modify the design. In this chapter we start by discussing coding style and form, which set the basis for the implementation. We then give a detailed description of how the knight's-tour example in the previous chapter is implemented. The complete implementation appears in Appendix B.

CODING CONVENTIONS

Implementing a design involves converting the class design into declarations and the method pseudocode into actual code. If the overall design is relatively complete, this process should be mechanical: translate each of the data elements into fields and each of the operations into methods, and then map the pseudocode into the implementation language. However, the programmer should look at coding as the task of "publishing" a program and should spend just as much effort on getting the style and form of the code correct as on getting its contents correct.

Programs should be designed and implemented for readability. This has several implications:

- There should be standard conventions for files, naming, and formatting code. What is important here is to adopt a set of conventions to make the code readable and consistent. File conventions should make it easy to find any class or method without having to look at every file in the system. Naming conventions should tell the reader of the code something about each identifier without having to look the identifier up explicitly. Formatting conventions should make the code as readable as possible.

- The programmer should make liberal use of comments. Comments should be used to provide design information and in general to make the code more logical and simpler to understand. Comments should be inserted as the program is written to best capture the author's intent.

- Language conventions enhancing readability should be used as much as possible. In C++, these conventions include the use of `const`, protection qualifiers (`private`, `protected` and `public`), type definitions, and, when programs become more sophisticated, exception declarations.

- Coding style should emphasize simplicity rather than efficiency or craftiness. A simpler program is easier to modify and evolve over time. Moreover, only a small fraction of a program is performance-critical. Since it is difficult to foresee exactly which portion this is, coding for efficiency is best done after the program is written and working.

Naming Conventions

The first set of conventions involves naming. The programmer has a variety of alternatives in defining names. Names can be all upper-case, all lower-case, or mixed-case. Names can begin with an upper-case or lower-case character or with an underscore. Words can be separated by an underscore as in `board_size`, by a change in case as in `addMove`, or not at all as in `numzero`. Words can be long or abbreviated, singular or plural.

The purpose of a naming convention is to use these various alternatives to make the program more understandable. The goals of a naming convention are first to enhance readability by making the program look good, second to provide consistency so the names help the reader understand the program, and third to make the program easier to write and debug. The principal means of achieving these goals is to use names in a consistent way so the reader can tell at a glance what type of entity each identifier refers to. A secondary goal is to ensure that a name contains enough information for the reader to find its definition easily. A full-scale naming convention is provided in Appendix A and a summary with examples is shown in Figure 3-1. In this section we briefly cover the high points of the convention. Most companies and teachers today have developed their own styles. What is important here is not the particular conventions used but the consistent application of a comprehensive standard.

The naming convention we use anticipates larger programs involving multiple programmers. In these cases it is important that each global or external name contain some information about the part of the system in which it is defined. We assume that the system is divided into separate packages and each package has its own unique name. The package name is then used as the prefix for all global or potentially global names from that package. For a sim-

Identifier Type	Examples	Description
Type name	Integer KnightBoard KnightSquare	Mixed-case with the first letter of each word (including the first) in upper-case. Defined types should begin with the package name.
Method name	process getBoardSize outputTour	Mixed-case with the first letter of each word except the first in upper-case.
Field name	the_board num_moves squares_	All lower-case with words separated by an underscore. If it consists of a single word, an underscore should be appended or prepended to the name.
Local variable	i numzero	All lower-case with no underscores.
Constant	DEFAULT_SIZE	All upper-case with underscore separating the name. Global constants should begin with the package name.

Figure 3-1 Summary of naming conventions.

ple program such as knight's tour, all names have the same prefix, in this case **Knight**.

Different name styles are used to distinguish among:

- *Type names*: Type names are mixed-case starting with an upper-case character and with an upper-case character starting any additional words. Types are generally global and begin with the package name.

- *Method names*: Method names are mixed-case starting with a lower-case letter. New words begin with an upper-case letter. Methods are defined inside a class and do not need the package prefix.

- *Field names*: Field names are all lower-case with underscores separating words. They should always contain an underscore (to distinguish them from local variables). Hence, field names consisting of a single word should have an underscore at either the beginning or the end. An alternate convention is to have field names always consist of more than one word. Another convention, sometimes used here, is to insist that all method names begin or end with an underscore. I don't like this convention as I find it makes the program less readable.

- *Local variables*: Local variables (parameters and names defined inside a method) should be all lower-case with no underscores.

- *Constant names*: Constant names, whether defined as constants, using the preprocessor, or inside an enumeration type, should be all upper-case with words separated by underscores. If the constant is accessible beyond the scope of a single file, it should begin with the package prefix.

In addition to these formatting conventions, names should be chosen for consistency. If the programmer wants to abbreviate "board" as "bd" in names, all names that would include the term "board" (including fields, methods, classes, and constants) should use `bd` rather than `board`. Similarly, consistent phrasing and terminology should be used for all names. For example, a set of items may be referred to in the singular or the plural, as in `board_squares`. If the items are used collectively, a plural name makes sense. But if the items are indexed, as in `board_squares[10]`, then a singular name makes the code more readable. The programmer should, for consistency, use either singular or plural names for collections throughout an application.

Overall we recommend

> **Adopt and adhere to a comprehensive naming convention.**

Standard Types

C++ provides the programmer with a wide variety of built-in types that are fairly standard and should be understood by most programmers and code readers. However, the basic type names do not adhere to our naming conventions and several of the types differ from one implementation of the language to another. For example, `long` on some systems will be 32-bit integers while on others it will be 64-bit integers. The type `long long` can be either 32, 64, or 128 bits depending on the implementation; the type `char` can be either signed or unsigned. Other types have names consisting of multiple keywords and tokens such as `unsigned long int` or `const char*`.

In order to make the program clear and to ensure portability, it is generally a good idea to develop a standard set of type names to represent the basic types. This lets the standard naming conventions be used throughout, facilitates porting the code to a new machine or compiler, and makes the code more readable.

Throughout our examples we use the standard set of type definitions:

```
typedef   int            Integer;
typedef   char           Boolean;
typedef   char           Character;
typedef   double         Float;
typedef   char *         Text;
typedef   const char *   ConstText;
```

Here **Integer** represents an arbitrary integer, **Boolean** is used for Boolean values, **Character** for characters, and **Float** for arbitrary floating-point values. (To simplify our code, we generally use `double` instead of `float` for all floating-point computations. On most machines, this is both more accurate and more efficient.) Finally, we define **Text** as a string pointer in which the string can be modified and **ConstText** as a string pointer in which the string cannot be modified. Note that if one's compiler supports it, the built-in type `bool` should be used as the basis for the **Boolean** type.

These definitions can either be defined for each program or be part of a standard header file included by all programs.

Pointers and Objects

An object-oriented language implements an object as a structure with operations. The structure, stored in memory, includes the data elements of the object and any additional information needed for the implementation of the methods. The methods are invoked with a pointer to this structure. In pure object-oriented languages such as Smalltalk, Eiffel, or Java, the pointer to the structure and the object are synonymous — the pointer acts as the object and the only way of accessing the object is through the pointer. The result is a simple, consistent view of objects.

C++, on the other hand, because it was derived from C, views the structure and a pointer to the structure as separate entities. This has advantages and disadvantages. It gives the programmer additional flexibility since objects can be placed on the stack, in the heap, or in static storage. It lets objects be declared and initialized before the program starts executing. It can make programs slightly more efficient by avoiding storage allocation and providing more direct access to the contents of an object. However, it also makes the language significantly more complex and can easily lead to confusion. Objects can be passed by using pointers or references to the data, or by copying the structure itself. Each of these has different semantics. Destructors are called implicitly for some objects and not for others, depending on their storage classification. Pointers to objects that no longer exist are easy to create and pass around. Different syntax is required for objects represented as pointers than for objects represented as structures.

Because the main objective in writing a program should be to get it working, the programmer should strive for simplicity and avoid the many pitfalls of the dual representation of objects in C++. Although there are exceptions such as iterators when using the standard library, we generally want to view an object as a pointer to its block of storage and deal with the storage itself only when we have to, as in creating a new object. Thus we actually define two type names for each class we define. The first type name, representing the pointer to the object, is the one we generally use. The second, representing the class, is used rarely. In C++, the object type name is declared with a forward reference to the class type:

```
typedef class KnightMainInfo *       KnightMain;
typedef class KnightBoardInfo *      KnightBoard;
typedef class KnightSquareInfo *     KnightSquare;
typedef class KnightHeuristicInfo *  KnightHeuristic;
typedef class KnightSolutionInfo *   KnightSolution;
```

Note that this introduces a new naming convention by which the type name for the actual class consists of the pointer type name followed by the text "`Info`". Note also that these lines should have appropriate comments describing the type (for which there is not enough room here).

The pointer type and its corresponding class type should be used consistently. Items being declared, whether variables, parameters, or data fields, should use the pointer type, either directly or in its `const` form if the data is not to be modified. When an object is created, the `new` statement should use the class type and access one of the constructors of the class. The result of the `new`, however, is a pointer type and can be assigned directly. Once pointers exist, the `->` form of reference should be used for both method and data access. Finally, the application should use the `delete` statement to free all objects explicitly.

Constants

C++ provides a variety of ways of defining and using constants. Constants can be used directly by inserting the appropriate number. Alternatively, they can be defined using the preprocessor, constant declarations, or inside enumeration types. Again, the plethora of ways of defining constants can lead to confusion and limit program readability.

The first rule for using constants should be to use symbolic constants almost exclusively. In general, the only numbers that should appear in a program are zero and one, and these should appear only in obvious contexts. Any other number should be defined as a symbolic constant and the symbol should be used in its place.

The second rule is to be consistent in how constants are defined. Because the preprocessor is really an extension to the language, it should generally be avoided. Thus most constants should be defined using constant declarations, as in:

```
const  Integer   DEFAULT_BOARD_SIZE = 8;    // if none specified
const  Integer   MAX_MOVES = 8;             // from a square
```

These should have meaningful comments to let the reader quickly understand their purpose. Enumeration constants should be used for defining constants inside class definitions (where constant declarations cannot be used with all compilers) and where there is a set of related integer constants. Considering these, we recommend:

> **Use symbolic constants defined consistently throughout.**

```
class KnightMainInfo {
private:
    KnightBoard the_board;          // board to compute tour over
    Integer board_size;             // size of the board

public:
    KnightMainInfo();
    ~KnightMainInfo();

    void process(Integer argc,ConstText * argv);    // main loop

private:
    Integer getBoardSize(Integer argc,ConstText * argv);
    void outputTour(const KnightSolution) const;
};
```

Figure 3-2 Declaration of KnightMainInfo.

WRITING THE CLASS DECLARATIONS

The first step in implementing an object-oriented design is to convert the design into a set of declarations. This process should be straightforward. The data elements and operations defined for each class are converted to fields and methods. The type names used in the informal design are converted to the standard and internal type names used in the application.

For example, the class **Main** in the knight's-tour example from Figure 2-12 is converted in the declaration for **KnightMainInfo** as shown in Figure 3-2. There are several things to note about this declaration. First, comments describe the meaning of each of the fields and methods. For readability, the methods are grouped by function, each grouping separated by a blank line. Here the groupings are the constructors and destructors, the processing routines, and the input and output methods. Blank lines should in general be used to improve readability of both declarations and code. Also, the elements of the class definition are given in a fixed order. Here we define the fields first, then the public methods, and finally the private methods. The public methods should always precede the private methods. The data elements can come either first (where they help the reader to understand what the object is about) or last (where they can be skipped more easily so the reader can see the actual interface). Finally, when a method is declared, argument names are provided to document any non-obvious parameter. The process method, for example, takes two parameters, the argument count and the argument value list. The names argv and argc are standard C or C++ names for these values.

Methods not called externally and field definitions are declared private rather than public. Field definitions should always be declared either private or protected. Methods should be declared at the highest appropriate level of

```
class KnightBoardInfo {

private:
    Integer board_size;         // size of the board
    KnightSquare * the_squares; // sq[board_size][board_size]

public:
    KnightBoardInfo(Integer size); // set up the board squares
    ~KnightBoardInfo();

    KnightSquare findSquare(Integer row,Integer col);

    KnightSolution findTour();      // find complete knight's tour
};
```

Figure 3-3 Declaration of KnightBoardInfo.

protection. In this case, the process method will be invoked by the actual main program and needs to be external. Similarly, the main object will be created and deleted by the main program so the constructor and destructor need to be public. Putting the elements of the class definition at the appropriate level of protection serves both to document the class interface by telling the reader explicitly what is meant for external and internal use, and to ensure that the interface is used properly by the remainder of the program.

Another language feature used in this declaration for improved readability and safety is const. Each method that is meant to treat the object as read-only should be declared constant, both to document this fact and to ensure it is actually true. Moreover, each parameter (other than ones with simple types such as int or float that will not be modified) should be declared const as well. For example, the method outputTour, which outputs the resultant tour or an error message, does not modify the **KnightMainInfo** object and is declared const. Its parameter, the solution, is not modified so it too is declared const.

Finally, even though they were not included in our initial design, we have added a constructor and a destructor for the class. While C++ is quite happy creating its own versions of these, it is generally better that the programmer define them explicitly, giving them the proper protection level and providing a placeholder for any appropriate initializations and clean-up code.

Taking all this into account, we proceed with the definition of the other classes of the knight's-tour example. The class **Board** is converted into a declaration for **KnightBoardInfo** as shown in Figure 3-3. This definition again differs slightly from the class specified in the design. In this case, we have moved the setup operation into the constructor for the class. This can be done when the operation only does relatively simple initializations; if the setup operation were to do nontrivial operations, then a separate method should be used. The reason for this is that constructors are somewhat special and virtual methods

```
class KnightSquareInfo {
private:
    Integer row_number;                      // row index
    Integer column_number;                   // colunm index
    Integer num_moves;                       // # of legal moves
    KnightSquare legal_moves[MAX_MOVES];  // available moves

public:
    KnightSquareInfo();
    ~KnightSquareInfo();

    void setup(KnightBoard,Integer row,Integer col);

    Integer numMoves() const;               // count for heuristics

    Boolean findRestOfTour(KnightSolution); // local path search
    void markUsed(KnightSquare);            // remove legal move
    void markUnused(KnightSquare);          // restore move
};
```

Figure 3-4 Declaration of KnightSquareInfo.

```
class KnightHeuristicInfo {

private:
    Integer num_moves;                        // # moves to consider
    KnightSquare valid_squares[MAX_MOVES];// squares for moves
    Integer move_count[MAX_MOVES];            // count for squares

public:
    KnightHeuristicInfo(Integer movect,KnightSquare * squares);
    ~KnightHeuristicInfo();

    KnightSquare nextMove();          // return next square or NULL
};
```

Figure 3-5 Declaration of KnightHeuristicInfo.

do not work correctly inside them. Another change we have made in implementing this class is to convert the two-dimensional array of squares into a dynamic one-dimensional array, since C++ does not support dynamic multidimensional arrays. The internal code for the methods, especially findSquare, will have to take this into account.

The definition for the **Square** class is closer to the original design, as shown in Figure 3-4. Note here that the number of legal moves is specified by a symbolic constant rather than by the number 8. Finally, the **Heuristic** class is shown in Figure 3-5 and the **Solution** class in Figure 3-6. The **Solution** class

```
class KnightSolutionInfo {

private:
    Integer board_size;         // size of board for solution
    Integer num_moves;          // size of current solution
    Integer * tour_index;       // idx[board_size][board_size]

public:
    KnightSolutionInfo(Integer bdsize);
    ~KnightSolutionInfo();

    void addMove(Integer row,Integer col);   // add next to path
    void removeMove(Integer row,Integer col);// remove last

    Integer findIndex(Integer row,Integer col) const;
    Boolean isValid() const;        // check if tour is complete
};
```

Figure 3-6 Declaration of KnightSolutionInfo.

again converts the dynamic two-dimensional array into a one-dimensional one.

WRITING THE METHODS

Once the declarations for all classes have been completed, the methods can be written. This process should again be a straightforward mapping from the design pseudocode into actual C++ code.

Just as with the class definitions, it is important in writing the actual code to aim for simplicity and readability. A program is like a book — it should be designed to be read by people, not just by the compiler. Moreover, simplicity in the code can only improve its clarity and the ability of later programmers to modify and adapt it to changing circumstances.

KnightMainInfo

Here we start with the implementation of the class **KnightMainInfo**. From the definitions shown in Figure 3-2, there are five methods to implement, starting with the constructor and destructor.

The constructor should initialize all the fields of the class, as shown in Figure 3-7. A programmer should not assume that a field will be set by a method other than the constructor before it is used. Similarly, it is not good practice to let the compiler initialize things for you, since C++ compilers generally do not. We also prefer to initialize fields using assignment statements

```
KnightMainInfo::KnightMainInfo()
{
    the_board = NULL;
    board_size = DEFAULT_BOARD_SIZE;
}


KnightMainInfo::~KnightMainInfo()
{
    delete the_board;
}
```

Figure 3-7 Constructors and destructors for KnightMainInfo.

rather than the special initialization syntax C++ provides. Assignments are well known and will not confuse the reader of the code. Moreover, C++ initialization is done in the order the compiler decides rather than that written by the programmer, so any initializations with side effects can have weird results.

The destructor should free any storage allocated for the class. In general, memory management is the most error-prone part of C++ programming. Each allocated item should be assigned an "owner," a single object that is in charge of that item, and this should be documented as part of the design. Then it is the responsibility of this owner to free the storage for the item at the appropriate time. We cover this issue in more detail in "Safe Memory Management" on page 93. In this case, the **KnightBoardInfo** object for the tour is owned by the **KnightMainInfo** class, which is in charge of both allocating and deleting it.

The input and output methods for class **KnightMainInfo** are shown in Figure 3-8. The input method does a bit of error checking and then gets the size from the command-line argument using the library function atoi. It also checks the result to ensure it is logical and sets it to the default value if not. These actions are examples of *defensive coding*, the practice of anticipating problems or errors in advance and checking for them in the code. Defensive coding should attempt to catch both user errors (as here) and possible programming errors. For example, the outputTour method checks for both a null solution and an invalid one. We return to defensive coding when we discuss debugging in Chapter 8, but our examples will be replete with instances of appropriate checks.

Another approach to defensive coding covered in more detail in Chapter 8 is to add *assertions* to the code. Assertions are Boolean conditions the programmer assumes to be true at a given point in the program. An assert statement (actually a macro in C and C++) is used to state the condition. The compiler generates code to test if the condition holds and to abort the program if not. Assertions are good for specifying necessary conditions but, because they cause the program to abort, are not useful for handling user errors.

```
Integer
KnightMainInfo::getBoardSize(Integer argc,ConstText * argv)
{
    if (argc < 2) return DEFAULT_BOARD_SIZE;

    Integer sz = atoi(argv[1]);
    if (sz <= 0) return DEFAULT_BOARD_SIZE;

    return sz;
}



void
KnightMainInfo::outputTour(const KnightSolution tour) const
{
    Integer r,c,i;

    if (tour == NULL || !tour->isValid()) {
        cout << "No valid tour found for " << board_size <<
            " x " << board_size << " board." << endl;
        return;
    }

    for (r = 0; r < board_size; ++r) {
        for (c = 0; c < board_size; ++c) {
            i = tour->findIndex(r,c);
            cout << setw(4) << i;
        }
        cout << endl;
    }
}
```

Figure 3-8 Input and output methods for class KnightMainInfo.

The final method for **KnightMainInfo** is the process method in Figure 3-9. While the code here follows directly from the pseudocode for the design, there are still several things worth noting. First, the code starts with local declarations. While C++ lets declarations be intermingled with the code, it is still generally better to put most declarations at the start of the function, since this gives readers a known place to look for them. If the variable is used only locally, it can either be placed in a local scope or declared where it is used. However, if the variable is used more than a few lines beyond where it would otherwise be declared, putting the declaration at the top makes more sense. Second, the code anticipates future changes. Not only does it call getBoard-Size to input the board size, it also checks the value returned. This is again an instance of defensive coding. However, it is actually more. If in the future we want to add a graphical interface that requests the board size from the user,

```
void
KnightMainInfo::process(Integer argc,ConstText * argv)
{
    KnightSolution sol;

    board_size = getBoardSize(argc,argv);
    if (board_size <= 0) return;

    the_board = new KnightBoardInfo(board_size);

    if ((board_size & 1) != 0 || board_size <= 4) sol = NULL;
    else sol = the_board->findTour();

    outputTour(sol);

    if (sol != NULL) delete sol;
}
```

Figure 3-9 The process method for KnightMainInfo.

```
KnightBoardInfo::KnightBoardInfo(Integer size)
{
    Integer i,r,c;

    board_size = size;
    the_squares = new KnightSquare[size * size];

    for (i = 0; i < size*size; ++i)
        the_squares[i] = new KnightSquareInfo;

    for (r = 0; r < board_size; ++r) {
        for (c = 0; c < board_size; ++c) {
            findSquare(r,c)->setup(this,r,c);
        }
    }
}
```

Figure 3-10 The constructor for KnightBoardInfo.

the user will probably be given the option of canceling the request. In this case the input method could either terminate or, more appropriately, return an invalid value to its caller. The check here anticipates this eventuality.

KnightBoardInfo

Initializing the board is a bit more difficult. The constructor for **KnightBoard-Info** is shown in Figure 3-10. The board is the owner of both the array of squares and the squares themselves. To set up the board, it must loop through the squares twice, the first time allocating the squares and the next time calling `setup` for each square. The reason for this is that setting up a square involves finding its legal moves, and these moves are represented by the squares it can move to. Hence, before `setup` can be called for a square, all the squares it can move to must have been created.

Another thing to note is that this code uses the `findSquare` method to find the square for a given row and column. There are several more efficient ways of looping through the squares and calling `setup`. One could loop through all the squares and then, for a given index, determine the row and column of that index. Alternatively, one could keep the loop in this code and exploit the fact that the squares are actually looked at in the order they were allocated and hence one could simply bump a pointer through the array of squares. However, both of these alternatives have disadvantages. First, they both are less intuitive to the reader — the reader would have to think a bit more to understand the resultant code and see what it did and why it worked. More importantly, they both make assumptions about how the two-dimensional board is encoded in the one-dimensional array. In the present code this encoding is known only by the `findSquare` method. This avoids any potential problem when the constructor and this method use different encodings (one row-major and one column-major), and the encoding can be changed easily by changing only a single method. This is an instance of *information hiding*. In general, just as we attempted to encapsulate design decisions in appropriate classes, it is a good idea to limit the scope of implementation decisions to a single method or a small set of related methods.

The remaining methods for **KnightBoardInfo** are shown in Figure 3-11. The destructor deletes both the individual squares and the array of squares, since both of these were determined to be owned by the class. The remaining methods follow immediately from the corresponding pseudocode. The only thing to note is the use of initializing declarations in the method `findTour`. Unless the variables being declared are obvious temporaries such as loop variables, it is generally a good idea to provide initial values at the time of declaration. (We really should have initialized `sol` in the `process` method shown in Figure 3-9.) This avoids any attempts to use uninitialized variables. Moreover, when a variable will remain constant throughout the routine, as in this case, providing its definition as part of the declaration acts as a form of documentation to make the code more readable.

KnightSquareInfo

The constructor, `setup`, and `numMoves` methods for **KnightSquareInfo** are shown in Figure 3-12. The constructor initializes all the fields even though the setup method will actually be called before any fields are used. This is again an instance of defensive coding. The design for setting up the individual squares is not, however, optimal. The row and column number for a square are fixed

```
KnightBoardInfo::~KnightBoardInfo()
{
    Integer i;

    for (i = 0; i < board_size * board_size; ++i) {
        if (the_squares[i] != NULL) delete the_squares[i];
      }

    delete [] the_squares;
}


KnightSquare
KnightBoardInfo::findSquare(Integer row,Integer col)
{
    if (row < 0 || row >= board_size) return NULL;
    if (col < 0 || col >= board_size) return NULL;

    return the_squares[row*board_size + col];
}


KnightSolution
KnightBoardInfo::findTour()
{
    KnightSolution sol = new KnightSolutionInfo(board_size);
    KnightSquare start = findSquare(1,2);
    KnightSquare sq0 = findSquare(0,0);

    start->markUsed(sq0);
    sq0->markUsed(start);

    start->findRestOfTour(sol);

    return sol;
}
```

Figure 3-11 The remaining KnightBoardInfo methods.

when the square is defined, but it would be cleaner and more logical to set them as part of the constructor rather than in the setup method. The setup method would then be constrained to finding the set of valid moves from the given square.

The numMoves method for **KnightSquareInfo** is quite simple, just returning the value of the field num_moves. This is an instance of a *access method*, a method that provides a procedural interface to some of the data of the class. Data fields represent the implementation and should be kept private or protected within a method, and other classes that need to access or set this

```
KnightSquareInfo::KnightSquareInfo()
{
    row_number = -1;
    column_number = -1;
    num_moves = 0;
}


void
KnightSquareInfo::setup(KnightBoard b,Integer r,Integer c)
{
    Integer i,j,k;
    KnightSquare sq;

    row_number = r;
    column_number = c;

    for (i = -2; i <= 2; ++i) {    // generate move combinations
        if (i == 0) continue;
        for (j = -1; j <= 1; j += 2) {
            k = (3 - abs(i)) * j;          // in i and k
            sq = b->findSquare(r+i,c+k);
            if (sq != NULL) legal_moves[num_moves++] = sq;
        }
    }
}


Integer
KnightSquareInfo::numMoves() const
{ return num_moves; }
```

Figure 3-12 Initialization methods for KnightSquareInfo.

should go through methods defined for this purpose. Using methods here lets the programmer control what happens to the class and change the implementation of one class without affecting any others. It also ensures that implementation decisions made for one class are independent of those made for another. Here, the numMoves method was specified as part of the design, and it is an accident of the implementation of the class **KnightSquareInfo** that it is actually a data field in the class.

Access methods are simple enough that they are often best represented as inline definitions within the class declaration. While inline methods are convenient and offer the compiler an opportunity for optimization, they should be used sparingly. The class declaration is intended to be a general definition of a class so the reader can get a feel for the class while ignoring the details. Inline methods that are more than one line long or contain complex expressions tend

```
Boolean
KnightSquareInfo::findRestOfTour(KnightSolution sol)
{
    KnightSquare sq;
    KnightHeuristic heur;
    Integer i;

    sol->addMove(row_number,column_number);  // add sq to soln
    if (sol->isValid()) return TRUE;         // check if done

    for (i = 0; i < num_moves; ++i)   // remove moves to square
        legal_moves[i]->markUsed(this);

    heur = new KnightHeuristicInfo(num_moves,legal_moves);
    while ((sq = heur->nextMove()) != NULL) {// try each move
        if (sq->findRestOfTour(sol)) return TRUE;
    }
    delete heur;

    for (i = 0; i < num_moves; ++i)   // restore moves to square
        legal_moves[i]->markUnused(this);

    sol->removeMove(row_number,column_number);// restore board

    return FALSE;
}
```

Figure 3-13 KnightSquareInfo::findRestOfTour method.

to interfere with such readability. Moreover, methods containing references to or using other classes should not be declared inline. Making these inline creates implicit dependencies on the order of class declarations and the order of include files that can both get in the way of readability and lead to errors if the code is modified later on.

The remaining methods for **KnightSquareInfo** are shown in Figure 3-13 and Figure 3-14. The findRestOfTour method is the heart of the knight's-tour search and the most complex method of the program, yet it still follows directly from the pseudocode we wrote in the design phase. There are several things to note here. The first is the use of spacing and comments to make clear what the procedure does. Blank lines are used extensively to separate the different steps in the search. Moreover, comments are used at each step to describe what is going on, making it easy for a casual reader to understand the code.

The method allocates a **KnightHeuristicInfo** information structure to help order the moves. This object is stored not in the class object but in a local variable within this method. Thus the method (rather than the class) should be

```
void
KnightSquareInfo::markUsed(KnightSquare sq)
{
    Integer i,j;

    j = 0;
    for (i = 0; i < num_moves; ++i) {
        if (legal_moves[i] == sq) ++j;
        else if (j > 0) legal_moves[i-j] = legal_moves[i];
    }
    num_moves -= j;
}


void
KnightSquareInfo::markUnused(KnightSquare sq)
{
    legal_moves[num_moves++] = sq;
}
```

Figure 3-14 The methods for removing and adding valid moves for a square.

considered the owner of the **KnightHeuristicInfo** object and should free it when it is finished.

The code for `findRestOfTour` is 26 lines long. If we were working with 24-line display terminals, it would not fit on one screen. In general, it is a good idea to make method bodies fit on one screen or page. This ensures their simplicity and lets the reader see the whole method at one glance. If a method needs to be longer than one page, it should be broken up into the main method and one or more private helper methods, each of which does fit on a page. Of course, as display technology improves, the number of lines that can be displayed increases. Today the maximum desired length of a routine is about 50 lines, so that this implementation of `findRestOfTour` is acceptable.

KnightHeuristicInfo

The class **KnightHeuristicInfo** is defined next. It consists of a constructor, a destructor (see Figure 3-15) and the `nextMove` method. The constructor implements the heuristics we specified as part of the design. However, it is probably too complex: constructors in general should only contain simple initialization code, and anything more complex should be included in separate methods. A case can be made, however, that the move setup done in this case is initialization. Moreover, placing the code in the constructor makes the calling code and the **KnightHeuristicInfo** class a bit simpler.

An alternative implementation for effecting the heuristics would be to have a single heuristic object for each square that is allocated only when the square

```
KnightHeuristicInfo::KnightHeuristicInfo(Integer ct,
                                        KnightSquare * sqs)
{
    Integer i;
    Integer numone = 0;
    Integer numzero = 0;

    num_moves = ct;
    for (i = 0; i < ct; ++i) {
        valid_squares[i] = sqs[i];
        move_count[i] = sqs[i]->numMoves();
        if (move_count[i] == 1) ++numone;
        if (move_count[i] == 0) ++numzero;
    }

    // check for unreachable squares
    if (numzero > 1 || (numzero == 1 && ct > 1)) num_moves = 0;
    // check for unreachable sequences
    else if (numone > 2) num_moves = 0;
    // if single sequence, use only it
    else if (numone > 0) {
        for (i = 0; i < ct; ++i) {
            if (move_count[i] > 1) move_count[i] = MAX_MOVES+1;
        }
    }
}


KnightHeuristicInfo::~KnightHeuristicInfo()
{ }
```

Figure 3-15 Constructor and destructor for KnightHeuristicInfo.

is created. Then there would be an additional method to set up the moves and implement the heuristics for a search instance. This would have the advantage that heuristic objects are not continually allocated and freed. It would have the disadvantage, however, of reusing an object for different purposes at different times (since the set of valid moves and their conditions will differ when one square is considered at different points of the search) and of requiring some thought to ensure that it is not used by the same square twice simultaneously within the search.

The destructor here does nothing. It is tempting in this situation either to omit it (C++ will define it for you) or to make it inline. However, it is a good idea actually to provide a destructor and place it next to the constructor in the implementation file. The class may change over time, and the changes should be consistent. If new data fields are added and storage must be freed when the destructor is called, the presence of the destructor in the code file will remind

```
KnightSquare
KnightHeuristicInfo::nextMove()
{
    Integer i,mv,ct;

    mv = -1;
    ct = MAX_MOVES+1;
    for (i = 0; i < num_moves; ++i) {
        if (move_count[i] < ct) {
            mv = i;
            ct = move_count[i];
        }
    }
    if (mv < 0) return NULL;

    move_count[mv] = MAX_MOVES+1;

    return valid_squares[mv];
}
```

Figure 3-16 Determining the next move based on heuristics.

the programmer to insert the appropriate delete statements and will provide a place for doing so. If the destructor were not present or were defined only in the header file, it would have to be created and thus would be more easily overlooked.

The nextMove method of **KnightHeuristicInfo**, shown in Figure 3-16, is a simple way to implement finding the minimum count move on successive calls. Alternative implementations would either sort the moves initially and just take moves one by one or would remove a move from the array after it had been used. (The latter could be done cheaply by moving the minimum move to the end of the array as it is being searched for and then decrementing the move count.) However, one should generally stress simplicity when implementing code. If the code turns out to be a performance bottleneck later on, it can always be rewritten. Moreover, performance problems are often difficult to predict a priori, and implementing complex code where it is not necessary only makes the task of programming more difficult and leads to more bugs.

KnightSolutionInfo

The final class to be implemented is **KnightSolutionInfo**, which maintains the solution as it is being built. The implementation here is fairly straightforward. The constructor and destructor are shown in Figure 3-17. This class must again implement a two-dimensional dynamic array in a vector. The vector is allocated dynamically based on the board size, is owned by the class, and hence is freed in the destructor. The actual work methods of the class are

```
KnightSolutionInfo::KnightSolutionInfo(Integer sz)
{
    Integer i;

    board_size = sz;
    num_moves = 0;
    tour_index = new Integer[board_size * board_size];

    for (i = 0; i < board_size*board_size; ++i)
        tour_index[i] = -1;
}


KnightSolutionInfo::~KnightSolutionInfo()
{
    delete [] tour_index;
}
```

Figure 3-17 The constructor and destructor for KnightSolutionInfo.

shown in Figure 3-18. Unlike the **KnightBoardInfo** class, where a single method implemented the array indexing, here it is implemented separately in each of the methods. Note that if the index method changes, we will have to change each of the methods appropriately. Adding a new routine to implement the indexing (or adding a new class to implement a 2D array) would be preferable in the long run, especially if the **KnightSolutionInfo** class were not as simple as it actually is.

FILE STRUCTURE

Although we have now shown the complete implementation, we have not actually shown how to write the corresponding program. Doing so requires the code to be placed into files and compiled. A good implementation requires files to be named, formatted and used carefully so that changes are localized and readability is enhanced. In this section we look at how to do this in the knight's-tour program. A complete listing of the knight's-tour solution is given in Appendix B.

C++ systems are composed of two types of files, header files and code files. The header files contain declarations only, while the code files contain the code using these declarations. Organizing these files properly, while not particularly important in a small system, becomes critical as systems get larger, especially when more than one programmer is involved. In order to get programmers accustomed to file structures that work for large-scale programming, we introduce them here and use them throughout the text.

```
void
KnightSolutionInfo::addMove(Integer r,Integer c)
{
    tour_index[r*board_size + c] = num_moves++;
}


void
KnightSolutionInfo::removeMove(Integer r,Integer c)
{
    tour_index[r*board_size + c] = -1;
    --num_moves;
}


Integer
KnightSolutionInfo::findIndex(Integer r,Integer c) const
{
    return tour_index[r*board_size + c];
}


Boolean
KnightSolutionInfo::isValid() const
{
    return num_moves == board_size * board_size;
}
```

Figure 3-18 Methods to build and return the solution.

In the discussion that follows, we assume the programmer is working on a single package or component of the system, i.e. a set of classes with the same name prefix that are logically related and serve a single purpose. In general, each such component is assigned its own directory to hold its files and separate it from other packages.

Header Files

All header files have a common structure. They should all start with a block comment that identifies the file and tells a bit about it, as in Figure 3-19. In a multiple-person project, this should include the author as well as a short description of the purpose of the file. Any version-management information should be included in this header. In general, the programmer should put enough information in the header to identify the file completely and let readers determine if they need to consider it for a given purpose. Care should be taken to maintain this information as the program evolves. If too much or too

```
/**************************************************************/
/*                                                          */
/*      knight_local.H                                      */
/*                                                          */
/*      Local definitions for the knight's tour problem     */
/*                                                          */
/*      Author: Steven P. Reiss, Brown University           */
/*                                                          */
/**************************************************************/


#ifndef KNIGHT_LOCAL_USED
#define KNIGHT_LOCAL_USED


#include <iostream.h>
#include <iomanip.h>
#include <stdlib.h>
```

Figure 3-19 The start of the header file knight_local.H.

detailed information is included here, it tends to become out-of-date and inaccurate.

Block comments can be handled in a variety of ways. They should be formatted so that the comment itself stands out and its contents are easy to determine. We prefer a block comment of the form

```
/**************************************************************/
/*                                                          */
/*      Label Goes Here                                     */
/*                                                          */
/**************************************************************/
```

with appropriate blank lines before and after. The overall block makes the comments obvious to the reader. The text is indented and surrounded by the block and is easy to find and read. This style is difficult to achieve in some editors, however. Alternatives are acceptable provided they stand out, let the text be easily read, and are used consistently. In general, however, C-style comments (/* ... */) spanning multiple lines should be avoided because they are the source of potentially hard-to-spot errors.

After the initial block header should come preprocessor constructs that ensure the file is included only once. These *guards* should always be present not only to let programmers include files in arbitrary order but also because some compilers automatically include files in an arbitrary order when processing templates. The #ifndef and #define lines here at the start of the file are matched by a corresponding #endif line at the end of the file. Following this should come any include files needed by this particular file. Placing these all up front lets the reader easily determine what the dependencies are and track down the other needed files.

After the standard header descriptions should come a set of standard definitions, including parameters, general type definitions, enumerations, and forward class definitions. Each of these should be preceded by a block comment letting the reader quickly find or skip any particular section, and the sections should be defined in a standard order. The various declarations should be commented appropriately. The standard sections from `knight_local.H` (with some comments omitted) are shown in Figure 3-20. Following these global sections should be the declarations of the actual classes. The order of the class declarations should be defined for readability, not for dependencies. (Dependencies should be handled by the forward type declarations.) In this case, we define the classes in a top-down fashion as done in the text, starting with **KnightMainInfo**, then **KnightBoardInfo**, **KnightSquareInfo**, **KnightHeuristicInfo**, and finally **KnightSolutionInfo**. The file should end with the `#endif` that matches the `#ifndef-#define` guard, and then a comment marking the end of the file.

Header files provide the declarations for all the code files. Especially when templates are used, it is important that declarations appear in header files rather than in code files. Each package has three levels of header files. At the top level are the definitions of classes and methods viewable outside the package. This file, typically called *package*.h where *package* is the package name, should hold as little information as possible and should give no hint about how the package is implemented. This ensures that the class interface presented to outside packages is clean and independent of the implementation. It also means that this file need not be changed every time the implementation changes and thus minimizes the amount of recompilation required by outside packages. In future chapters we discuss ways of defining and implementing such header files. For the knight's-tour example, there are no external packages and hence this file is omitted.

The second level of header file contains global definitions for the package. This file, generally called *package*_local.H, should start with a block comment describing the project and identifying the file. Like all header files, it should be guarded to ensure it is included only once. The `#include` lines in this file should specify dependencies for this include file and should specify any global include files to be used generally by all the files in the package. In the knight's-tour example shown in Figure 3-19, we include the definitions for the C++ streams library (`iostream.h`) with manipulators (`iomanip.h`), and the standard C library (`stdlib.h`). Other common include files are `string.h` for the string library, `unistd.h` for more of the standard C library, and `ctype.h` for character manipulation functions.

Class definitions can occur either in this file or in the third level of headers, class-specific files. These files should be named *package_class*.H, where *class* is replaced by the class name without the package header or the "Info" suffix, for example, `knight_main.H`. If a package is complex, it is generally a good idea to break up the header definitions so each class or closely related set of

```
/*************************************************************/
/*                                                         */
/*      Local Type Definitions                             */
/*                                                         */
/*************************************************************/

typedef int              Integer;
typedef char             Boolean;
typedef const char *     ConstText;
typedef char *           Text;
typedef char             Character;
typedef double           Float;




/*************************************************************/
/*                                                         */
/*      Parameters                                         */
/*                                                         */
/*************************************************************/

const  Integer    DEFAULT_BOARD_SIZE = 8; // if not specified
const  Integer    MAX_MOVES = 8;          // max from any square

const  Boolean    TRUE = 1;
const  Boolean    FALSE = 0;




/*************************************************************/
/*                                                         */
/*      Class Type Definitions                             */
/*                                                         */
/*************************************************************/

typedef class KnightMainInfo *        KnightMain;
typedef class KnightBoardInfo *       KnightBoard;
typedef class KnightSquareInfo *      KnightSquare;
typedef class KnightHeuristicInfo *   KnightHeuristic;
typedef class KnightSolutionInfo *    KnightSolution;
```

Figure 3-20 The standard declarations in knight_local.H.

classes has its own header file. This makes it easier to find specific classes, isolates changes and minimizes recompilation. It also lets the programmer easily view multiple class declarations simultaneously by bringing up editors or windows on separate files. These files should be structured similarly to the local include file: they should contain a header comment, the `#ifndef-#define` guard to protect against multiple inclusions, include files (including the local include file in this case), and the various global definitions needed exclusively for the class being defined. Then they should provide the class definition.

The basic guideline here is to put each class definition in a separate header file. Any exceptions to this guideline should then be justified by the programmer. If two classes are closely related, for example if one is used to implement the other, then it makes sense to put the implementation class in the same include file as the class it is serving. Similarly, if a class hierarchy is being defined, it often makes sense to define all the classes in the hierarchy in the same file. A class that defines a primitive type for a package that will be used throughout the package, for example a class defining a color for a graphics package, might be more logically placed in the local include file. If a package is very simple, all the class definitions can be placed in the local include file. In general, classes should be allocated to include files to enhance readability and make it easy for a programmer to find appropriate information.

When defining multiple class header files, the programmer should take care to avoid complex dependencies, since these complicate the program and lead to errors as the system evolves. A class header file should in general depend only on the definitions in itself, the package-local header file, and the package-global header file. It should not depend on the contents of other class header files. This is easily accomplished when all classes are treated as pointers, as we have recommended, and no complex code is included in inline functions in the class header files. The package-local header file should `typedef` the pointer names as forward references to the various classes. This is sufficient for declaring fields, parameters and function return values. Each code file should then include all the class header files it requires.

Code Files

Code files should also be structured for readability. In general, there should be one code file for each class being defined. Again, exceptions to this rule can be made when there is a simple helper class for a given class or a set of closely related classes, for example, variations within a class hierarchy. The files should be named *packageclass*.cxx (or whatever extension is used for C++), for example `knightmain.cxx`.

Code files should start with a block comment naming the file and defining its purpose. In a multiperson project, this header should also specify the author, version-control information, and a brief revision history. Following the header should be the set of `#include`s needed by this file., which should include the local include file and a minimal set of class-specific include files. Following these should come local definitions and then the methods and functions being defined. The file should end with a tailing comment that again names the file.

Code files should contain a minimal set of local definitions. Type definitions, including enumerations, needed exclusively by this file should be placed in the class-specific include file for whatever class is being defined, as should any constants or parameters. Putting all these in a standard location makes it easy for the programmer to find them while reading the code. The only local definitions that should occur are the definitions of static class variables and static definitions of local non-class support functions and storage. In general, it is wise to avoid the need for non-class storage and functions, as these are scoped and named differently from class methods and storage, and only serve to complicate the system. Private static methods and static fields should be used in their place.

The presentation of the method bodies in the code files should be logical and easy to read. The order of presentation should be the same as that in the class declaration. This lets the class declaration be used as a table of contents and ensures the same logical associations used in defining the class are maintained in its implementation. Each method or group of methods should be preceded by a block header letting the reader quickly identify what is being declared and what its purpose is. If the method is in any way complex, this header should elaborate on the complexity, whether it is a complex interface or a sophisticated algorithm. Generally, method bodies should be kept to one screenful in size so the reader can view the whole method at once. Longer methods should be split into logical submethods as needed. As we have noted, blank lines and comments should be used liberally both to improve the readability of the code and to describe any aspects that are not obvious to the potential reader.

SUMMARY

An object-oriented design is implemented in stages. The first stage involves creating the header files from the class designs. Here one takes the class descriptions developed as part of the design, isolates the interfaces inherent in these descriptions, and then translates these interfaces into the appropriate implementation language. While this task should be fairly straightforward, it must be done so as to ensure the program works and can evolve. The important points to remember here are:

- Make the header file readable. Use appropriate block comments, single-line comments, blank lines, and formatting to make the file easy to look at and understand.

- Use a comprehensive naming convention.

- Put definitions in header files in a fixed order. We generally use the order: block comment, guard, included files, local type definitions, parameters, forward type definitions, enumeration types, class definitions, and then any other global definitions.

- Split the header files into a global file for external use, a project-global file containing common definitions for local use only, and individual class files containing class-specific definitions.
- Define the classes in a header file in a logical order that stresses readability.

The second stage is to create the code files containing the method implementations. This involves translating the pseudocode developed as part of the design into actual code in the implementation language. Much of this should again be straightforward, but again care must be taken to ensure that the result is a high-quality and lasting implementation. To achieve this result:

- Write the code so it can be read. Use blank lines liberally and insert meaningful comments where appropriate. Use block comments to identify each method.
- Place methods in the code file in the same order as in the class definition. The file itself should also follow a fixed format such as: block comment, included files, local type definitions, local storage and parameters, and then the method definitions.
- Code defensively.
- Insure that the code is as simple and straightforward as possible.
- Use information hiding to isolate implementation dependencies as much as possible.
- Ensure that all constants (other than possibly 0 and 1) are named.
- Use your naming conventions consistently.
- Generally place only one class in a code file.
- Keep the code for each method or function short enough to fit on one screen.

EXERCISES

3.1   What other enhancements improve code and header file readability? For example, could and should you define a standard formatting convention?

3.2   Implement the tic-tac-toe program designed for Exercise 2.1.

3.3   Implement the eight-queens program designed for Exercise 2.2.

3.4   Modify the code given above to include the modified designs for paths from Exercise 2.3 or the arbitrary board sizes of Exercise 2.4 (or both).

3.5 Implement the alternative approach to the knight's-tour program designed for Exercise 2.5.

3.6 One way of testing code readability is to try reading the code. Take code from someone else in the class for any of Exercises 3.2 through 3.5 or some other assignment and review it. Determine if the code seems to be correct and then comment on its readability, making specific suggestions on making it more readable.

3.7 Design and implement a program that makes word-search puzzles. These are squares of letters in which you are to find a set of words that can be hidden horizontally, vertically, or diagonally and either forwards or backwards. The program should take as input a list of words to be included and the size of the desired puzzle.

3.8 Investigate the various approaches taken to file compression and then design and implement one of these approaches. In a course, see whose program achieves the best compression for some set of sample files.

Chapter 4

How to Use C++ Effectively

C++ is a large and complex language. Parts of it are nonintuitive, other parts are poorly defined, and still others have complex and inefficient implementations. It is thus easier than most languages to use incorrectly. Many of its features are quite specialized and are unnecessary or unsuitable for general programming. These features are best avoided. Other features are very beneficial when used correctly and extensively, but are not encouraged by the language and are typically overlooked by programmers. The purpose of this chapter is to provide guidelines on how to use C++ effectively so that C++ programs are more likely to work, be readable, and be maintainable.

CLASSES AS POINTERS

Unlike pure object-oriented languages in which an object and a pointer to it are the same thing, C++ differentiates between the two as discussed in "Pointers and Objects" on page 51. C++ lets one define and pass classes around as structures or allocate storage and view things as pointers.

The advantages of viewing classes as structures, in addition to backward compatibility with C, are efficiency and convenience. Classes viewed as structures can be allocated either statically or on the stack. Classes represented as pointers should always be allocated in heap storage using the `new` operator. Dynamic allocation of storage can be time-consuming (although today's storage-allocation routines are much faster than they were ten years ago, when memory allocation was a real bottleneck). It also requires additional statements for creating and deleting objects, and forces the programmer to keep track of who owns each object so the object can be deleted at the proper time. All this adds to the complexity of the program.

The advantages of using structures are outweighed, however, by the disadvantages. Viewing objects solely as pointers tends to yield a cleaner and simpler program. One important part of simplicity and understandability of a system is consistency. Viewing objects sometimes as pointers and sometimes as structures is confusing for the reader and the programmer. Using objects in just one way lets the program be understood without having to sort out this issue. Using pointers also provides a degree of portability to and consistency with other object-oriented languages such as Java.

Treating objects as pointers also tends to make one's use of the C++ language a lot clearer. C++ provides a separate syntax for accessing fields or invoking methods of objects viewed as pointers versus objects viewed as structures. Using only pointers lets the programmer consistently use the `a->method()` notation rather than requiring `a.method()` in some contexts and `a->method()` in others. Second, the programmer is sure that virtual methods are used when the object is a pointer. Objects viewed as structures sometimes use virtual methods (for example when they are passed as reference parameters) and sometimes do not, causing further confusion and misunderstanding. C++ also uses a pass-by-value semantics for calling sequences. When an object represented as a structure is passed to a routine, a temporary object is created using the copy constructor of the object and this copy is passed on. Any changes the routine makes to the object are made in the temporary copy, which may not be what was intended. (If the programmer means to make temporary changes, this is better made obvious to the reader by making an explicit copy for this purpose.) If pointers are used consistently, then what is passed is a pointer to the object. This is both more efficient and more often meets the intent of the programmer. Finally, C++ introduces a number of implicit calls using constructors, destructors and conversion operators. If objects are viewed as pointers, these calls become explicit in the code and the code actually states what is happening in the program. If objects are viewed as structures, C++ will insert constructor and destructor calls that are hidden from the programmer and not obvious to the reader.

We thus recommend:

> **Use pointers to represent classes.**

This has several implications. First, as noted, the pointer type and the object type should both be declared, with the pointer type being the name used most often. One of the header files, generally the local header file, should contain a forward type definition introducing the class name and defining the pointer type. For example,

```
typedef class KnightMainInfo * KnightMain;
```

defines both the name `KnightMainInfo` as a class to be declared later and the name `KnightMain` as a pointer to an instance of this class. Note that we make the pointer type name shorter, and thus easier to use, type, and remember, in order to encourage its use over that of the class name. The actual class name should only be used where absolutely necessary, as when using the `new` operator and when calling a static method.

There are three exceptions to this general guideline, all dealing with advanced uses of C++. The first involves the creation of a class to represent a pointer. This can be done to provide automatic control of memory through reference counting or to separate an external interface further from the actual implementation. In this case, the class is meant to be treated as if it were a pointer and hence is an actual class and is passed around as such. Note, however, that such a class can be designed to be treated exactly as if it were a pointer, so that the fact that it is a class is hidden from both programmer and reader.

The second exception arises when the system requires a simple data structure that should be treated as if it were a primitive object such as a point in a graphics program. Here the overhead of allocating, keeping track of, and freeing storage for the small objects throughout the implementation is excessive and makes the code much more complex than it would otherwise be. The program would be more readable and simpler in this case if the data is represented as a structure rather than as a pointer. A structure should only be used in this case, however, if the object is truly simple, i.e. if it contains only simple data, is relatively small, and can be copied with no harmful effects. To distinguish such structures from standard classes, the programmer should declare it as a `struct` rather than a `class`.

The third exception involves classes that are meant to act as primitive elements of the language. For example, in order to add complex numbers to the language one can define a class **Complex** that can be used as a basic arithmetic type. This means that the programmer can mix it freely with integer and floating-point numbers, can apply all the basic arithmetic operations to it in a natural way, can use it for comparisons, can input and output to it directly, and so on. Because one wants to use it with the standard operators and in expressions, it is much more natural to define such a class directly and not to use an intervening pointer. We will see an instance of such a class when we define rational numbers in Chapter 12.

CLASS IMPLEMENTATIONS

C++ offers language features serving both to ensure program correctness and to document the code. These include protection levels within a class and the use of `const` declarations. Both of these should be used as much as possible.

Protection

C++ offers multiple protection levels in a class. Public methods constitute the external interface of the class; they are accessible to other classes and the programmer should make few assumptions about how they are used or the validity of the values being passed in. Private methods and data, on the other hand, are accessible only to members of the class; they constitute the internal interface and define the implementation. The programmer presumably has sufficient control over these that documented assumptions about their parameters, calling order, etc. can be made without extra checking in the code. Protected methods are a special case used only in inheritance; these methods are accessible to subclasses of the class as well as the class itself.

The protection of an item in a class declaration serves both to control access to the class and to document how the programmer expects the method to be used. Thus:

> **Use the most restricted protection level possible for each method and data element.**

Moreover, since data elements directly reflect the implementation, they should never be publicly accessible. Here we insist:

> **Data elements should always be either private or protected.**

Following these guidelines does several things. First, it ensures that the reader can understand the target scope of each method. Second, it minimizes the size of the external interface of a class. Since the external interface essentially defines how the class is viewed from outside, this tends to simplify the class and its use in the system. Third, it lets the compiler check that methods are used only where the programmer expects them to be, thus avoiding potential problems later on.

If a class is so simple that it is essentially a container for some related data items such as the X and Y coordinates of a point, then it can be reasonable to make its data accessible. This should be done by declaring it as a `struct` rather than a `class`, so as to inform the reader. Note that for C++, structures and classes are the same except that the data and methods of a structure are public by default while those of a class are private. In general, a structure should include few if any methods (since methods imply an implementation that should be hidden) and should be as simple as possible. Moreover, all of a structure's methods should be public.

In addition to these levels of protection, C++ offers the notions of friend classes and friend functions. Once a class or function is declared as a friend of a given class, it has full access to the private (and protected) data and methods of the class. However, because friend declarations let the program avoid the normal constraints imposed by the protection mechanisms, they introduce additional complexity by forcing the reader to be aware of exceptions to the standard rules, and thus make it difficult to understand when and where methods can be called and data set. Because of this we recommend:

> **Avoid the use of friend declarations.**

There are two situations in which the use of friends is helpful in C++. Some overloaded operators can only be defined in C++ by using friend functions.

This occurs when the parameter of the class type to the operation is not the first argument, for example when the output function `<<` is overloaded. In these cases, the operator should be defined as a friend function within the class definition. Friend classes can be used for two very closely related classes. For example, one might want to define an iterator whose workings are closely related to a class's implementation. Normally, the iterator would need public access to the class implementation, but making it a friend lets the implementation remain private. It is acceptable to use friend classes in such cases provided the two classes have related names, are both declared in the same header file, and are both defined in the same code file.

Constant Declarations

The other self-documenting facility C++ provides involves the use of `const` in declarations. C++ uses the keyword `const` to represent a variety of things. Consider the method declaration:

```
const char * const member(const ClassPointer obj) const;
```

The first `const` describes the following `char`, indicating the character is read-only. The second `const` modifies the pointer preceding it, indicating the pointer itself is read-only and cannot be changed. The `const` inside the parameter list relates to the subsequent class pointer name. If we assume that `ClassPointer` was defined using a `typedef` to be a pointer to the class **Class-PointerInfo**, this indicates that the parameter `obj` points to a constant object. The final `const` in the declaration refers to the method itself and indicates that the method does not modify the object and can be used if the object is constant. The parameter `obj` in this case, being constant, can be used only to invoke constant methods.

Constant declarations serve both as documentation and as a check on the programmer. Compilers ensure that the code of a constant method does not call any non-constant methods or modify any of the data elements of the class. Moreover, the constant declaration informs both the programmer and any readers of the code of this fact and lets them make the corresponding assumptions without having to check the code. Constant methods are also simpler since they are guaranteed not to modify the class. Thus we recommend:

> **Use const as much as possible in declarations.**

`Const` should be used to indicate which parameters are input-only parameters versus in-out or output-only parameters. As many methods as possible should be declared constant. Note that it is difficult to add constant declarations to existing code because a constant method can only call other constant methods and thus constant declarations must be present throughout. It is much easier to start with the design and specify as such everything that might possibly be declared constant. The initial code can then reflect these decisions. As methods are added that were expected to be constant but are not, the programmer should reevaluate the design to verify that the method should indeed be non-constant, and then should remove as few constant declarations as possible.

Parameters

Const is only one of the options C++ offers in declaring parameters. Parameters in C are all passed by value. A const parameter is thus one that is passed but cannot be set — it is effectively an input parameter. C++, on the other hand, provides two ways of defining parameters for returning values. The first is compatible with C and uses pointers: a pointer to the value to be returned is passed by value to the method and the method sets the value by going indirectly through the pointer.

The alternative is to use reference parameters. These are effectively implemented the same way as pointers: the pointer to the object is passed to the called routine. However, neither the caller nor the called routine need be aware of pointers. The routine is called exactly as if the parameter were passed by value. Similarly, the routine itself can access and assign to the parameter, treating it as an instance of the declared type. This means that reference parameters are more convenient to use and lead to more straightforward code than parameters passed as pointers. Moreover, because the pointer usage is hidden from the programmer, errors such as attempts to dereference a NULL pointer are much less likely.

There are two situations in which reference parameters cannot be used. The first arises when compatibility with C is needed, and thus does not apply to method calls, but might apply to external functions. Since C does not provide reference parameters, pointers must be used in this case. The second situation arises when the output parameter is optional. A pointer parameter lets the programmer pass a NULL value that the routine can then interpret to mean that the resultant value need not be computed or stored.

Reference parameters both document the fact that a parameter is to be used as output and make the program simpler. Hence we recommend:

> **Use reference parameters whenever a value is to be returned by a function as a parameter.**

This recommendation should be qualified by noting that output parameters, whether they use references or pointers, should not be needed very often. A routine that needs to return a single value should be written as a function. Output parameters are needed only when multiple values must be returned. Routines returning multiple values are, however, inherently more complex and should be avoided where possible.

Reference parameters can also be declared const. A constant reference parameter is like an input variable but uses copy-by-reference semantics; that is, a pointer to the value is passed rather than the value itself being copied. This offers a convenient and efficient way for passing complex objects. If a structure (or a C++ class not represented as a pointer) needs to be passed as a parameter, a reference parameter should be used. If the structure is an input parameter, a constant reference parameter should be used. The only difficulty here is that different compilers treat constant reference parameters differently when an expression is passed, sometimes creating a temporary for the call and sometimes giving an error message.

Since we recommend using pointers to represent classes, we generally need not worry about using reference parameters for the passing structures. A class pointer can be passed to a method to let that class be modified. A constant pointer to the class can be passed to indicate a class parameter that will not be changed directly or indirectly.

Parameter types in general are a source of complexity in a C++ program. For simplicity, we recommend:

> **Use simple types for parameters wherever possible.**

Simple types include all the built-in types, including those introduced by the standard libraries (see Chapter 7), enumeration types, names defined as pointers to simple types, and names defined as pointers to classes. Classes should always be passed using a pointer or a constant pointer to the class. If the application requires structures that are not classes, these should either not be used as parameters or should be treated similarly to classes by using pointers. If such structures must be passed, they should at least be passed by reference. Arrays defined directly in C++ should be passed only where necessary, since the language actually treats these as pointers and does no bounds checking. In general, if an array is passed, an additional parameter should be passed with the bounds of the array. Pointers defined using the "*" notation should be passed only when they are used explicitly to allow a return value. All other pointers should be defined using a `typedef`.

The programmer should also keep the types of parameters simple and consistent so as to make the code comprehensible, enhance reuse, and avoid potential misunderstanding. This means the order of similar parameter sets should be the same. For example, when an array and its bounds are passed, the calling sequence should consistently be `array,bounds` (or consistently `bounds,array`). Parameter names should be provided in the declaration for any parameter whose use is not obvious from either its type or the name of the function.

Overloading

One of the more controversial features of C++ is the ability to overload functions and methods. Overloading can take two forms. The user can define multiple methods with the same name but different argument types. The compiler then considers the number and types of arguments in a given call and, using a set of little-understood rules for disambiguation, chooses the proper instance of the method to call. Overloading also occurs when the user provides default values for parameters, thereby letting different calling sequences be used for the same method.

Overloading is controversial because, while it generally makes the code more complex, it can sometimes make it more straightforward and easier to read. Overloading is omitted from many languages because it adds significant complexity to the language that shows up in the programming-language definition and the compiler. The program becomes more difficult to read because it is no longer obvious what function is called from a given site. The language and compiler complexity in C++ is reflected in the complexity and obtuseness of the corresponding sections of the C++ reference manual.

However, overloading can simplify a program by reducing the number of distinct methods the programmer needs to remember and making the code more natural. Consider a drawing program that lets an application set the color of an object using a setColor method. A color can be specified in a variety of ways — by name, by pixel value, or by using red, green, and blue values. The application could define methods for each of these:

```
void setColorByName(const char * color);
void setColorByIndex(int pixel);
void setColorByRGB(float red,float green,float blue);
void setColorByRGBValue(unsigned r,unsigned g,unsigned b);
```

This makes it clear to the reader which method is being called. However, it also requires the programmer to remember (or look up) the names for set-Color for each type of call depending on the circumstances, and makes the resultant code more difficult to read. Using an overloaded function setColor could make more sense here.

A related instance in which overloading can simplify code occurs in setting attribute values in a library. Some libraries, such as Motif and OpenGL, give the user a collection of classes. Objects of these classes have a set of associated properties each of which has an associated type. The library interface needs to provide methods to set each of these properties, accepting arguments of the appropriate type. OpenGL defines a large set of routines for this purpose, one for each type of argument list. For example, there are 24 different functions for specifying the vertices of an object being drawn, all differing only in their names and their argument types. Motif, on the other hand, defines only a single function for setting the hundreds of different properties. While the Motif interface is defined for C and is not type-safe, it is easy to imagine a corresponding C++ interface using a single name and overloading it for the different parameter types. Such an overloaded version of the Motif interface is much more intuitive and easier for the programmer to remember and is the preferred design in this case.

Another use of overloading occurs with constructors, which are special methods that are called implicitly and hence cannot easily be defined with different names. We cover these in "Constructors" on page 89.

Overloading based on the number of arguments is easier to interpret than overloading based solely on argument types, because argument counting can be done without knowledge of the underlying expression types. However, even here one must be careful. Arguments are often added to a method as the program evolves. The addition of a new argument to one method should not cause problems due to sudden ambiguities between it and another method of the same name. Moreover, even though the resolution process is easier, overloading here still requires additional work from both the compiler and the reader.

Default arguments provide an alternative to overloaded functions. They let a library define functions taking a range of parameters that are rarely used but are needed in certain circumstances. These functions can then be used most of the time with their default parameters, providing the programmer with a simplified calling sequence. For example, a graphics library might have a method to specify the colors of an object. Objects, depending on their type, can have between one and three different colors, but generally have one. The library can provide a single method to handle this case:

```
void setColors(const char *,
               const char * = NULL,
               const char * = NULL);
```

This method can then be called with one, two, or three colors depending on the circumstances. The alternatives to using overloading here are always to pass three colors, which adds complexity to the calling code when the additional colors make no sense, or to define three different methods based on the number of colors, which complicates the interface and requires the programmer to remember three different method names.

Default parameters can also be used to merge two different methods into a single method, thereby simplifying the interface of a class. Here the fact that the additional parameter has a value other than its default causes one implementation to be used rather than the other. For example, the method

```
void displayInfo(const char * text,unsigned howlong = 0);
```

is used in a library package to display a message on the screen. If the second parameter is not provided, the message becomes the default message and is displayed continuously. If the second parameter is provided, the message is displayed only for that number of milliseconds and then the current default message is restored. The use of default parameters in this case, however, is questionable. The complexity of using a single method for two different purposes, combined with the need for the reader or programmer to understand the two different applications, tends to outweigh the simplicity of fewer methods in the interface. Moreover, it is generally not a good idea to have parameters that affect control flow directly.

From this discussion, we recommend:

> **Use overloading and default parameters sparingly.**

While C++ lets the programmer overload global functions and operators, over-loading should be used only for methods and only if it greatly simplifies the external interface of an object. It must both reduce the number of methods in the interface and provide a natural and obvious calling sequence for its intended purpose. Default parameters are not quite as bad as overloaded methods, but should also be used frugally and when the simplicity they bring to the interface far outweighs their inherent complexity.

Operator Methods

While the overloading of methods is somewhat controversial, the overloading of operators C++ provides is more so. Global operator definitions add complex-ity to a program, generally making the program much more difficult to under-stand and read. They should be avoided. Operators applied to class operands, however, while generally not a good idea, do have their uses.

When programmers first see that they can define new operators for a class, they tend to go all out and define lots of operators, planning to simplify the use of the class by using expressions rather than method calls. The end result, however, is a program that is totally incomprehensible to the reader (and to the programmer a year or so down the road). The meaning of the various oper-ators tends to be ad hoc and hence not apparent to the reader. Combining calls and relying on operator precedence makes things even more problematic. Operators are also somewhat difficult to define and use correctly: the differ-ence between x++, ++x, and x+1 for a class object is not apparent to the reader (or the programmer). Moreover, getting the return type correct, especially for assignment operators, can be confusing.

The only cases in which operator definitions are useful are those in which their application is natural and can be understood without knowing the pro-grammer's assumptions. There are several such instances. One involves using the >> and << operators for standard I/O. These have already been defined and overloaded as part of the standard I/O library. When appropriate, it makes sense to define these operators for new classes so that the classes can be used directly for input or output. Because the context of their use has become stan-dard, the extension of these to a class for the same purpose is easily under-stood by the reader and the programmer.

A second instance in which operator methods are acceptable arises when defining a class with natural operations. For example, if one were to extend C++ to support a type for rational numbers, defining the basic operators on this type would make sense since the reader can assume that the type instances represent numbers and the operators applied to them have their natural meanings. This is done in the standard C++ library for complex numbers. Note that if this is done for the class, then it should be done completely, so that rational (or complex) numbers can be used in any context in which they would make sense. This means that if one operation is defined, all relevant operations should be defined, and that operations should be defined not only for pairs of rationals, but for rationals mixed with integers (and possibly floats) as well. This use of operators is quite limited since very few classes have natural operations.

A third instance in which operator methods can be justified involves clean extensions to the language to handle classes. One such extension involves iterators. An iterator is a class used to step through a data structure, looking at each element in turn. Iterators can be defined for lists, trees, arrays, and hash tables, as well as arbitrary user structures. An iterator class typically has a setup method in which it is defined for a given structure, a test method to check if there are more items, a method to return the current item, and a next method to step to the next element. For example, a list iterator might have an interface like:

```
class ListIter {
    ListIter();

    void setup(const List&);
    int more() const;
    void next();

    ListItem current() const;
};
```

This iterator could be used in a C++ program by using the `for` statement:

```
ListIter li;
List list;

for (li.setup(list); li.more(); li.next()) {
    ListItem itm = li.current();
    ...
}
```

The normal use of a `for` statement, however, uses operators:

```
for (i = 0; i < 10; ++i) { ... }
```

or

```
for (p = string; *p != 0; ++p) { ... }
```

We can extend the definition of **ListIter** with operators:

```
class ListIter {
    ListIter();

    void setup(const List&);
    int more() const;
    void next();

    ListItem current() const;

    ListIter& operator =(const List& l){ setup(l);return *this;}
    operator int() const             { return more();  }
    ListIter& operator ++()          { next(); return *this; }
};
```

Then the `for` statement for iterating through a list is written as

```
for (li = list; li; ++li) { ... }
```

The assignment in the first part of the `for` uses `operator =` to set up the linked-list iterator. The test in the middle part uses the conversion operator. (Since C++ expects an integer value in this context, it attempts to convert the class object to an integer and thus uses the given conversion.) Finally, the increment part of the `for` uses `operator ++`.

Operators can be used in such cases if they are used consistently for all iterators throughout the code. Other instances in which operators are needed for extending the language are the definition of the `->` operator when defining a class that should act like a pointer, and a definition of an assignment operator for assignable classes.

Another instance in which operators are useful involves treating objects as functions. The standard library has algorithm templates requiring a function argument: for example, it provides a `sort` template taking a comparison function as its argument. Because explicit function pointers are error-prone and add significant complexity, it is desirable to pass an object here rather than a function. To let the object be used as a function, the library uses `operator()`. This lets the code be read as if the passed object were a function, ensures that the template takes only class parameters, and lets the function object encode any additional parameters that might be needed.

This brings us to the guideline:

Define operators only inside classes and only where their use is obvious and natural.

Operators should be defined only when they help the reader understand what is happening, not merely when they make the code shorter. Note that the use of pointers to represent classes sharply limits the utility of operator definitions and should remove much of the temptation to create operators in inappropriate circumstances.

Class Variables

C++ lets variables be declared at a variety of levels in a variety of ways. In general, however, one should restrict variable definitions to as narrow a scope as possible and strive for consistency. Variables are necessary within a routine and can be used freely there. Variables that must exist beyond the scope of a routine are more troublesome because their domain is broader and it is more difficult for the programmer or the reader to keep track of how and where they might be used.

When such variables are needed, the best approach in C++ is to make them private or protected static class members. This restricts their scope to the given class and ensures that access can occur only in methods of the class. The alternatives, making the variable file-level static data or making the variable a global program variable, should be avoided. File-local variables should be implemented as static class data. General global data should be avoided by modifying the program design. Where needed, it should be implemented as a class in itself (see "Singleton" on page 334) or by using static methods of some known class. Thus we recommend:

> **Avoid non-class storage.**

C++ STORAGE MANAGEMENT

In this section we look at issues in the creation and deletion of class storage in C++. We start by looking at the use of constructors and destructors. Then we give a general discussion of techniques for safe memory management.

Constructors

C++ is large, complex, and not always intuitive. As an example, consider what the following statements might have in common:

```
Move m;
Board b = 5;
Square sq(4,5);
function(sq,m,b);
b = 6;
Square(4,5);
new Square(4,5);
: field(5)
}
```

While these comprise a diverse range of statements (declarations, expressions, and an end of block), C++ lets all of them represent function calls. Some are obvious, such as the call to `function`. Others are not so clear. The first three are constructor calls, `Move()`, `Board(5)`, and `Square(4,5)`. The fifth, assuming `b` is a class type, may also represent either a constructor call or a call to the assignment operator. The subsequent line is an explicit constructor call of **Square**. The invocation of `new` and the initialization of a field or subclass may also represent a constructor call. The call to `function` might also represent additional, hidden function calls, for example, invoking a copy constructor for each of its arguments. Finally, any end of block may represent a destructor call.

Implicit function calls such as these make C++ difficult to read and impede the programmer in understanding exactly what is happening. At the same time, they can make programming significantly easier by hiding many unnecessary details. One of the tasks of the programmer here is to use the language wisely so that implicit calls that are innocuous (such as those that merely initialize a class to default settings) are used to simplify the code and ensure safety, while calls that actually do something are made explicit.

One way to do this is to treat classes as pointers. A declaration or assignment of a pointer to a class does not imply a function call. Any constructor for such an object is given explicitly using the `new` operator. Moreover, there are no constructor or conversion calls when passing such an object as a parameter, nor are there implicit calls for the destructor. All this tends to make it clearer to the programmer and the reader exactly what the code is doing.

To understand and simplify implicit functions, one must first understand constructors. C++ treats constructors as functions. However, constructors are always called implicitly. For instance:

- Any declaration of a class object is a constructor call.

- Any assignment to a class object in which the right-hand side is not of the same type and no explicit assignment operator that can be used has been defined is handled by a constructor call.

- Any parameter that is a class object and is not a reference parameter is passed using a constructor call.

- Any expression in which a temporary of a class type is required creates a temporary using a constructor call.

- A subclass constructor either implicitly or explicitly (using an initializer) calls its superclass constructors.

- A constructor either implicitly or explicitly (using an initializer) calls constructors for any fields that are class objects.

- A `new` expression for a class represents a constructor call for that class.

In addition to being called implicitly, C++ also creates certain constructor methods for a class without telling the programmer. If the programmer does not create a constructor for a class, then C++ defines a default constructor:

```
Class::Class();
```

calling the default constructor for any superclasses and then the default constructors for any data fields that are class objects. In addition, the compiler creates a copy constructor of the form

```
Class::Class(const Class&);
```

unless the programmer has defined a constructor that can take an object of the class type (that is, can act as a copy constructor). The copy constructor calls the copy constructor for each superclass and calls either the assignment operator or the copy constructor for each data field of the class.

These intricacies involving constructors are the source of many misunderstandings and programming problems in C++. To simplify and clarify the code and to avoid potential pitfalls, the programmer should not let C++ do a lot of hidden work and should attempt to make most things explicit. Thus we first recommend:

> **Define a constructor for each class.**

The programmer should define at least one constructor, even if it is the default constructor and does nothing. This makes explicit what it going on, offers a location for setting breakpoints while debugging, and gives a place to add appropriate initializations as the program evolves.

If a class is to be treated as a pointer to a structure so that only the pointer will be passed around and used in expressions, the above is generally sufficient. However, if a class is to be used otherwise, we strongly recommend:

> **Define both a copy constructor and an assignment operator for any class that is to be passed as a structure.**

This ensures that the programmer can specify the correct semantics for copying an object and not rely on whatever the compiler generates. It again provides hooks for adding whatever code is needed later to handle copying correctly.

In general, if objects are to be copied, it is best to define explicit methods to copy them and not to use copy constructors at all. Copying a complex object containing instances of or references to other objects is inherently ambiguous: the programmer must differentiate between a shallow copy, where references to other objects are copied, and a deep copy, where new instances of referenced objects are made. Defining an explicit method here lets the program use the method name to specify the type of copy. Even for simple objects, using an explicit method makes it much clearer that a copy is being made and a function is being called.

Constructors themselves are special functions in C++, handling the initialization of superclasses and data fields implicitly. When a class object is initialized, C++ ensures that the objects from each of its superclasses and each of its class data fields are also initialized by calling the appropriate constructors.

The programmer can make these constructor calls explicit by using initialization syntax, as in

```
Class::Class(int a, int b)
    : SuperClass(a), field1(b), field2()
{ ... }
```

The initializer elements are calls to the appropriate constructors for the fields. If the field is not a class, then the elements represent assignments of the parameter to the field.

There are advantages and disadvantages to using initializers within constructors. The advantages come from making the various constructor calls explicit. This shows the programmer and the reader that constructor calls are being made here, indicates which constructor is being called, and lets the programmer specify a constructor other than the default constructor. Initializer syntax is actually the only way a constructor call can invoke anything other than the default constructor on a superclass or a class field. Using initializers also can be slightly more efficient, since if they are not used the default constructor is called in any case. Finally, initializers are the only valid way of assigning to a constant data field.

However, using initializers here has three disadvantages. First, while initializers are specified in a given order, the compiler actually implements them in the order in which the original declarations are given. If any of the constructors have side effects or if order is important, the resulting program may not work as expected. Second, the parameters for the initializers all must be readily available, generally computed from the parameters of the constructor itself or constants. It is difficult to pass anything complex or conditional to an initializer. Finally, initializers detract from the readability of the program. Almost everywhere else in the language, values are assigned via an assignment operator, and thus programmers and readers look for assignment operators to see where things are set and changed. The assignment of values in an initializer is not as intuitive and straightforward as in a simple assignment statement.

From these pros and cons and our bias towards consistency and simplicity, we recommend:

> **Use initializers only for superclasses and constant data members.**

If the default constructor for a superclass is both simple and sufficient, we generally omit the corresponding initializer, although it can be left in to indicate the implicit call. We do not recommend the use of initializers for data fields. Since most data fields are not class structures (especially if classes are represented as pointers), using assignments within the constructor is both more readable and more consistent with assignments and initializations in the rest of the program. If you prefer to use initializers, use them completely and consistently, i.e. either for the minimum we recommend or for everything.

Destructors

Just as constructors are called implicitly whenever a class object is created, a destructor is called whenever the object is removed. Each implicit constructor call is paired with an implicit destructor call. Constructors called for declarations have corresponding destructors called at the end of the scope in which the declaration occurs. Constructors called when using the `new` operator have destructors called when the corresponding object is freed by the delete operator. Constructors for superclasses are called automatically when a subclass constructor is invoked. Similarly, when a subclass is deleted, the destructor for each of its superclasses is called implicitly. Finally, constructors called for temporary objects such as parameters have destructors called at the end of the statement in which the temporary occurs.

A class object is generally responsible for its own data. Just as the constructor is useful for initializing this data, the destructor is useful for cleaning up. This generally means freeing any storage that was allocated for the object and is no longer needed once the object is removed. Just as we recommend that constructors always be defined, we also recommend:

> **Define a destructor for every class with a constructor.**

This should be done even in the normal case when no action is necessary, if only to provide a hook for future changes to the program. Note that even if the programmer does not define an explicit destructor, C++ defines one for the class that does nothing. Note also that a destructor, whether defined explicitly or created by C++, automatically calls the destructors for any class fields of the object and any superclasses. Thus, the code within the destructor should deal only with the local, non-class fields of this object.

Safe Memory Management

Memory management is probably the biggest problem when using C++. Memory-management errors are both easy to create and difficult to detect. Whole companies have been formed just to help programmers find real or potential memory problems within programs. The best way to write working C++ code is to plan memory management as part of design and keep it at the forefront during implementation and maintenance.

There are three types of memory-management problems. Since C++ does not check array bounds, problems occur when insufficient storage is allocated for an array. We recommend this problem be dealt with by using defensive coding techniques:

> ### Always check array indices against their bounds.

This can be done in a variety of ways. One should check parameters and input values to ensure that whatever array is being accessed is valid. Whenever an array is passed to a function, its size should also be passed so that such checking can be done. If output from a function is being put into an array, then the function should check that only the specified amount of output is inserted.

This problem manifests itself most clearly in dealing with character strings. A good C++ program should always check that a string buffer has enough space to hold whatever string is being put into it and should either truncate or generate an error if it does not. Again, whenever a buffer is passed to a function, the length of that buffer should also be passed. Another technique here is to use the class **ostrstream** from the C++ library for dealing with string buffers, which does explicit bounds checking whenever an element is inserted. Perhaps the best technique for strings, however, is to use the standard library **string** class that does its own checking, which we cover in "Independent Objects" on page 162.

Another way of checking array bounds is to create classes to represent arrays. The classes can then define appropriate indexing operations that do bounds checking. While this can be done on an instance-by-instance basis, it is easier to create a template class to do it in general. The standard vector template class provided with C++, however, does not do bounds checking (a major drawback). We illustrate in Chapter 12 how to construct an appropriate array template based on the standard template class.

Other memory-management problems involve pointer management and arise frequently when pointers are used to represent classes. The first and most obvious of these involves dangling references, which occur when storage is created and then freed but the pointer to the storage is still being used. Since C++ tends to reuse storage in order to minimize program size, the result is that the storage is reallocated and used simultaneously for multiple purposes, yielding weird and wondrous results somewhere down the road. A partial solution to this is to be sure to set any pointer to an object to NULL when deleting the object.

A second type of pointer-management problem occurs when memory is allocated and never freed, even after all pointers to it have been removed. This rarely leads to immediate problems, but tends to make the program larger than necessary at run time: programs typically run much longer than the original programmer anticipated and such *memory leaks* tend to accumulate. For example, we wrote a programming environment and tested it on our own programs, running it for an hour or two at a time without memory-leak problems.

When we released the environment to students, however, they stayed in the environment for twelve or more hours and memory leaks became significant.

While no fixed rules guarantee a program will not have memory-management problems, a few guidelines can minimize the problems that do arise. The first is:

> **A class is responsible for its own data.**

This means that any non-class data allocated for an object such as strings or arrays should be freed when the object is freed. It also means that classes should not pass back pointers to internal data that might be freed, since the validity of such pointers cannot be guaranteed outside of the class. The deletion code for any local class data should be added to the destructor as the data is added to the class.

Managing dynamic data within a class is more difficult if the class is not treated as a pointer and can be copied. If the default copy constructor is used in this case, then both the original class and the new copy will contain pointers to the same dynamic data. Then, when the copy is freed, the destructor for the copy will delete the storage that is still being used by the original object, or the free storage will be omitted and there will be memory leaks. If dynamic data is used with a class that is not treated as a pointer, then a copy constructor and assignment operator should be defined and any dynamic storage should be duplicated in the copy.

Making dynamic data local to a class and keeping it that way takes care of non-class dynamic storage, but dynamically allocated classes generally must be treated differently since these will be passed around and can have indeterminate lifetimes. The solution we recommend to managing class storage is to assign each object an *owner* that is responsible for managing that object's storage. The owner can be another object, a function, or a method.

Consider our implementation of the knight's-tour problem. The **KnightMainInfo** object was owned by the function `main`, which both allocated and freed it. The **KnightBoardInfo** object was owned by the **KnightMainInfo** object, which created it in the `process` method and deleted it in the destructor. The various **KnightSquareInfo** objects were all owned by the **KnightBoardInfo** object, which allocated them in the constructor and freed them in the destructor. The **KnightHeuristicInfo** objects were owned by the `findRestOfTour` method of **KnightSquareInfo**. Finally, the **KnightSolutionInfo** object was owned initially by `KnightBoardInfo::findTour`, which created it, and then ownership was passed back to `KnightMainInfo::process`, which used and freed it.

A good object-oriented design for C++ includes information on who owns each object. Objects can have many potential owners, but there can only be one actual owner at a time. For example, the **KnightSolutionInfo** object in our program had two owners, the creating method and the receiving method. In a drawing package, a graphics object might have a dynamically assigned owner.

If it is a top-level object on the display, it might be owned by the drawing-area object; if it is a subobject in a group, it might be owned by the group object; if it was recently deleted, it might be owned by either the cut buffer or the undo list. This information should be considered part of the design. Moreover, the programmer should track, maintain, and document this information as the code is being written. Here we recommend:

Assign an owner to each object whenever possible.

We illustrate the use of object ownership for storage management as we consider further examples throughout this text.

The "whenever possible" qualifier in this recommendation admits that in some situations, ownership is not a viable option for memory management. Consider a wrapper object used in a C++ interface to strings in the Motif user interface package. Motif defines its own type of string so it can represent multiple character sets and allow font changes. The wrapper class we define, **BaumString**, encapsulates a Motif string, letting it be easily created from a C string and providing method access to the various functions Motif defines for strings. **BaumString** objects are created by the library but are actually managed by the application. As such, it is impossible within the library to assign an owner and ensure the object is freed correctly. A second exception arises when a class might have multiple potential owners. For example, a program that maintains a symbol table may have symbol objects. The symbol objects may have one owner actually creating and using them and, at the same time, have other owners that are the hash tables used for symbol-table lookup.

The issue is how to handle these cases cleanly and without incurring memory-management problems. There are several alternatives. The easy one is to use garbage collection, as is done in Java. Here the language itself does storage management, automatically freeing storage once all references to that storage have disappeared. Unfortunately, this solution is not currently available to C++ programmers and alternatives are needed.

One alternative for the library-application problem is to put the onus of storage management on the application. Here the library should explicitly document that storage returned from a given method or function is dynamic and must be freed by the caller. (Some libraries even provide separate free routines for each type of storage to make clear what is going on and isolate the allocation storage management from library storage management.) This requires the application programmer to be more careful and to work harder, but makes writing the library easier.

An alternative that splits the work between the library and the application is to do some sort of *reference counting*. Here each object keeps a count of its users. When an application routine gets a handle to the object, it increments the count. If it passes the object to other routines or objects, they also increment the count. Whenever an object or routine is finished with the library object, it decrements the count. Counters can be incremented and decremented by adding two methods to the library object:

```
LibObject::addRef();
LibObject::removeRef();
```

The first of these increments an internal counter on the object. The second decrements the counter and, if it reaches zero, actually deletes the object. (This is discussed in more detail in "Wrapper Classes" on page 118.) As we get into more sophisticated examples, we will see how such reference counting is actually used. Note that, with appropriate use of C++ classes representing pointers, it is possible (but somewhat difficult) for all the reference counting to be done automatically without any special calls of the application. Note also that reference counting works only if there are no cycles of pointers among reference-counted storage.

C++ TYPES

The typing model of C++ is complex in that it augments the already messy model used in C with classes. To use the language effectively, the programmer must avoid some of the typing features and make good use of others.

Typedefs

The syntax for defined C++ types, inherited from C, is often nonintuitive. Consider the declaration:

```
const char (* (*x)(char * const,int))(rtn);
```

This declares the variable x as a pointer to a routine taking two arguments and returning a pointer to a const char, i.e. a string. The variable is initialized to the actual routine rtn. Such declarations are nearly impossible both to write as a programmer and understand as a reader. However, C++ provides a variety of techniques whereby the type system can be used to make such code more readable.

The first helpful language feature here is the use of typedef to define new type names. Using typedef lets us simplify the above declaration:

```
typedef const char *    ConstText;
typedef char *          Text;
typedef ConstText       (*RoutinePtr)(const Text,int);

RoutinePtr x = rtn;
```

The resulting code, while longer, is much easier to understand. Moreover, the definitions are more consistent. For example, the const for the first parameter of the routine can be put before the type name rather than afterwards, and the variable being declared is put after the type name in the actual declaration.

Typedefs are also useful for standardizing types and type names throughout a system, for ensuring the names of built-in or library types conform to the system's naming conventions, and for letting types change when porting or maintaining a system. We thus recommend:

Use typedefs extensively.

Typedefs should be used, as we saw in the knight's-tour example, in defining a standard set of types (`Integer`, `Boolean`, `ConstText`, `Text`, etc.), in defining the names of the object types that are actually pointers to classes, and also in defining any complex type.

Enumerations

Another very useful typing feature in the language is enumerations. Enumerations can be used for their intended purpose of specifying a related set of constants of which only one is applicable at a time. They can also be used inside a class definition to define a single constant local to the class, as in:

```
class Sample {
public:
    enum { EMPTY };
    ...
};
```

Here the constant `Sample::EMPTY` can be used and has whatever protection (private, public, or protected) is in effect when the `enum` definition occurs. While some compilers allow standard constant declarations within a class (using `static const ...`), most do not and enumerations are thus the preferred method here.

Enumerations can also be used to define sets of related flags, as in:

```
enum PinSide {
    PIN_SIDE_NONE = 0,
    PIN_SIDE_FRONT = 0x1,
    PIN_SIDE_BACK = 0x2,
    PIN_SIDE_TOP = 0x4,
    PIN_SIDE_BOTTOM = 0x8,
    PIN_SIDE_LEFT = 0x10,
    PIN_SIDE_RIGHT = 0x20,

    PIN_SIDE_ALL = 0x3f
};
```

Here combinations of the flags may be passed. Because enumerations provide a logical way to associate a group of related constant names as well as to define a type name that can then be used further to document parameter or variable types, we recommend:

> **Use enumerations to define any related set of constants and all class constants.**

Naming conventions should be adhered to when defining enumeration types and constants. All enumeration constants should be viewed as constants, as reflected in our basic conventions as all upper-case names with underscores separating words. Moreover, enumeration constants not defined within a class, such as those of **PinSide** above, should have a name prefix indicating the package (PIN in this case) and the type (SIDE). Enumeration constants defined inside a class can omit part or all of this prefix, since the class name must be used to reference it globally.

Pointer Types

While type definitions and enumerations are useful language features, C++ also includes typing capabilities that should be avoided. In particular, C++ extends the notion of pointers to include pointers to class fields and methods. In C pointers are used extensively, in particular to return values and implement dynamic calls using pointers to functions. In order to provide similar features in C++, the language was extended to associate a class with a pointer, since class fields and class methods are treated differently from standard types. The result is some messy syntax (::*, ->*, and .*) and generally incomprehensible code. Moreover, because C++ provides both reference parameters and virtual methods, such pointers are rarely needed and can be easily avoided. Hence we recommend:

> **Do not use pointers to class fields or methods.**

Conversion Functions

Constructors in C++ can serve multiple purposes. Their obvious application is to initialize the storage for a class. They can also be used, however, to convert data from an arbitrary type into an object of a given class. Suppose, for example, we want to extend the language by adding the class **RatNum** for rational numbers. In this case it is desirable to be able to mix integers or floating-point numbers with rational expressions. This requires that we let C++ implicitly build rationals from either integers or floating-point numbers and that we can generate the floating-point equivalent of a rational. Conversions from arbitrary types to elements of the class **RatNum** can be handled by defining appropriate constructors:

```
RatNum::RatNum(long value);
RatNum::RatNum(double value);
```

C++ then uses these constructors in a context in which an integer or floating-point value is present and a **RatNum** is called for. Note that just having these two constructors is probably not sufficient. Some compilers, on meeting an `int` or a `short` in an expression, get confused about whether the `int` should be converted to a `long` or a `double` before being used to call the constructor. In general, if one defines a conversion function for both integers and floating-point, one must define conversions for each type of integer and floating-point value that might be used.

The conversion from a rational to a floating-point number cannot be handled with a constructor but must be done with a separate conversion operator:

```
RatNum::operator double() const
```

This function is again called implicitly by the compiler if a **RatNum** object is used in a context where only a floating-point value can occur.

Conversion functions can also be used for convenience. Consider the **BaumString** wrapper class mentioned earlier in the chapter. Most programmers writing Motif programs use simple C strings. To simplify the use of Motif, our implementation of **BaumString** lets a **BaumString** object be created from either a C string or Motif string (**XmString**):

```
BaumString::BaumString();                   // Null string
BaumString::BaumString(const char *);       // C string
BaumString::BaumString(XmString);           // Motif string
```

Moreover, we let **BaumString** objects be used wherever a Motif string could be used:

```
BaumString::operator XmString() const;
```

This lets us declare methods taking a **BaumString** as an argument and pass it directly to Motif. The programmer can call these methods with a simple C string, a Motif string, or a **BaumString** created previously.

While conversions can be convenient, they are also the source of many problems within C++. Conversion functions, by their nature, represent implicit calls that are not obvious to the programmer and may cause the program to do something unexpected that is not obvious from reading the code. Moreover, if too many conversions are defined, the compiler will begin to complain about ambiguous conversions. For example, if both the conversions:

```
ClassA::ClassA(const ClassB&);
ClassB::operator ClassA() const;
```

are defined, the compiler will not know which to apply when converting an object of type **ClassB** to one of type **ClassA**. Because of these potential problems, we recommend that conversions be limited to cases in which a reader would easily understand what is happening:

> **Use conversions only where there is a natural mapping between the two types.**

Constructor-based conversions should be used rather than operator-based conversions wherever possible. Moreover, as noted, if a conversion from an integer or floating-point type into a class is defined, then conversions should be defined for all other numeric types. Note also that using pointers to represent classes avoids most of the cases where C++ uses conversions implicitly. In addition, the more recent C++ standards have introduced the notion of an explicit constructor (defined using the `explicit` keyword in front of the constructor definition). Such a constructor is guaranteed not to be called implicitly by the compiler. However, many compilers do not yet support this feature.

COMMENTS

We end our discussion of using C++ effectively by considering comments. C++ provides two types of comments, inline comments beginning with `//` and C-style comments delineated by `/*` and `*/`. Both should be used extensively in coding along with blank lines to enhance the readability and understandability of the text. Throughout our discussion we have emphasized:

> **Write code to be read as well as executed.**

To be useful, comments should be both appropriate and meaningful. One should assume the reader can understand the code, so that the comments should not just duplicate what the code says, but go beyond it. Comments should provide additional information relating to design or a higher-level view of what a particular section of code is doing. Any code that is not straightforward and hence self-documenting should have an associated comment.

Comments should also provide a formatting structure that makes the program look good. Each file, section, class, and routine should start with a block comment identifying the item and providing enough information that a reader knows whether to read the item in more detail or skip it. The block comment should be separated by white space and should stand out. For inline comments describing declarations or code fragments, we generally use C++-style comments.

In any case, commenting code is something programmers need to do by habit. Many programmers, for expediency, write the code first, get it working, and comment it afterwards (for example, just before handing it in as homework). This strategy has several disadvantages. First, comments written after the fact tend to be faulty. Programmers may or may not recall every detail of the code and, when trying to add comments in a hurry later on, will not always be accurate. For similar reasons, such comments also tend merely to echo the code rather than give the reader additional information. Finally, if comments are not inserted until the end, they are not available to help the programmer while debugging and getting the program to work in the first place. Adding comments as you write the code also has its own advantages. In particular, the comments can act as placeholders for other things to be done, serving as stubs that let one come back later and fill in the details. Hence we strongly recommend:

> **Comment code as it is entered.**

One other use of comments is to be placeholders for code not yet written or reminders to the programmer of potential problems with the code. In both cases, the programmer wants to be sure to get back to the code at some later time. Here some commenting convention should be adopted that makes comments of this sort look different from normal informative comments and lets all such comments be readily located. For example, formatting the comment as

```
// ########## Check for special case of x = 0 here
```

not only highlights the comment but also lets the programmer find what is left to be done by searching all source files for the text string "##########".

SUMMARY

This chapter describes guidelines for making effective use of C++. These include:

- Use pointers to represent classes.
- Use the most restricted protection levels possible.
- Data elements should always be private or protected.
- Avoid the use of friend declarations.
- Use `const` as much as possible in declarations.
- Use reference parameters whenever a value is to be returned.
- Use simple types for parameters wherever possible.
- Use overloading and default parameters sparingly.
- Define operators only where their use is obvious and natural.
- Avoid non-class storage.
- Define a constructor for each class.

- Define both a copy constructor and an assignment operator for any class that is to be passed as a structure.
- Use initializers only for superclasses and constant data members.
- Define a destructor for every class with a constructor.
- Always check array indices against their bounds.
- A class is responsible for its own data.
- Assign an owner to each object whenever possible.
- Use `typedef` extensively.
- Use enumerations to define any related set of constants and all class constants.
- Do not use pointers to class fields or methods.
- Use conversions only where there is a natural mapping between the two types.
- Write code to be read as well as executed.
- Comment code as it is entered.

To these should be added the recommendations in the previous and following chapters.

EXERCISES

4.1   The best way to test program readability is to try to read a program. This is difficult for one's own code but much easier for someone else's. Take a program someone else has written and analyze it purely in terms of how understandable the code is. Come up with a list of suggestions on making it more readable.

4.2   None of the guidelines given here is absolute or agreed to by all programmers. Take one or two of the guidelines you disagree with and explain when and why it should be violated.

4.3   Find an instance in some of your own code that violates one or more of the guidelines presented in this chapter. Try to modify the code to meet the guideline(s) and compare the results. Which version seems better? Why?

4.4   The need to track the ownership of objects is probably the most difficult guideline presented in this chapter. Take one of your own programs and describe, for each dynamically allocated object, who owns that object when.

4.5 Many newspapers run a simple daily cryptogram. This is a quote or common saying that has been encrypted by a simple letter transposition whereby each letter is mapped to some other letter (e.g. A→C, B→X, C→M, ...). Write a program that inputs such a cryptogram and attempts to decode it. You can assume that your program has access to a list of valid words. (Note, however, that the quote might contain proper names and the like that are not valid words.)

4.6 Design and implement a program to make a crossword puzzle. The program should take as input a list of words to be included and the desired size of the puzzle. Assume that there is a file containing a list of valid words for the puzzle. The crossword puzzle can either be dense (American-style) or open (English-style). The first version of the program should create only the puzzle, not the clues. The program should be designed, however, so that it could eventually be extended to output the set of clues as well.

Chapter 5

Designing with Inheritance

One of the central features of object-oriented design and object-oriented programming is inheritance. Inheritance is the ability to define new classes as refinements of previous ones. Its presence in object-oriented languages provides a framework for both organizing and implementing a system. It provides a way to simplify programming and a foundation for reusing code by letting the code of the superclass be shared by all its subclasses. It offers the ability to refine and extend existing code through virtual methods. Moreover, it offers an organizational structure for code, documenting similar items using the class-subclass relationship, and providing a basis for describing the varying behavior of different entities in a system.

In this chapter we consider a variety of designs that can be implemented using inheritance in the context of an example application involving symbolic differentiation. We discuss how each use of inheritance can be applied, alternative implementations, the pros and cons of these versus inheritance, and we give our recommendation. We also describe strategies for designing with inheritance.

SYMBOLIC DIFFERENTIATION

Suppose we want to write a system to do symbolic differentiation. The system should input an expression and output its derivative with respect to x. Since the rules for differentiation are fairly mechanical, this is not a very difficult problem. (Integration is much more challenging.) We start with a more precise problem statement:

> You are to write a program that does symbolic differentiation. It should read from standard input a sequence of strings, each consisting of an arithmetic expression in infix form containing the operators +, -, *, /, and ^ (exponentiation with an integer exponent), integer constants, and single letter variables. Each equation appears on a separate line. Blank lines and lines starting with "#" should be ignored. For each equation that is input, the program should compute the symbolic derivative with respect to x and output the result to standard output. The result should be simplified as appropriate.

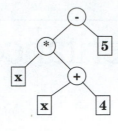

a) Expression tree for x*(x+4)-5

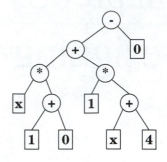

b) Tree after taking derivative

c) Tree after simplification

Figure 5-1 Symbolic differentiation using expression trees.

In order to design a program accomplishing this task, we must understand exactly what it should do. The input is given in terms of strings, but strings are not the easiest thing to manipulate in C++. Moreover, infix (standard-form) expressions are not amenable to direct application of the rules for differentiation. It is much better to view the input expressions by using expression trees. Figure 5-1a shows an input expression and the corresponding tree, which contains both internal nodes representing operators and leaf nodes representing constants and variables.

Given such a representation, the rules for differentiation can be viewed as tree transformations mapping a tree containing the source expression into a tree containing the derivative, as shown in Figure 5-1b. This was derived by applying the rules

```
d(A-B)  = d(A)-d(B)
d(A+B)  = d(A)+d(B)
d(A*B)  = A*d(B) + d(A)*B
d(Constant) = 0
d(x) = 1
```

The result is a relatively complex expression that would not make too much sense to the user and hence must be simplified, again by applying tree transformations in the form of simplification rules. In this case, we use the rules:

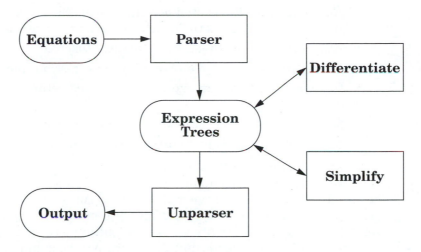

Figure 5-2 Data-flow diagram for symbolic differentiation program.

```
A  -  0  =>  A
A  +  0  =>  A
A  *  1  =>  A
1  *  A  =>  A
```

and we get the tree in Figure 5-1c, which is equivalent to the result x+(x+4).

The program thus must read the input, convert the input into expression trees, transform the expression trees to obtain the derivative, transform the resultant trees to simplify the result, and then convert the final expression tree into a textual form for output. This is shown in the data-flow diagram in Figure 5-2.

The process of converting the input strings into expression trees is called parsing; its inverse, generating the output from the trees, is called unparsing. Parsing generally involves first breaking the input into logical units or tokens and then analyzing the tokens to produce the desired output. In this case the tokens are operators, variables, and integers.

From this description of the problem and its solution, we can come up with an initial set of potential classes. From a description of the basic data elements involved, we get:

- *Input Stream*: the sequence of strings being input.
- *Tokens*: the components of the input stream.
- *Expression Tree*: the tree for the current expression.
- *Expression Nodes*: the nodes of the tree, including both internal operator nodes and leaf nodes representing variables and constants.
- *Output Stream*: the output from the program.

In addition, the algorithms used provide the following candidate objects:

- *Main*: organizes the overall algorithm, calls the parser, and then differentiates and simplifies the result for each input expression.
- *Token Stream*: the sequence of generated tokens.
- *Parser*: converts a token stream into an expression tree.
- *Differentiator*: takes an expression tree and returns the differentiated tree.
- *Simplifier*: takes an expression tree and returns a simplified tree.
- *Unparser*: the algorithm to turn an expression tree into a string.

The central component of the data-flow diagram is the expression tree. This is a strong candidate for a top-level object and is a good starting point in the design. Expression trees, if viewed as intelligent active data, can be told to generate their own derivative, to simplify themselves, and to output themselves. The rules for differentiation can be built into the expressions.

Simplification, however, is much trickier since it can have a much wider set of rules, must deal with integer arithmetic, and might need to apply rules multiple times. Our design will be simpler and more extensible if we separate the simplification rules from the expressions. Hence we add a class to hold the simplification rules and assume that this class is used by the expression trees in doing simplification. An expression node simplifies itself by first asking the set of rules to check if any rule matches the given node. If so, the result of the match is returned. If no rule matches, then the expression node attempts to simplify its subexpressions and build a corresponding result. Finally, the node handles constant arithmetic.

The parser can be built using any of the standard techniques for parsing arithmetic expressions. These include recursive-descent parsing, operator-precedence parsing, or even use of a parser generator such as *lex* and *yacc*. To design our solution to the symbolic differentiation problem, we can ignore implementation details and just assume there is a class **Parser** containing a method `parse` that converts an expression from an input stream into a suitable expression tree. This elision of detail is an example of information hiding during design. Elision here lets us concentrate on the problem at hand without data overload. Details of the parser implementation are covered in Chapter 8.

Given this description of how the program will work, we build the initial object diagram in Figure 5-3. This diagram gives a top-level view of the resultant system, not the complete set of objects. As we implement the design, we will refine the set of classes appropriately.

NATURAL INHERITANCE

We start refining the top-level design by considering the expression tree class **Expr**. An expression tree actually consists of tree nodes of two distinct types:

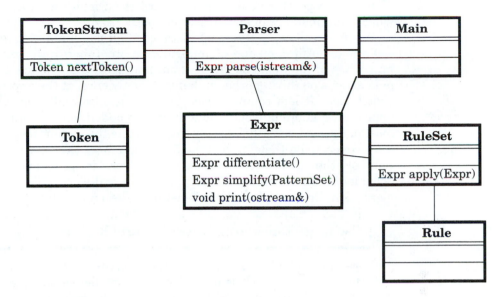

Figure 5-3 Top-level objects for symbolic differentiation.

```
Expression
    Operator Node
        Binary Operator
            Addition
            Subtraction
            Multiplication
            Division
            Exponentiation
        Unary Operator
            Minus
    Leaf Node
        Constant
        Variable
```

Figure 5-4 Hierarchy of expression node types.

leaf nodes represent either variables or constants; interior nodes represent either binary or unary operators. Each node represents a subtree of the original tree and hence should be considered an expression tree on its own. Thus, we actually want to view an expression tree as a node and all of its subtrees.

Figure 5-4 shows how the various types of expression-tree nodes can be arranged into a hierarchy from the general to the specific. This grouping represents an instance of an *is-a hierarchy* in which each child component is an instance of its parent component. For example, an addition node is an instance of a binary operator node, which in turn is an instance of an operator node, which is an instance of an expression node.

When a problem contains an instance of an is-a hierarchy, inheritance is a clear and natural means of implementation. Inheritance lets the common properties of the items be factored out and defined only once. It lets the common actions on the items be implemented only once, at the appropriate level of abstraction. It lets common code be written once and then reused for each appropriate subitem. It lets new items be added with minimal effort, since most of the common code already exists. It lets the rest of the program be written to operate on the generic type **Expr** and ignore the details of implementation of the actual expressions. Moreover, it provides language-based documentation describing the mapping from real-world objects into the implementation. Because of all these benefits, we recommend:

> **Use inheritance to express a natural hierarchy.**

Here this guideline means we should create a hierarchy of tree nodes rooted in the top-level class **Expr**. There is some flexibility in designing a class hierarchy and care should be taken to design the proper one. In this case, the breakdown of the nodes into a hierarchy in Figure 5-5 may not be the correct one. It might be too complex, containing levels such as **Operator Node** that need not be there. It might be too specific, providing multiple leaf nodes that are essentially equivalent. It might be too simple, omitting hierarchical levels that provide common functionality. It might be too general at the lowest level, containing leaf nodes with multiple functions that should be treated differently. Finally, it might be too current, addressing only the immediate needs of the application and not anticipating future demands or extensions.

Designing a Natural Hierarchy

The first step in determining the correct hierarchy is to decide on the set of leaf nodes. Here the designer should attempt to understand what the hierarchy will be used for, considering both current and future needs of the application. We have specified three top-level operators on the expression tree, differentiate, simplify, and print. Print treats the binary operators pretty much the same, possibly differentiating based on priority if we don't want the output to contain excess parentheses. Simplify, because it defers the actual checking to the **RuleSet** object, also does not need to special-case each specific operator. However, differentiate will be substantially different for each of the binary operators, for unary minus, and for the constant and variable nodes. Because of this, we assume that the leaf nodes of the hierarchy include each of these cases separately. Using the package prefix Derive, we thus need the leaf classes **DeriveExprConst**, **DeriveExprVar**, **DeriveExprAdd**, **DeriveExprSub**, **DeriveExprMul**, **DeriveExprDiv**, **DeriveExprExp**, and **DeriveExprMinus**.

Care should be taken to anticipate the future uses of the classes so that the resultant hierarchy does not need major reorganization as the system evolves. The hierarchy should be designed to accommodate the future, while putting more emphasis on the current needs of the classes. If the hierarchy models a true natural hierarchy, most future demands should fit comfortably.

The next step in defining the hierarchy is to factor out commonalities. Here one wants to consider what properties are shared among classes and what properties distinguish each class. Generally there is a range of properties from which the hierarchy designer must choose. The appropriate set of properties depends on the classes and how they will be used. In the case of expression trees, the properties that distinguish the various nodes include:

1. The arity of the node (leaf, unary, binary).
2. Whether the node is an operator or a non-operator.
3. The precedence of an operator node (multiply and divide have higher precedence than add and subtract).
4. Whether differentiation is simple, yielding a tree of about the same complexity, as with `d(A+B) = d(A)+d(B)` or `d(A-B) = d(A)-d(B)`, or complex, requiring both differentiating and copying the current tree, as with `d(A*B) = A*d(B)+B*d(A)`.
5. Whether or not constant arithmetic can be applied (everything but a variable can potentially do constant arithmetic).

The job of the hierarchy designer, once this list has been enumerated, is to order the items so as to arrive at a single hierarchy that does the refinements most appropriate for the given problem. Intermediate classes based on the distinctions should be created during design, even if they eventually turn out not to be needed. At the same time, the hierarchy should remain simple, with the smallest number of classes compatible with the above guidelines.

Hierarchies should reflect the natural distinctions among their elements and should not be too broad or too deep. A deep hierarchy generally yields more opportunities for reuse and provides locations for attaching new methods in a natural way; it also lets the reader understand the original programmer's distinctions among the various classes. However, deep hierarchies can also make it difficult to understand how the resultant code works. Control flow in such a hierarchy often yo-yos up and down the hierarchy, making it hard to follow what is happening. This also makes the code difficult to read, since understanding how one class works requires understanding all the other classes above it in the hierarchy.

While depth in a natural hierarchy facilitates reuse but can make code hard to follow, breadth indicates a variety of alternatives and less extensive commonality and reuse. It is unusual for a natural hierarchy to have breadth without corresponding depth. A broad but shallow hierarchy indicates that the actual objects are all quite different from each other and do not share common properties or methods. This usually indicates that the designer hasn't

```
DeriveExprInfo
  DeriveExprOp
    DeriveExprBinOp
        DeriveExprAdd
        DeriveExprSub
        DeriveExprMul
        DeriveExprDiv
        DeriveExprExp
      DeriveExprUnaryOp
        DeriveExprMinus
  DeriveExprLeaf
    DeriveExprVar
    DeriveExprConst
```

Figure 5-5 The class hierarchy for expression nodes.

done the job properly in selecting what elements constitute a natural hierarchy or in determining the common factors of those elements. In general, a good hierarchy design will balance depth and breadth.

Returning to the five properties that characterize the various expression-tree nodes in the symbolic differentiation problem, we note that item (1) is a special case of item (2), since only non-operators are leaf nodes. The precedence of a node is needed only for sophisticated printing and is probably better handled as a value associated with the leaf nodes than as something entering into the design. Finally, items (4) and (5) probably don't matter greatly in the eventual solution. Thus we get the hierarchy shown in Figure 5-5, which looks pretty much like the classification of the tree nodes in Figure 5-4. Note here how we have named the classes. The names start with the package prefix, Derive, followed by the hierarchy prefix, Expr. It is generally a good idea to include both of these in the names of subclasses so that the reader sees important information about the class just from its name. Note also that the root name has been changed to reflect the fact that the design class **DeriveExpr** is actually defined as a pointer, and the underlying class is called **DeriveExprInfo**.

In addition to the natural hierarchy implicit in the expression trees, our design contains a second hierarchy in token types. There are basically three types of tokens: those indicating a specific character such as "+" or "*", those representing a variable and containing the variable name, and those representing an integer and containing the integer value. These are used during parsing to reflect the input stream in a structured manner. The parser must decides what to do next based on the type of token. For example, if "A*B" has been scanned and the next token is "+", then the parser builds a multiplication subtree. However, if the next token is "^", it delays, since it must build an exponentiation subtree first. These decisions could be embedded in the token class hierarchy, but this would create a high degree of coupling between this hierarchy and the parser class. We prefer to make these classes independent, thus letting different parsing algorithms be easily substituted without any

```
DeriveTokenInfo                    DeriveTokenInfo
    DeriveTokenChar                    DeriveTokenConst
    DeriveTokenConst                   DeriveTokenVar
    DeriveTokenVar
```

Figure 5-6 Alternative hierarchies for tokens.

change in the token class hierarchy. To achieve this, we simply define an enumeration type reflecting the type of token and add a value of this type and an access function for it to each class in the token hierarchy.

There are basically two ways of constructing the token hierarchy, as shown in Figure 5-6. The first method creates leaf nodes for all the token types. The leaf node for characters, however, has no functionality of its own — it shares all its functionality with the other types of tokens and hence would be completely implemented by **DeriveTokenInfo**. The second method reflects this by omitting the unneeded class. We prefer the first alternative to the second, applying the recommendation:

> **Intermediate classes in a hierarchy should be abstract.**

Hierarchies must be designed to change over time. As the overall system evolves, new classes will be needed and new functionality will have to be added. It is easier to insert new classes and methods into a hierarchy in which all the intermediate classes are abstract, since then the interfaces to the methods are cleaner, and changes made in the intermediate classes are guaranteed not to directly affect concrete instances. Moreover, it generally turns out that some future modification will differentiate the concrete class from the original abstract one.

Special Cases of Natural Inheritance

Natural hierarchies are not always obvious or common, and often those that do exist are quite small and shallow. Because inheritance provides benefits in terms of easier implementation, cleaner code, language support for special cases, and reuse of code, the designer should work on identifying hierarchies in a problem in which object-oriented design will be used. This process goes hand in hand with the design step of consolidating the set of potential classes to identify a smaller set of top-level classes. If the designer can identify natural hierarchies among the potential classes, the subclasses should generally be eliminated from the top-level design, leaving only the root of the hierarchy.

In some situations a designer may be tempted not to use a hierarchy. Additional complexity is involved in defining, creating, and using multiple classes. If the differences among the items are trivial, the code and the application will be simpler if a hierarchy is avoided. Here, if the potential classes all have the same behaviors but have a small number of parameters used by (but not controlling) that behavior, the elements are better represented as a single, parameterized class in which the parameters are either set at initialization or can be changed dynamically. For example, if all binary operators in an expression tree are treated in the same way except for the text they print, it would probably be better to have a single class containing a constant data field (set when an object is created) indicating the character to print. Note, however, that in many cases such simple initial differences become magnified as the design progresses and a hierarchy might later be justified.

A second reason to avoid inheritance in implementing a natural hierarchy arises if the system needs to convert from one type of item to another — for example, if the tree transformation will be done in place so that the `simplify` method actually modifies the current tree. In this case, each object might potentially have to contain properties for itself and anything it might be converted into. In general, object-oriented languages are not particularly good at converting one class of object into another.

Several alternative approaches can be used here. The hierarchy could be discarded so as to leave only one type of object that would contain the properties for all types of objects and would have a flag indicating the object type. Methods such as `derivative` would then case on this flag to implement the different transformations. Changing object types here is as simple as changing the flag. This approach has the drawbacks, however, that common code may or may not be factored out in the correspond switch statements, that new objects become more difficult to add since the code for them is distributed among a variety of methods, and that the language is not being used to its fullest extent.

Another alternative is to use delegation and prototypes. Here a class hierarchy would be created to reflect the different possible behaviors and how they are implemented. One instance or prototype of each of these classes would be created. The actual objects used throughout the application would be of a different class and would contain a reference to one of the prototype objects. Any operation on one of these objects would be delegated by calling a similar operator on the prototype. We will see examples of this in Chapter 9.

The third alternative, which we have chosen in our design, is to create new objects rather than modify existing ones. Thus, the `differentiate` and `simplify` methods both return a new expression tree that is the result of taking the derivative or simplifying the original expression. It is then the responsibility of the caller to use this result appropriately. This approach can be more complex and less efficient since memory management is needed to ensure that expression nodes are removed at the right time and expression trees must be copied for some of the differentiation rules. However, it tends to yield much cleaner and simpler code in the long run and makes the resultant program easier to understand, debug and maintain.

INTERFACE INHERITANCE

While natural hierarchies are the principal motivation for using inheritance, inheritance is used in a number of other situations. One such situation involves separating an interface from its implementation.

In a complex system composed of multiple packages or in a library designed to be used by a variety of applications, a class must generally provide a certain functionality and the implementation of this functionality should be hidden from its users. In C++ this is typically handled by a *package*.H file containing the external interface that is separate from the local include and source files defining the implementation. Ideally, the externally visible include file should not contain any of the implementation details. This ensures that the implementation can be changed without affecting external applications and lets the package be maintained by changing local include files and their implementation, without having to recompile or otherwise modify the components that use it.

This separation of the definition of an interface from its implementation is central to all aspects of large-scale design. Although it is costly in both code size and execution time for small-scale systems, these costs are completely outweighed by the simplicity, ease of debugging, and ease of implementation that such information hiding brings to moderate-sized and large-scale systems. Anyone interested in developing such systems should get into the habit of specifying the interface first, independently of the implementation.

Suppose we want multiple programmers to implement the symbolic differentiation program, one programmer for the expression tree hierarchy and one for the main program and the parsing methods. We would then want to isolate the implementation of the expression trees from its implementation. This should be done by having the include file used by the parser to describe expression trees provide only an interface and no implementation.

The cleanest and simplest way of creating such an interface is through inheritance. The include file describing expression trees for the parser and other external applications defines an abstract class that provides only the interface. In C++, this is typically done by defining a class with pure virtual methods so that the method signatures are present, but any implementation is deferred to the subclasses. The local include files then give a subclass of this abstract class that defines the actual implementation. This subclass provides implementations of the abstract methods specified in the superclass and defines the storage and private methods needed to effect this implementation. Other languages provide language constructs for implementing this directly, for example Java interface classes.

Interface inheritance can be used for a wide range of applications. Its most obvious use is in specifying an external interface to a portion of the system independently of the underlying implementation. However, it is equally useful within a system component when alternative implementations are needed or when a library component needs to address external data abstractly.

Multiple implementations of a class are commonly needed when a system must work in multiple environments. For example, in the knight's-tour problem in Chapter 2 we discussed the notion of an abstract user interface that would be implemented textually in some circumstances and graphically in others. One way to build a system incorporating such flexibility is to design an abstract interface class that represents the user interface and then use inheritance to define subclasses for both a textual and a graphical interface. This technique is also useful when a system should be independent of a particular operating system, windowing system, database tool, etc.

Interface inheritance is also useful when creating an external interface for a package. Suppose we want to design a graphical editor package to manipulate arbitrary graphical objects that are defined independently by applications using the package. Here the editor can define an abstract interface for a graphical object but does not define any instances of that interface. Instead, an application wanting to use the editor package would define subclasses of this abstract interface. All interactions between the graphical editor and the objects it supports are through this abstract interface, and the specific functionality of the editor for a particular application is determined by the externally defined subclasses.

Implementing interface inheritance is fairly straightforward, as shown in Figure 5-7. The top part of the figure shows the definition of the public interface to expression trees. **DeriveExpr** is defined as a pointer to the abstract class **DeriveExprInfo**. This class in turn defines only those methods needed externally, and then only as pure virtual methods with no implementation. The destructor is defined here so that the external interface can explicitly delete expressions. Note that it is declared virtual so that the destructor for the proper subclass is actually called. The bottom part of the figure shows the definitions from the local include file for implementing expression trees. In addition to defining concrete versions of the methods specified in the interface, it defines any needed local storage and local methods. In this case, because, the class is the root of a hierarchy, it defines all the methods as virtual and introduces new virtual methods for internal use.

Factory Classes

There is one problem with this separation of the interface from the implementation: the outside user of the class **DeriveExprInfo** has no way of actually creating an object of that type. The type itself is abstract and hence cannot be created directly. Moreover, the subtypes that can be created are not defined in the external include file used by the outside application.

Several techniques can be used to let the external application create items of the internal class while still preserving the isolation of the interface from the implementation. The simplest approach is to add static methods to the external class to do the creation. Here we could add:

```
typedef class DeriveExpr * DeriveExprInfo;

class DeriveExprInfo {

public:
    virtual ~DeriveExprInfo()                              { }

    virtual void print(ostream&) const = 0;
    virtual DeriveExpr differentiate() const = 0;
    virtual DeriveExpr simplify() const = 0;
};
```

```
class DeriveExprData : public DeriveExprInfo {

public:
    DeriveExprData();
    virtual ~DeriveExprData();

    virtual void print(ostream&) const;
    virtual DeriveExpr differentiate() const;
    virtual DeriveExpr simplify() const;

protected:
    virtual DeriveExpr clone() const = 0;

    virtual Boolean matchTree(DeriveExpr tree) const;
};
```

Figure 5-7 Using inheritance to separate the interface from the implementation.

```
    static DeriveExpr createConstant(int value);
    static DeriveExpr createVariable(const char * name);
    static DeriveExpr createAdd(DeriveExpr,DeriveExpr);
    static DeriveExpr createSub(DeriveExpr,DeriveExpr);
    static DeriveExpr createMul(DeriveExpr,DeriveExpr);
    static DeriveExpr createDiv(DeriveExpr,DeriveExpr);
    static DeriveExpr createExp(DeriveExpr,DeriveExpr);
    static DeriveExpr createMinus(DeriveExpr);
```

to the class **DeriveExprInfo**. The application would then call these rather than calling the corresponding constructors. This approach is flexible in that a variety of creation methods can be defined, including ones that can create arbitrary subclasses. One could even define a method

```
    static DeriveExpr createFromString(const char * source);
```

that parses the initial string to produce the appropriate expression.

It is not generally desirable, however, to define a variety of static methods in the interface class. An alternative is to define a new class whose sole pur-

```
typedef class DeriveExprFactoryInfo *DeriveExprFactory;

class DeriveExprFactoryInfo {

public:
    DeriveExprFactoryInfo();
    ~DeriveExprFactoryInfo();

    DeriveExpr createConstant(int value) const;
    DeriveExpr createVariable(const char * name) const;
    DeriveExpr createAdd(DeriveExpr,DeriveExpr) const;
    DeriveExpr createSub(DeriveExpr,DeriveExpr) const;
    DeriveExpr createMul(DeriveExpr,DeriveExpr) const;
    DeriveExpr createDiv(DeriveExpr,DeriveExpr) const;
    DeriveExpr createExp(DeriveExpr,DeriveExpr) const;
    DeriveExpr createMinus(DeriveExpr) const;
};
```

Figure 5-8 A sample factory class.

pose is to create the objects. Such a class is called a *factory class*. An example
factory for expressions is shown in Figure 5-8. While this looks similar to adding the static methods to the external class, a factory class is more flexible. A
standard set of parameters is often required for all the items being created.
For example, in the knight's-tour example, all square objects needed to be
passed the board object in their constructor. Here, the standard parameters
could be passed to the factory class when it is created and the creation methods in the factory would be simplified. A more detailed discussion of factory
classes and methods is found in "Factory Patterns" on page 330.

Wrapper Classes

An alternative to using inheritance to separate the interface from the implementation is to use a wrapper class. This is a class containing a private
pointer to the underlying data, whose methods correspond to the public interface; the implementation of these methods involves delegating the actual work
to the underlying object. Figure 5-9 shows a wrapper class for expression tree
nodes. Here the internal class, **DeriveExprInfo**, is defined only in a forward reference: the actual definition of the class appears only in the internal include
files, and the class **DeriveExpr** defines a wrapper for it. The idea is that the
wrapper class should be used just like the pointer type defined previously.

   This approach has some advantages. First, it allows a complete separation
of external from internal methods. The implementation of DeriveExpr::dif-
ferentiate, for example, would typically be:

```
class DeriveExprInfo;

class DeriveExpr {
private:
    DeriveExprInfo * _data;

public:
    DeriveExprData();
    DeriveExprData(DeriveExprInfo *);
    ~DeriveExprData();

    void free();

    DeriveExpr differentiate() const;
    DeriveExpr simplify() const;
    void print(ostream&) const;
};
```

Figure 5-9 A sample wrapper class.

```
DeriveExpr
DeriveExpr::differentiate() const
{ return _data->differentiate(); }
```

Here the work is actually done by the corresponding method in **DeriveExprInfo**. However, unlike inheritance, this need not be the case. This method can add error checks such as testing if _data is NULL, and it can call a sequence of methods if that is more appropriate. Second, the wrapper class provides a substitute for a factory class: it is easy to add the necessary create methods directly to the wrapper. A third advantage is that the use of a wrapper class lets a library implement internal storage-management techniques such as reference counting.

Wrappers have disadvantages as well. First, they require a different syntax. The methods of the wrapper class must be invoked using the dot syntax, as in expr.differentiate(), and this is additional overhead. A second disadvantage involves the complexity of memory management. There are two distinct ways of using wrappers. In one approach there is a one-to-one correspondence between a wrapper and the object it points to. Here the constructor and destructor of the wrapper can be used directly to create and destroy the object. However, this type of wrapper requires the user to define an assignment operator and a copy constructor so that when such an object is copied, the contents are duplicated. Because this is inconvenient and expensive, wrappers are generally maintained as if they were pointers, with multiple wrappers able to refer to the same internal class. Here constructing or deleting a wrapper does not create or destroy the underlying object, so that additional methods must be defined to do so. Figure 5-9 contains a method

```
typedef class DeriveHolderInfo * DeriveHolder;

class DeriveHolderInfo {
private:
    int ref_count;

protected
    DeriveHolderInfo();
    DeriveHolderInfo(const DeriveHolderInfo&);
    virtual ~DeriveHolderInfo();// don't allow explicit deletes

    DeriveHolderInfo& operator =(const DeriveHolderInfo&);

public:
    void addRef();
    void releaseRef();
};
```

Figure 5-10 A mix-in class for reference counting.

free() that acts as an effective destructor. Because of these disadvantages, we generally recommend:

> **Use factory classes or methods rather than wrappers.**

MIX-IN INHERITANCE

Another way to use inheritance is to extend a class implementation by providing features orthogonal to the class. Reference counting, persistence, and the ability to include a class into a collection can all be added in this way.

Suppose we want to avoid doing normal new-delete-style storage management in our symbolic differentiation program and instead do reference counting. Recall that this means that each object maintains a count of the number of references to itself. When code in the application gets hold of such an object, this count is incremented; when the code is done with the object, the count is decremented; when the count goes to zero, no one has a reference to the object and it can be deleted. Using reference counting in the differentiation program would let us reuse expressions rather than copying them and would generally simplify the code.

Rather than independently defining the appropriate methods and checks for each class to be reference-counted, we can define a new class that implements the feature. An example of such a class is shown in Figure 5-10; it contains an integer for the reference count, defines protected constructors, destructors, and an assignment method, and then defines the actual interface.

The interface has a method called by the client when it uses a pointer to the class and another method called when the client is done with the pointer.

This is an example of a *mix-in*, a class designed to be inherited by an arbitrary class in order to provide additional functionality. In this case, we can make any class into one that does reference counting simply by having that class inherit from **DeriveHolderInfo**. Of course, we would also have to change the rest of the application to add `addRef` and `releaseRef` calls appropriately.

While mix-ins are quite convenient to use, they are also quite difficult to define correctly. The problem is that they must be designed to work with an arbitrary class; hence they must be independent of the operation of the rest of the class and can make few assumptions on how the class is used. Whatever assumptions they do make must be made explicitly so that their users know what they are getting into. For example, the user of **DeriveHolderInfo** must

- Explicitly call `addRef()` whenever there is a new holder of a pointer to the storage;
- Explicitly call `releaseRef()` whenever a holder that called `addRef()` is finished using the pointer;
- Not call delete explicitly; and
- Ensure that each call to `addRef()` is matched with a single call to `releaseRef()`.

Ideally, the set of assumptions should be small and the code for the mix-in will make checks where possible to ensure that the assumptions are followed.

Even with this set of assumptions, the code for the mix-in, as shown in Figure 5-11, is somewhat tricky. First, we defined a dummy reference count to handle the case where the object has been created but there are no pointers to it yet. This value must be checked both when adding and deleting a reference. Second, we added a copy constructor and an assignment operator (recall that defining one means you should define the other) to handle the case in which the underlying object is copied. Here we set the new object's reference count to UNUSED, assuming the client will call `addRef` for the new object.

In general, because mix-ins are difficult to implement correctly, we recommend:

Do not define mix-ins.

We feel that mix-ins are complex enough that they should be left to the sophisticated programmer. If mix-ins are available and have been well tested, they can be used for their intended purpose. When using a mix-in, however, one should be sure to understand and follow the assumptions made by its creator.

Mix-ins are one instance of using inheritance for defining additional properties of an object. In general, adding properties in this way both is difficult to implement correctly and complicates the resultant code. This is especially true if multiple properties are added or if a property is added in the middle of a

```
const int              DERIVE_REF_COUNT_UNUSED = -1;

DeriveHolderInfo::DeriveHolderInfo()
{ ref_count = DERIVE_REF_COUNT_UNUSED; }

DeriveHolderInfo::DeriveHolderInfo(const DeriveHolderInfo&)
{ ref_count = DERIVE_REF_COUNT_UNUSED; }

DeriveHolderInfo::~DeriveHolderInfo()
{
   if (ref_count > 0) {
      cerr << "DERIVE: Illegal delete" << endl;
      abort();
   }
}

DeriveHolderInfo&
DeriveHolderInfo::operator =()
{ ref_count = DERIVE_REF_COUNT_UNUSED; }

void
DeriveHolderInfo::addRef()
{
   if (ref_count >= 0) ++ref_count;
   else if (ref_count == DERIVE_REF_COUNT_UNUSED) ref_count = 1;
}

void
DeriveHolderInfo::releaseRef()
{
   if (ref_count-- > 0) return;
   if (ref_count < 0) {
      ++ref_count;
      if (ref_count == DERIVE_REF_COUNT_UNUSED) ref_count = 0;
   }
   if (ref_count == 0) {
      delete this;
   }
}
```

Figure 5-11 Implementation of a mix-in class for reference counting.

hierarchy. In both of these cases, multiple inheritance must be used. Multiple inheritance is difficult for both programmer and reader to understand since finding the relevant methods is more difficult and it is not obvious what should happen when different parents have common methods or a common ancestor. Multiple inheritance also is much more difficult for the compiler to implement.

```
enum DeriveCallbackType { DERIVATIVE, SIMPLIFY };

typedef void (*DeriveCallbackRtn)(DeriveCallbackType,
                DeriveExpr,DeriveExpr);

class DeriveExprInfo {
...
    DeriveExpr differentiate(DeriveCallbackRtn = NULL) const;
    DeriveExpr simplify(DeriveCallbackRtn = NULL) const;
...
};
```

Figure 5-12 Modifications of DeriveExprInfo for a callback routine.

INHERITANCE FOR CALLBACKS

Most of the obvious applications of inheritance involve augmenting a subclass with methods and information from its superclass. It can also be used, however, to let the subclass interact with other classes in the application in a structured manner.

Suppose we want to augment our symbolic differentiation program with a graphical front end showing the tree being modified, so it can be used to teach students how to do differentiation. In order for such a front end to work, it must be notified whenever an expression tree is modified so that it can update its presentation appropriately. Rather than redesign the whole application to apply one transformation at a time or retain all the intermediate trees, we can implement this by having the transformation code call the front end each time a change is made. Since the front end initially calls the differentiation code, which then calls back to the front end, such invocations are named *callbacks*.

We want both the `differentiation` method and the `simplify` method to call the front end each time a transformation is applied. A function outside the given class that is invoked whenever an event in the class occurs is called a *callback function*. The callback function in this case would look something like:

```
void callback(DeriveCallbackType,DeriveExpr o,DeriveExpr n);
```

where the first parameter identifies the type of transformation (derivation, simplification, and so on) and the second and third parameters provide the old and new expression trees, which can be subtrees of the overall expression.

We don't want to include this function or knowledge of it explicitly in the code for symbolic differentiation, since it will be defined in and used by the front end and the differentiation code should make no assumptions about what the front end looks like or contains. Instead we want the front end to pass the function to the differentiation code and then have the code call back to the function at the appropriate time. We can modify the interface for **Derive-Expr** to include the appropriate callbacks as shown in Figure 5-12. Here we have added the appropriate type definitions and then put the callback routine as an optional parameter of both `differentiate` and `simplify`. We presume that the implementation checks if this pointer is non-`NULL` whenever a transformation is made and, if so, calls the passed function.

There are several difficulties with this function-oriented approach. First, the function to be invoked probably needs more information. If it is a windowing interface, then it probably needs a handle to tell it what window to update. Even if not, since it will be passed subtrees, it must keep track of the overall tree and will need a data pointer to that tree. The typical way to do this in C is to pass `differentiate` and `simplify` an additional data element that is then passed to the callback routine. This value is typically declared as a `void *`, letting it point to arbitrary data and then be interpreted appropriately by the callback routine.

Callback routines are in general messy and error-prone. The functions in the front end will be called from some arbitrary location. That these functions are callbacks will not be obvious from the source, and understanding this and how and when they are called will take the reader some time. Using a `void *` parameter to pass data back and forth only makes matters worse, since this violates type safety and it can take considerable checking on the programmer's or reader's part to ensure that the data the callback routine expects is actually what is passed to it. Moreover, as different callback functions tend to have different parameters, each new application of callbacks typically requires at least one new type definition.

Inheritance lets a programmer circumvent these problems and provides a cleaner implementation of callbacks. Here, the code issuing the callback defines a generic callback object that provides methods corresponding to whatever callback functions are needed. Instead of passing a pointer to the callback routine and its data, the application simply passes a pointer to a callback object. When a callback is to be invoked, the code calls the appropriate method of the passed callback object. To make this work, the front end specifies the callback implementation by defining a subclass of the callback class and passing a pointer to it. This subclass contains whatever data is needed to process the callback and defines actual implementations of the callback methods. Callback methods are thus invoked within the callback object that already has the necessary data.

Figure 5-13 shows how to use this for our symbolic differentiation example. The top part of the figure shows the modifications needed in the code for differentiation. Here we define the abstract callback class and its associated properties. We also modify the `differentiate` and `simplify` routines to take a pointer to this class. The bottom part of the figure shows a subclass of this abstract class that a front end might create to use callbacks; the subclass includes the local data needed to process the data, appropriate constructors and destructors, and an implementation of the callback method.

Using callback classes defined with inheritance has several advantages. It simplifies the resultant code by avoiding the need to define a new type for the

```
typedef class DeriveCallbackInfo * DeriveCallback;

class DeriveCallbackInfo {
public:
    enum Type { DERIVATIVE, SIMPLIFY };

public:
    virtual void transformCB(Type,DeriveExpr,DeriveExpr) = 0;
};


...
class DeriveExprInfo {
...
    DeriveExpr differentiate(DeriveCallback = NULL) const;
    DeriveExpr simplify(DeriveCallback = NULL) const;
...
};
```

```
typedef class DemoCallbackInfo * DemoCallback;

class DemoCallbackInfo : public DeriveCallbackInfo {
private:
    DemoWindow for_window;
    DemoTree current_tree;

public:
    DemoCallbackInfo(DemoWindow);
    ~DemoCallbackInfo();

    void transformCB(Type,DeriveExpr,DeriveExpr);
};
```

Figure 5-13 Declarations for a callback class.

callback routine, by eliminating the void * parameter, and by localizing the definitions needed for callback. It makes explicit, in the name of the class and its methods, that the methods will be invoked as callbacks, and it uses the language to guarantee that these callbacks have the appropriate data available. It also makes it easier to have multiple types of callbacks. If a callback class is used, an additional type of callback is just an additional method. If it is not used, multiple functions might have to be passed to the library code and multiple types might have to be declared. Another advantage is that the callback class can provide additional functionality. If there are multiple callbacks, the generic class can define default implementations of the callbacks. The application-specific subclass for handling callbacks is often a logical place to put the methods needed to process the callback. Finally, we note that a callback class need not be distinct. We could have implemented the callbacks of Figure 5-13 just as easily by treating the callback functionality as a mix-in and then having the window class **DemoWindowInfo** inherit from **DeriveCallbackInfo** and provide an implementation of the `transformCB` method.

Because callback classes offer all these advantages and fit better into the object-oriented scheme of things, we recommend:

> **Use inheritance to provide callbacks.**

The only exception to this might be when compatibility with C is necessary.

So far, we have used callbacks only to convey information from a package back to the caller of the package. Callbacks, again defined using a callback object interface, are also useful for passing intermediate information from a calling package to the callee. For example, consider a library package that displays a graph given a set of node and arc objects. To be reusable, the package should be written so that it can be used with arbitrary node and arc objects. At the same time, it needs to know something about the nodes and arcs in order to lay out the graph and assign colors, shapes, and sizes to the nodes and arcs. This can be accomplished in one of two ways. First, the package could define a global callback object defining callbacks that take a node or arc and return the necessary information. Second, the package could use mix-ins to define a "drawable" node and arc. Such mix-in interfaces would then be inherited by the node and arc objects of the application.

BEHAVIOR INHERITANCE

While mix-ins provide behavior orthogonal to the class being defined, inheritance can also be used to provide arbitrary behaviors to a class. Consider the expression tree we are using for symbolic differentiation. Instead of defining this in terms of the different types of tree nodes, as done so far, we could simplify our definition by having the root of the hierarchy inherit tree behavior from a general-purpose tree class. Then our implementation of the expression trees could concentrate on the differentiation and simplification and not on maintaining the trees.

Here we would start by defining a general-purpose tree-node class to embody tree behavior. This class might look something like the simple binary tree node in Figure 5-14. The constructor can take zero, one, or two subtrees. It has a virtual destructor since it is designed to be inherited, and provides access functions to the nodes; further functionality could be added as necessary. Note that the name of this class does not begin with `Derive`. This is intentional: the class is designed to be used in other applications where a tree is needed. This class would be used in our example by simply having **DeriveExprInfo** inherit from **TreeNodeInfo**.

```
typedef class TreeNodeInfo * TreeNode;

class TreeNodeInfo {
private:
    TreeNode left_child;
    TreeNode right_child;

public:
    TreeNodeInfo(TreeNode = NULL,TreeNode = NULL);
    virtual ~TreeNodeInfo();

    TreeNode leftChild() const;
    TreeNode rightChild() const;
};
```

Figure 5-14 A general-purpose tree class.

Behavior inheritance has its advantages and disadvantages. Its primary advantage is that it lets one design classes for a particular purpose that are otherwise independent of the rest of the application. Such classes can be reused both in other parts of a large application and in other applications. A library of such classes enables one to put together a new application with a minimum of new code. Note that this advantage springs from the class and not directly from how it is used. The benefits of having a tree class can be achieved equally well by defining **DeriveExprInfo** so that it contains a **TreeNode** as one of its data elements.

The disadvantages of using inheritance here have to do with complexity and maintainability. Designing a class that can be used to inherit a behavior, with its associated data and methods, is difficult to do correctly, as noted with mix-ins. While using inheritance here might simplify the initial coding of a system, it tends to make the system more complex and difficult to maintain in the long run. Even in the simple example here, the internal code for the expression trees needs to get a left or right child that is an expression tree and not a general tree node, and thus must cast the value returned from leftChild() to the appropriate type. Note that this particular complexity can be alleviated by using templates, as described in Chapter 7.

A second concern is that objects in complex applications tend to have several behaviors. This typically means that multiple inheritance is used to associate all the different behaviors with an object. For example, a graphical object in a drawing package might inherit from a drawing-properties object, a list-management object, and a manipulation object to handle resize. As noted before, multiple inheritance is problematic in that its behavior is neither well defined nor well understood and thus adds considerable complexity to the application.

A third concern is that the resultant hierarchies are not natural. Hierarchies should be designed to group common properties and to order these so that the most essential ones are considered first. Behavioral inheritance tends to obscure these properties and often leads to hierarchies that are not easily extended or maintained.

Because of all these concerns, we recommend:

> **Do not use inheritance solely to obtain behaviors.**

There are several reasonable alternatives for the programmer to consider. The first is to integrate behavior inheritance into a natural hierarchy. Behaviors are properties commonly considered when designing a hierarchy, and thus the existence of inheritable behaviors typically implies that there is a natural hierarchy. Behaviors considered in this way tend to be integrated in a more natural order and to be added linearly, removing the need for and complexities of multiple inheritance.

A second alternative is to use delegation to embody the desired behavior as fields of the object. Consider the drawing object described above. Instead of inheriting drawing properties, it could have a field containing a pointer to a drawing-property object. This still lets the definition of a common object manage and apply drawing properties, but avoids the use of inheritance in implementing it. The result is generally cleaner and easier to maintain.

GUIDELINES FOR USING INHERITANCE IN C++

So far we have discussed how to design with inheritance. The implementation of inheritance in C++ is a source of many potential difficulties because the language provides a wider range of features for using inheritance than do most object-oriented languages. These must be used with caution to simplify programs and enhance their readability.

Levels of Inheritance

C++ provides a variety of levels of inheritance. Inheritance can be public, private, and, in some compilers, protected. The different types of inheritance essentially determine the visibility of the fields and methods of the superclass within the subclass. Public inheritance is what programmers typically mean by inheritance. Here the public methods of the superclass remain public in the subclass, while those that are protected remain protected. (Private methods in the superclass, by definition, are not accessible in the subclass.) Private and protected inheritance are more restrictive. Here the public and protected methods of the superclass are accessible in the subclass, but effectively become either private or protected members, respectively. Hence, in either case, the inherited public elements are not accessible outside of the class.

Restricted inheritance seems to have potential benefits in that it reduces the visibility of members where possible and lets one define restrictions by using inheritance. However, it does so at a large cost in programmer understanding and simplicity. Most object-oriented languages provide only one type of inheritance (essentially public) and that is how most programmers and code readers will interpret inheritance when they see it. Anything else is basically unnecessary and adds complexity to the system. Thus we recommend:

> **Always use public inheritance.**

Note that the C++ language assumes inheritance is private unless told otherwise. Thus:

```
class Sub : Super { ... };
```

declares **Sub** to be a private subclass of **Super**. Programmers should get into the habit of always specifying public inheritance here:

```
class Sub : public Super { ... };
```

and consider it an error to omit the inheritance type.

Private inheritance can be used effectively in C++ in defining restrictions. For example, to define a class representing a stack, one can start with a class that implements a list, inherit it privately so that the normal list operations are not visible, and then define push and pop operations for the stack in terms of the underlying list operations. The result is a class that can be used only as a stack. We recommend that such use be avoided so that inheritance is used consistently. This can be done by allowing the extra operations, by explicitly overriding them in the stack class, or by implementing the stack as a non-inherited class with a data field containing the list.

Multiple Inheritance

In addition to providing different levels of inheritance, C++ offers the ability to have multiple superclasses through multiple inheritance. Multiple inheritance is controversial since it adds substantial complexity to the language with only minor benefits. The run-time implementation of classes that utilize multiple inheritance is something few programmers except those writing compilers truly understand. Accessing data or members of classes defined with multiple inheritance is often inefficient. Moreover, if such classes are passed by value (rather than as pointers), they are likely to lose their subclasses. Other difficulties arise in attempting to determine which member is called for a class, especially if the member name occurs in more than one superclass, and in determining how to lay out storage when the same superclass occurs more than once.

There are two cases in which multiple inheritance might be beneficial. The first comes from the inheritance of interfaces rather than classes, a distinction made in Java and Modula 3 but not in C++. An interface is essentially a class with methods but no associated data. Implementing interface inheritance is substantially simpler than implementing general class inheritance since the data elements need not be accessed and inheriting the same interface multiple times induces no problems. It still has trouble with methods in multiple interfaces that have a common name and thus result in name ambiguities. While inheriting multiple interfaces has its applications, natural instances where this is needed are hard to find and probably do not arise in most programs. The other instance where multiple inheritance is useful comes from mix-ins, as described in "Mix-in Inheritance" on page 120.

Given the complexity associated with multiple inheritance and the relative complexity of the situations where it is actually useful, we recommend:

Do not use multiple inheritance.

Note that multiple inheritance can be effectively implemented through delegation. Here one of the potential superclasses of an object is actually stored as a data element of the object. Then the methods for that superclass are implemented by calling the appropriate methods on the contained object. Delegation provides considerable flexibility and is easy to implement. It is often preferable even to simple inheritance and should definitely be used in preference to multiple inheritance.

Virtual Methods

Inheritance is useful both for extending and refining classes. Classes are typically refined by redefining some of the methods of the superclass in the subclass. The language is then set up so that the method called is determined at run time from the actual class of the object. Such methods are called *virtual*.

In traditional object-oriented languages such as Smalltalk, all methods are considered virtual and the system determines which method to call dynamically. C++, because of concerns for efficiency and its derivation from C, chose to allow both virtual and nonvirtual methods. If a method is not declared virtual, then the compiler determines which instance of it to call from the static type of the object, which generally means that the method in the superclass is used even if it was redefined in the subclass.

In very few instances do methods of the same name exist in a superclass and a subclass when the programmer wants such static semantics. Most of the time, methods either are designed so that they need not be redefined at all (access methods are typically of this ilk), or are meant to be virtual with the corresponding semantics. The reason for not using virtual methods, efficiency, is not as important today as it used to be. Moreover, today's compilers are quite capable of determining that a particular call is static and generating an efficient calling sequence in most cases.

While the default for methods should be that they are virtual, C++ assumes just the opposite. It requires the user to define a method as virtual if it is to be overridden and used dynamically. We recommend:

> **Use virtual methods almost exclusively.**

The only exception to this rule is methods that the programmer is 100% sure will never be overridden during the extended life of the program. In this case, the lack of the virtual keyword should be treated as documentation to this effect.

Omitting the virtual designator is one of the common errors in C++. Not only is it not detected by the compiler, but its effects are subtle and difficult to detect. This is especially true for destructors. If the destructor of a class in a class hierarchy is not declared virtual, then deleting an element of the class does not invoke the proper destructor for that object. Hence one should always:

> **Make destructors virtual throughout a class hierarchy.**

SUMMARY

In this chapter we showed how inheritance in an object-oriented language can be used for a variety of different applications and provided guidelines for each. In particular, the types of inheritance we talked about and the important points about them include:

Natural Inheritance:

- Use inheritance to express a natural hierarchy.
- Define a natural hierarchy by first determining the leaf nodes, then factoring out common elements from these nodes, and finally building a single hierarchy that balances breadth and depth.
- Make the intermediate nodes of the hierarchy abstract.

Interface Inheritance:

- Use inheritance to isolate the interface of a class or class hierarchy from its implementation.
- Provide factory classes or methods to support constructing the implementation objects when interface inheritance is used.

Mix-in Inheritance:

- Use mix-in inheritance if it is provided and needed, but do not attempt to define new mix-in classes.

Callback Inheritance:

- Use inheritance to provide callbacks.

Behavior Inheritance:

- Do not use inheritance to acquire behaviors.

In addition to these general principles on inheritance, we discussed the use of inheritance within C++. Here we recommended the following:

- Always use public inheritance.
- Do not use multiple inheritance.
- Use virtual methods almost exclusively.
- Remember to make destructors virtual.

EXERCISES

5.1   One obvious example of a natural hierarchy occurs in a drawing program in which the user can place various shapes upon the screen. Provide a simple description of such a program and, using that description, define and justify a natural hierarchy for the graphical objects.

5.2   Suppose you were to design the knight's-tour example of the previous chapters with a completely separate interface and implementation so that each class could be implemented by a different person. Show what the interfaces would look like and how the implementation classes would be created.

5.3   Describe how a mix-in class could be used for persistence by designing an appropriate class interface. Do not worry about how the class would be implemented.

5.4   Design the interface for a class that would allow an application to set alarms and get called back when an alarm occurred. Do not worry about how the class would be implemented. Instead, concentrate on designing the best interface from the potential user's point of view.

5.5   Describe (with examples) how inheritance could be used in the solar-system example in Chapter 1. Look for at least one instance each of a natural inheritance, interface inheritance, and callback inheritance.

5.6   To understand why multiple inheritance is complicated to implement, a good exercise is to look at how it is implemented. Using the appropriate manuals (or experimentation), write up a brief description of how your compiler implements multiple inheritance.

Chapter 6

Design Notations

In this book we use pictures as well as text to describe our design solutions to various problems. The notation used so far has been somewhat ad hoc and informal. Informal diagrams are fine when one is doing an individual design. But as problems become more complex, designs need to fill other roles and be understood in other contexts. They need to be shared with other programmers developing a common project. They need to be understood by their designer and other programmers as changes become necessary, often years after the program was originally written. In these cases it is important to have standard design notations with fixed meanings that everyone can understand and agree to.

The notations most relevant to object-oriented design were recently standardized as the Unified Modeling Language (UML).[1] UML consists of eight types of diagrams useful in varying degrees to describe all aspects of object-oriented design and programming. In our experience, the most relevant and hence most important of these are the static structure and message-trace diagrams. Static structure diagrams describe the relationships among the various classes and hence provide a useful view of the system design. Message-trace diagrams describe complex run-time relationships among classes.

UML, while providing useful and standard notations, is geared to larger projects and full-scale software engineering. The other diagrams UML provides are use-case diagrams showing the relationship between actors and actions, state and activity diagrams to show flow of control, collaborative diagrams to give another view of run-time relationships, component diagrams to show high-level structure, and deployment diagrams to coordinate hardware and software. These are all more applicable to large projects and convey little if any additional meaning for smaller systems. Moreover, even the UML notations that are useful for smaller systems contain many features and subtle nuances that are not relevant or important for inexperienced designers.

In this chapter, we introduce a subset of UML's static structure and message-trace diagrams that we feel are important for designers to understand

---

1. For more information on UML and its current definitions, see Rational Software's web site at `http://www.rational.com/uml`.

and use consistently. Our examples are based on the differentiation program of Chapter 5.

DESIGN NOTATIONS

The truth of the old saying that a picture is worth a thousand words is especially obvious in understanding and designing systems. Pictures let one show both the components and the relationships between these components at a single glance. Their convenient shorthand lets the designer quickly compare and contrast different design alternatives. They also provide a framework for more detailed analysis and for the actual textual description of a system.

Diagrams are most effective when designed to convey the proper information. Different information is important at different times during system development. Initially, the task is to understand the problem, not necessarily to describe its solutions. Several types of diagrams are useful for this purpose, including data-flow diagrams (which we have used informally in the previous chapters) and state-transition diagrams. These become both more relevant and more important as the problem size increases. We cover these types of diagrams in more detail when we consider larger systems in Chapter 15.

Once the problem has been understood, one needs to develop and describe a design. Here the relevant information is the set of classes arranged hierarchically, their components, and a description of how the classes interact. This information is derived from the three steps involved in object-oriented design: determining the objects, characterizing the objects, and defining the implementation.

The first piece of information to be conveyed by the diagram is the set of classes composing the design. This must be done in a hierarchical way so that the viewer is presented only with a small number of classes at any one time. Any implicit relationship between these classes, such as containment or hierarchy, should be included in the diagram. The information added when characterizing the classes includes the set of data fields and methods of each class, in order to show what the designer means by the class name. Finally, the diagram must provide a high-level view of the implementation inherent in the design. The important information here is how the different classes interact.

To accommodate all this, we need a representation that shows the appropriate classes arranged in a hierarchical fashion as well as the components of each class. It must also illustrate the relationships among these classes that are relevant to the implementation. While a number of different representations have been developed to do just this, it is important to settle on a single, standard representation. One wants a representation with a generally understood meaning so that, once written, it can be understood not only by its creator in the next few days, but by other programmers or designers (or even by the creator three or four years hence). One wants to be able to share representations and let different designers work together on a common design.

Just as important as agreeing on a common representation with a common meaning is selecting a representation that is supported by design tools. Design is an iterative process. Diagrams, especially complex diagrams that attempt to encode all sorts of design information in little space, can be difficult, time-consuming, and messy to draw by hand. Without a reasonable editor, the designer will be loath to update the diagram continually to reflect improvements in the design. In addition, if the designer happens to lack artistic talent (i.e. can't draw well or write legible annotations), a hand-drawn diagram will probably be useless. Finally, if a standard representation with well-understood semantics is used, a drawing tool for that representation can, at least potentially, take the next step beyond the design and generate and maintain the skeletal implementation files corresponding to the diagram.

The most common object-oriented design representation is the Object Modeling Technique (OMT) designed by Rumbaugh, which has been updated and is included as the static structure diagrams of the Unified Modeling Language (UML). Static structure diagrams are a formalization of the informal object diagrams used in previous chapters. They describe the sets of objects, use multiple descriptions to show the design hierarchy, describe the contents of an object, and use arrows to indicate the relationships among them. The formal representation describes precisely what each aspect of the diagram means and provides different graphical notations to encode many of the design details in the diagram.

However, static structure diagrams in their full generality are too complex to be useful to beginning designers, since many of their graphical encodings are not relevant. Moreover, while the basic diagrams are easy to learn and use, learning the full set of encodings and using them consistently is difficult and not generally worthwhile for inexperienced designers or smaller systems. In the next section we define what we feel is a useful subset of the components of a static structure diagram and show how it is used. The following section considers how diagrams and an appropriate diagram editor can be used to build a design.

STATIC STRUCTURE DIAGRAM BASICS

UML static structure diagrams look much like the diagrams we have been drawing informally to describe object-oriented designs. Their two principal components are classes and relationships. Classes provide the set of classes and direct information about each class. Relationships provide the other information, including the class hierarchy and how the various classes are related structurally.

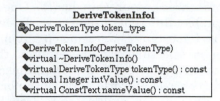

Figure 6-1 UML representation of a class.

Class Notations

Classes themselves are described using a three-part box, as in Figure 6-1. At the top of the box is the name of the class being defined, in this case the root of the token hierarchy, **DeriveTokenInfo**. Below this is the set of data fields characterizing the class that is defined using C++ syntax as much as possible. (This is allowed but not mandated by the UML definition.) Some object-oriented design tools insist on the default format, which uses Pascal syntax, so that the field declaration line would be written as:

```
token_type : DeriveTokenType
```

In general, we find it clearer and more straightforward to use the syntax of the implementation language rather than the artificial syntax defined by UML.

The third part of the class-description box contains the operations of the class. We again use C++ syntax here, though the standard UML syntax is more like Pascal:

```
DeriveTokenInfo(type : DeriveTokenType)
~DeriveTokenInfo() {virtual}
tokenType() : DeriveTokenType {virtual,const}
intValue() : Integer {virtual,const}
nameValue() : ConstText {virtual,const}
```

Here the function name appears first, along with the parameter list. The parameters are given as the formal parameter name, followed by a colon, followed by the type. After the parameter list come a colon and the return type of the function if it returns a value. Finally, optional properties are given inside braces after the definition. The tool we happen to be using for the examples in this text, Rational *Rose*, lets us use C++ syntax up to a point. It does not understand the syntax nor does it allow the direct entry of the final const; we thus precede the const with a colon to force the tool to display it.

The icon at the start of the data fields and operations in Figure 6-1 indicates the visibility of the corresponding item: a plain icon indicates public, an icon with a lock indicates private, and an icon with a key indicates protected. Standard UML indicates this by preceding the definition with "+" for public, "#" for protected, or "−" for private. Here the tool we are using replaces these text symbols with icons to make the diagram more understandable. If one is

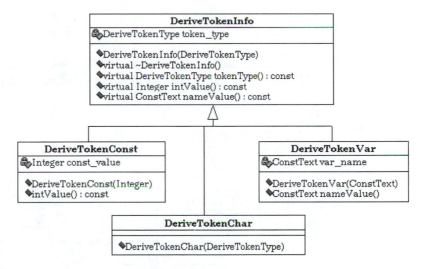

Figure 6-2 UML generalization denoting a class hierarchy.

using a tool that makes it convenient to indicate protection, then this information should be present. If the tool requires typing the extra symbol, we recommend using only the more restricted terms and avoiding the bother of always entering "+" when defining the public interfaces during top-level design.

Relationship Notations

Lines are used in a static structure diagram to express relationships among the different classes. Two basic types of relationships can be defined, inheritance and containment. Different graphical properties and textual annotations are used to qualify these and make the overall diagram more explicit.

Inheritance among the classes is called *generalization* in UML and is denoted by lines containing an open triangle pointing to the superclass. For example, Figure 6-2 shows the simple hierarchy defined in the previous chapter for the different types of tokens needed for expression parsing.

Containment relationships are more complex. Containment in general represents a *has-a* relationship. For example, in the knight's-tour problem, the board class has a set of square classes and the main class has a board class. There are actually two types of has-a relationships to be considered here. The first is actual containment, i.e. a *contains-a* relationship: in the knight's-tour example, a board contains a set of squares. The other type of containment relationship is *knows-about*, which is a little less direct but just as important. In the above example, the main class knows about the board class but, since the main class doesn't represent a actual entity, it cannot actually contain the corresponding board.

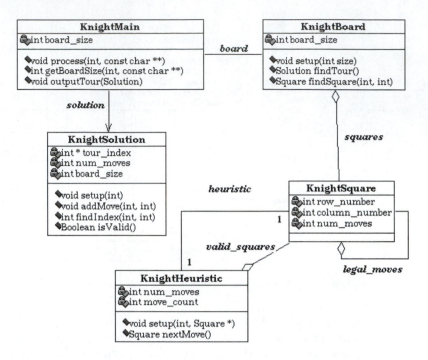

Figure 6-3 Static structure diagram showing knight's-tour solution.

A UML static structure diagram can indicate containment in two ways. The first is just to specify the data field in the class definition. Doing this is consistent with defining other fields, but does not show the actual relationships among the classes. The preferred way is to use an *association* relationship drawn as a line between the two classes. Properties of this line, for example its arrowheads, are used to characterize the relationship further. The line is generally labeled with a name describing the relationship.

Consider the diagram in Figure 6-3, which shows our solution to the knight's-tour problem discussed in Chapter 2. Several types of relationships are shown here. The arrow from **KnightMain** to **KnightBoard** is a simple line with a label and denotes a simple containment relationship. The line from **KnightBoard** to **KnightSquare,** on the other hand, starts with a diamond, which denotes an aggregation. In this case the board contains a set of squares. Similarly, each square contains a set of squares denoting its legal moves and each heuristic contains a set of squares denoting valid moves to be considered.

Associations in such diagrams are usually considered bidirectional. For example, the link between **KnightMain** and **KnightBoard** indicates that each main object is associated with a board object and each board object is associated with a main object. This lets the designer express the relationship between the objects without committing to an implementation for that relationship. The relationship could be implemented, for example, as a single link

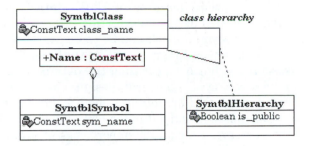

Figure 6-4 UML static structure diagram for a symbol table.

in **KnightMain** (which is what we actually did), as a single link in **KnightBoard**, as cross-links in both these classes, or even as a separate class representing the relationship between the two that is pointed at by one or both of the original classes. The particular implementation would be decided later in the development process based on the needs of the implementations of the two classes. Where such flexibility is not desired, an association can be defined as one-way by using an arrow, as on the arc from **KnightMain** to **KnightSolution**. This indicates that the main object can find the solution, but not the other way around.

Associations can also be qualified by describing the arity of the relationship for each of the classes involved. This is denoted by an expression at one or both ends of the line. For example, the line between **KnightSquare** and **Knight-Heuristic** in Figure 6-3 explicitly states that this relationship is one-to-one. This expression can be a single number or a range of numbers. An arbitrary value is denoted here with an asterisk.

Two other properties that can be used in defining an association, qualifiers and association classes, are illustrated in Figure 6-4 for a symbol-table example. The class **SymtblClass** represents a class object containing the class name and the set of symbols defined in the class. This set or aggregation is *qualified* by the Name box. A qualifier designates a means for partitioning the set of elements. Here the qualifier Name indicates that the symbols of the class are partitioned and hence accessed using a string. This would be implemented using an appropriate data structure such as a hash table or an ordered tree within the **SymtblClass** class. Methods would presumably be added to find or enter names using this data structure.

The class **SymtblHierarchy** in Figure 6-4 is an example of an *association class*. The association class_hierarchy represents a 1-n relationship between classes, with each class having multiple subclasses. The design of the symbol table requires storing additional information about each of these associations, specifically whether the inheritance is public or private. The class **SymtblHierarchy** is used to contain this information. It is associated with the hierarchy by the dotted line, which indicates that each instance of the association will be represented by an object of this class.

These various features of UML static structure diagrams let the user encode detailed design information. When the diagrams are used to create a design, however, they should be thought of as secondary. The designer should first draw a basic diagram, noting the candidate classes, generalizations, and associations but not providing the details. This should be used to get a good understanding of the overall design. Only when such a design is understood (and presumably acceptable) should the designer add specific information such as methods and data members. Further refinements to associations, visibility, or parameter and member types should be made when a more detailed design is required and only when the given design mandates the additional constraints. Keeping the diagram as simple as possible at each design stage lets the designer be expressive without constraining the eventual implementation too much or getting too bogged down in details.

EXPRESSING DESIGNS USING DIAGRAMS

Static structure diagrams provide a convenient and useful representation of a complete design. They also can be used effectively as a tool for creating that design in the first place.

Top-Level Design

Design starts by finding candidate classes. A static structure diagram can be useful in this process to record the candidate classes as they are identified and to help prune them. The first step here is simply to place all the candidate classes in a diagram. Then the various classes can be organized into logical groupings that can be used to restrict the set of objects needed for top-level design.

In discussing the symbolic differentiation problem in the previous chapter, we identified the classes shown in Figure 6-5. The first step in using this diagram is to group the classes so that related classes are near to one another. This gives us a way to select an appropriate top-level set of classes. Figure 6-6 shows these classes grouped into five sets: classes related to overall control, classes for simplification based on pattern matching, algorithmic classes, classes for tokens, and the large number of classes related to expression trees.

The next step is to use these groupings and all other information available to select the appropriate set of top-level classes. This is done by eliminating as many of the given classes as possible:

- In the first cluster we keep **Main** to give us a means for overall control. We discard **InputStream** and **OutputStream** as too low-level (we will use the standard C++ library for these). We also omit **Callback** for now, since we won't be implementing a graphical front end.

Figure 6-5 Candidate classes for symbolic differentiation.

- We keep **RuleSet** in the second cluster and eliminate **Rule** since it is an implementation feature of the **RuleSet**.
- All the algorithmic classes except for **Parser** are eliminated. Unparsing and differentiation will be handled by the various types of expression nodes. Simplification will be handled by the **RuleSet** in conjunction with an expression node.
- We keep **TokenStream** and **Token** from the fourth cluster, and eliminate the specialized token types from the top-level design. As with **Rule** and **RuleSet**, these will show up when we implement **Token**.
- Finally, we keep only **ExpressionNode** and **ExpressionFactory** from the last cluster. The overall expression tree is represented by its root node, so we can eliminate **ExpressionTree**. The other classes here will be involved in the implementation of **ExpressionNode** but are not needed at the top level.

The result of this is the set of classes shown in Figure 6-7.

The next step in object-oriented design is to characterize the objects. This is reflected in three ways in the static structure diagram. First, any data fields that do not refer to other classes in the diagram are added to the field part of the class definitions. Second, any data fields that do refer to classes are

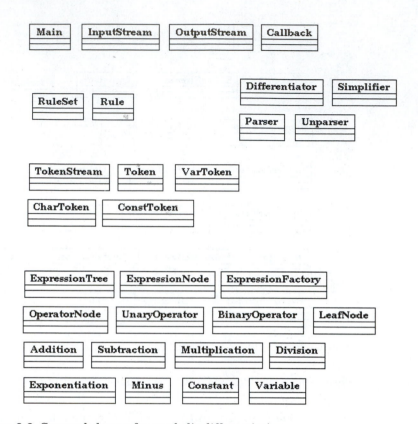

Figure 6-6 Grouped classes for symbolic differentiation.

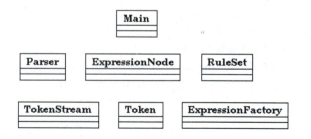

Figure 6-7 The set of top-level objects for symbolic differentiation.

reflected as associations of the appropriate type. Finally, any methods that are known at this point are added to the operator part of the class definitions.

Doing this for the symbolic differentiation example of Figure 6-7 yields the diagram in Figure 6-8. Here we have changed the class names to reflect our naming conventions, added the various standard methods discussed in the

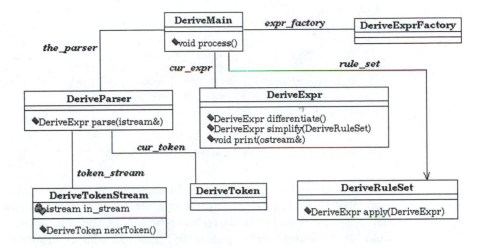

Figure 6-8 Static structure diagram for symbolic differentiation.

```
void
DeriveMain::process()
{
    expr_factory = new DeriveExprFactory
    rule_set = new DeriveRuleSet
    the_parser = new DeriveParserInfo(cin,expr_factory)
    loop
        cur_expr = the_parser->parse()
        if (cur_expr == NULL) break;
        expr1 = cur_expr->differentiate();
        expr2 = expr1->simplfy(rule_set)
        call expr2->print(cout)
    repeat
}
```

Figure 6-9 Pseudocode for top-level symbolic differentiation.

previous chapter, and defined data fields such as `in_stream` for **DeriveToken-Stream** and the various associations.

After the initial object characterization is done, we are ready to define the implementation of the top-level classes. We start at the main entry point, `DeriveMain::process` in the pseudocode shown in Figure 6-9. Here we have changed the class **DeriveParser** so that its constructor takes both the input stream and the factory object for building expressions. Next the parser object is defined by writing pseudocode for parsing. The top-level parsing code looks for a line containing an expression, sets up the token stream, and parses it as noted in Figure 6-10. Here the actual parsing must know the token types and uses the expression factory object to create the different types of expression

```
DeriveExpr
DeriveParser::parse()
{
    get next input line containing an expression
    let ist =  a new istrstream for the line
    token_stream = new DeriveTokenStream(ist)
    cur_token = token_stream->nextToken()
    return parseExpr()
}
```

Figure 6-10 Pseudocode for parsing an expression.

nodes. Noting this causes us to add the various methods for creating expression objects to the **DeriveExprFactory** object and the methods for accessing token information to the **DeriveToken** object. In addition, we need to add a data field for the input stream passed to the parser and an association between the parser and the expression factory.

We defer the definition of the remaining parsing methods until we consider the more detailed design of the various components of the problem. The definition of `DeriveTokenStream::nextToken` requires an understanding of the implementation of **DeriveToken** and its hierarchy. Similarly, the methods associated with expressions require the definition of the expression hierarchy, and the rule set method needs to be understood in terms both of the implementation of the rule objects and of how it will be used by expressions. With this in mind, we show the resultant top-level static structure diagram in Figure 6-11.

Second-Level Designs

As a system becomes more complex, a single static structure diagram becomes insufficient. When making an object-oriented design, one attempts to consider the system in such a way that only a few classes, say 5-10, need be considered at any one time. The top-level design tries to elide as many of the details of class implementation as possible for the small set of top-level classes. This means that helper or support classes, as well as all members of a class hierarchy other than the root, are generally not included in the top-level design and hence should not be detailed in the corresponding top-level static structure diagram. In order to design and understand these second-level classes, we need to draw additional diagrams.

Our top-level design for the program provides a framework that lets us isolate the implementation of different parts of the system. In this case there are four separable components. The first is the implementation of tokens. This involves both the class hierarchy implicit in **DeriveToken** and the implementation of the **DeriveTokenStream** class that returns the next token. If these classes are not particularly simple, we could hide their implementation, as we did with expressions, by adding a token factory class. If we don't do this here, we

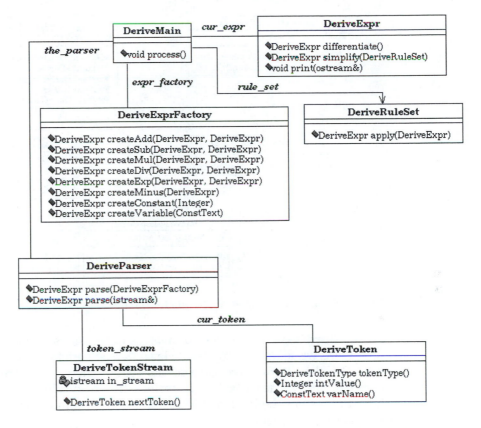

Figure 6-11 Top-level static structure diagram for symbolic differentiation.

end up with a second-level static structure diagram describing the token implementation similar to that in Figure 6-12.

There are two things to note in this diagram. The first is that we duplicated the classes relevant to token processing from the top-level design diagram. Any secondary diagram should start with the relevant classes from the top-level diagram, although it can include more implementation details for these classes, such as the data members and additional methods needed in implementing the more detailed design. The second point is that the token hierarchy is reflected completely in this diagram while the top-level diagram only included the root class, **DeriveTokenInfo**. This is typical of secondary diagrams and class hierarchies.

The second component is the parser. As it turns out, a recursive descent parser can be implemented without adding any classes, so the second-level structure diagram here contains only the **DeriveParser** class augmented with the additional private methods needed for the actual parsing.

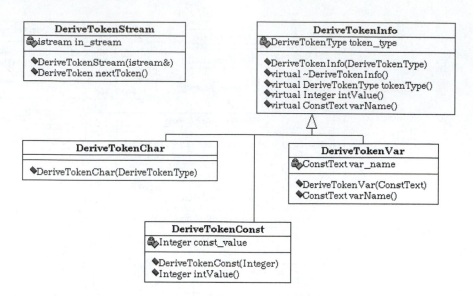

Figure 6-12 Static structure diagram for the token implementation.

The third second-level design involves expressions and the expression factory. Here we make the top-level class, **DeriveExprInfo,** be abstract and introduce the class **DeriveExprData** and the rest of the expression node hierarchy beneath this, as described in "Interface Inheritance" on page 115. Then we have to consider the implementation of the three primary methods: `differentiate`, `simplify`, and `print`.

The `differentiate` method requires that for each leaf node of the expression-tree hierarchy we create a method to build a new expression representing the derivative. For some of the nodes this requires duplicating a subtree. For example, applying the rule

```
d(A*B) = A*d(B) + d(A)*B
```

requires copying the two subtrees of the multiply node as well as taking their derivatives. To accomplish this, we add a `clone` method to the local root of the hierarchy. This method, which is implemented in each leaf node, does a deep copy of the tree. A *deep copy* of a data structure duplicates each element of that structure; a *shallow copy* duplicates only the top element, reproducing only the pointers to second-level elements. Using assignment or the default copy constructor yields a shallow copy, hence the need for a new method. The definitions of the `differentiate` method and the new `clone` method are relatively similar for all the classes. They are shown for the class **DeriveExprMul** in Figure 6-13. In both of the methods in this figure we choose to build the subtrees directly since we don't have a handle to the factory object.

Printing an expression also requires a method in each leaf node. However, in this case, the print methods for each of the binary operators are quite simi-

```
DeriveExpr
DeriveExprMul::differentiate()
{
    leftclone = lhs_expr->clone();
    leftdiff = lhs_expr->differentiate();
    rightclone = rhs_expr->clone();
    rightdiff = rhs_expr->differentiate();
    t1 = new DeriveExprMul(leftclone,rightdiff);
    t2 = new DeriveExprMul(leftdiff,rightclone);
    return new DeriveExprAdd(t1,t2)
}


DeriveExpr
DeriveExprMul::clone()
{
    leftclone = lhs_expr->clone();
    rightclone = rhs_expr->clone();
    return new DeriveExprMul(leftclone,rightclone);
}
```

Figure 6-13 Implementation of differentiation for multiply.

lar, outputting a left parenthesis, the left-hand expression, the operator, the right-hand expression, and a right parenthesis. The only difference among the five routines is what operator is output. To simplify these methods, we make use of the hierarchy and define the print method in **DeriveExprBinaryOp**. To make this work, however, we need to introduce a new virtual method returning the operator name, which we call op. Since unary operators can be handled similarly, we define a print method in **DeriveExprUnaryOp** and make the virtual method op an abstract method of **DeriveExprOp**.

Finally, the simplification method uses the set of simplification rules embodied in the **DeriveRuleSet** object that is passed in. Since this method is the same for all expression nodes, we define it at the root of the concrete hierarchy. Figure 6-14 shows the static structure diagram that reflects the expression hierarchy and these implementation decisions.

MESSAGE-TRACE DIAGRAMS

While differentiation of an expression is a simple transformation of the tree based solely on the type of tree node, simplification is more complex, involving repeated application of a variety of patterns or simplification rules as well as constant arithmetic. In designing the simplification aspects of our symbolic differentiation program we must consider how the simplification rules are

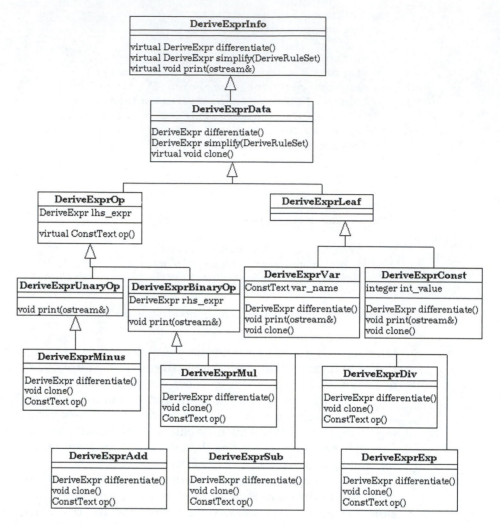

Figure 6-14 Design for expression management.

expressed, what the various rules are, how to apply them, and how and when to do constant arithmetic.

Rules for simplification can be expressed in terms of expression patterns. For example:

A - 0 => A

A + A => 2 * A

where the variable A matches any subexpression. The first decision here is whether to build the set of simplification rules into the program or let it be defined externally. Since it is difficult to determine whether a set of patterns is

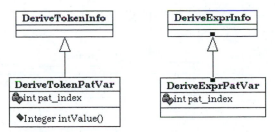

Figure 6-15 The additional classes for handling pattern variables.

complete enough to do all the simplification we need, it is desirable to make the set of patterns extensible and hence to define them externally. This lets us add patterns as needed and experiment with different pattern sets — it hides or abstracts out what the pattern set should be.

Simplification rules are defined in terms of expressions. Within our program we are using trees to represent expressions. It is thus natural to view the two expressions composing a rule as trees as well. These trees differ from the expression trees we have been dealing with in needing to support an additional type of node, one representing the variable A in the above patterns.

Pattern trees can be developed in two ways: by building a new expression-tree class hierarchy just to represent patterns or by extending our existing hierarchy by adding a new node type corresponding to a pattern variable. While the first alternative lets us separate the two implementations, the second is much simpler and lets us reuse much of the mechanism we have already designed. In particular, it lets us use the existing parser to read in the set of simplification rules from a data file.

In defining the pattern rules we need to allow multiple variables in an expression, so that rules such as

   A + B => B + A

can be expressed. We denote pattern variables with a question mark and a single digit, letting up to ten variables be defined. Thus the above patterns would actually be given in the data file as:

   ?1 + 0 => ?1

   ?1 + ?1 => 2 * ?1

   ?1 + ?2 => ?2 + ?1

where everything other than a pattern variable is interpreted literally.

To achieve this we need to add two classes to our existing hierarchies as shown in Figure 6-15. First, we need to define a new type of token to represent a pattern variable. This is represented by the class **DeriveTokenPatVar** as a subclass of **DeriveTokenInfo**. The class has one data field to hold the variable `index` and uses the `intValue` virtual method to return the corresponding value. Here

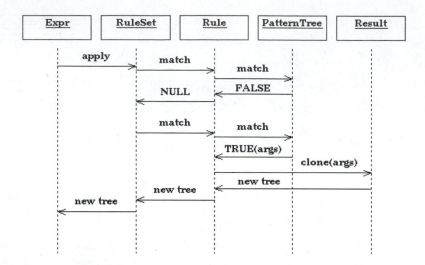

Figure 6-16 Message-trace diagram showing simplification.

we need to augment the `nextToken` method of **DeriveTokenStream** to create pattern-variable tokens.

The second class we need to add is new type of expression node for a pattern variable. This is the class **DeriveExprPatVar,** which will be defined as a direct subclass of **DeriveExprInfo**. To let pattern-variable nodes be created we need to extend our previous design in two simple ways. First, we need to add a new method `createPatVar` to the expression factory class so that pattern-variable nodes can be built by the parser. Then we have to extend the parser to handle pattern-variable tokens as primitive elements.

Our next task is understanding how to use patterns to simplify an expression tree. The top-level method we need to define is `simplify` in the class **DeriveExprData**. This method takes a **DeriveRuleSet** object holding the set of rules as an argument and attempts to simplify the tree corresponding to the given node. While there are various alternative implementations, the basic idea is to match patterns against the node and, if a match is found, to replace the node with the second part of the simplification rule. If no match is found, then the routine should build a clone of the current node with any subexpressions replaced by their simplified form. The expression returned by `simplify` is thus guaranteed to be a new subtree that can be deleted and treated independently of the original subtree, thus simplifying memory management.

Figure 6-16 reflects the dynamics of the matching part of simplification. Here vertical lines represent individual objects, horizontal lines represent messages, and time is indicated by the vertical dimension, reading from top to bottom. This *message-trace diagram* is a part of UML.

This particular diagram shows what happens when `simplify` is called for an expression. The first thing the expression object does is to call the `apply`

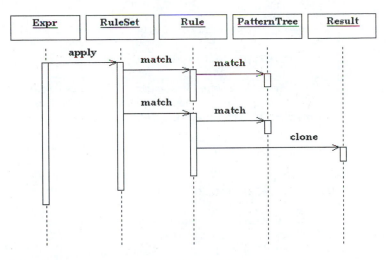

Figure 6-17 Message-trace diagram showing focus of control.

method of the rule set. The rule-set object then calls the `apply` method on a rule object in the set. The rule tests whether it is applicable by calling the `match` method on its pattern-expression tree. For the first object, this returns `FALSE`, indicating that no match was found. The rule-set object then tries another rule, and here the `match` routine returns `TRUE` along with the set of trees that matched the pattern. At this point the rule-set object calls the `clone` method of the result-expression tree passing in the set of matching trees. The result of this is a new tree that is returned to the original `simplify` method and is the result of the simplification.

Message-trace diagrams are useful for detailing how objects interact over time. They are particularly good for documenting complex interactions among a set of objects where the code might be both distributed and complex. They can be extended in natural ways to indicate timing constraints and parallelism. Note that while static structure diagrams deal with classes and show the overall program structure, message-trace diagrams deal with individual objects and generally show only one or two cases of how the objects are used.

Message-trace diagrams should be used to give the designer and the reader of the design a better understanding of any complex interactions among objects in the target system. They can have a variety of different forms and the designer should choose the one most suitable to the task at hand. Figure 6-16 uses arrows for both the call and its return value. One can also omit the return arcs and use the vertical lines to show the *focus of control* for each object, as in Figure 6-17. The extended regions on the vertical lines here indicate times when the object has been called and has the focus of control.

The actual `simplify` method must be defined for leaf, unary, and binary nodes. The pseudocode for the binary case is shown at the top of Figure 6-18.

```
DeriveExpr
DeriveExprBinOp::simplify(DeriveRuleSet drs)
{
    DeriveExpr rslt = drs->apply(this)
    if (rslt == NULL)
        rslt = clone(lhs_expr->simplify(drs),
                     rhs_expr->simplify(drs);
    return rslt->constEval()
}


DeriveExpr
DeriveRuleSet::apply(DeriveExpr e)
{
    for each rule r in the set
        rslt = r->match(e)
        if (rslt != NULL) return rslt
    return NULL
}


DeriveExpr
DeriveRule::match(DeriveExpr e)
{
    DeriveExpr pats[10];
    clear pats[0..9] to NULL
    if (source_tree->match(e,pats)) then
        return target_tree->clone(pats)
    else return NULL
}


Boolean
DeriveExprAdd::match(DeriveExpr e)
{
    DeriveExprAdd * a = dynamic_cast<DeriveExprAdd *>(e);
    if (a == NULL) return FALSE;
    return lhs_expr->match(a->lhs_expr) &&
           rhs_expr->match(a->rhs_expr);
}
```

Figure 6-18 Pseudocode for simplification.

The other two cases are just simplifications of this. In this pseudocode we introduce three methods. First, the method apply of the class **DeriveRuleSet** applies all the patterns in the rule set to an expression and returns a new tree if one matched and NULL otherwise. The second method, clone, builds a copy of the current node with appropriate subtrees, and must be defined explicitly for

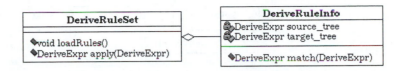

Figure 6-19 Static structure diagram for the rule set.

each subtype of **DeriveExprBinOp**. Finally, the method `constEval` checks if both subexpressions are constant and if so returns a modified tree containing the result of evaluation.

We continue the design process by defining these newly introduced methods. We start with the `apply` method that applies the rule set to a tree by applying each rule of the set in turn until one is found that matches, and returning the result, as seen in the pseudocode for the `apply` method in the top-middle of Figure 6-18. Here we use the `match` method for a rule to check if the rule matches the given tree and returns the resultant tree if so. The pseudocode for this is shown at the bottom-middle of the figure. This code uses the `match` method for the source tree and a `clone` method for the target tree. Note that these two methods take an additional argument, an array of pattern expressions containing the trees that match the corresponding pattern variables. The structure diagram for **DeriveRuleSet** and **DeriveRuleInfo** based on this is shown in Figure 6-19.

These definitions require us to go back to the class **DeriveExpr** and add the two new methods. (Note that both the source and target trees of the rule are expression trees.) The added `clone` method is similar to the `clone` method already defined for differentiation. The differences are that it takes an extra parameter, the trees matching source-pattern variables, and that it needs special handling when the target node is a pattern variable. The easiest way of defining this is to use the existing `clone` method itself, add the extra parameter with a default value of `NULL` for the differentiation case, and then define the `clone` method of **DeriveExprPatVar** to return a copy of the proper subtree from the array of matching trees.

The `match` methods for expression trees are a bit more complex since they require checking two objects to see if they are of the same type and then testing if they contain the same values. The simplest approach here is to use the run-time typing features of the language, as illustrated at the bottom of Figure 6-18.

Finally, we need to define the methods for constant evaluation. Figure 6-20 shows a message-trace diagram indicating how we expect constant evaluation to work. The `isConstant` method of an arbitrary expression node tests whether the node represents a constant value and returns the value if so. The `evaluate` method, shown here for binary operator nodes, takes two integers and does the appropriate arithmetic. Finally, if constant evaluation succeeds,

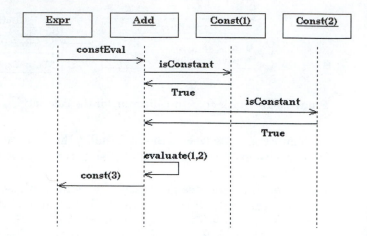

Figure 6-20 Message-trace diagram showing constant evaluation.

```
DeriveExpr
DeriveExprBinOp::constEval()
{
    if lhs_expr is constant with value v1 AND
            rhs_expr is constant with value v2 then
        return new DeriveExprConst(evaluate(v1,v2))
    else
        return this
}
```

Figure 6-21 Pseudocode for constant evaluation.

a new constant tree is built using the result of evaluation. The actual pseudocode for the method is shown in Figure 6-21.

USING DESIGN DIAGRAMS

The design notation we are using here, and those introduced in later chapters to deal with larger-scale programming, have a variety of applications. In this section we look at these applications and their limitations.

The primary purpose of the diagrams should be to help the developer understand the problem and its solution. Static structure diagrams are a convenient means for visually organizing and pruning the set of candidate classes. They provide, at a glance, a view of complex relationships among the different classes. Often, just by looking at a class diagram, the programmer can see areas that are too complex or classes that are too closely coupled.

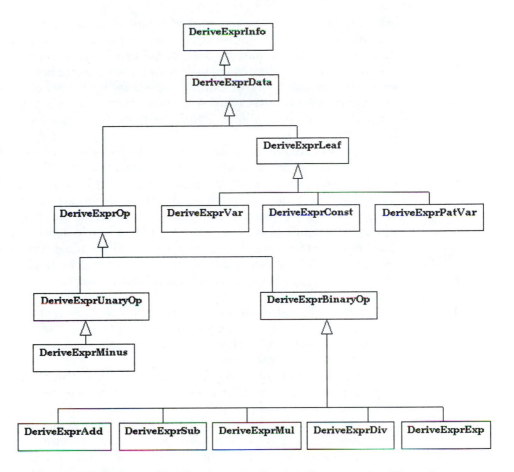

Figure 6-22 Static structure diagram showing just the expression hierarchy.

Finally, designs at the early stage at which such diagrams are made are easy to change and improve.

But static structure diagrams have their limitations. They can easily become overwhelming and confusing. A static structure diagram that includes more than five to ten classes is generally difficult for a reader to understand: Figure 6-14, for example, is probably too complex to be useful. Since most of the subclasses are pretty much the same, it would probably be better to use a diagram such as Figure 6-22 merely to display the hierarchy and then augment this only with new or different methods. Alternatively, the different methods could be put in separate diagrams: for example, a separate diagram could describe the operation of the binary operators.

Static structure diagrams show only the structure of the classes and not the call relationships or how the methods of the classes are intertwined. This information, which is also essential in analyzing and understanding an object-oriented design, must be provided by annotations to the diagrams or in separate diagrams. Textual annotations should generally accompany any design diagram. The class names are meaningful to an outside reader only when they are fully described. Similarly, the simple names used to label associations provide a minimum of information. The designer either should create a textual description to accompany the structure diagram or, when using a tool that supports annotations, should attach the more detailed information directly to the diagram.

Message-trace diagrams are designed to provide dynamic information and are quite useful in helping the developer understand an implementation involving complex interactions among objects. However, these diagrams also have their limitations. They have difficulty showing relationships involving large numbers of objects, again because they become too complex to be useful. Moreover, each diagram can illustrate only a single specific case involving a fixed number of objects. This means that multiple diagrams might be needed to understand fully how a complex method should be implemented. Finally, the diagrams elide considerable helpful information that must then be added as annotations.

The second function of design diagrams is to document the overall design. As a program evolves, it is important for programmers who need to modify it to understand how it was built and why. A good description of the design can only aid in such maintenance.

Creating and maintaining these diagrams for use in documentation, however, is a laborious task that is usually not done. The easy part of the task is including full annotations with the various diagrams so that they are useful even when the original designer has left or forgotten how they were created. The more difficult part is maintaining the diagrams as the code is written and the design evolves. Design diagrams are most useful when a system is actually being designed. Once the system starts to be implemented, most programmers use the diagrams for reference, but do not continually update them. In order not to waste the effort that went into creating these diagrams in the first place, programmers must get into the habit of continually keeping them up to date.

A second problem with static structure diagrams as documentation is that they eventually become too complex. If the diagram includes every method in the public and private interfaces of each class, not even the simplest diagram can be displayed in an organized fashion on one page. The solution we recommend here is to use the design diagrams to reflect only the public interfaces, which should be kept simple enough to fit.

The final use of design diagrams is to provide a basis for implementation, as in this chapter. Static structure diagrams give an outline of what the class definitions should look like and a basis for defining pseudocode for the various methods. Message-trace diagrams let the programmer understand what the pseudocode should look like in the more complex cases. Design diagrams are particularly useful here in that they offer a lot of information in a relatively compact space and can easily be modified as the design evolves.

However, design diagrams are not necessarily the only or the best representation even in this case. When a problem is relatively simple or when the system has been designed hierarchically to the point that each particular problem is simple, it is often clearer and more convenient to use include files and the actual class definitions as a further basis for design. Once the initial set of classes is determined, all the design steps can be done using header files in lieu of the static structure diagrams. Data fields and candidate methods can be added to the class definitions. As methods are considered in turn, new methods can be added or previous ones modified to reflect the current state of the implementation.

Using header files in place of structure diagrams has its pros and cons. The disadvantage is that header files do not show the big picture, including the overall nature of class hierarchies or the relationships between classes. For a complex design this is a serious problem, but once the design is simple enough it is not really an issue. The principal advantages are that it forces the programmer to commit to an actual implementation, defining more precise interfaces, and that, when the design is completed, the finished product can be used directly in the resultant application.

In general, designs use both diagrams and header files. The exact mix is determined by the complexity of the problem, the inclinations and habits of the designers, and whether or not the design diagrams must be preserved and maintained for future program development.

SUMMARY

A wide variety of notations has been developed for expressing object-oriented designs, many of which have recently been standardized as part of the Unified Modeling Language (UML). Of these, two are particularly useful, in a somewhat restricted form, for intermediate-level programming.

The first, static structure diagrams, are useful for representing object-oriented designs in terms of classes and their relationships. In this chapter we showed how to use these as a visual aid in the basic object-oriented design process. In particular, we discussed using them:

- To identify the initial set of classes;
- To determine an appropriate set of top-level classes;
- To describe the details of the design; and
- To define multiple levels of design.

The second, message-trace diagrams, provide information about the dynamics of an object-oriented design, illustrating how a particularly complex aspect of the design is implemented. These are useful for understanding complex run-time interactions among the objects of the design.

EXERCISES

6.1   Using UML and a suitable UML editor, construct the initial set of classes and a high-level description of the design of the solar system example of Chapter 1. Show the UML diagrams at various stages of the design.

6.2   Using UML and a suitable UML editor, build the top-level and second-level class diagrams for the problem described in Exercise 1.2, Exercise 1.3, or Exercise 1.4.

6.3   Using the UML notation and the framework outlined in this chapter, do a top-level design for a tic-tac-toe program. The program should have a textual interface that numbers the squares from 1 to 9, reads the next move from the user, and prints out a nice-looking tic-tac-toe board when appropriate. The user should be given the choice of going first or second. The program should support different levels of difficulty, some of which let the user win at times.

6.4   Using a set of message-trace diagrams, take a program you have written recently and explain how it works.

6.5   Implement the differentiation program described in this and the previous chapter. Note what design changes are needed as you do the implementation.

6.6   An alternative design for the differentiation program would isolate the expression trees from all the operations on the expression trees using a visitor (see "Visitor" on page 348 for details). Redo the design outlined in this chapter for such an implementation. Show how simplification would work by using a message-trace diagram.

6.7   Design and implement a program to play Scrabble against the user. The program should maintain the pool of letters, check the legality of the user's move, keep score, and, of course, find the best move (both offensively and defensively) when it is its turn. Use static structure diagrams and message-trace diagrams to show how the program would work.

Chapter 7

Using Object-Oriented Libraries

Simplicity is a primary goal in both the design and implementation of software since simpler designs and programs tend to be easier to develop and maintain. The simplest code to write is code that is already written for you. This generally takes the form of a library.

Traditional libraries provide sets of functions that applications can use where needed. Object-oriented programming goes beyond this to allow the definition of reusable objects and of parameterizable objects using templates. In this chapter we look at object libraries in general and at the Standard Template Library (STL) in particular, showing how to use such libraries effectively to simplify implementation.

OBJECT LIBRARIES

One of the biggest selling points of object-oriented programming is the ability to reuse code. This is generally done by giving the programmer a suite of object definitions providing much of the basic functionality that would otherwise have to be coded by hand. Large built-in object libraries of this type are key to the success of Smalltalk and Java. Smalltalk provides over 900 classes with a wide range of functionality covering input and output, basic and complex data structures, graphics, animation, multiprocessing, interrupts, and a particularly heavy emphasis on user interfaces. Java is being equipped with libraries that support input and output, 2D and 3D graphics, multiprocessing, database access, client-server computing, mail, electronic commerce, and multimedia.

Types of Libraries

Libraries have been used for a long time. Specialized Fortran libraries, such as Matlib, offer scientific programmers a broad range of numeric routines. Much of the success of the C language under UNIX can be attributed to the large (for the time) standard C library. Similarly, the Macintosh is easy to program because of the large suite of basic functionality provided in the Mac Toolbox libraries.

Object-oriented languages let libraries easily grow larger and more powerful and thus make implementing a system in the language that much simpler. The organizational structure that objects provide makes it easy to add functionality without the complexity of a large set of unorganized names or of large parameter lists. Objects let one build sets of library routines for data-structure management that are difficult in standard languages. Finally, some object-oriented languages support *type parameterization* whereby a single instance of a piece of code can be applied for a variety of different types, i.e. where some of the types used by the code can be viewed as parameters. C++ provides such functionality through templates. Type parameterization lets a library define generic data types that can be easily customized and used effectively in a broad range of applications.

Object libraries contain two types of objects, independent objects and dependent ones. *Independent objects* are wholly implemented in the library and do not depend on any user types or code. Common examples in object libraries include a reasonable implementation of a string type to replace C strings that are actually character arrays, the standard I/O types representing files and streams, types to allow manipulation of dates and times, and graphical user-interface frameworks. These are convenient to use because they offer standard types that should be portable among implementations, organize functionality in a meaningful way, and provide additional functionality that is shared among a broad range of applications. For example, most string classes do storage management within the class and offer such additional operations as concatenation and substring extraction.

Dependent objects are in a sense more interesting. These are data structures that interact with data in the application. For example, an object library might provide a linked-list type to support lists of arbitrary application objects. Other common data structures supported by object libraries include expandable arrays and various types of associative storage such as balanced trees and hash tables. Dependent objects can also provide algorithmic functionality. For example, a sort function can be defined that sorts an array of arbitrary application objects.

Because object libraries can simplify programming, and because C++ was originally developed without a standard library, a significant number of different libraries have been created. Many of the early ones, such as that from National Institutes of Health currently supported by the GNU project, were rooted hierarchies loosely based on experiences with Smalltalk. Here the library defined a generic **Object** class from which all library objects and any application objects that will use the library inherit. The generic class provides the basic functionality needed by other library classes, which allows application objects to be placed into containers such as linked lists or hash tables. It supports serialization (converting objects to and from byte streams for input and output) and typically offers run-time type checking through appropriate methods. This root-class-based approach to libraries, however, is messy and unnecessarily complex in C++. It imposes an additional class hierarchy on all user objects, and essentially forces the application to use a large portion of the library even if it needs only a small part.

A better approach has evolved with the introduction of templates in C++. Templates permit the definition of object libraries that do not require the user to accept the whole library in order to use a small part. Moreover, they produce cleaner code and impose fewer restrictions on the application. Even here, there has been a variety of libraries, each working with different compilers on different sets of machines. But over the past few years, a standard library has been defined for C++. This library, the Standard Template Library or STL, is based on templates and should eventually be available with all C++ implementations. Because this library should become the standard, we use it throughout the rest of the text. We note, however, that other template libraries are generally similar in nature and, once the user is familiar with one, adapting to another is straightforward.

Dependency Analyzer

To facilitate study of object and template libraries, consider the following simple problem:

> You are to write a program that takes a list of file pairs representing dependencies as input and produces a valid order for compiling the files as output. The input consists of lines containing two strings, the name of file A and that of file B. Blank lines and lines beginning with a pound sign (#) should be ignored. The input line should be read to mean that file A depends on file B. The constraint imposed by the problem is that if A depends on B, then B should be compiled (and hence output) before A is.

This is a classic example of a problem requiring a *topological sort*. We can view the overall input as a graph in which the files are the nodes and the dependencies are represented as arcs. Topological sort works by maintaining a count of the number of incoming links for each node. This count represents nodes that have not yet been output. The algorithm maintains a work queue that contains nodes to be considered and output. Initially the queue contains all nodes with no incoming arcs. At each point in the process, a node is taken off the queue, output, and then the link count of any nodes that were dependent on that node is decremented by one. If the count on any of these goes to zero, then that node is added to the queue. The process continues until the queue is empty and all nodes are output.

The candidate classes here are:

- **Node**: this represents a file, keeps track of the number of incoming links, and records all outgoing links.

- **NodeSet**: this maintains the set of all nodes, doing lookup to match string names as needed. It is also responsible for reading in the dependencies, setting up the set of nodes, and doing the topological sort.

- **Arc**: this represents a dependency link between nodes.

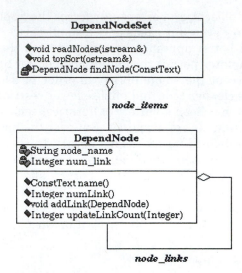

Figure 7-1 Classes for the dependency analyzer.

We can reduce this set by noting that, since no information is actually associated with a dependency, we can view the links as simple associations between nodes. This yields the static structure diagram of Figure 7-1.

The first class, **DependNodeSet**, contains the list of all nodes. It has two basic methods. The first, readNodes, reads pairs of nodes from an input stream. For each name, it either finds the corresponding node or creates a new one if none exists. This implies that it needs to keep an index of all existing nodes and look up the names in that index. We use an appropriate data structure and the private method findNode for this purpose. The second method, topSort, does the topological sort, outputting the names in the proper order to the given output stream.

The second class, **DependNode**, represents a node and does the appropriate bookkeeping. It maintains the node name and the count of active incoming links, and provides methods to access and manipulate these. We defer the specific implementation of topological sort and the corresponding methods to later in this chapter, in the section "Iterators" on page 174.

INDEPENDENT OBJECTS

The current C++ standard defines a number of independent objects that can be used to simplify and standardize programs. Prominent among these are classes to support strings and input/output. While these may not be implemented immediately in all current compilers, they should be soon. Moreover, most compilers offer a reasonable alternative. For example, Sun offers the

Rogue Wave classes including **RWCString**, while Microsoft offers the MFC classes which include **CString**.

The most important primitive type that is missing from the C++ language is a string type. Strings in C++ are inherited from C, which means they are implemented by using arrays of characters, with the string consisting of a null-terminated sequence of (ASCII) characters.

Using C strings has a number of disadvantages, most of them arising in memory management. First, the programmer must allocate space for them in advance. This means that the programmer must know the maximum length that the string could have or must constantly check that the allocated length is not exceeded. Not allocating enough space for a string is the source of numerous hard-to-find bugs. A second disadvantage is that the programmer must keep track of the storage of each string and free it at the appropriate time. This can involve tracking strings through all parts of the program that might have a pointer to them and is also a source of errors, either from freeing a string too early and thus having dangling references to it or from not freeing a string at all and thus having memory leaks. A third disadvantage is that some common operations such as concatenation and substring extraction are not supported directly or via the standard C library.

The C++ standard defines a **string** class that does its own storage management and supplies a broad range of operators. The definition in Figure 7-2 illustrates some of the basic functionality of this class. Note that any methods here that take an argument of type `string&` may also take an argument of type `const char *`, thus allowing compatibility with C strings. The `c_str` method is used to convert a standard **string** object to a C string.

The standard string type also supports several operators, as shown in Figure 7-3. Most of these, such as assignment, accept either a C string or a simple character in place of a **string** object parameter. The various comparison operators (`==`, `!=`, `<=`, `>=`, `<` and `>`) are defined appropriately for strings, as are the input and output stream operators (`<<` and `>>`). The addition operators provide an alternative syntax for concatenating strings.

Our dependency analyzer will use standard strings for storing the node name. Because this class or its equivalent is generally available and is much safer and more convenient than C strings, we recommend:

> **Use the built-in string class for all strings.**

The other independent classes that are widely used today are the standard input and output streams libraries distributed with all C++ compilers. The basic classes **istream** and **ostream** here provide fundamental input and output capabilities. The classes **ifstream** and **ofstream** extend these to files in the underlying file system. The classes **istrstream** and **ostrstream** let input and output be done from and to character arrays. Programmers should be familiar with all these classes. Moreover, the string stream classes should be used for

```
class string {
    string();
    string(const char *);            // build string from C string
    string(const string&);

    string& operator =(const char *);
    string& operator =(const string&);
    void clear();

    int length() const;
    bool empty() const;

    const char& operator[](int) const;
    char& operator[](int);

    string& append(const string&);      // concatenation
    string& append(char);
    string& insert(int,const string&);  // insert at position
    string& erase(int pos,int ln);      // erase at pos for len
    string& replace(int pos,int ln,string&);

    int find(const string&);            // search for substring
    int find(char);
    int rfind(const string&)            // reverse search
    int rfind(char);

    string substr(int pos,int ln);

    int compare(const string&);
    int compare(int pos,int ln,const string&);

    const char * c_str() const;
};
```

Figure 7-2 Excerpts from the built-in class string.

all input and output conversions and internal formatting rather than doing string manipulation directly, since both these classes keep track of the boundaries of the input and output arrays and provide convenient access to the necessary functionality. Because of their portability, better error checking, and object-oriented nature, we recommend:

> **Use C++ streams for all input and output.**

Note, however, that the current implementation of streams is being replaced with a template-based implementation as STL becomes more prevalent. The operations and use are mostly the same, but some of the names will change.

```
class string {
...
    string& operator =(const string&);
    string& operator =(const char *);
    string& operator =(char);

    friend string operator +(const string&,const string&);
    friend string operator +(const string&,const char *);
    friend string operator +(const string&,char);
    string& operator +=(const string&);
    string& operator +=(const char *);
    string& operator +=(char);

    friend bool operator ==(const string&,const string&);
    friend bool operator ==(const char *,const string&);
    friend bool operator ==(const string&,const char *);
    friend bool operator !=(const string&,const string&);
    friend bool operator !=(const char *,const string&);
    friend bool operator !=(const string&,const char *);
    friend bool operator <=(const string&,const string&);
    friend bool operator <=(const char *,const string&);
    friend bool operator <=(const string&,const char *);
    friend bool operator >=(const string&,const string&);
    friend bool operator >=(const char *,const string&);
    friend bool operator >=(const string&,const char *);
    friend bool operator >(const string&,const string&);
    friend bool operator >(const char *,const string&);
    friend bool operator >(const string&,const char *);
    friend bool operator <(const string&,const string&);
    friend bool operator <(const char *,const string&);
    friend bool operator <(const string&,const char *);

    char operator[] (int pos) const;
    char& operator[] (int pos);

    friend ostream& operator <<(ostream&,const string&);
    friend istream& operator >>(istream&,string&);
};
```

Figure 7-3 Operators defined for the standard string type.

For example, **istrstream** will become **istringstream** and will be based on C++ standard strings.

While strings and input and output are ubiquitous, other independent classes are used less frequently. Programs that manipulate dates and times should look into corresponding classes for inputting, outputting, storing, and comparing these values. Programs that need to be international should look into the locale classes that provide generic methods for managing strings, money, dates, etc. for this purpose. Unfortunately, at this point no generally available standards exist in these cases, so programmers are best advised to learn what is available on the systems they are targeting and to use whatever is appropriate. In addition, they should know and make use of the full C library where it isn't duplicated by C++ class functionality.

DEPENDENT OBJECTS

The power of today's object libraries comes from giving the programmer data structures that utilize arbitrary application types. This lets the programmer build lists, hash tables, dynamic arrays, and other structures without having to worry about pointer manipulation, complex algorithms, or debugging problems.

Such structures have been implemented in several ways. In C they are supported by a variety of routines that either are limited in the types they support (for example, the standard hashing functions support only character strings as keys), or require the programmer to cast the application's data to and from void * or its equivalent. Some object-oriented libraries define a generic superclass, say **Object**, from which all application classes inherit. Then the data structures, which are generally containers, are designed to hold **Object** instances and hence can hold arbitrary application objects. This scheme, used in Smalltalk and Java as well as the NIH C++ library, requires either run-time type checking (which Smalltalk, Java, and some C++ implementations provide) or casting to get access to the stored objects. Another alternative is to use the C++ preprocessor facilities to define a unique instance of the container class for each application class. Because the preprocessor is limited in functionality and tricky to use, however, this is always a bit messy and difficult to debug and use and is recommended only as a last resort.

Today's libraries implement these dependent objects by using the template facilities of C++. *Templates* are in effect smart macros. They are supported by the compiler and the language. Instantiation is automatic so that the user effectively declares an instance of a template type just by using it. Moreover, duplicate instances are merged by the system.

At the same time, templates are powerful and messy. The process of template instantiation is Turing-complete, that is, it can involve an arbitrary (and potentially infinite) computation. Templates are implemented differently on different compilers and what works on one machine may not work on another. The syntax for templates is inherently messy and ambiguous. Most importantly, templates are difficult to implement so that they work correctly with arbitrary subclasses. Most algorithm implementations make assumptions about how the base user type should be accessed. For example, the template might need to know the conventions for keeping track of dynamic storage for the user type. We thus recommend:

> **Leave the writing of templates to advanced programmers.**

While we don't in general recommend writing templates, application templates that are not truly generic are useful in some instances, as we see in Chapter 12.

Once templates are written correctly, they are easy to use. A template can be thought of as an extended type. For example, the Standard Template Library defines the template type **list**. If we want to create a list of **DependNode** objects, we simply use the type:

```
list<DependNode>
```

The name **list** here is the name of the template class and the arguments to the template appear inside angle brackets. Most templates take one or more types as their arguments. In this case, the argument is the type of each node of the linked list.

The templated class name, **list<DependNode>**, can be used anywhere a regular type name can occur. However, it is generally not a good idea to use these names freely. C++ syntax uses "<" and ">" both in expressions and as a terminator for template definitions. Moreover, ">>" is a separate token within the language. Because templates can in principle take expression arguments and other templates, syntactic ambiguities can arise in unexpected places. Second, templates that involve multiple arguments can be tricky to track. If the programmer does not use exactly the same set of arguments each time a template is used, the compiler might not complain, but the code may not work as intended. Templated names are also complex and the standard template names violate our naming conventions by not beginning with an uppercase letter. The code is cleaner and easier to read if these complex names are replaced with a simple name that has been `typedef`'d to the template. Defining type names for templated types also lets one easily change the template being used, for example substituting a vector for a list, without having to modify code throughout the application. Finally, defining type names in this way allows one to change library implementations rather easily when this is needed for portability purposes. For all these reasons and to ensure consistency, we recommend:

> **Define an application type name for each templated name.**

This can be done in one of two ways. If one is simply going to use the templated type, as is normally the case, one should use a `typedef`:

```
typedef list<DependNode>   DependNodeList;
```

Alternatively, if one wants to add additional functionality to the template for the particular type, the name can be defined as a subclass definition:

```
class DependNodeList : public list<DependNode> {
    ...
    void decrementCounts();
};
```

The ability to subclass a templated definition to provide additional functionality is one of the benefits of using a class library. It lets one place structural operations in a logical framework within the design. However, it should be used not to provide behavior inheritance but only to extend what is logically a container. A data type that uses a container while providing significant other functionality, such as the set of nodes in our dependency analyzer, should have the list defined as a data field and not through inheritance, for all the reasons stated in "Behavior Inheritance" on page 126. In particular, using a data field here simplifies the code by separating independent concerns, avoiding multiple inheritance, and ensuring that the inheritance hierarchies are natural. It also promotes code maintainability and evolution by making it easier to change the code by changing a class implementation instead of a whole class hierarchy. Thus

> **Inherit from a library class only to provide extensions of that class, not to define an application type.**

Dynamic Vectors and Lists

The templated class **vector<T>** defines an extensible one-dimensional array that supports the range of operations shown in Figure 7-4. The template assumes that the type T has default and copy constructors. In addition to the operators listed, it supports equality and lexicographic comparison if the type T has equality (`operator ==`) and a less-than (`operator <`) operator.

The standard template definition for vectors has both strengths and weaknesses. The class provides a dynamic array that can easily be expanded using the `push_back` method. The class itself handles all the necessary storage management. Operators are available to add, remove, and sort vectors. At the same time, the class does not, as one might expect, do bounds checking. The indexing operators return garbage (or abort the program) if the index value passed to them is out of range. A better implementation of the template would provide a safe implementation of this class.

A safe implementation can be achieved using subtyping, as shown in Figure 7-5. The first two type definitions in this figure are our standard type definitions. The third defines a new local type name, **String**, representing the library string class, and the fourth defines **DependNode** as a pointer. The fifth defines a name for the simple template with unsafe indexing. We defined a

```
class vector<T> {
    vector();

    bool empty() const;
    int size() const;

    T& operator [] (int);
    const T& operator [](int) const;

    T& front();
    const T& front() const;
    T& back();
    const T& back() const;

    void push_back(const T&);
    void pop_back();

    iterator insert(iterator,const T&);
    void erase(iterator);
    void erase(iterator first,iterator last);
};
```

Figure 7-4 Basic methods for the vector template class.

name here because we need to access the parent type from inside the index methods and it is more convenient to do this with a named type. The subclassed vector type provides a default constructor and destructor as well as the indexing operators. Here we have decided to return NULL if an invalid index is passed in. This could just as easily have raised an exception or triggered an assertion.

The subclass of Figure 7-5 defines a vector of **DependNode**, not a vector of **DependNodeInfo**. That is, the elements of the vector will be pointers to **DependNodeInfo** objects. The actual class definition for **DependNodeInfo** and the basic method definitions are shown in Figure 7-6. Note that the templated object, the vector of nodes, is a real object and not a pointer to an object. This requires us to use the dot notation, as in

```
depend_on.push_back(dn)
```

rather than the points-to notation we prefer.

An alternative to using a dynamic array or vector to hold the links for a node would be to use a linked list. The Standard Template Library provides a doubly-linked-list template type, **list<T>**, for this purpose. The basic operations for this type are shown in Figure 7-7. Linked lists share many of their operations with dynamic vectors. They allow quick access to the first and last element, maintain the size, and support a push and pop for the end of the list. They differ from vectors in that they support push and pop directly from the front of the list as well as the end and they do not support indexing

```
typedef const char *                    ConstText;
typedef int                             Integer;
typedef string                          String;
typedef class DependNodeInfo *            DependNode;

typedef    vector<DependNode>           DependNodeVectorUnsafe;


class DependNodeVector : public DependNodeVectorUnsafe {
public:
    DependNodeVector()                                        { }
    ~DependNodeVector()                                       { }

    DependNode operator[](int v)
        {   if (v < 0 || v >= size()) return NULL;
            else return DependNodeVectorUnsafe::operator[](v);
        }
    const DependNode operator[](int v) const
        {   if (v < 0 || v >= size()) return NULL;
            else return DependNodeVectorUnsafe::operator[](v);
         }
};
```

Figure 7-5 Definition of a safe vector template.

(`operator []`) for accessing an arbitrary element of the list. Additional list operations let the application reverse or sort the list. Sorting uses the less-than operator (`operator <`) of the element type. We define a list of **DependNode** objects as:

```
typedef list<DependNode>        DependNodeList;
```

This is what we will actually use to implement the topological sort for our dependency program.

Associative Containers

Another basic data structure we need for the dependency program is a symbol table for the node set class. A *symbol table* provides a mapping from a key, generally a name, to a value of an arbitrary type. Three basic types of containers can satisfy this need. First, we could use a linked list or vector of names and define a lookup operation that scans the list for the desired name. This is inefficient and would require us to write the lookup operator. A second choice would be to use a hash table. This would be ideal since it supports almost-constant-time insertion and lookup, the only capabilities that we need. Unfortunately, hash tables are not currently supported by the Standard Template Library, so this choice would again require a significant amount of work. The third solution is to use a sorted associative container such as a balanced tree.

```
class DependNodeInfo {
private:
    String node_name;
    Integer num_link;
    DependNodeVector depend_on;

public:
    DependNodeInfo(String);

    ConstText name() const         { return node_name.data(); }
    Integer numLink() const        { return num_link; }

    void addLink(DependNode dn);
    Integer updateLinkCount(Integer ct);
};


DependNodeInfo::DependNodeInfo(String nm)
{
    node_name = nm;
    num_link = 0;
}


void
DependNodeInfo::addLink(DependNode dn)
{
    depend_on.push_back(dn);
    dn->updateLinkCount(1);
}


Integer
DependNodeInfo::updateLinkCount(Integer ct)
{
    num_link += ct;
    return num_link;
}
```

Figure 7-6 Class definition for DependNodeInfo.

These both support insertion and lookup and, in addition, can easily access
their elements in sorted order.

The standard library supports four types of sorted associative containers,
sets, multisets, maps, and multimaps. In sets and multisets, the key upon
which the associative lookup is based is kept in the object, while in maps and
multimaps the key is kept separately from the object. Both support essentially

```
class list<T> {
    list();

    int size() const;
    bool empty() const;

    T& front();
    const T& front() const;
    T& back();
    const T& back() const;

    void push_front(const T&);
    void push_back(const T&);
    void pop_front();
    void pop_back();
    void remove(const T&);

    void reverse();
    void sort();
};
```

Figure 7-7 Basic list-template operations.

the same set of operations. Multisets and multimaps differ from sets and maps respectively by allowing multiple instances of an item with the same key.

Most applications in which one actually builds a symbol table call for a map data type, since one wants to create a new node only if there is no previous one. If you use a set data type here, you would have to create a new node in order to check if an old one previously existed, since the container will extract the key from the node itself. The basic definitions of both the map and set classes are shown in Figure 7-8; the multimap and multiset classes are similar. These definitions are incomplete: many of the useful operations of the templated classes require the use of iterators, which are described in the next section. Note that the map template supports an indexing operator that takes the key type as its index. This provides a clean and simple syntax for using a map as an associative array and is the preferred means for storing and accessing map elements.

The actual definition of the map data type is complicated by the fact that the algorithms to implement the type require a comparison function to compare two keys. This function should be part of the template parameters since different instances of the template may require different comparison methods. For example, a symbol table with a string key might want a case-sensitive or a case-insensitive comparison method. Templates, however, should be defined only with type parameters, not with functions or variables. The Standard Template Library gets around this by embedding the comparison function into a class using the `operator ()` construct, as in

```
class map<K,T,C> {
    map();

    bool empty() const;
    int size() const;
    int count(const K&) const;

    T& operator [] (const K&);
    const T& operator[] (const K&) const;

    int erase(const K&);
};

class set<T,C> {
    set();

    bool empty() const;
    int size() const;
    int count(const T&) const;

    int erase(const T&);
};
```

Figure 7-8 Basic methods for map and set template classes.

```
class StringComparer {
    bool operator()(const String& x,const String& y) const
        { return x < y; }
};
```

The template is then coded to use this class as a function to do the comparison. This comparison class is what is passed as the third parameter for a map template, the second for a set template.

Actually, the programmer need not define this class if the less-than operator of the type is used, the most common case, since the template library provides a templated type **less<T>** that serves this purpose. Thus we can define the map type we need to associate string names with **DependNode** objects as:

```
typedef map<String,DependNode,less<String> > DependNodeTable;
```

(Note that the space between the two ">" characters is needed to prevent C++ from interpreting it as a shift operator.) Given this, the **DependNodeSet** class is defined as shown in Figure 7-9.

One of the difficulties a programmer faces in using vector, list, set, and map container types is managing the storage of the container's elements. If the elements are actually restricted to the container, then the container object should be designated as the owner of its contents and should be responsible for deallocating the storage for the elements when it itself is destroyed. This will be reflected in our implementation of the destructor for **DependNodeSetInfo.** If the

```
typedef class DependNodeSetInfo * DependNodeSet;

class DependNodeSetInfo {
private:
   DependNodeTable node_table;

public:
   DependNodeSetInfo()                        { }
   ~DependNodeSetInfo();

   void readNodes(istream&);
   void topSort(ostream&);

private:
   DependNode findNode(const String&);
};
```

Figure 7-9 Class definition of the set of nodes.

elements exist both in and out of the container, this process becomes more complex. Here the programmer must ensure that each element has only one owner and that the owner is responsible for the element's storage. Even in this case, it is generally easier to leave the container as the owner.

The readNodes method shown in Figure 7-10 is implemented by reading lines from the given stream, checking if they are valid, and then using a string stream to extract the two names. The technique of reading a line and then processing it is generally preferred to straight use of C++ streams if the input is line-oriented. The findNode method described in the next section is used to look up and create a new node as needed.

ITERATORS

Before we can use a map or set type or do anything with a list other than simple insertion and deletion, we need to introduce the notion of iterators used by the Standard Template Library. An *iterator* is a class that lets the program look at each element of a collection in order. For example, a list iterator lets the program step through a list so as to look at each element in the list in turn. Iterators also serve as placeholders in a collection and thus act as the basis for location-dependent operations on collections.

The Standard Template Library uses iterators extensively with the various container types. The iterators for the different container types share common methods and usage. The iterator class for a container is accessed as Container::iterator, and should be defined with a user class name using a

```
const       int           MAX_LINE_LENGTH = 2048;

void
DependNodeSetInfo::readNodes(istream& inf)
{
    Character lbuf[MAX_LINE_LENGTH];
    String from,to;

    while (inf) {
        inf.getline(lbuf,MAX_LINE_LENGTH);
        if (inf.eof()) break;
        if (lbuf[0] == 0 || lbuf[0] == '#') continue;

        istrstream ist(lbuf,strlen(lbuf));
        ist >> from >> to;
        if (ist.fail()) break;
        findNode(from)->addLink(findNode(to));
    }
}
```

Figure 7-10 The readNodes method for DependNodeSetInfo.

typedef. Thus, when we define the symbol table for **DependNodeSet**, we should define both the map type and its iterator:

```
typedef map<String,DependNode,less<String> >   DependNodeTable;
typedef DependNodeTable::iterator              DependNodeTableIter;
```

Then we can define the iterators for the vector and list of **DependNode** objects:

```
typedef DependNodeVector::iterator     DependNodeVectorIter;
typedef DependNodeList::iterator       DependNodeListIter;
```

The library provides both an iterator for each type and a reverse iterator that is accessed as `Container::reverse_iterator` and goes through the elements in reverse order by default.

All iterators are currently bidirectional. The C++ operators ++ and -- have their normal meaning on iterators, moving the iterator to the next or previous value respectively. The unary * operator is used to access the current item pointed to by the iterator. Finally, iterators can be compared to each other. Comparison is typically used to terminate an iterator loop. Each container type provides a standard set of methods for defining and using iterators. The method `begin` returns an iterator for traversing the container, while the method `end` returns an iterator that can be used to test if the traversal is complete. This makes writing code to iterate through a container relatively simple. For example, Figure 7-11 shows simple code to loop through a list, printing each element in turn.

In addition to the `begin` and `end` methods, each container class defines methods that use iterators to access and modify the container. These methods are shown in Figure 7-12. Some of these use an additional template type

```
typedef list<int>          IntList;
typedef IntList::iterator  IntListIter;

void
traverse(IntList& l)
{
    IntListIter li;
    int v;

    for (li = l.begin(); li != l.end(); ++li) {
        v = *li;
        cout << "Next element is: " << v << endl;
      }
}
```

Figure 7-11   Using iterators to loop through a list.

```
class vector<T> {
    iterator insert(iterator,const T&);
    void erase(iterator);
    void erase(iterator first,iterator last);
};

class list<T> {
    iterator insert(iterator,const T&);
    void erase(iterator);
    void erase(iterator first,iterator last);
    void splice(iterator,list<T>&);
};

class set<T> {
    iterator insert(iterator,const T&);
    pair<iterator,bool> insert(const T&);
    void erase(iterator);
    void erase(iterator first,iterator last);
    iterator find(const T&) const;
};

class map<K,T> {
    iterator insert(iterator,const pair<const K,T>&);
    pair<Iterator,bool> insert(const pair<const K,T>&);
    void erase(iterator);
    void erase(iterator first,iterator last);
    iterator find(const T&) const;
};
```

Figure 7-12   Basic container methods using iterators.

```
DependNode
DependNodeSetInfo::findNode(String nm)
{
    DependNode dn = node_table[nm];

    if (dn == NULL) {
        dn = new DependNodeInfo(nm);
        node_table[nm] = dn;
     }

    return dn;
}
```

Figure 7-13 Finding a node by using a map template.

defined in the library, **pair**. This is a simple structure containing two elements that can be accessed as the fields `first` and `second` respectively. This type can be accessed as `Container::value_type,` which should be redefined with a user type name if it will be used. The iterator methods also follow certain conventions, using the empty iterator (which is defined by the `end` method) to indicate an empty value. For example, the various `find` methods return either an iterator pointing to the element found or an empty iterator if none was found.

Now we are ready to look at how to use the various containers and their iterators in our dependency analyzer example. The next method we consider is `findNode` for the class **DependNodeSetInfo**, which looks up the given name in the table and inserts it if is not present, as shown in Figure 7-13. The first line here looks the name up in the table using the indexing operator provided by the map template. If the name is not found, this line actually adds an element to the table using the default initializer for the value type of the table. The C++ standard insures that this is NULL if the value type is a pointer (as in this case). Thus, we test if the returned value is NULL and if so create a new node and add it to the table. This is the simplest (and generally the best) way to use a map, treating it as an associative array. Even if the routine were just doing a lookup and not doing an insertion if the element didn't exist, this approach is probably better, since it is simpler and the extra empty table elements have little impact on the program.

The code for the actual topological sort makes use of both vector and map iterators. It maintains a queue of nodes that are ready to output as a linked list of nodes using the type **DependNodeList**, which we defined to be **list<DependNode>**. This list is initialized to contain all nodes without incoming links in the first part of the routine shown in Figure 7-14. The work queue is set up as empty when it is declared. The code then steps through the symbol table using a map iterator. For each entry it extracts the corresponding node

```
void
DependNodeSetInfo::topSort(ostream& ost)
{
    DependNodeList workqueue;
    DependNodeTableIter tbliter;
    DependNode dn;

    ost << "\nThe dependency order is:" << endl;

    for (tbliter = node_table.begin();
            tbliter != node_table.end();
            ++tbliter) {
        dn = (*tbliter).second;
        if (dn->numLink() == 0) workqueue.push_back(dn);
    }

    while (!workqueue.empty()) {
        dn = workqueue.front();
        workqueue.pop_front();
        ost << "\t" << dn->name() << endl;

        DependNodeVectorIter liter;
        DependNode ldn;

        for (liter = dn->links();
                liter != dn->linksEnd();
                liter++) {
            ldn = *liter;
            if (ldn->updateLinkCount(-1) == 0)
                workqueue.push_back(ldn);
        }
    }
}
```

Figure 7-14 Topological sort code using iterators.

from the iterator, checks if the number of incoming links is zero, and if so adds it to the work queue.

The second part of the routine takes the first element off the work queue, outputs it, and then updates the incoming link count for all items that were dependent on that node, adding to the work queue any that now have a link count of zero. In order to implement this, we have to add two methods to the class **DependNodeInfo** to provide access to the array of links and let the top-Sort method loop over the links using iterators. These are:

```
DependNodeVectorIter links()  { return link_list.begin(); }
DependNodeVectorIter linksEnd(){ return link_list.end(); }
```

Finally, we note that the generic containers of the template library are designed to have common interfaces. Many of the methods, such as the default constructor and destructor, `size`, `empty`, `insert`, and `erase`, are provided by all the containers. Other operations such as `push_front` and `pop_front` are provided by a subset of containers in which the operations make sense. This lets the programmer change, with a minimum amount of effort, which container is used for a particular function in an application. For example, if we change the `typedef` line for **DependNodeVector** to use a list instead of a vector:

```
typedef list<DependNode>        DependNodeVector;
```

the program will still compile and work without any other modifications. This also has the advantage that one can transfer much of one's knowledge of how to use one of the templates to using the others.

THE REST OF THE LIBRARY

The string class and the list, map, and set data structures we have mentioned are only a part of the standard C++ library. The library provides a host of other useful features including additional templated data structures and standard algorithms.

Data-Structure Classes

In addition to the basic data structures of vectors, lists, maps, multimaps, sets and multisets, the Standard Template Library also supports a *deque*. This is a two-ended queue that is a cross between a doubly linked list and an array. It allows fast insertion at either the front or the back and allows indexed access to the elements. It provides all the methods of the **vector** template as well as a `push_front` and a `pop_front` method similar to the **list** template.

The template library supports some specialized data structures that are built on the more general containers. These include:

- *stack<Container>*: A stack implements a `push`, `pop` and `top` method. Stacks in the template library are viewed as an overlay of some other type of container, and the type provided in the definition is that of a container, i.e. a vector, a list, or a deque. Thus the user would declare a list-based stack of integers as `stack<list<int> >`. The only advantage of a stack template is that it restricts the interface so that the other methods of the underlying representation cannot be used.

- *queue<Container>*: This supports a simple queue using either a list or a deque in a manner similar to **stack<C>**. It restricts the operations on the resultant class to `push`, `pop`, `front`, and `back`.

- *priority_queue<Container,Comparator>*: This template supports a priority queue using either a vector or a deque. It provides `push`, `pop`, and `top` operators where the top operator returns the element with the highest priority. The comparator class parameter defines the less-than operator upon which the queue priority is based.

In the definition of the `topSort` method in Figure 7-14 we used a linked list to represent the work queue. Since the work queue is actually used only as a queue, we could define a queue template:

```
typedef queue<list<DependNode> >       DependNodeQueue;
```

and use this type for the local variable `workqueue`. To do this we would have to replace the `push_back` method with `push` and the `pop_front` method with `pop`.

Algorithm Classes

Most libraries provide access to algorithms rather than implementations of data structures. The standard C library, for example, offers algorithms for input and output conversion, sorting, hashing, string manipulation, and so on. Because of the nature of C, many of the corresponding routines either are restricted or offer an unsafe and complex interface. For example, the `dbm` database functions work only with character string keys, while the available sort function, `qsort`, makes the user create a comparison function and pass the width as well as the size of the structure to be sorted, and requires considerable casting from `void *`.

The Standard Template Library attempts to provide a cleaner interface to much of this and to additional functionality as well. Some of this interface is embedded in classes. For example, all the standard library string functions are available as methods on the class **string**. Others, such as the database functions of `dbm`, are implemented in the map or set-templated data structures.

Much of the rest of the functionality that would otherwise require a generic or restricted interface is provided by the library via algorithm templates. These are effectively functions that take parameters of an arbitrary type and are created automatically by the compiler on demand.

The simplest such functions are templates that yield the minimum and maximum of two values. The library defines generic functions:

```
const T& min(const T&,const T&)
const T& max(const T&,const T&)
```

that are templated over arbitrary types **T** that provide a less-than operator. If the appropriate library header file (`algo.h`) has been included, the user can simply assume that `min` and `max` work for all types:

```
int i = min(5,6);
```

The simple templated functions of this sort are shown in Figure 7-15. In addition to `min` and `max`, a `swap` function is provided to exchange two elements. Although not shown here, the `min` and `max` functions have an additional form

```
template<class T>
void swap(T& a,T& b)

template<class T>
const T& min(const T& a,const T& b)

template<class T>
const T& max(const T& a,const T& b)
```

Figure 7-15 Simple templated functions in the standard library.

that takes a comparison object rather than using the built-in less-than operator for the given type.

Another simple example is a generic find function that works over any type that supports an iterator, such as a linked list, vector, map, or set. This function is defined using a template over the iterator type **Iterator** and the element type **T** as:

```
Iterator
find(Iterator first,Iterator last,const T& value)
```

If we define:

```
typedef list<int>        IntList;
typedef IntList::iterator  IntListIter;
...
    IntList l;
    IntListIter li;
```

then to find the element matching 6 in the list `l`, we can use the `find` function:

```
li = find(l.begin(),l.end(),6);
```

which returns either an iterator pointing to the element or `l.end()` on failure.

The `find` function is just one of the searching functions provided by the library. An alternative version, `find_if`, takes a predicate object rather than a value of type T. A *predicate object* is a simple class that has one method defined, `operator(const T&)` or equivalent. Here the predicate is called for each element from the iterator and the function returns an iterator pointing to the first element for which the predicate returns true. Thus, for the above example, we could define a predicate class:

```
class Pred {
public:
    operator() (int v)           { return v == 6; }
};
```

and then use the code:

```
    Pred p;
...
    li = find_if(l.begin(),l.end(),p);
```

```
template<class Iter,class T>
Iter find(Iter first,Iter last,const T& value)

template<class Iter,class Pred>
Iter find_if(Iter first,Iter last,Pred p>

template<class Iter>
Iter adjacent_find(Iter first,Iter last)

template<class Iter,class T,class Size>
void count(Iter first,Iter last,const T& value,Size& n)

template<class Iter1,class Iter2>
bool equal(Iter1 first1,Iter1 last1,Iter2 first2)

template<class Iter1,class Iter2>
Iter1 search(Iter1 first1,Iter2 last1,Iter2 first2,Iter2 last2)
```

Figure 7-16 Templated searching functions in STL.

The template library provides a variety of other templated searching functions, some of which are shown in Figure 7-16. In addition to find and find_if described above, these include:

- *adjacent_find*: This function returns an iterator pointing to the first instance in which two consecutive elements of the underlying structure match.

- *count*: This function returns a count of the number of instances of a value in the section of the collection denoted by the first and last iterator. The result is passed back in the Size& parameter, which should be initialized to zero.

- *equal*: This function checks if the subsequence denoted by the first two iterator parameters exactly matches the subsequence starting at the point indicated by the third parameter.

- *search*: This function finds a subsequence within a sequence. The first two parameters denote the sequence in which to search. The second two parameters define the subsequence. The function returns either an empty iterator or a pointer to the start of the first match.

The above functions use a pair of iterators to indicate a sequence of elements for searching purposes. The template library offers additional functions that provide a set of standard operators on sequences defined in this way. For example, to take a list of integers, copy it, and then replace each element with its square, we could use the transform functions:

```
template<class Iter,class OutIter>
OutIter copy(Iter first1,Iter last1,OutIter first2)

template<class Iter1,class Iter2>
Iter2 swap_ranges(Iter1 first1,Iter1 last1,Iter2 first2>

template<class Iter,class OutIter,class UnaryOp>
OutIter transform(Iter first,Iter last,OutIter rslt,UnaryOp op)

template<class Iter,class T>
void replace(Iter first,Iter last,const T& oval,const T& nval)

template<class Iter,class T>
void fill<Iter first,Iter last,const T& value)

template<class Iter,class T>
void remove(Iter first,Iter last,const T& value)

template<class Iter,class Pred>
void remove_if(Iter first,Iter last,Pred p)

template<class Iter>
Iter unique(Iter first,Iter last)

template<class Iter>
void reverse(Iter first,Iter last>

template<class Iter>
void rotate(Iter first,Iter middle,Iter last)

template<class Iter>
void random_shuffle(Iter first,Iter last)
```

Figure 7-17 Standard templated sequence-manipulation operators.

```
   class Square {
   public:
       int operator(int v)        { return v*v; }
   };
...
   IntList l,l1;
...
   copy(l.begin(),l.end(),l1.begin());
   transform(l1.begin(),l1.end(),l1.begin(),Square());
```

Note that both functions take an iterator parameter to denote where to put
the output. The declarations for these and some of the other sequence-manipulation functions are shown in Figure 7-17. These functions include:

- *copy*: This function copies the sequence indicated by the first pair of iterators to the place indicated by the third parameter.

- *swap_ranges*: This function swaps the sequence denoted by the first pair of iterators with the sequence that starts at the location indicated by the third iterator.

- *transform*: This function applies the provided unary operator to each element of the sequence defined by the first two parameters and stores the result starting at the location specified by the third parameter.

- *replace*: This function replaces all the elements in the sequence denoted by the first two parameters that match the value given by the third parameter with the value given by the last parameter. Other replacement functions make a copy of the list and let a predicate object be used to check for the match.

- *fill*: This function replaces the contents of the denoted sequence with copies of the given value.

- *remove*: This function removes all values in the given sequence that match the given value. Like *replace*, it is available in a form that makes a copy of the list and a form with a predicate object.

- *unique*: This function eliminates all duplicate elements from the given sequence. It assumes that the elements of the sequence are in sorted order so that duplicates correspond to consecutive matching elements.

- *reverse*: This function reverses the elements of the given sequence. It is also available in a form that copies the sequence into a new sequence.

- *rotate*: This function rotates the elements of the given sequence around the given middle element. It is also available in a form that creates a new list rather than operating in place.

- *random_shuffle*: This function randomizes the order of the elements of the given sequence.

As noted, many of these functions have more than one form. For example, those that require matching a given value generally have one form that takes a value and a second form that takes a predicate object (similar to `find` and `find_if`). Also, some of the functions are restricted in the type of objects to which they can apply; for example, the `random_shuffle` function requires a vector type object.

In addition to these routines for manipulating sequences, the library provides templated functions for sorting and searching sequences that are vectors. These provide an interface that is simpler than the standard library `qsort` routine and is type-safe as well, and should be used in preference to either `qsort` or writing your own sort methods. These functions use either the built-in less-than operator or a comparison object that defines the method

```
bool operator()(const T&,const T&)
```

```
template<class VIter>
void sort(VIter first,Viter last)

template<class VIter,class Compare)
void sort(Viter first,Viter last,Compare comp)

template<class VIter>
void stable_sort(VIter first,Viter last)

template<class VIter,class Compare)
void stable_sort(Viter first,Viter last,Compare comp)

template<class Iter,class T>
bool binary_search(Iter first,Iter last,const T& value)

template<class Iter,class T,class Compare>
bool binary_search(Iter first,Iter last,const T& v,Compare cmp)

template<class Iter,class T>
Iter lower_bound(Iter first,Iter last,const T& value)

template<class Iter,class T,class Compare>
Iter lower_bound(Iter first,Iter last,const T& v,Compare cmp)

template<class Iter>
Iter min_element(Iter first,Iter last)

template<class Iter,class Compare>
Iter min_element(Iter first,Iter last,Compare cmp)

template<class Iter>
Iter max_element(Iter first,Iter last)

template<class Iter,class Compare>
Iter max_element(Iter first,Iter last,Compare cmp)
```

Figure 7-18 Sorting functions in the Standard Template Library.

to emulate that operator. The functions defined here are shown in Figure 7-18 and include:

- *sort*: This function sorts an array or a portion thereof.
- *stable_sort*: This is similar to sort except that the algorithm used is a stable one, i.e. elements that are equal are guaranteed to keep their order under the sort.
- *binary_search*: This does a fast search within the sequence for an element that matches the given value. It assumes the given sequence is sorted.

```
template<class Iter1,class Iter2>
bool includes(Iter1 frst1,Iter1 last1,Iter2 frst2,Iter2 last2)

template<class Iter1,class Iter2,class OutIter>
OutIter set_union(Iter1 first1,Iter1 last1,
        Iter2 first2,Iter2 last2,OutIter r)

template<class Iter1,class Iter2,class OutIter>
OutIter set_intersection(Iter1 first1,Iter1 last1,
        Iter2 first2,Iter2 last2,OutIter r)

template<class Iter1,class Iter2,class OutIter>
OutIter set_difference(Iter1 first1,Iter1 last1,
        Iter2 first2,Iter2 last2,OutIter r)

template<class Iter1,class Iter2,class OutIter>
OutIter set_symmetric_difference(Iter1 first1,Iter1 last1,
        Iter2 first2,Iter2 last2,OutIter r)
```

Figure 7-19 Set functions in the Standard Template Library.

- *lower_bound*: This is similar to `binary_search` except that it returns the iterator corresponding to the value where the item should be. If the item is present, it returns an iterator for the first instance of that item. If the item is not present, it returns an iterator where the item would be inserted.
- *min_element*: This function finds the minimum element in the given sequence. The sequence need not be ordered.
- *max_element*: This function finds the maximum element in the given sequence. The sequence need not be ordered.

As an example, suppose we want to sort an array of integers and then check if it contains the value 255. This can be done as:

```
typedef   vector<int>      IntVector;
...
  IntVector l;
...
  sort(l.begin(),l.end());
  if (binary_search(l.begin(),l.end(),255) { ... }
```

Finally, the Standard Template Library provides several functions that let any of the container types be treated as sorted sets. Here it provides the set operators shown in Figure 7-19, including:

- *includes*: This function tests if the set denoted by the first pair of iterators contains the set denoted by the second pair of iterators.

- *set_union*: This function builds the union of the two sets, discarding duplicate elements of the second set. The result is returned using the output iterator.
- *set_intersection*: This function is similar to set_union except that it constructs the intersection of the two given sets.
- *set_difference*: This function builds the difference of the two sets, i.e. it returns a set containing all elements of the first set that are not in the second.
- *set_symmetric_difference*: This function computes the symmetric difference, returning a set containing all elements that appear in either the first or second set but not both.

The actual template library includes all these functions as well as additional functionality that is not used as frequently. Because the use of these functions simplifies the resultant code and avoids bugs (since the library is already debugged), we recommend:

> **Learn what is in the STL and use it where appropriate.**

The reader should become familiar with these and other library functions by reading the C++ manual or an appropriate C++ text.

SUMMARY

Object libraries are a powerful mechanism for simplifying software development. They offer significant amounts of already tested and debugged code that can be reused in a new application relatively easily. The hardest part of their use is learning what is available and how to use it. Time invested in such learning is generally repaid with interest in terms of time saved in writing and debugging the current and future applications.

The standard C++ library, called the Standard Template Library because it is based mostly on the template facilities of the C++ language, includes a variety of different types of classes that are useful in one's applications. These include:

- *Basic Classes*: This currently means a practical and safe string class as well as the various streams classes provided for input and output. It will be extended with classes to support common objects such as times and dates.
- *Basic Data Structure Templates*: These include lists, dynamic vectors, sets, and mappings that are essentially associative arrays. These will be sufficient for constructing most of the complex data structures necessary in one's applications. The only basic structure missing is a hash table

(which can be implemented as a map), which is present in some versions of STL (notably that of Silicon Graphics).

- *Advanced Structure Templates*: These provide additional common data structures by building on the basic templates listed above. They include stacks, queues, and priority queues.

- *Basic Algorithms*: In addition to data structures, the STL provides a variety of algorithms using templated functions. These include basic functions such as min, max and swap; functions for searching through the standard data structures; functions that provide sequence operators over the standard data structures; functions that provide set operators over the standard data structures; and functions for sorting those data structures that can be accessed randomly.

EXERCISES

7.1   Write a program to find prime numbers up to a value given in the user's input.

7.2   Write a program that takes a text document and splits it into a list of words, discarding all punctuation, spaces, and formatting commands. Use the STL string facilities exclusively.

7.3   Design a program to take a list of words and a document and check that each word in the document appears in the list of words. (This is basically how a spelling checker works.) What STL data structures are appropriate to your design?

7.4   Write a program that counts the number of occurrences of each word in a document and prints out the k words that occur the most frequently. The program should map plurals to their singular form.

7.5   Write a program to take a set of documents and produce an *inverted index*: a data structure that maps each word in a document to the locations in the document where it is used (for example, line and character number or just word number). Your program should let the user ask about individual words and should print out the number and location of the occurrences of these words.

7.6   What data structures or functions do you feel are missing from the Standard Template Library? Describe what they would look like and how they might be used.

Chapter 8
Debugging and Testing

Developing a software system is a complex task. It starts from an understanding of the problem to be solved and proceeds to a well-structured, simple object-oriented design that is then translated into readable code. The next step is making the resultant implementation work. This is the task of debugging and testing.

Debugging is one of the most difficult and time-consuming parts of software development. It is also one of the least understood and least liked. In this chapter we first distinguish debugging from testing and explain the purpose and methodology of each. We then cover design and coding techniques targeted at minimizing and simplifying debugging. Next we explore different approaches to debugging, and finally consider testing as a means of finding bugs.

DEBUGGING AND TESTING

Once the code for a software system is written, it is the programmer's job to convert that code into a working program. This means finding and fixing any problems in the code. It also means demonstrating that the code works, or at least demonstrating some confidence that the code won't fail in a catastrophic manner when the first real user attempts to do something with it.

The first step in this process is to test the implementation. Here the programmer runs the program or parts of it in order to determine which parts of it work and which do not. On the surface, testing seems relatively simple. It might involve writing some extra code to emulate missing parts of a system, but other than that, it just means finding sample data and running the program. Real, effective testing, however, is a difficult task because it is a destructive rather than a constructive process.

Testing is the process of running a program with the intent of finding bugs. It is difficult because people by nature assume that what they do is correct and tend to overlook minor deficiencies in their own handiwork. Thus it is easy, when running a program, to overlook or ignore results that are inconsistent with one's expectations. It is also easy subconsciously to choose test cases that show that the program works rather than ones that find problems. To be good at testing the programmer must practice what is called "egoless" programming, consciously attempting to make the program fail. Because this is difficult, real software is tested in practice by a different group of programmers from that responsible for the code. We discuss various testing techniques and approaches later in this chapter.

Once testing has found a problem, debugging can commence. *Debugging* is the task of determining the exact nature of a suspected programming error and fixing it. Finding the problem and fixing it are two separate tasks, both of which can be difficult and time-consuming. Debugging is a part of programming that is generally not well liked: it takes a certain mindset (again egoless) to want to find problems with one's own code. After all, we all write perfect, bug-free code — it's the next person (or the compiler or the operating system) whose code has bugs!

Debugging can also be quite complex. It is puzzle-solving with a huge puzzle. When a problem occurs in a program, there is no a priori means for limiting that problem to any section of the code: it can occur anywhere. The programmer doing the debugging must understand the program as a whole all at once and take all possibilities into account. In a small system, this isn't too difficult. In a large system, however, especially one designed and built by multiple people, it can be a huge task. As programs grow larger, the interrelationships among the different parts of the program become more involved and the difficulty of isolating, tracking down, and fixing a problem tends to grow significantly faster than the size of the program.

The bulk of debugging, estimated to take up as much as 95% of the time, involves finding the cause of a suspected problem. While many bugs are quite simple to track down, especially when the coding error is close to the point where the problem was detected, others can be much more difficult. Several types of bugs tend to arise in a software system:

- *Syntactic bugs* reflect typing or transcription errors. Many of these are caught by the compiler, but some slip by and must be detected later on. They are often easy to find (and even easier to fix), but occasionally they are subtle and, because they are easy to overlook when reading the code, difficult to track down.

- *Design bugs* — faults in the overall or detailed design of the system — are relatively easy to find but often difficult to fix since they can require rewriting a significant part of the system.

- *Logic bugs* are flaws in the logic of a function or method. These are similar to syntactic problems in that they are generally easy to fix but can be subtle and difficult to track down.

- *Interface bugs* occur when an object or method is used in a way other than it was intended, for example with arguments in the wrong order, or when the assumptions made by the caller are different from those of the callee. These problems are often difficult to track down, especially if the interface code and the code using the interface are the responsibility of different programmers, but are generally easy to fix.

- *Memory bugs*, for instance if storage is freed that will be used later, or if storage is overwritten at one point and then used later on, are especially difficult to track down. Fortunately, tools and techniques exist to ameliorate these problems by detecting potential problems nearer to their source.

The remainder of debugging involves fixing a problem once it is identified. While this often just involves correcting a single line of code, it can entail redesign, recoding, and further testing. More importantly, even in the simpler cases, programmers are not likely to take into account the full consequences of changing existing code to avoid a problem, with the result that new problems are introduced. Bug fixes are often themselves buggy. Moreover, it has been observed that code in which bugs have previously been found is more likely still to contain bugs. Thus careful attention must be paid here as well.

DEFENSIVE PROGRAMMING

The easiest way to do debugging is to avoid it. The second easiest way is to ensure that bugs that are identified are local problems found where and when they occur. Both these approaches are the goals of *defensive programming*, where the programmer attempts to anticipate potential problems and design and code the system so that they are avoided or at least detected as early as possible. This approach is a lot like defensive driving: one anticipates what can possibly go wrong and takes steps to prevent problems before they occur.

Defensive Design

While debugging is typically considered to involve code and the coding process, a substantial amount of debugging can be avoided by appropriate action during system design. Several of the design objectives we have been encouraging throughout this text help serve this purpose. These are instances of *defensive design*.

The first such objective is simplicity of design. Simplicity tends to make programs easier to understand, write, and maintain. In addition, simplicity makes programs easier to debug. A simple design is easier to understand and code. It is less likely to have hidden errors when dealing with special cases. It is less likely to be the source of misunderstandings in which the code does not do what the designer intended. Simplicity in the overall structure tends to make problems easier to locate, since there are fewer problem sources and fewer levels of interaction to be considered in determining problem causes. Simplicity in class interfaces helps in identifying the function of each class and limiting the number of ways in which objects can be modified and used.

Simplicity in the algorithms used to implement the class results in simpler, less buggy code.

A second design feature we have stressed is encapsulation. Here we have emphasized that the coupling between classes should be minimized so that classes are as independent of each other as possible. This helps in debugging because bugs in a loosely coupled environment tend to stay within a given class. That is, if the symptoms of a problem occur in a given class, then the actual problem is likely to be in that class. The more classes depend on one another, the less likely this is to be true. Each class should be designed as much as possible so that its proper functionality does not depend on other classes at the same level of design.

A third design approach to minimizing debugging is designing with error in mind. We have not considered this fully in our previous discussions because it is more important for larger programs. A significant fraction of the bugs in a piece of software occurs in the error-handling code for several reasons. First, this code is generally not the primary focus of the design and often is not as well thought out as the code handling the working cases. Second, it is generally not used as much as the code for normal cases and hence is not as well tested. Third, this code often has secondary status and programmers typically add it on or throw it together without enough thought.

To alleviate this, the design process must focus on error handling as much as on normal operation. Part of the design process should be developing and answering a lot of "what if" questions. These questions ask how the program should react if the user, another system, or another component of this system does something unexpected. The designer of a component should attempt to identify as many of these exceptional cases as possible and ensure that the design can deal with all of them.

All three of these approaches tend to make the program more robust and easier to debug and maintain in the long run. We thus recommend:

Design defensively.

Another design tactic that can help minimize debugging involves analyzing a design to identify problems early on. A general practice, especially with large programs, is to do *design reviews*. Here the design is presented to a review panel that may consist of upper-level management, other software developers, a senior designer, or outside consultants. In a classroom situation, the panel could be an individual teaching assistant, the teacher, or other class members. The original designer learns a lot about the design in putting together a coherent presentation. Moreover, the reviewers provide a new viewpoint on the design, one that does not necessarily make the same implicit assumptions as the original designer. Even if a design review is not called for, it is a good practice for a designer to:

> **Review a design before implementing it.**

Note that this again requires the designer to be self-critical and practice ego-less programming. The purpose of the design review should be to identify problems more than to demonstrate that the design works.

Another approach during the system design that helps alleviate or eliminate problems later on is to make all assumptions and conditions explicit. When a method is designed, the designer typically makes some assumptions about the input values, the state of the object when the method is called, and what the method does. It is generally a good idea to make all such assumptions explicit, incorporating them into the design. This means formally defining preconditions and postconditions. A *precondition* for a method specifies the assumptions that are made on the input parameters and the state of the object when the method is invoked. A *postcondition* for a method specifies assumptions that can be made on the output values of the method and the state of the object when the method returns.

Preconditions, postconditions, and any other assumptions that the programmer makes about the code should be stated explicitly. They should be made part of both the detailed documentation for the code and part of the code itself, both as comments in the code and as actual code to test the various conditions as appropriate.

As an example of these techniques for defensive design, let's go back to the symbolic differentiation program of Chapter 5. One of the tasks we put off during our discussion was the design of the parser. The parser was implemented as the class **DeriveParserInfo** supporting one method:

```
DeriveExpr parse(istream&)
```

which takes an input stream corresponding to one line of the input and returns the expression tree corresponding to that line.

The first step in designing this class defensively is to note that the user will not always input a valid expression and thus the method must be able to deal with errors. We thus must determine how to reflect such errors to the caller. The simplest approach would be to just return a NULL value if the input is in any way invalid, and this works fine if a single error message, say "Invalid Expression," suffices.

If a more detailed description of the error is desired, however, then the method needs a way to return error values. This can be done by defining a new type of expression node, **DeriveExprError**, that indicates an error and contains the error message. Such a node type would be useful in other aspects of the program as well; for example, it can be used during simplification to handle division by zero. This change would involve modifying essentially the whole design since such a node would have to be detected at various points in the computation and each part of the system would have to handle error nodes appropriately.

A better alternative is to use exceptions. C++, Java, and most modern programming languages provide exceptions as a means for structured error handling. Because exceptions are designed for unusual conditions such as errors, they are generally simpler and more straightforward to use than implementing error cases within an existing framework. In the symbolic differentiation program, using exceptions lets us concentrate on the normal cases while still handling the error cases. It also lets us isolate error handling and not have it pervade the whole system.

Exception handling is defined in terms of protected code, handlers, and the ability to raise an exception. A routine can specify a section of its code as protected and provide exception handlers for it. The exception handlers are code fragments to be invoked if an exception occurs within the protected code or in any code called by that code. Once an exception handler is set up, any code invoked from a protected region that detects an error can raise an exception corresponding to that error. An exception is raised using a special statement that creates an instance of an exception object. Because an object is used here, it is possible to parameterize the exception, creating it with a set of arguments (such as the reason for the error) that can later be used by the appropriate handler. When an exception is raised, the environment determines the innermost handler for the given exception, exits all intervening routines (invoking destructors to clean up as necessary), and passes control to the code of that handler. Note that this is all done dynamically based on the actual calling order. We go over how to code this in more detail later in this chapter.

To specify error handling for the parser using exceptions, we define an exception to indicate a parsing error. Exceptions in C++ should be defined using classes. Thus, we define a new class **DeriveParseError**. We can then specify that the parse method can raise this exception by changing its declaration to

```
DeriveExpr parse(istream&) throw(DeriveParseError)
```

This declaration begins to define the assumptions that are inherent in the parse routine. To define this method fully, we should further specify these assumptions as preconditions and postconditions, using annotations in the static structure diagram and comments in the header file. In the latter case the result would be something like the declarations shown in Figure 8-1.

The parse method is implemented in conjunction with the class **DeriveTokenStream**, whose purpose is to break up the input stream into individual tokens and sequentially return the appropriate token objects. A further analysis of the design should ask what happens if a token is invalid, say if the input stream contains "4x" or "&&&." There are two ways of dealing with this. The first is to define an error token and let the parser generate an appropriate error message, assuming that the error token is not valid wherever it occurs. If the parser is sophisticated and does error recovery, this is generally the best

```
DeriveExpr parse(istream&) throw(DeriveParseError);
    // Preconditions:
    //      istream& represents a single expression
    //      The expression is over the operators +,-,*,/,^
    //          and unary -, allowing parentheses, integer
    //          values, and single-character variables.
    // Postconditions:
    //      If the expression is valid, then the returned
    //          value is a valid, non-NULL, expression tree
    //      Otherwise the exception DeriveParseError is thrown


DeriveToken nextToken() throw(DeriveParseError);
    // Preconditions:
    //      The token stream has been initialized with an istream&
    //      The token stream may be at the end of the stream
    // Postconditions
    //      Blank space is ignored and the next valid token is
    //          returned. EOS is returned at the end of the stream
    //      DeriveParseError thrown if the next token is invalid
```

Figure 8-1 Declarations showing preconditions and postconditions.

approach. The alternative is to let the token stream object raise the **Derive-ParseError** exception if it detects an invalid token. This is simpler in our case since this is just what the parser would do and the parser would require additional checks to detect the error token. Thus we could define the nextToken method of **DeriveTokenStream** as shown at the bottom of Figure 8-1.

Informal preconditions and postconditions at the design level can be very helpful. However, if they state the obvious and duplicate other material, they can become burdensome to both the programmer, who has to enter them continually, and to the reader, who is given a wealth of useless information. They should be used at the design level to indicate assumptions that may not otherwise be obvious but are necessary for understanding and eventually implementing the corresponding methods. They can also be used as a more formal presentation of exactly what the routine will do. For example, the conditions for nextToken above provide a concise statement of what is expected of the routine and should be a good basis for determining how to implement it.

Defensive Coding

Defensive design is aimed at producing programs that have few problems to begin with. However, as programmers are generally human, they make mistakes. Since it is impossible to catch all these mistakes before the program is run, debugging will still need to be done. *Defensive coding* involves writing the code so as to simplify this debugging.

The first step in defensive coding is to be suspicious. One should not trust one's own code, much less code written by other programmers. One should always be questioning whether the code will work and whether code that it calls does the right thing. One should be wary of all possible errors and add whatever code is needed to check for them. Never make the blind assumption that things will work.

There are a variety of specific applications of such distrust. First, methods, especially methods in the public interface, should check that the values of incoming parameters are within the expected ranges. This includes checking for NULL pointers, index parameters out of range, invalid enumeration types, and so on. We illustrated several of these checks in examples in previous chapters. Second, one should check that the value returned by an outside method is valid. For example, other programmers' error checking might return a NULL value if an error is detected. While this should be noted as part of the design of the routine, often it is not. Checking the return in this case can identify a problem cleanly before it propagates further. Third, one should always check for error conditions returned by other routines: it is silly for a routine to return an error status if the caller doesn't check for that status.

Handling error conditions is one of the leading causes of problems and one of the things that makes debugging difficult. As noted in the previous section, part of the design process should be specifying what conditions are errors and what each method should do if an error is detected. This can involve aborting or throwing an exception, but more generally entails returning some sort of error flag or status indicator. In either case, the error conditions and values should be an explicit part of the method specification. Moreover, any routine calling the method should check the returned value to ensure that an error did not occur. There are any number of programs on UNIX that do not check status on a write and cause substantial problems such as corrupted files if a file system becomes full.

Checking input and return values is especially helpful when multiple programmers are working on a project. Such projects are very difficult to debug since it is often hard to determine whose code is to blame for a problem, since programmers are (and should be) loath to look at other people's code, since people typically assume their code works and someone else's does not, and since not all the programmers will be present when debugging is done. Here it is important to be able to identify whose code is at fault. Moreover, all the programmers will want to make sure that they can blame the problem on someone else. Checking input and return values from external methods provides a mechanism for doing just that.

In addition to checking input and return values, it is sometimes a good idea to check intermediate values and class fields to be certain that the code is working properly and being used correctly. Such checks, especially if done inexpensively, can help detect potential problems with complex algorithms or with complex interactions among classes. These checks can range from making sure that data fields of the class have been initialized correctly when a routine is called to ensuring that the `else` part of a sequence of `if` statements corresponds to the proper condition by replacing it with an additional test.

Another helpful technique is to ensure that variables and fields are initialized to meaningful values. C++ in general does not initialize stack or heap storage. Such storage often starts out zero, but not always. As we have noted, it is a good idea always to initialize variables and fields and not depend on the compiler to do it for you. It is also important here that the initialized storage not be given a value that could lead to future errors. If the storage is not yet used, it should be given a value indicating it is undefined. For a pointer, this would be a `NULL` value. For an enumerated type, this should be a special enumerant that indicates an undefined or null value. Indeed, when defining an enumeration type, it is a good idea to add an enumerant to indicate an undefined or unspecified value. This should be the first enumerant with a value of zero, to handle the case where initialization was overlooked.

Another coding technique that aids debugging is one we have been emphasizing all along: keep the code simple. Simple, straightforward code is generally easier to read and understand and, by its very nature, is less likely to have logic errors or other difficult bugs. Whenever the code is not straightforward, programmers should add comments to tell the reader and to warn themselves of what is going on. Moreover, they should double-check the code.

Double-checking code is a good idea in general. Code written without any prior thinking is more likely to have errors than code that is well thought out and has been reviewed. Just as a design review works well in finding problems with a design, a *code review* can be used to identify problems with a block of code before they show up as bugs in other parts of the system. This review should consider the code line by line. It should concentrate on what the code should be doing and check that it actually does that. Special attention should be paid to error and exceptional conditions that might arise in order to ensure that the code handles them correctly. Other things that can be checked quickly here are that variables are initialized before they are used, that there are no infinite loops, that all the code is reachable, and that comments exist for any unusual code or cases.

One technique I have found quite helpful is simply to read the code and justify to myself or others that it actually does what I want. Again, this works only if the audience (myself included) is suspicious and wants to find holes in the code rather than to demonstrate that the code works. Reading code critically can identify an amazing number of real and potential problems, which is another reason that code should be written so it can be read. I find that by writing the code once, reading it over to justify it, and reading it over a second time while typing it in, I can produce almost bug-free code the first time.

All these techniques help the programmer identify and isolate problems quickly and easily. While some of the techniques can be applied after the fact when problems are discovered in the code, it is generally easier and more productive to code defensively from the start and to include all the necessary checks and conditions in the original code when it is fresh in one's mind and well understood. As such, we strongly recommend:

> **Code defensively.**

Assertions

One way of adding all this defensive code in a clean and structured manner is by using assertions. Assertions are defined as part of the C++ language and implemented using a header file (generally `assert.h`). Once this file is included, the programmer can place a line

```
assert(<condition>)
```

where the condition is an arbitrary Boolean expression. This generates a conditional call to a function that prints out the condition, file name, and line number and then aborts if the condition is not true. Moreover, all such checks can be disabled by turning on the NDEBUG flag, although that is generally not a good idea when developing the code.

Assertions are a means to implement preconditions and postconditions in the code as well as the various checks that are part of a defensive programming style. Assertions placed at the beginning of a routine can check the parameters and class variables to ensure that any preconditions for the routine are met. Assertions placed before the return of a routine can check that postconditions are met. Other assertions can check the return value of routines and internal consistency conditions.

Assertions have one disadvantage, however: if the condition is not true, then the routine that is called prints the message and terminates the program, precluding any attempt at error recovery. This is okay when the program is being developed and bugs can be found and fixed quickly. However, it is not a good idea in a released system that has actual users (unless the condition is inherently unrecoverable), in a large system where one wants to find multiple problems per run or where aborting would trash necessary data files, or in a library that might be used by a large number of applications. (These are the reasons for the NDEBUG flag.)

In general, a little analysis should be done when considering using assertions. If the error condition being checked is truly a fatal error, then an assertion should be used. If the condition most likely reflects an error in the calling code and there is a reasonable mechanism for returning an error indication, then an error should be returned instead. This lets the calling code handle the error as it sees fit, by aborting itself, by recovering, or by passing the problem on to its caller. For example, a library routine that is passed a pointer and is supposed to return some value based on that pointer, say the size of the widget that the pointer represents, might check for a NULL pointer and return a size of zero to tell the caller the widget doesn't exist. Finally, if the condition is one that can or should be recovered from, returning an error indication or throwing an exception might be better than inserting an assertion. However, in general we recommend:

Use assertions liberally.

Exceptions

Exceptions provide a structured way of dealing with errors. In the previous sections we saw that they can be a clean way to return an error condition from a method and suggested using them in place of assertions where recovery may be called for. Both of these are valuable tools for the programmer.

In general, exceptions are a fairly powerful but not well understood part of C++. Just like any other part of the language, they can easily be misused and abused to create unreadable, undebuggable, and unmodifiable code. Thus it is important to understand how they should and should not be used. Our first recommendation is that exceptions be limited to what they were designed for:

Use exceptions only to indicate and return error conditions.

Exceptions should not be used as a way of returning normal values from a routine nor as a means of jumping out of a set of routines without going through the normal returns.

Each exception should be associated with an error condition and used exclusively for that condition. The exception should be defined as its own class. While C++ lets arbitrary types be used for exceptions, it is much cleaner and more straightforward to use separate classes:

Use classes to define exceptions.

The data for the exception class should hold whatever information is needed to identify the cause of the error. This is generally an error message, but could also be pointer to the objects that had a problem along with information on where the problem was detected. For example, in a program that manages a symbol table, an exception might contain an optional pointer to the offending symbol and an indication of the current source line. Putting this information in the exception is helpful in printing an appropriate error message, taking the appropriate recovery actions, and debugging. The exception class should define constructors that let these fields be set. The `throw` statement in C++ is effectively a constructor call and this is the only way that these fields are set.

Finally, C++ allows, but does not require, the availability of exceptions to appear in the routine header. Thus, we can declare

```
DeriveExpr parse(istream&) throw(DeriveParseError)
```

but could just as easily omit the throw part. While the throw clause is not actually used by most compilers, it does offer significant information to the programmer, to potential users of the code, and to the reader of the code. We thus recommend:

If a routine can throw an exceptions, declare it to do so.

Declaring an exception in this way reminds users of the method that the routine might throw the given exceptions. Hence the caller should handle the exceptions either directly with a `catch` statement or indirectly by indicating that it throws the exception itself. If no caller handles the exception, the program will abort when the exception is raised, which is probably not the desired behavior.

An Example

Let's now go back to the parser for symbolic differentiation. We have already discussed how to use defensive design to anticipate potential parsing errors. We continue by illustrating how to code the routine defensively.

The class **DeriveParserInfo**, derived from the static structure diagram of Figure 6-12, is defined as shown at the top of Figure 8-2. In addition to this declaration, we need a class to hold the exception that indicates a parse error, **DeriveParseError**. This is shown at the bottom of the figure. Note that we use the word `Error` at the end of the class name, so that the reader knows instantly that it is an exception.

The constructor for **DeriveParserInfo** is responsible for initializing the fields, as shown at the top of Figure 8-3. Note that it initializes all the values, even `cur_token` and `token_stream`, which are used only internally to the parse method.

We can then define the actual parse routine to set up the token stream and then call a secondary routine, `parseExpr`, to parse the current expression. This routine, which has the preconditions and postconditions noted in Figure 8-2, has the effect of setting the variable `current_token` to be the value of the token that follows the expression. This lets us use the routine recursively to handle expressions inside parentheses, but requires us to check that we actually scanned the full string from the top-level call. The code for the actual parse routine is shown at the bottom of Figure 8-3.

In this routine we first initialize the resultant expression to NULL. Then we make an assertion that the token stream is NULL. This is used to ensure that the routine is not called to parse multiple expressions simultaneously and serves as a check that we are managing memory correctly. The next statement resets `cur_token` to NULL; it should already be NULL at this point, but we are suspicious and want to make sure it has a well-defined value when we start

```
class DeriveParserInfo {
private:
    DeriveTokenStream token_stream;
    DeriveExprFactory expr_factory;
    DeriveToken cur_token;
public:
    DeriveParserInfo(DeriveExprFactory);

    DeriveExpr parse(istream&) throw(DeriveParseError);
    // Preconditions
    //      cur_token is set to the initial token
    // Postconditions
    //      cur_token is the token after the expression
    //      returns a non-NULL expression or throws
    //          DeriveParseError if the expr is not valid
};


class DeriveParseError {
private:
    String error_message;
public:
    DeriveParseError(String& msg)     { error_message = msg; }

    ConstText message() const         { return error_message; }
};
```

Figure 8-2 Class declarations for the parser.

parsing. After allocating the token stream we attempt to parse the expression, using a try-block so that if an error occurs, we can still delete the token stream object. Note that the catch clause of this block removes the token stream and then rethrows the same exception (this is the meaning of the `throw` statement without any arguments) so it will actually be handled by the caller.

The code to delete the `token_stream` is actually two statements rather than one. We first do the delete, freeing the storage that was allocated, and then we clear the pointer to NULL. This is defensive action to avoid having pointers around that point to unallocated storage. Next we clear the current token, freeing it and resetting the pointer. The expression parser should leave the current token set to an end-of-string flag, and before freeing it we ensure it is not NULL and get the token type to check this. Finally, we check the value returned by expression parser. Rather than asserting that it should be non-NULL, we check that it is not and raise our normal error exception if it is.

The actual parsing is based on the precedence of the various operators using an approach called *recursive descent parsing*. The top-level routine, `parseExpr` in Figure 8-4, parses the "+" and "-" operators that have low prece-

```
DeriveParserInfo::DerivePraserInfo(DeriveExprFactory f)
{
    token_stream = NULL;
    expr_factory = f;
    cur_token = NULL;
}


DeriveExpr
DeriveParserInfo::parse(istream& ist) throw(DeriveParseError)
{
    DeriveExpr exp = NULL;
    assert(token_stream == NULL); // not reentrant
    cur_token = NULL;
    token_stream = new DeriveTokenStream(ist);

    try {
        cur_token = token_stream->nextToken();
        DeriveExpr exp = parseExpr();
    }
    catch (DeriveParseError err) {
        delete token_stream;
        token_stream = NULL;
        throw;
    }

    delete token_stream;
    token_stream = NULL;

    if (cur_token == NULL)
        throw DeriveParseError("Syntax error");
    DeriveTokenType typ = cur_token->tokenType();
    delete cur_token;
    cur_token = NULL;
    if (exp == NULL || typ != DERIVE_TOKEN_EOF)
        throw DeriveParseError("No expression");

    return exp;
}
```

Figure 8-3 DeriveParserInfo constructor and parse methods.

dence. It uses a secondary routine, parseTerm, to handle all expressions of
higher precedence; parseTerm is similar except that it handles the "*" and "/"
operators and calls parseFactor to handle operators of higher precedence.
The parseFactor routine is also similar, handling the exponentiation operator
and calling the parseAtom routine in Figure 8-5 to deal with items of the highest precedence. In both cases, we are careful to initialize our local variables.

```
DeriveExpr
DeriveParserInfo::parseExpr() throw(DeriveParseError)
{
    DeriveExpr lhs = parseTerm();
    DeriveExpr rhs = NULL;

    for ( ; ; ) {
        if (cur_token->tokenType() == DERIVE_TOKEN_PLUS) {
            nextToken();
            rhs = parseTerm();
            lhs = expr_factory->createAdd(lhs,rhs);
        }
        else if (cur_token->tokenType() == DERIVE_TOKEN_MINUS) {
            nextToken();
            rhs = parseTerm();
            lhs = expr_factory->createSun(lhs,rhs);
        }
        else break;
    }

    return lhs;
}
```

Figure 8-4 Code for parsing expressions.

Moreover, the `parseAtom` routine explicitly places a default case in the switch statement even though it does nothing, in order to provide a placeholder and tell the reader we haven't forgotten it. The check here for an invalid expression is based on the variable `atm` being NULL. This is defensive action as well, since the only way this should occur is by going through the default case of the switch statement. By putting the check after the switch statement, we can check the return value of all the other cases as well.

DEBUGGING TOOLS

Over the last three decades tools have evolved to aid the programmer in the difficult task of debugging. These include machine-language debuggers that require the user to work at assembly level, symbolic debuggers that let the user control a running program in terms of the source, and a variety of tools for finding memory problems.

The typical debugging tools today are source-level symbolic debuggers. These let the programmer refer to their source files to identify where in the program they are or want to be. They display values symbolically and enable the programmer to refer to values by using source-language expressions.

```
DeriveExpr
DeriveParserInfo::parseAtom()
{
    DeriveExpr atm = NULL;

    switch (cur_token->tokenType()) {
        case DERIVE_TOKEN_CONST :
            atm = expr_factory->createConst(cur_token->intValue());
            break;
        case DERIVE_TOKEN_VAR :
            atm = expr_factory->createVar(cur_token->varName());
            break;
        case DERIVE_TOKEN_MINUS :
            nextToken();
            atm = parseAtom();
            atm = expr_factory->createMinus(atm);
            break;
        case DERIVE_TOKEN_LPR :
            nextToken();
            atm = parseExpr();
            if (cur_token->tokenType() != DERIVE_TOKEN_RPR)
                throw DeriveParseError("Unbalanced parenthesis");
            nextToken();
            break;
        case DERIVE_TOKEN_PAT :
            atm = expr_factory->createPat(cur_token->intValue());
            break;
        default :
            break;
    }
    if (atm == NULL) throw DeriveParseError("Syntax error");

    return atm;
}
```

Figure 8-5 Code for parsing an atomic expression.

While a wide range of symbolic debuggers are available today, most of them share the same basic functionality. The essential features of the debugger are the ability to examine and control the execution of the program using the following commands:

- *Run*: Start execution with a particular set of arguments. Most debuggers let the program be rerun with the same or different arguments without exiting the debugger.

- *Breakpoint*: Set a breakpoint in the source code. A breakpoint is a location at which execution stops so that the programmer can examine the state of the system. Breakpoints can generally be set either with a debugger command or by clicking on the source in the editor.

- *Tracepoint*: Set a tracepoint in the source code. A tracepoint is similar to a breakpoint except that rather than stopping execution, the debugger reports where execution is and possibly prints other information; then program execution continues.

- *Display*: Display the contents of a user variable or expression. This command generally lets the programmer enter an arbitrary source-language expression and view the value. Some debuggers support the graphical display of user data structures.

- *Assign*: Let the programmer change the value of a variable. This command lets the programmer set an arbitrary memory location to an arbitrary value.

- *List*: Let the programmer examine the source code.

- *Stack*: Let the programmer examine the current execution stack showing what routines have been called with what arguments and from where.

- *Continue*: Continue execution of the program after a breakpoint.

- *Step*: Single-step the program. This command lets the program continue executing for a single source line and then returns control to the debugger. Different versions of the command give the programmer control over how to handle routines called in the source line, either by skipping over them or by stopping at the first line of the first called routine.

- *Trap*: Stop the program and return control to the debugger if the program receives an interrupt, fault, or a C++ exception.

- *Call*: Execute an arbitrary routine with a given set of arguments.

As machines have become more powerful and languages more complex, debuggers have become more sophisticated. Advanced features found in modern debuggers include:

- *Watchpoints*: Watchpoints are value-based breakpoints. The programmer specifies a variable or an expression denoting a memory location. When the designated variable or memory changes value, the debugger stops execution and returns control to the programmer.

- *Conditional breakpoints*: These are standard breakpoints (or tracepoints or watchpoints) that are qualified by an arbitrary expression. When the breakpoint would normally occur, the debugger evaluates the expression: if it is true, execution halts, otherwise execution continues.

- *Multiple thread support*: As more programs (and languages) support threaded execution, debuggers are providing commands that let the programmer control and examine individual threads of control.

- *C++ expressions*: Some debuggers today provide full support for C++ expressions: they handle overloading and conversions in the expressions to examine and display the actual type of a dynamically allocated data structure.

All these capabilities are useful and, taken together, can make locating a suspected problem a great deal easier. While the user interfaces and command sets on many debuggers are complex and sometimes nonintuitive, it is worth investing the time to learn to use them to their full advantage. Thus we strongly recommend

---

Use the debugger to locate problems.

The alternative here, inserting print statements into the program, should only be used as a last resort. Not only does it take more time to insert such statements (because of the need to recompile and rebind each time), but the process is both overkill and error-prone. Producing lots of trace output that then must be evaluated is substituting bulk for thinking and generally ends up taking more of the programmer's time. Moreover, the whole process of adding statements to the code tends to introduce new errors through typing mistakes, misplaced statements, or even expression side effects.

Other debugging tools are also becoming available, either independently or as part of modern debuggers. The most useful of these tools help detect memory problems. These tools generally monitor all calls to the system memory allocation and freeing routines to detect spurious or incorrect calls and to keep track of the state of storage. Some of them also track all reads and writes done in the program and check that they are valid. These tools can detect a range of problems including:

- Attempts to free unallocated storage.
- Attempts to access uninitialized memory.
- Attempts to read from or write to unallocated or freed memory.
- Access beyond the end of an allocated memory block.
- Memory leaks.

While these tools can be a big help in finding problems that are generally very difficult to locate, they do have some drawbacks. The principal problem is that they tend to slow program execution significantly (often by one or two orders of magnitude). A secondary problem is that most of them generate spurious error reports, either memory leaks that are not leaks or memory-access errors that are not errors. A third problem is that they can miss some errors. They can miss the use of a dangling pointer if the storage it pointed to was freed and then reused for something else. They can miss memory leaks if a data location happens to contain a valid address for the leaked block even if the location is an integer data field. Still, these tools are invaluable and we recommend:

> **If a memory-checking tool is available, learn to use it.**

In particular, we suggest that part of testing a program for potential problems should be running it with a memory checker to check for unsuspected access violations and memory leaks. We recommend using these tools when your program exhibits some weird behavior that could arise from a memory problem. The part of such tools that checks for memory leaks should be used over several long and diverse runs of the system to look for potential memory leaks that might not show up under simpler circumstances.

DEBUGGING TECHNIQUES

Debugging tools, like any other, can be misused. Just as it doesn't make sense to use a screwdriver to hammer in a nail, it doesn't make sense to use a debugger or memory checker to locate and fix all problems. Instead, one should develop an understanding of how to use these tools most effectively and should approach debugging accordingly.

Debugging has two basic steps. The first, more difficult one is locating a suspected problem. This is where the tools are the most useful and where the programmer needs to be the most creative. The second is repairing the problem. Caution needs to be taken here not to introduce new errors and to fix the problem correctly and completely.

To consider debugging further, we look at a simple (buggy) program to compute the mean and median of a sequence of input values. Here we define a class that accumulates values and then can be queried for the mean or median of those values. Figure 8-6 shows the header file for the class. The method `addValue` adds a value to the data, the methods `mean` and `median` return the result, and the method `clear` resets the set for next time. The actual code that implements the **StatSetInfo** class is shown in Figure 8-7 and the driver program that tests the class is shown in Figure 8-8. Running this program gives us the following output:

```
Test 1: 2 elements (1..2), mean = 1.5, median = 1
Test 2: 200 elements (1..200), mean = 100.5, median = 100
Test 3: 51 elements (0*0..50*50), mean = 842.686, median = 25
```

The output looks almost correct. The only value that is obviously off is the median for Test 3, which should be 625 rather than 25.

```
typedef bool                    Boolean;
typedef double                  StatValue;
typedef vector<StatValue>       StatVector;
typedef StatVector::iterator    StatVectorIter;
typedef class StatSetInfo *     StatSet;


class StatSetInfo {
private:
   StatVector the_data;

public:
   StatSetInfo()                    { }
   ~StatSetInfo()                   { }

   void clear();
   void addValue(StatValue v)       { the_data.push_back(v); }

   StatValue mean();
   StatValue median();
};
```

Figure 8-6 Header file for statistics-debugging example.

Error Location

Finding a suspected problem in a large system can be very difficult. The programmer is presented with a symptom: the program aborts or produces the wrong answer. The task is then to identify the specific part of the system that produces that symptom. While this is sometimes trivial, as when the program aborts on a line containing an obvious typographical error, it is generally quite complex. The cause of a symptom can be that certain variables have unexpected values or that the program is executing code where it shouldn't be at this point, i.e. the cause of one symptom is itself another symptom of the problem. This can cascade many times until the problem is finally located in a section of the code very different from where the error was originally detected.

Debugging in general, and error location in particular, should be viewed as a form of puzzle solving. Just as one does not put a jigsaw puzzle together by blindly trying to connect pairs of pieces, one should not attempt to do debugging without considerable thought. The key to debugging is that it involves thinking. The cardinal rule of debugging is:

> **THINK.**

Thinking about error location can take two forms. One can work *inductively*, starting by analyzing the various symptoms and working from there to find

```
void
StatSetInfo::clear()
{ the_data.erase(the_data.begin(),the_data.end()); }


StatValue
StatSetInfo::mean()
{
    if (the_data.size() == 0) return 0;

    StatVectorIter vi;
    StatValue v = 0;

    for (vi = the_data.begin(); vi <= the_data.end(); ++vi)
        v += *vi;

    return v/the_data.size();
}


StatValue
StatSetInfo::median()
{
    if (the_data.size() == 0) return 0;

    StatVector nv(the_data);
    sort(nv.begin(),nv.end());

    int i = nv.size()/2;
    StatValue v = nv[i];

    return i;
}
```

Figure 8-7 Class implementation for statistics debugging example.

the actual cause, or one can work *deductively*, thinking about all the potential problems and then eliminating suspects on the basis of the clues.

In inductive debugging one works from the particulars to the whole. The first step is to analyze all the pertinent data. Here the programmer should consider not only what fails but also what works. The data should then be organized with the aim of identifying an hypothesis. This is generally best done by looking for contradictions. Once the programmer has a hypothesis, it must be checked to ensure that it indeed is the cause of the error and, moreover, that it completely explains the error. Only after this is done should the error be fixed.

```
main(int,const char **)
{
    int i;
    StatSet ss = new StatSetInfo;

    for (i = 0; i < 2; ++i) ss->addValue(i+1);
    cout << "Test 1: 2 elements (1..2), mean = " << ss->mean() <<
        ", median = " << ss->median() << endl;

    ss->clear();
    for (i = 0; i < 200; ++i) ss->addValue(i+1);
    cout << "Test 2: 200 elements (1..200), mean = " <<
        ss->mean() << ", median = " << ss->median() << endl;

    ss->clear();
    for (i = 0; i < 51; ++i) ss->addValue(i*i);
    cout << "Test 3: 51 elements (0*0..50*50), mean = " <<
        ss->mean() << ", median = " << ss->median() << endl;

    delete ss;

    return 0;
}
```

Figure 8-8 Test driver for statistics-debugging example.

In the statistics example of Figure 8-6 through Figure 8-8, we want to determine why the median value in the third test case is wrong. We begin by organizing what seem to be the relevant symptoms. The obvious one is that the third test case fails to compute the median, so we note:

Test 3 (0*0..50*50): Median was 25, should be 625

The question that follows is whether the median computation is bad. Data relevant to that involves the other two test cases where the median was correct:

Test 2 (1..200): Median was 100, should be 100 or 101

Test 1 (1..2): Median was 1, should be 1 or 2

Moreover, given that the answer is bad, we need to check whether the data is bad. Thus we add to our observations

All tests computed the mean correctly

which tends to imply that the input data was correct.

Having noted the various symptoms, we look for contradictions in order to form an hypothesis as to what may be wrong. Here we look for some difference between the third test case, where the program failed, and the first two, where it worked. There are two differences: the number of elements in the third case was odd where it was even in the first two, and the third case involved a geometric sequence rather than an arithmetic one. We know that the program computes the median by sorting the array and taking the middle element, so there is little difference between the computation in the odd case versus the even case. Moreover, we note that in the third case the program returns the index of the median element rather than its value; this could be the problem.

Before checking if this is indeed the problem, we see whether it is consistent with all the above symptoms. This problem would not affect the computation of the mean. Moreover, in the second case, the median element should be element 99 or 100 (assuming the array is zero-based), so the output value 100 is consistent with the hypothesis. Similarly, the first case also is consistent. We next check the code and find that the median function is indeed returning i rather than v. We fix this and our program now produces the output:

```
Test 1: 2 elements (1..2), mean = 1.5, median = 2
Test 2: 200 elements (1..200), mean = 100.5, median = 101
Test 3: 51 elements (0*0..50*50), mean = 842.686, median = 625
```

and we are happy.

We now release the statistics class to a set of users, only to get back complaints that it sometimes computes the mean incorrectly. We go back to our test cases and double-check that the answers are indeed as correct as they look. The first two turn out okay, but the third is not. Using the formula for the sum of squares, we find the mean for the third case should be 841.66667 rather than the 842.686 value that was output, and we have another bug to find.

Here we use deductive debugging, working from the general to the specific. The first step is to enumerate possible causes of the error. These are generally vague and incomplete explanations of what type of thing might have gone wrong. One next attempts to eliminate as many of these explanations as possible from the available data, generally information about what works and what doesn't. Once as many of these explanations as possible have been eliminated, the remaining ones should be refined to be as specific as possible. Each can then be checked using the debugger, adding more test cases as needed.

In the statistics example, there are a number of potential reasons that the mean computation is slightly off:

- The data is inaccurate, either because of how it was set up by the test program or because of how it is stored.

- The computation itself is bad, possibly using the wrong divisor or summing the sequence incorrectly.

- The computation is correct, but the value returned or printed is not correct.

We proceed to order these explanations in order of their probability. The first does not seem all that likely: the mean is generally computed correctly (the first two cases were correct), the medians are now correct, and very little can go wrong here, especially since all the test values are integers to begin with.

The third also seems unlikely but more possible, since there is no value the program computes that is close to the median and might be returned accidentally, the test driver just prints the result and does nothing else with it, and the inaccuracy is small and thus can't be attributed to returning the integer part of the mean rather than the whole value. This leaves the second explanation, that something is wrong with the computation itself, as the most likely.

The code in Figure 8-7 for computing the mean is relatively simple. After checking for the case of an empty array, it sums the values and then returns the sum divided by the size. Again we enumerate possible hypotheses for what could be wrong:

- The sum is not initialized correctly.
- The sum is not computed correctly because one or more elements are left out or added.
- The quotient is not computed correctly.

Again, we can order these on their likelihood. A quick check of the code shows that the sum is initialized to 0 and that the quotient computation is correct. Thus we focus on how the sum is computed. Looking closely at the for statement using the iterator, we note that the end test is wrong. The iterator returned by `the_data.end()` is one beyond the end of the array, so the check should be either < or != and not <=.

Before correcting this problem, we should check if it explains the facts. The program, as it currently exists, adds one extra element to the sum. This element arises from memory allocated for the array and hence is likely to be zero in most cases. Thus it generally does not affect the computation and the mean should be correct in many cases, as it was in the first two test cases. Problems arise when the array is allocated in reused storage or when the array is reused with a smaller set than a previous use. This is exactly what happened in the third case, with the fifty-second element of the array being left over from the prior case. This should have added 52/51 = 1.0196 to the mean value, which is exactly what happened.

Fixing this problem, we now get the output:

```
Test 1: 2 elements (1..2), mean = 1.5, median = 2
Test 2: 200 elements (1..200), mean = 100.5, median = 101
Test 3: 51 elements (0*0..51*51), mean = 841.667, median = 625
```

and everyone is happy. Note that this problem almost wasn't detected by our test program and would not have been detected if we had done test three before test two or if we had run the tests separately. Don't expect simple test programs to find all errors in a system, even if the system itself is simple.

In real life, debugging is not this simple or straightforward. One generally proceeds with a combination of inductive and deductive reasoning, noting as many symptoms as possible, generating hypotheses about what might be wrong, testing the hypotheses against the symptoms and with the debugger, and eventually tracking down the problem. The process can often be frustrating, with many dead ends and blind alleys, with hypotheses that are eliminated once and later shown to be true, and with errors that seem to have no possible cause.

Debugging is best managed by keeping track of all the little things. Programmers should be careful to note, either on paper or mentally, all the symptoms, both working and nonworking, of the problem at hand. They should construct and check specific hypotheses based on these symptoms rather than blindly attempting to track down a problem. The debugger should be used as an aid to thinking and testing rather than as a means to its own end. Experimentation with the program should be used only as a last resort.

Even with great care, particularly difficult problems often stymie the programmer so that no hypotheses are available and all attempts at tracking the problems down fail. Several techniques can be used in these cases. One effective approach is to walk away from the problem. Sleeping on it, thinking about it a bit at dinner, musing on it briefly in the shower, and generally getting one's mind off if it and dealing with the rest of life is often very effective in identifying alternative hypotheses. Another good approach, especially for logic or algorithmic problems, is to describe the problem to someone else, since the process of coming up with a description that someone else can understand often suggests new hypotheses. Moreover, the listener does not start with the same biases that the programmer does and may well spot something the programmer overlooked.

Error Logging

Debugging is also something one gets better at with experience. If one has seen a particular error before, or at least something similar, then it is easier next time to create hypotheses about what is going wrong. A good way for beginning and intermediate programmers to reinforce this experience is to keep track of your errors, either informally or in a written error log. The information that should be kept includes:

- When in the overall process the error was made.
- Who made the error.
- What exactly was done incorrectly.
- How the error could have been prevented.
- How the error was found.
- How the error could have been detected earlier and with less work.

The programmer can then use this information in two ways. The first is to identify other potential errors. If the programmer used the wrong variable name in one location, it is likely to be used incorrectly in a second location as well. Whenever an error is found, the programmer should check whether the same error was made in other parts of the system. Second, tracking this information will help the programmer find problems quicker in the future by identifying similar situations. Here it can point the programmer to programming styles and techniques that avoid potential problems or simplify debugging.

Error Repair

While the difficult part of debugging is locating the error in the system, fixing the problem is also not trivial. Sometimes, as in the examples earlier in this section, the fix involves an obvious error that is easily corrected and will only improve the program. Just as often, however, the fix involves significant program changes that, while they may fix the particular bug, adversely affect other parts of the system.

How to approach error repair depends on the nature of the problem. For complex problems, programmers should go back to the design stage of program development. Here they should determine how to best fix the problem at the design level, using the various tools provided for design, such as static structure and message-trace diagrams as well as pseudocode for the various methods. Simpler problems that affect only one method can be handled at the detailed design level, possibly by writing pseudocode or at least rethinking that method. The simplest problems, those that affect only one or two lines of code, can be fixed at the code level.

The major difficulty with repairing program errors is that fixing the program often doesn't. Several factors come into play here. The first is that one bug in a section of code can indicate the presence of others. This can happen if the first problem occurred because the programmer either didn't understand the code when it was being designed or written or was not paying close attention to what was typed as the code was entered.

Second, the programmer should remember that the probability of the fix being correct is not 100%. Something that looks obviously wrong can in fact be correct in its particular context — the actual error occurred somewhere else. Alternatively, the fix, because it was made without as much thought as went into the initial design and coding, might just be wrong. Fixes are especially vulnerable in large systems, where the interplay among a wide range of classes and methods can be complex and not particularly well understood. Changing even one line of code can have far-ranging effects on the rest of the system. The programmer must carefully analyze all the ways a method is used in the system to ensure that fixes for one problem actually work for the problem case and all other cases as well.

A third difficulty is that fixing one problem can create new errors. This can happen when the fix is incomplete or incorrect or if the original code is actually needed as it was for some other case. When making any change, the programmer must consider not only the case that failed, but all the other possible cases as well. This is especially true when the return value of a method is affected by the change. Error repair must be viewed in the same light as design and coding: the programmer must have the whole gestalt of the system in mind.

Another issue that arises with fixing bugs is determining what to fix. If a program aborts because it is accessing a NULL pointer, the programmer can either change the code so that the pointer is not NULL at that point or check for a NULL pointer and avoid the access. The first change fixes the problem, the second fixes the symptoms. The better change here is to fix the problem by insuring that the pointer cannot be NULL on entry, since the fact that it is NULL probably indicates some other error in the code. The best thing to do, however, is to fix both the problem and the symptom. Here, we not only prevent the pointer from being NULL, but also add a check in the code where the bad access occurred, either to avoid the access and continue on or to check with an appropriate assertion that the problem doesn't occur in some other way.

Finally, we note that, while defensive programming is aimed mainly at simplifying the task of error location, some things can be done during design and coding to simplify later error repair. The primary focus here is on simplicity and encapsulation. Simpler code is just going to be easier to fix: it is easier for the programmer to understand and changes made to it are more likely to be correct; special or odd cases are less likely to arise. Encapsulation helps in larger systems by limiting the program scope to be considered when making a fix. A change that is limited to a single method or a single class is much more likely to be correct than one that affects multiple classes and their interactions.

Memory-Management Problems

Memory-management problems, as we noted, are among the most difficult to find because they tend to reveal themselves at a considerable distance from where the problem actually occurred. However, the programmer can use a variety of techniques and precautions to minimize the occurrence of such problems and make them easier to find. In this section we look at the two primary types of memory-management problems, access beyond the end of a block of storage and freeing storage that is still being used.

Reading or writing beyond the end of an array is generally an avoidable problem. It occurs most often when the programmer sets up an array and then accesses elements with an index that is either less than zero or greater than the bounds of the array. As we noted, the programmer should always do bounds checking on array access. This includes not only doing the obvious when using arrays, but also avoiding the use of library functions that do not do bounds checking, such as the standard C string library (strcpy, strcat, sprintf). Here the C++ streams library or the standard C++ string type should be used instead. Other good defensive techniques include passing the dimension along with any array pointer, adding assertions in or after loops to ensure that bounds weren't exceeded, and checking buffer sizes on reads.

Access beyond the end of a structure is less common unless the programmer uses the old C technique of embedding a variable-length array at the end of the structure and doing dynamic allocation, a trick that can and should be avoided in C++. The only other common case in which this occurs is when casts are done and a structure of one type is accessed as if it were another. In C++ this happens most frequently when a cast is made from a supertype to a subtype. The solution here is to avoid the use of unsafe casts, restricting oneself either to using the built-in C++ run-time typing (if available) or implementing one's own routines to do the appropriate down-casting.

Freeing storage while it is still being used is a more difficult problem to track down and to prevent. The key here is to ensure that each block of storage has a unique owner and that this owner is the correct one, i.e. that if the owner does not know about the storage then no one else does either. Beyond this, programmers should take several precautions. First, when deleting a block of storage, they should clear the pointer to that storage, so as to eliminate at least one possible dangling reference. Second, the destructor for a class should clear the contents of the class and somehow mark the object as invalid. The various methods that access the class can then check if the object or field is still valid. While this doesn't prevent such access, it at least helps to find the problem earlier and makes it easier to track down.

Both of these types of problems are common enough that the programmer should suspect them if the program is behaving in an otherwise strange manner. If the program aborts and the stack is totally clobbered, it generally means that the user overwrote automatic (stack) storage. If the program aborts inside a system allocation routine such as `malloc` or `free`, it generally means that the programmer wrote something beyond the end of a block or wrote into storage that had been freed. If the program is behaving randomly, it often means that the programmer is accessing uninitialized or previously freed storage.

The easiest way to find these problems, once the programmer realizes they may be occurring, is to use any available memory-checking tools. A useful technique for locating allocation problems is to set a breakpoint in the destructor for a class to keep track of when and where objects are deleted. Another useful technique is to use watchpoints to see when the affected storage was overwritten. Another alternative is to do a binary search over the program's execution. Here one uses breakpoints to focus in on the precise time when the storage in question is being clobbered. These techniques really only work, however, if the problem is easily repeatable. If it isn't, defensive techniques and lots of thinking are one's best alternative.

TESTING

While debugging involves fixing problems that have been identified, testing involves the identification of problems. Overall, testing gives the programmers and the users of a system some assurance that the system probably works. Since it is impossible to test any but the most trivial system with all possible inputs and outputs, testing cannot prove that the program is correct: it can only give some sense of confidence that the program probably works. It is thus important that testing be as complete as possible, considering as many cases as possible and demonstrating that the program works under a wide variety of circumstances.

The only way to do this is to view testing not as a constructive process of showing a program is correct, but as a destructive process that tries to break it. Testing should be viewed as the process of executing a program with the intent of finding errors, and test cases should be constructed with the intent of demonstrating that the program is not correct. A successful test case is one that finds a problem with the program, not one for which the program works. It is only when repeated and concentrated attempts to make a program fail themselves fail that one gets any confidence that the program works.

Approaches to Testing

Testing can be done at various levels and in various ways. It can be done formally or informally; it can be done off-line or by actually executing the program; it can be done at the design level or at the actual code level; it can be done once or it can be done repeatedly.

Static testing is testing done without actually executing the program. The simplest form of such testing is that the programmer reads the code to check that it says what was meant. This can be extended to informal proofs or justifications that a particular method does what it is supposed to and to hand-simulation of the complicated parts of the system. The most effective non-execution testing, however, occurs when the programmer attempts to justify the code to another person whose job is to be skeptical. This can be done informally, but formal presentations called *code inspections* and *walkthroughs* have been developed for large-scale projects.

Most testing, however, is *dynamic testing* done by executing the program or at least parts of it. While a program is being developed, *module testing* can be used to test individual components and *integration testing* can be used to test how components fit together. After the program is complete, *system testing* attempts to find problems with the overall system. Each of these levels of testing can be done with or without knowledge of the actual code. In black-box testing, the test driver and test cases are built without any knowledge or assumptions about the code being tested; in white-box testing, the actual code is taken into account.

Module testing — testing individual classes or small sets of classes — is generally done by the programmer responsible for the classes. Here the programmer creates a driver program that sets up data structures and makes the appropriate calls on the class. Figure 8-8 is a driver program to test the **StatSetInfo** class. While drivers can be difficult to write, this approach to testing can save time and effort later on. Module testing has the advantage that it lets the programmer initially test a class in a controlled context rather than as a small part of a larger system. This makes it easier to generate test conditions and to check if the output is valid. While it is not needed for simple classes or relatively small systems, it should be used when a complex class will be part of a larger system. It should also be used when creating reusable or library classes, when multiple programmers are involved in building a system and should test their code before releasing it to others, and when a set of classes that is the core of the system is to be developed first.

While module testing is a bottom-up approach, testing the low-level classes of a system, integration testing is a top-down approach. Here the programmer starts with the overall system framework, generally the top-level classes, possibly with a primitive user interface. Once this is tested, new functionality can be added and tested in the context of the overall system. This approach often requires that the programmer initially write stubs or dummy routines for code to be added later. In some cases these routines can be quite complex and require as much work as writing the drivers for module testing. Top-down testing has the advantage that the user sees the overall system and that further pieces are added in the context in which they are to be run. It also lets the actual system user interface serve as the test-case driver, eliminating the need to write separate drivers and actually testing the user-interface code in the process. It has the disadvantage, however, of often making it difficult to test the individual components fully; also, finding problems can be more difficult in that the whole system, not just a single class, must be considered.

For small to moderate-sized applications, the programmer should combine top-down and bottom-up approaches. Module testing should be used to verify any library components that will be widely used in the system and to verify the workings of any complex data structures or algorithms. Integration testing should be used for the remainder.

The programmer should first write the top-level classes and the outlines of the user interface. If the application uses a graphical interface, this would include the main window with its menus and display areas. Then further functionality should be added to the program one step at a time. This might involve implementing one or two of the menu buttons or a dialog box or creating a graphical display. After each piece of functionality is added, the program should be thoroughly tested and any bugs found should be fixed.

This approach has the advantage of presenting the programmer with an early working system (albeit one with much reduced functionality). This allows experimentation with the user interface, lets the programmer demonstrate the system and show what it will eventually do, and provides strong motivation for adding the necessary functionality to get there. It also lets components be tested one by one in their final context. Moreover, the ability to play with the system encourages additional testing. Note that this approach works best when the system is to be put together from relatively independent components. We cover this approach to design when we discuss large-scale program development in Chapter 16.

Module and integration testing are useful while developing a new system. Once the system has been completed, however, testing begins in earnest. System testing is the attempt to find problems in a complete program. It is generally done not only when the program is first completed, as a simple extension of integration testing, but also as the program evolves, continually testing new changes and environments and ensuring that the previous functionality still works.

In industry, such system testing is often done by an independent group of programmers. This encourages the view of testing as a destructive process, since the testers have no stake in the program and hence are more likely to develop test cases that cause it to fail. In smaller applications, this must be done by the individual egoless programmer. Testing here is not a simple task. It takes creativity and intelligence to figure out all the possible ways a program might be used and to identify combinations of inputs and actions that might cause it to fail.

System testing is often called *regression testing*. Here the same test cases are used over and over. This is generally a good approach since it provides a wide range of test cases and makes sure that error repair does not introduce new problems. The name "regression testing" stems from the fact that one is testing to ensure that the program doesn't regress by exhibiting problems in cases that previously worked. In general, system testing is a monotonic process: one is always adding new test cases while maintaining all the old ones. Whenever a new problem is found with the system, a test case that exhibits that problem should be added to the test suite. Whenever a new feature is added, tests of that feature should also be added. Then, whenever a new version of the system is available, all previous test cases should be run against it.

A variety of tools is available commercially to automate this process. These tools let new tests be added readily and are a convenient way to run a whole suite of tests and check the outputs quickly.

Test Case Selection

In all approaches to testing, the most difficult part is choosing test cases that are likely to find errors. Recall

> **A successful test case is one that finds a bug.**

Once a program works on the simpler cases, it is often difficult to construct test cases that actually find bugs. However, there are techniques and approaches that can help.

In Figure 8-6 through Figure 8-8 we used module testing to check the workings of the **StatSetInfo** class. In doing this, we avoided using some of the techniques and approaches that should be used, and the result was that the class was not adequately tested. These were mistakes both in how we used testing and in our selection of test cases.

The first error in how we used testing was not to make the expected output part of the test case. In the example, we used three sequences and knew exactly what the inputs were to be. However, we did not compute the expected outputs in advance and did not include them as part of the test case. If we had, then we would have detected immediately that the mean computation in the third test case had a problem.

Our second error was not to examine the results of each test thoroughly. If we had, we would have realized right away that not only was the median computation wrong for the third test case, but the mean was incorrect as well. In general, when one goes to the trouble of constructing a test case and running it, one should go over the output with a fine-tooth comb to find all possible indications of problems. A test case can often indicate multiple problems with the program, and even minor ones should not be overlooked. Moreover, it is important to look at each test case to check not only that the program did what it was supposed to, but also that it did not do what it was not supposed to. Extra output, spurious warning messages, flashing screens, and so on, that should not be present are just as much bugs as incorrect answers or program aborts.

In addition to not using our test driver to its fullest, we also did not provide an adequate test of the system. The goal of testing should be to cover all possible executions. While we cannot test the program on all possible inputs, we can approach this. Test coverage refers to the fraction of the program actually tested by a sequence of test cases. The minimum coverage one should expect is that every statement is executed at least once in the process of testing. This is called statement coverage. Our test program did not do this: it never tested what happens if one asks for the mean or median of an empty set, the one conditional branch that is in the code. Beyond this, testing can ensure that each branch is taken at least once, or that each logical condition that appears in an `if` or `while` or `for` statement takes on all possible values. These are called decision and condition coverage respectively. Programming tools exist to determine the level of test coverage and to report statements that were not executed by a test suite to the programmer. In general, test cases should be as dissimilar as possible, while those we used were quite similar to each other.

Finding tests that cover all possible statements is difficult if not impossible without looking at the code. Even then, some statements that represent defensive programming will, we hope, never be executed. Still, it is reasonable to check that most if not all of the program is executed by some test case. A variety of secondary goals can help to achieve this.

The first is to test for invalid and unexpected conditions as well as for what the program expects. This could involve providing illegal input such as typing in a word where an integer is expected, or just pushing random buttons in the application in some meaningless order. The program should be checked to ensure that it either ignores or appropriately handles the meaningless input or provides reasonable error messages.

The second approach is to test for boundary conditions. If a program wants an input between 1 and 10, try it with 0, 1, some intermediate value, 10, and 11. If it's going to fail, it will probably fail right on the boundary of what is legal and what is not. If it asks for a string, try giving it an empty string as well as a string that is as long as its internal buffer (and one that is longer). Our driver program did not try the boundary conditions of an empty set or a set with one element. Note that boundary conditions can occur on both input and output. For example, if a program computes line intersections, one should consider the boundary conditions of parallel lines, as well as lines with zero and infinite slope.

A third approach is to make the test cases as varied as possible. The test cases in our driver program were lacking here: they all presented the input in ascending order. This means that any problem with the sorting used for computing the median would not have shown up, nor would an error such as returning the middle element of the original array rather than of the sorted array.

Selecting the right test cases and taking a reasonable approach to the overall testing process are important aspects of software development. Without adequate testing, programs will be buggy. Overall, we strongly recommend

> **Always test your code thoroughly.**

SUMMARY

The first step in debugging and testing is defensive programming. This is split into defensive design, where the programmer attempts to design a system so as to minimize errors, and defensive coding, where the code is written to anticipate errors and locate them rapidly. Both of these techniques attempt to minimize the amount of debugging needed.

No matter how well these are done, however, debugging and testing will still be necessary. The first and generally most difficult step in debugging involves locating the problem. Some guidelines here include:

- THINK.
- If you reach an impasse, sleep on it.
- If you reach an impasse, describe the problem to someone else.
- Use debugging tools as a second resort.
- Avoid experimentation. Use it as a last resort.

One the problem is identified, it must be fixed. This is not always a simple and straightforward process. Some of the rules to keep in mind in this phase of debugging include:

- Where there is one bug, there is likely to be another.
- Fix the error and the symptoms.
- The probability of the fix being correct is not 100% and drops as the program gets bigger.
- Beware of a fix that creates new errors.
- Error repair is a design process.

While debugging involves isolating and fixing problems, testing involves finding problems in the first place. Testing is a difficult process because it is generally a destructive one: a successful test case is one that finds a bug, not one that shows no bug is present. Some things to keep in mind while testing include:

- A necessary part of the test case is the expected output.
- Avoid attempting to test your own programs.
- Thoroughly inspect the results of each test.
- Test cases must be written for invalid and unexpected, as well as valid and expected input conditions.
- Check that the program does not do what it is not supposed to do.
- Avoid throw-away test cases unless the program is a throw-away program.
- Plan testing with the assumption that errors will be found.
- The probability of the existence of one or more errors in a section of code is proportional to the number of errors already found in that section.
- Testing is an extremely creative and intellectually challenging task.

EXERCISES

8.1   You are given a program that reads in three numbers representing edge lengths and outputs the type of triangle (acute, obtuse, isosceles, equilateral, right) that the edges create when put together. Provide a comprehensive list of test cases for this program.

8.2   You are working on a simulator for a imaginary simple machine. Your current task is the dump command, which doesn't seem to be working correctly. The dump command has two forms:

```
dump <address>-<address>
dump <address>.<count>
```

where the default address is 0 and the default count is 1. All addresses are given in hex. The command should always dump eight bytes at eight-byte intervals.

For testing purposes, memory is filled with a pattern:

```
00 00 44 44 88 88 cc cc
00 00 44 44 88 88 cc cc
...
```

The result of several test cases is then:

```
dump .e
    EXPECT:     0008 : 00 00 44 44 88 88 cc cc
    ACTUAL:     Invalid command syntax
dump 21-24
    EXPECT:     0020 : 00 00 44 44 88 88 cc cc
    ACTUAL:     0020 : 44 44 88 88 cc cc 00 00
dump .11
    EXPECT:     0000 : 00 00 44 44 88 88 cc cc
                0010 : 00 00 44 44 88 88 cc cc
                0020 : 00 00 44 44 88 88 cc cc
    ACTUAL:     0000 : 00 00 44 44 88 88 cc cc
                0010 : 00 00 44 44 88 88 cc cc
```

What are the likely error(s) in the code?

8.3   Take code that you have written for a previous assignment, determine the preconditions and postconditions for each method, and then augment the original code with defensive code to check these conditions. Run the code under a variety of conditions to see what problems can be detected.

8.4   Maintain an error log (as described in "Error Logging" on page 213) for your next (or current) programming assignment.

8.5   Take someone else's program and attempt to find a problem with it simply by reading the code. (You can try this with your own code as well, but it is much more difficult.)

8.6   Draw up a sequence of test cases for a tic-tac-toe program. (This is more difficult than it looks since the program must be treated as a black box, few assumptions can be made regarding its behavior, and some of the inputs depend on previous outputs.)

8.7   Write a program to implement a simple version of the Basic language. The program need only allow statements of the form:

```
<line> LET <variable> = <expression>
<line> IF <condition> THEN <line>
<line> PRINT <expression>
<line> STOP
```

where <line> is a line number (all lines are numbered in a Basic program), variables are all one-letter (A...Z) with case ignored, all data is floating-point, expressions can use the standard arithmetic operators, and conditions can use the various comparison operators.

8.8   Develop a suite of test cases for the program of Exercise 8.7 and a script that will run them. Determine what level of test coverage is provided by the test cases.

Chapter 9

Graphical Application Concepts

Most of today's applications involve graphical user interfaces. Here the interface itself is usually the most complex and difficult part of the system, often requiring half or more of the actual code. Moreover, the eventual success or failure of the application probably rests more on whether users like the interface than on how well the application actually works. Developing a high-quality user interface is thus an essential part of designing and implementing software.

User-interface development is a complex process. It is difficult at best to predict a priori how well a proposed interface will be received by its users, and its success or failure can depend as much on external factors as on the interface itself. The features and usage patterns assumed by the programmer may be quite different from those of the actual users. Moreover, the complexity and quality of the interface is often inversely proportional to the complexity of the underlying code — it is generally much easier to implement a poor-quality, complex interface than a better, simpler one with similar functionality.

Graphical and non-graphical applications differ in a variety of ways. Today's graphical user interfaces are typically based on an underlying system model where the system, not the application, has control. Here the system waits for the user to take some action, deciphers that action, and then calls an appropriate routine in the application's code. The application must describe the user interface to the system and operate using the calls that the system then makes to it. The result is an inverted control structure that imposes a different orientation on the design. This, combined with more complex input processing and the difficulty of maintaining dynamic graphical output, tends to make designing graphical programs difficult.

In this chapter we begin to consider issues in designing applications for today's graphical user interfaces. We cover the appropriate underlying program structures, how to manage a variety of input types in terms of events, and the basic concepts of graphical output. In addition, we cover the fundamental issues involved in designing the user interface and the code to support it. We attempt to discuss this material in a generic way, emphasizing the similarities between a C++ interface to Motif under UNIX and the Microsoft Foundation Classes (MFC) under Windows. We assume the reader has access to appropriate manuals or texts describing one of these or a related system in detail.

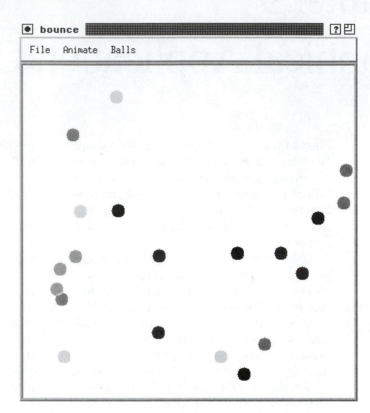

Figure 9-1 Sample window for the bouncing balls application.

A SAMPLE GRAPHICAL APPLICATION

To illustrate the intricacies of designing applications with graphical user interfaces, we again consider a sample program. In this case, we are designing a program that bounces balls around a window:

> You are to write a program to display a window containing balls that bounce off the four sides. The balls should be squares, circles, or diamonds and should start with a random nonzero initial X and Y velocity. When they hit a side, they should be reflected at the appropriate angle. You do not have to worry about the balls intersecting with each other. When a ball hits a side, it should change its color and velocity. If it hits the left or right side of the window, the X velocity should be set either to a random value in the appropriate direction or to the negative of what it was before. The Y velocity should be set similarly when it hits the top or bottom of the window. A sample display might look something like Figure 9-1.
>
> The application should let the user control the action. The user should be able to specify the number of balls, the maximum velocity, the set of colors the balls will cycle through, the type of bounce, and the drawing style of the balls. The

drawing style includes both the shape and whether the ball is drawn as a single solid shape or as a shape plus a solid, thick solid, dotted, or thick dotted outline. The user should be able to add and remove balls dynamically and to restart the animation. Finally, the user should be able to save and reload the parameter settings.

This application illustrates many of the principles involved in a graphical application. It requires a user interface with menus, dialogs, mouse, and keyboard input to let the user control the properties of the balls and of their interaction. It requires drawing a variety of different shapes and styles within a window. It also requires support for animation in the drawing area.

A traditional approach to designing this application notes that there are two principal classes in the design. The first represents a ball. It includes all the properties of each ball (shape, color set, current color, drawing style, position, X and Y velocity) and is in charge of updating the ball's position and properties at each time unit. The second, representing the ball manager, contains all the balls; controls the number of balls, adding or removing balls as appropriate; and handles updating all the balls at each time unit.

To understand the classes needed beyond these two and to see how to put together the actual application, we need to understand the workings of the underlying graphical libraries and the restrictions they impose on the application. In particular, we need to know:

- *Program structure*: The different user-interface libraries make various assumptions about the structure of the application. These constrain the selection of the classes representing the overall program structure and the user interface.

- *Inputs*: Values entered by the user in menus and dialogs, as well as mouse and keyboard input, must be provided to the application. The design must address how the application obtains and interprets such input.

- *Outputs*: The design here must deal with how the balls are drawn, how animation is handled, what happens when two or more balls pass through each other, and what the application must do to draw the necessary menus and dialogs.

- *Events*: These determine how the animation is controlled. For smooth animation, the application needs to update the ball position and redraw the display 10 or more times per second. The design must specify how the application shares control with the user interface to accomplish this.

In the next sections we look at these issues as we continue to design the bouncing balls application.

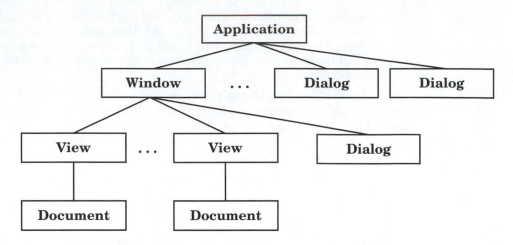

Figure 9-2 Basic application architecture in MFC.

PROGRAM STRUCTURE

The Microsoft Foundation Classes make very explicit assumptions about the class structure of an application, as illustrated in Figure 9-2. The first assumed class is a top-level class representing the application. It is responsible for dealing with command-line arguments; automatic instantiation of the application via drag and drop, print, or clicking on a file associated with the application; and interaction with other applications using event mechanisms such as ActiveX. The application itself typically has a single top-level window, though multiple top-level windows can be controlled by an application, some of which are dialog boxes.

The window class in this architecture represents a top-level window of the application. This includes the frame surrounding the application, the pull-down menu bar, any control panels, and one or more interior windows for the application's own display. There are two basic types of top-level windows. The first uses the top-level window as the display, showing a single application window immediately within. This is used for simple applications such as our bouncing balls program. The second allows multiple interior windows and uses the top-level window as a container for those windows, as in Microsoft's *Visual C++* environment or Microsoft *Word*.

Dialog boxes used by the application are each typically given their own class to manage their data and user interaction. These classes are attached to the overall application architecture at a location appropriate to the particular function of the dialog. Global dialog boxes such as a file open manager are generally attached to the application class, while those specific to a given window or view are generally attached directly to the corresponding window or view class.

A view class is used to give the user information from the application. In our case, the view class will contain the window in which the balls bounce around. In a more sophisticated example such as *Visual C++*, views are used for text and dialog editing, display of the build output, help browsers, and so on. The view class also handles any direct user interaction with the displayed information, including keyboard and mouse input.

While the view class displays the application information to the user, it does not contain that information. For this it relies on an underlying document class. This class deals with the contents of the information and not how it is displayed. This represents a separation between the user-interface layer of the application and the domain layer containing the actual application data. Such an organization can support multiple displays of the same contents, each involving different presentation strategies.

The impetus for separating the document from its display comes originally from the Smalltalk model-view-controller approach to user interfaces. Here the user interface is divided into three pieces. The *model* contains the underlying representation of the application data and corresponds to a document class. The *view* provides a read-only or editable display of a model. There can be multiple views for a single document or multiple documents in a single view. This corresponds to a combination of the view and window classes in the MFC approach. The third piece of this approach, the *controller*, separates input and event management from the display. In the MFC approach, all the levels can handle different types of input and it is up to the application to provide the appropriate handlers at each level.

This approach is also quite similar to what is typically done in a Motif application, although not as rigorously or as formally as with MFC. Here there is typically a class for the application, such as the **KnightMain** class we introduced in the knight's-tour problem. This class manages access to the X11 display and handles scanning the initial argument list. Then there is a class for each top-level window, either a dialog or the main application display. The main window typically includes a menu bar that this class manages, as well as one or more windows for the application to use for its own displays. These application windows are managed by separate classes corresponding to MFC views. They may either include the data being displayed or have the data in a separate class corresponding to a MFC document.

Separating the interfaces into classes in the manner suggested by MFC and used with Motif is an attempt to isolate the different aspects of the application. The top-level or application class is responsible for the overall control. It should not know what is to be displayed or how it should be presented. The window classes are responsible for managing the top-level window and user interaction. They should be flexible enough to handle a variety of different display strategies and standardized enough that applications are consistent with one another. The view classes handle the actual display of application data. Separating these from the data lets appropriate functionality be built in without complicating the data at the heart of the application. Moreover, it lets view

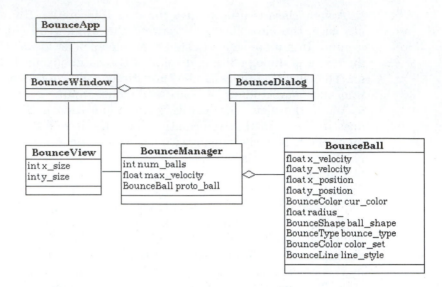

Figure 9-3 Top-level static structure diagram for bouncing balls.

classes be defined so that they can be reused in new applications or for other functions in the same application. It also provides a framework for applications in which multiple views of the same data can be available to the user simultaneously, as in a spreadsheet with both a textual and a graphical view of some data.

We next apply this approach to the bouncing balls application. Here we want a top-level class that handles overall control, including loading and storing parameter settings, reading command-line arguments, and setting up the rest of the system. This corresponds to the application class in the MFC framework. Below this will be a class to handle the top-level window, its menu bars, and any top-level user interaction with the system. This corresponds to the window class. At the same level we need additional classes for each of the dialog boxes that will eventually be needed to handle user input. We next need a class to handle the actual drawing of the balls and managing the display area. This corresponds to a view class. Finally we need a class to hold the application data, in this case the state and properties of all the balls. This corresponds to the manager class we previously included as one of the basic classes implied by the problem description.

This leads us to the top-level design for the bouncing balls shown in Figure 9-3. Here the class **BounceApp** represents the top-level application. It is responsible for initializing everything and handling the command line. It sets up a class **BounceWindow** that takes care of the root window, separating it into a menu bar and a display area and handling interaction with the menu bar. The class **BounceDialog** is a placeholder for the various dialog boxes that will be needed once we refine the user interface. In general, each dialog box will have its own class that will be a subclass of this. Note that the dialog classes include a reference to the manager so that they can set and access properties using appropriate methods. The **BounceView** class is then responsible for managing the drawing area, handling interactions among this area, the user, and the system.

The user will interact with the proposed system through several levels of the design. The program's menus and corresponding buttons are managed by the window class. Dialog boxes in which the user can provide more detailed input are each managed by their own class. Direct user interaction with the display, using either the mouse or the keyboard, is handled by the view class. This multiple-class approach to input management, while not ideal, is needed to ensure that the class associated with the display area where the input occurs is the one to interpret the input. Input management within the application can be significantly different. The application generally defines a series of functions corresponding to abstract operations on its internal data. Most, if not all, of the input handlers invoked when the user takes an action are very simple routines that call these abstract operations rather than attempting to process the input directly. This allows a cleaner separation of the application from the user interface, letting the user interface change more easily to meet changing demands. We discuss this in more detail in the next section.

The actual data in the bouncing balls application is contained in the **BounceManager** and **BounceBall** classes. The **BounceManager** class contains data fields for the number of balls, the maximum ball velocity, and the set of balls. The **BounceBall** class indicates the ball's current velocity, position, and color as well as the various settings inherited from the manager when the ball was created that are needed either for drawing or for computing its next position.

The **BounceManager** class in this application must also be able to create new balls with the current set of properties. This could be done by adding data fields for each of the properties of a ball, providing methods for other parts of the application (notably the dialog box classes) to set these fields, and then using these fields to set the properties of a new ball.

A simpler and cleaner way to do this, however, is to use *prototypes*. Here the **BounceManager** class holds a single ball object representing a prototype instance of a ball, rather than individual fields for each of the ball's properties. When a new ball is needed, the manager creates it by *cloning*, i.e. creating a duplicate of the prototype. This lets the default properties of a ball be stored without being declared in multiple places and without multiple classes needing to know what those properties are.

The concept of storing prototypes and cloning them to create new instances is a generally useful one with a variety of applications. In the bounce program it lets us hide the properties of a ball from the ball manager. It lets other classes interact directly with the prototype ball, and makes the task of creating a new ball with the right properties a method of the ball class rather than the manager class. In other applications it can greatly simplify the creation of objects, especially objects that are actually sets of objects. It can offer significant information hiding and allow easy property and mode setting. For example, in a drawing editor, a prototype can be used to represent the current shape to be created when the user clicks on the display. The prototype here not only indicates the properties of the shape, but also encodes the shape itself in the subclass of the object, something that would be difficult to do any other way.

Finally, the evolving design for the bouncing ball program should consider memory management issues. In this case the application objects will own, i.e. create and free, the window and dialog objects. The window object will own the view object. The view object will own the manager object, and the manager object will own the various ball objects.

CONTROL STRUCTURE

The primary difference between a graphical and a non-graphical application is how control is managed. In a non-graphical system such as the knight's-tour problem, the application has control. The main program calls whatever routines are necessary, these routines call whatever other routines are necessary, and the work eventually gets done. Such applications can operate this way because all the work is done in the context of the application.

In a graphical application, however, much of the work is done outside the application. The program has to respond to user interactions that may or may not affect the workings of the application. It needs to track the mouse and update the cursor as it moves around the screen. It needs to highlight buttons as the mouse passes over them. Menus need to be popped up or pulled down in response to mouse actions. During a drag-and-drop operation, whatever is under the mouse must be highlighted if it is a suitable drop target. The problem facing graphical libraries and applications is how to ensure these tasks are done while still letting the application do its work.

The earliest solution to this problem used polling. Here the application creates a loop in which it first waits either for an input event such as mouse movement or a keystroke, or for a system event such as a time-out. When it gets such an event, it looks at the event type and calls the appropriate routine, either a system routine or an application routine. This is the approach taken in most Macintosh applications and in UNIX programs that use only X11 and not Xt, Motif, or some other higher-level library. It has the advantage that the application remains in control. It has the disadvantage that the application needs to handle all the decoding of the input events, which adds significant complexity to the system and is an easy source of errors. It imposes restrictions on the processing the application can do, since it often must respond to new events in a timely fashion. Finally, while there is a significant amount of commonality in how different applications need to handle events, it is difficult to make the event loop part of the library because of the differences among applications. The result is a more complex application and somewhat messy interfaces to the library.

The current response to these issues is to structure the library in terms of events and callbacks. An *event* is an indication to the program that something external to the program, such as user input or a time-out, has occurred. A *callback* is a routine in the application that is called not from the application itself but rather from a library or its equivalent. In such a solution the application defines the high-level events it wants to handle, such as the selection of a particular menu button. In doing so it provides a function to be invoked when the event occurs. The main loop and the decoding and handling of basic event interactions are handled within the library. When the library determines that an application-defined event has occurred, it calls the appropriate function to process it.

This approach has several implications. First, the library and not the application has control most of the time. Rather than the application calling the library to get something done, the library calls the application when something should get done. This means that actions taken by the application must be structured to fit into routines that can be called from the library and will return control without processing additional events. The actions taken here must be relatively fast and simple since complex actions would inhibit further event processing. Some of these complications can be avoided using multiple threads of control, as discussed in "Multiple Threads of Control" on page 383, but this is not common in most current applications and libraries.

The complexities of an event and callback approach can be seen in the knight's-tour program. Suppose we want to provide a graphical interface to knight's tour to animate the construction of a tour. Here the library would have control and would call our code periodically to find the next move and update the board. This call could be made either in response to a timer or when the user requested the next move. In either case, we would have to restructure our knight's-tour solution completely. The current solution takes complete control to find all the moves. In order to find only the "next" move, we would have to eliminate our recursive control structure and encode the recursion in the various classes. The resultant code would be significantly more complex and much less clear.

Similar difficulties can arise when an application expects the user to take certain actions in a given order. Consider an exchange command in which the user selects "Exchange" from a menu and then chooses the two objects to be exchanged. Here the application gets a callback when the exchange command is invoked. It needs to set internal flags indicating it is now looking for the arguments for this command. The object-selection callback can check this flag, update it after the first object is selected, and then execute the command after the second one. However, all other callbacks in the application need to check these internal flags to ensure that the user follows the proper sequence of actions. This adds so much complexity that most applications today assume that arguments are given first and the command is given last or that arguments are given in a controlled environment such as a dialog box.

A second implication is that the application must set up the various callbacks. The application must create all its windows, menus, buttons, and so on at initialization time. This includes defining the layout and contents of each as well as the appropriate callback to be used. Once all these are set up, then the library routine representing the event loop can be invoked and the rest of the work of the application can be done through callbacks. Because most application code dealing with the user interface involves the setup process, it makes sense for the classes of the user interface to correspond to the different windows, menus, and buttons that must be created initially.

This fits into the program structure outlined in the previous section. The top-level or application class is responsible for the overall initialization. The window classes are responsible for controlling the initialization of the top-level windows and their corresponding menus and buttons. The view classes are responsible for setting up the user display areas. Classes for dialog boxes are responsible for setting up the dialog window. Additional classes can be created for components such as the menus of the window class, but these would be internal to the higher-level class and are considered an implementation detail.

A third implication of the use of events and callbacks is that everything the program does must be viewed as an event associated with an appropriate callback. If the program needs to do animation, as in the bouncing balls example, it must define a callback that is invoked often enough to update the screen to give the effect of smooth animation (10 to 30 times a second). If the program needs to get information from another program, it must view messages on an interprocess communication channel as events recognized by the library event loop. This has led user-interface libraries to add categories of events: they now have *time-out events* that provide callbacks after a given amount of elapsed time and *file events* that provide a callback when a file is in a ready state for either reading or writing. Files, in the general sense in which they are defined in today's operating systems, are used for terminal input as well as most types of interprocess communication. Finally, the libraries provide an *idle event* whose callback is invoked if the event loop can find nothing else to do. This lets programs do background processing under some very limited circumstances.

An event-and-callback control structure is easy to extend and fits in nicely with libraries. In particular, hierarchies of events can be defined in which the basic library handles the low-level events and passes on others as callbacks. The passed-on events can include simple program interaction such as type-in and composite events such as the selection of a button in a pull-down menu or the double-click of a mouse button. Higher-level libraries can then be defined to process these callbacks, take appropriate action, and make higher-level callbacks. For example, a dialog-box class can be defined to handle all the internal interaction of the dialog box and present a callback to the application only when the user chooses "`Accept`."

The control structure of the application is thus influenced most by the need to process input. A secondary consideration is the need to handle multiple graphical applications on a single machine simultaneously. If there are multiple active applications, then the actions of one can affect the others. Moreover, different applications must be able to interact with the user simultaneously. In UNIX, the X11 architecture incorporates a separate process to manage the display, and the individual applications send commands and receive events from the X11 process. This is convenient since it separates the graphics component from the operating system and provides a high degree of separation among different applications. However, it means that the input and output of the program are asynchronous: output commands may not be executed immediately; inputs are queued up and sent to the application for later processing; windows created by the application may not be immediately available for drawing. Similar constraints are imposed by the various Windows operating systems.

To accommodate all this, graphical libraries have augmented the input-event mechanism with *window events*. The principal such event is an *expose* event informing the application that all or a portion of one of its windows needs to be drawn. This can occur because the window just became visible for the first time, because the window was previously obscured by another application that has just terminated or had its windows moved, or because the window was resized or deiconified. Other events tell the window that it was moved, resized, iconified, deiconified, or that the mouse moved into or out of the window.

From an applications point of view, this implies that drawing to a window must be viewed as an asynchronous event done only when triggered by a window expose event. Drawing to a window is thus done in callback routines rather than under application control. This again reflects the inverted control flow inherent in the event-callback approach to graphical programs.

USER-INTERFACE CONCEPTS

In order to talk, one must understand the language. In order for a program to talk to the library supporting the graphical user interface, the programmer must understand the vocabulary, syntax, and semantics of the language comprising the library interface. The vocabulary of a graphical interface contains concepts such as the events described in the previous section, contexts, displays, visuals, colors, fonts, and images. The syntax of the interface deals with the basic components supported by the library and how to put them together. The semantics of the interface deals with the callbacks and how they are used by the application.

Type	Application
XtContext	Connection to the X11 display. Supports the main event loop with I/O, time-out, idle, and user-interface events and callbacks.
Display	Represents the display supported by an XtContext connection. Supports X11 resource files and provides basis for top-level windows.
Screen	A display can have multiple monitors, each of which is represented by a screen.
Visual	A method of accessing the display. Controls how pixels are displayed.
Pixel	Integer value used to represent a color that can be 8, 16, 24, or 32 bits wide.
Image	Representation in the application of an icon or other pixel pattern.
Bitmap	1-pixel-deep image stored in the server.
Pixmap	Arbitrary-depth image stored in the server.

Figure 9-4 Basic types of the X11/Motif user-interface library.

All systems today use bitmapped raster graphics to display information. The overall screen is divided into bits or *pixels* and has a certain resolution, say 1280 by 1024, and a given number of colors, say 256. This means that there are 1024 rows, each of which contains 1280 pixels. Each pixel on the screen can display one of 256 colors. Screen space and colors are limited resources in this environment and are managed by the operating system in Windows, or by some common lower-level package such as X11 on UNIX. The interface to this resource manager is included in the user-interface library.

Both UNIX and Windows define a number of additional concepts on top of the basics of displays. Because the two systems use slightly different names and terminology, we discuss them separately in the next two sections.

Basic Motif Concepts

UNIX, using X11 and Motif, offers a lower-level interface to the underlying display hardware than does Windows. This makes the UNIX approach somewhat more flexible, since the programmer has greater control over how the hardware is actually used. It also makes graphical programming more complex and difficult, since the programmer must be aware of low-level display details.

The basic elements of the UNIX interfaces shown in Figure 9-4 start with an **XtContext** object. This represents a connection to the X11 server and provides the basic functionality of the main event loop. It lets the user define time-out, file-based, and idle events along with their associated callbacks.

Such a connection is always associated with a display that represents the resources controlled by the X11 server handled by an object of type **Display**. In addition to the functionality of an **XtContext**, the **Display** object can be used to manage resource files and as a basis for defining top-level windows. Each X11 display can consist of multiple monitors that can each have different properties; each monitor is represented by an instance of type **Screen**. This type is not used extensively in X11 since the screen object is also accessible from the display using the integer screen number and most displays involve only one monitor.

Screens can be used in a variety of ways. For example, a color monitor might be used as a black and white display, a gray-scale display, a color display with 256 specific colors, or a color display supporting a range of colors based on red, green, and blue values. These are represented in X11 as *visuals* through objects of type **Visual**. When X11 starts up, each screen is associated with a default visual that is used by most applications. Applications may, with some effort, change the visual used for particular windows within the application.

Within a visual, each pixel represents a color by an integer value. Colors are created in the display hardware by mixing some value of red, green, and blue. Thus, the integer value for each pixel must be mapped into an appropriate red-green-blue triple of values for the display hardware. The different types of visuals correspond to different ways to accomplish this mapping. The two most common types of visuals are *true color* and *pseudo color*. The number of bits used to represent a pixel (one for simple black and white, eight for 256 colors, or 24 for 16,777,216 colors) is called the *depth* of the display.

The simplest type of visual is a *true-color* one. Here the bits in the original integer value are allocated among the three colors. For example, in a 24-bit (16,777,216-color) true-color visual, eight bits are used for each of the colors, while in an eight-bit (256-color) true-color visual, three bits are used for red and green and two bits are used for blue. When lots of bits are available in the graphics hardware, this type of visual is preferred. The human eye can discern only about a million different colors, so a 24-bit visual suffices to display all possible colors. However, if the hardware has fewer colors available, using a true-color visual limits the range of colors for any particular application.

Pseudo-color visuals let applications make more effective use of the limited set of available colors, but at a cost. Here the system introduces a *colormap* that serves as a translator between pixel values and color values. The colormap translates each pixel value into a full 24-bit color value. If the application specifies a pixel value of 117, then the 117th entry in the colormap is used. This lets the application specify any 256 colors out of the full range of 16 million colors using the eight available bits, rather than the limited predefined set a true-color visual provides. The problem with pseudo-color visuals is that they introduce a new resource, the colormap, that must be shared among applications.

While some of the items in the user interface are simple shapes such as lines, rectangles, arcs, and polygons, much of the interface is composed of more complex items such as icons and text. Icons are a special case of *images*, predefined sets of bits that are drawn on the screen. X11 lets the user define such icons in the application by using objects of type **Image**. Each image consists of pixels that can be packed in various ways. Each pixel can represent one, eight, or 24 bits; the number of bits generally matches the number of bits or depth of the visual of the corresponding window.

Because X11 uses a client-server architecture, an **Image** structure must be conveyed from the application to the server before it can be used. To facilitate this, X11 lets the application create windows in the server with arbitrary depth, copy images to these windows, and draw into them. Such a window is called a **Pixmap** or, in the special case of a depth of one, a **Bitmap**. In drawing a bitmap, it is possible to draw the one-bits in an arbitrary color and either to draw the zero bits in a separate color or to ignore them. Each pixel in a pixmap represents the color in which it is to be drawn, so that the color is stored with the image.

Text is drawn in X11 as a special case of bitmaps and images. When the application needs to draw a text string, it must specify a font to use. The font is essentially a mapping from the character code to a bitmap describing how that character should be drawn on the screen. Fonts are typically named and the graphics library handles the mapping from font names to the actual fonts.

A complex textual display within an application may display text in a variety of different fonts in a single string. For example, a mathematical formula might involve special symbols and Greek letters as well as standard names. Motif introduces a complex string type, **XmString**, to represent such strings. Most applications do not use this capability, preferring simple C-style strings. Motif requires, however, that most string parameters to its various functions be passed as **XmString** values, thereby requiring the programmer to do the type conversion.

Basic Microsoft Foundation Class Concepts

The graphics model provided by the Microsoft Foundation Classes is a bit simpler. Much of the initial complexity of the X11 interface comes from the fact that X11 is written on top of the basic operating system and can be used for displaying applications remotely. Further complexity comes from the fact that X11 was originally written when display technology was quite diverse and it was important that applications use as much as possible of the capacity of the display hardware. In addition, X11 was designed to work on a wide variety of different systems, not just a single UNIX platform.

Microsoft Windows, and MFC on top of it, is integrated into the operating system. Here the operating system takes care of the different display technologies, does the basic event management, and gives the program a simpler programming interface. The basic system assumes that the user has only one display.

The clearest example of this is MFC's color model. While X11 exposes the complexities of colormaps, different visuals, and pixels, MFC lets the programmer use a simple color model based on specifying a **COLORREF**, a 24-bit red-green-blue value. The operating system automatically maps this color value into whatever is appropriate for the underlying graphics hardware. In theory, this frees the programmer from worrying about the underlying display hardware and simplifies the application. In practice, however, the programmer must realize that the more basic graphics displays can show only a small set of colors and that the basic display techniques used limit the range of any one color to a relatively small set of values. The result of this is that images may not look as they were designed to.

Windows actually goes beyond this by offering a colormap through a **CPalette** object for hardware that can show only 256 colors. While Windows reserves twenty colors, the application can freely choose the remaining ones. However, since graphics cards capable of doing 16- or 24-bit color are becoming more common, new applications should probably be written using only **COLORREF**s.

X11 differentiates between a simple one-plane bitmap and a multiplane pixmap and also between an image kept in the applications memory and one kept in the X11 server. The result is that there are three distinct X11 data types, **Image**, **Bitmap**, and **Pixmap**. Windows makes no such distinction: any off-screen image is kept as a bitmap using the class **CBitmap**. A bitmap can have a single plane (one bit per pixel) or multiple planes. Moreover, because the display is actually handled by the operating system, bitmaps are all kept in the application's memory.

Text in Windows is drawn much as in X11, using fonts that contain bitmaps describing how each character should be displayed. The MFC type for a font, **CFont**, provides the same capabilities as the X11 equivalent: both let the user specify a font family and then specify an arbitrary font size for that family.

USER-INTERFACE COMPONENTS

Modern user interfaces are built out of low-level components supported by the underlying library called *widgets* in Motif and *controls* in MFC. These are items such as push buttons, scroll bars, or labels. Each can display itself under different conditions and can obtain and pass on input of the appropriate type to the application.

Programmers should understand and utilize these basic components when building user interfaces. It is generally a poor idea to create new modes of interaction or new primitive components when a suitable interface can be built from existing library components. Not only are the library components already written and debugged, they also provide interfaces with which the user is familiar since they are used on other applications within the system.

User-interface libraries provide several types of components. Primitive components such as a push-button provide the basic input and output of the interface. Higher-level components such as a scrolled list combine various primitives to provide additional functionality. Container components provide facilities for laying out and organizing the various components. Top-level components provide access to the windows and views discussed in the previous section.

Basic widgets or controls give the user a simple interactor. An *interactor* is a single entity combining input and output behavior and should be thought of as an object in the sense of object-oriented programming. It has both internal data and a set of user-callable methods. It handles its own interaction with the underlying windowing system, knowing when to draw or redraw itself, how to draw itself when the mouse moves or clicks over it, what to do if the user types over it, and so on. It maintains an internal state that includes any value it is designed to return to the user. It provides methods or functions whereby the application can set or inquire values from this internal state. Finally, it provides callbacks to inform the application when the value changes.

Motif Components

The basic interactors offered by Motif are shown in Figure 9-5. The top one, a *label widget*, is used just to display text without any interaction. Immediately below this is a *separator widget* that consists of a line and is used only for output. (In the figure, separator widgets actually appear between the other basic interactors.) The second box in the figure contains a *push-button widget*. This can highlight when the mouse moves over it and displays itself as depressed if the mouse clicks on it. A click-release of the mouse on a push button produces a callback to the user application. A *toggle-button widget* appears below the push-button; this acts similarly except that it maintains a binary or ternary internal state, with the check box on the left indicating the current state. Clicking on the widget both changes the state and generates a callback to the application. Below these two push buttons is an *arrow widget*, which is similar to a push button except that it displays an oriented arrow rather than a text label.

Below these various types of push buttons are two widgets that show a range. The first is a *scale widget*, typically used to show a single numerical value within a range with a slider. It can be labeled, as here, or unlabeled. The scale widget maintains an internal state corresponding to the current value. When the user drags or clicks on the slider, this internal value is changed and an appropriate callback to the application is generated. Below the scale widget is a *scroll-bar widget* used to indicate a subset of values within a range. It

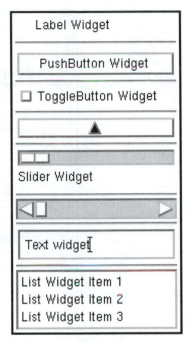

Figure 9-5 Basic Motif widgets.

maintains an internal state specifying the starting point and size of the subset, lets the user interact with the scroll bar in the usual ways, and provides a callback that is invoked whenever the internal values change.

Below the scroll bar is a *text widget*. Motif provides two types of text widgets. The more complex offers multiple lines of text and supports a full range of editing. The one shown here, a *text-field widget*, provides only a single line of text and a limited range of editing commands. The text widget makes a callback to the application whenever the text changes. Another callback is invoked when the focus moves out of the text region to let the application wait until editing is complete before receiving control from the library.

The final widget in Figure 9-5 is a *list widget* that displays a set of items and lets the user select one or more of them. Its internal state maintains the set of items and the currently selected item or items. It provides callbacks whenever the user selects or deselects an item.

The event-callback mechanism lets more complex components be built up from the basic ones. Both Motif and MFC offer several such higher-level components. Figure 9-6 shows some of the higher-level Motif components. At the top is a *menu-bar widget*. This consists of a sequence of push buttons tied to menus called *cascade button widgets*. Clicking on one of these causes the corresponding menu to pop up. Clicking on any of the menu buttons (which are again widgets) then invokes an appropriate callback. The application need not

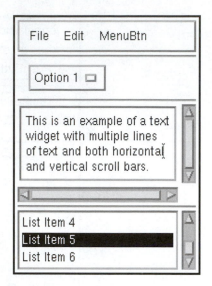

Figure 9-6 Higher-level Motif widgets.

handle any of the intermediate callbacks and only has to worry about the menu item that is finally selected.

Below the menu bar is an *option-button widget*. This is another cascade button, but one that is tied directly to a list of alternative values. Clicking on the button pops up the list of values, letting the user select one. The currently selected value is then displayed in the button. This widget provides a callback when the user changes the value associated with the option button.

A *scrolled-text widget* appears below the option button. This combines a text widget supporting multiple-line editing with horizontal and vertical scroll bars. The resultant widget behaves as if it were a text widget, providing callbacks to the application when the text changes or editing is complete. A *scrolled list widget*, the last item in the figure, is a list widget with scroll bars and provides the internal state and callbacks of the list widget.

User interface libraries provide components to lay out and organize the various interactors. Motif views these again as widgets. There are four primary types of container widgets. The first, a *row-column widget*, lays items out in either rows or columns with various packing options. It is easy to use as long as its rectangular layout is appropriate. Specialized forms of row-column widgets are used for pop-up and pull-down menus and *radio boxes*, regions containing a set of related buttons of which the user generally selects only one at a time. The second, a *form widget*, is much harder to use but lets almost any layout be created based on simple constraints among the components.

The third container type provides decorations around a window. Motif provides several widgets of this type. A *frame widget* provides a frame around its single constituent. A *paned window widget* provides space for two constituent widgets and a resizing control between the two. A *scrolled window widget* provides scroll bars around an arbitrary widget.

The fourth container type provides default window layouts. A *main window widget* provides a default top-level application view with a menu bar, a view area, scroll bars if necessary, and status windows. Another widget of this container type, *dialog widgets*, provide standard dialog boxes of various types with accept and cancel buttons at the bottom. Specialized forms of these widgets provide selection dialogs for items from a list and for files.

Beyond the various components, Motif uses widgets as an interface to all aspects of the user interface. It provides a variety of *shell widgets* as an interface between the application and X11, letting the application interact with the underlying windowing system. An *application-shell widget* is used for the initial top-level window in an application. A *top-level-shell widget* is used for any additional top-level windows and a *dialog-shell widget* for dialog boxes. Motif also contains a *drawing-area widget* that provides a window into which an application can draw. This widget provides callbacks for mouse and keyboard input as well as for redrawing the window of the widget.

Motif, although it takes an object-oriented approach to widgets, is actually written for C, not for C++. This means that the widgets, their properties, and their callbacks are implemented in a non-object-oriented framework. Functions are provided to create widgets of the various types. Common functions let the user set and access properties of any widget, but the widget must be passed explicitly, as must the property name.

There are three approaches to using Motif with C++. The first is to use it as is, making the normal C calls from C++. This works, but does not take advantage of the power of C++.

The second approach is to encapsulate the Motif widgets you need in your own classes. Wherever you need to create a Motif widget, you actually create a new class serving as a wrapper for that widget. All access to the widget is done through the class interface. This isolates the Motif-specific portions of the program and restricts the C-style (and unsafe) calls to a restricted set of classes. Moreover, where the classes have common elements, such as multiple classes for different push-button widgets, C++ inheritance can be used to simplify the interfaces.

The third alternative is to acquire a package that provides C++ wrappers to Motif. Such packages define C++ classes that mirror the widget hierarchy. They provide type-checked methods for each of the parameters widgets can have, thereby ensuring that only valid properties are set or accessed for a widget and that values are used correctly. They also provide simplified access to some of the types Motif complicates. For example, we previously noted that Motif defines its own notion of a string, **XmString**, to accommodate multiple fonts and extended character sets. Most programs, however, use simple character string internally. The Motif wrapper packages provide automatic conversions between simple C strings and Motif strings.[1]

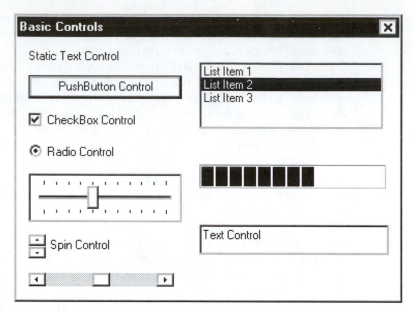

Figure 9-7 Basic MFC controls.

Microsoft Foundation Classes Components

The controls provided by the Microsoft Foundation Classes offer similar functionality to the Motif widgets. The controls have a slightly different look and feel, but are used in essentially the same way as their Motif equivalents.

Figure 9-7 shows a sampling of the basic controls MFC provides. The label in the top left of the figure is a *static text control* that lets the user place inactive text anywhere in a window or dialog box. Directly below this are three types of buttons. The top one is a simple *push-button control*. The second and third are equivalent to a Motif toggle button: a *check-box control* is used when multiple choices are allowed, while a *radio control* is used where only a single choice is allowed.

The MFC equivalent of a scale widget is the *slider control* shown under the radio control. Unlike the widget, this control does not automatically display the associated value or provide a label field. If a value is to be displayed, the programmer must create a second area (either a static or regular text control) and put up the corresponding value under program control. An alternative to using a slider to input numeric values in MFC is to use a *spin control*. This consists of two arrow buttons that let the user quickly raise or lower a value,

---

1. One such package is Motif++ by Ronald van Loon, who can be contacted at rvloon@motif.hacktic.nl. Another is BAUM by the present author, available from ftp.cs.brown.edu as part of the Forest package in file forest.tar.Z.

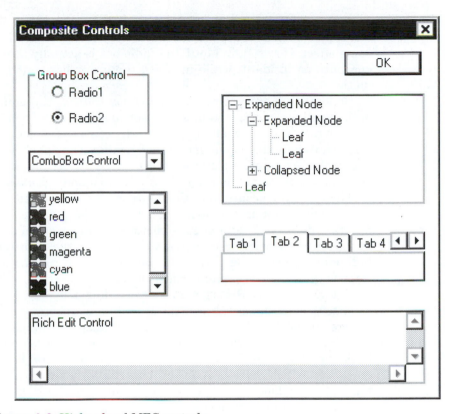

Figure 9-8 Higher-level MFC controls.

and can be associated directly with a numeric display so the user can see the current value.

A *scroll-bar control*, shown in the bottom left of the figure, is the equivalent of a Motif scroll-bar widget. Both horizontal and vertical scroll bars are available. A *list box control*, shown at the upper right of the figure, allows the user to select one or more items from a list. As with Motif list widgets, list box controls are generally not used directly, but rather inside a composite that allows scrolling if the list gets too long.

Below the list box control is a *progress control*, which has no Motif equivalent. It shows how much of an operation has been completed so far, and hence is used for output only, not as an input mechanism.

The final basic control is a *text control*, which is the equivalent of both the Motif text-field widget and the Motif text widget. It can be used as a single-line editor, like a text-field widget, or as a multiple-line editor, like a text widget. In addition, it can be used directly to input numeric values, with the control itself ensuring that the input text represents a valid number.

Windows and MFC also support more complex or composite controls, as shown in Figure 9-8. The box at the top left is a *group-box control*. While this control provides no input, it does offer a label and a box to show that the various controls inside it are related. Motif uses a radio-box widget to achieve the same effect. However, in Motif, the radio box is actually the parent of the various buttons inside it, while in MFC, the group-box control is primarily cosmetic.

Beneath the group box is a *combo-box control*, the equivalent of a Motif option-button widget. It allows the user to select one of a set of items by clicking down on the arrow at the right of the control and then clicking up on the selected item in the pop-up menu that results. The list shown below the combo box control is an example of a *list control*. It is essentially a list-box control with an optional scroll bar and the ability to display icons as well as text.

The remaining controls in the figure do not have Motif equivalents (except for the OK button in the upper right). The first is a *tree control* that lets the program display a hierarchical structure such as a set of directories and files. The user can expand and contract elements of the hierarchy and can select individual elements. It provides a convenient and consistent way for applications to give the user a hierarchical choice.

Below the tree control is a *tab control*, which lets the user select one of a set of pages. Typically, a tab control is tied to a display below it. As the user selects one of the tabs, the contents of that display change to show a different set of options or controls. In this way, a tab control acts as a set of tabs into a book of dialog boxes. Tab controls are often used in what Windows calls a *property sheet*, which consists of one or more dialog boxes with a tab control at the top and is used for setting properties. Figure 9-9 shows the standard Windows property sheet for networking.

The final control in Figure 9-8 is a *rich edit control*. This is a full-function editor available for insertion into an application. Our experience with earlier toolkits we and others developed showed that having such functionality available makes building many applications much easier. It also standardizes the editing interface provided by a range of applications. While Motif does not currently provide such functionality (the text widget is a poor substitute if real editing needs to be done), the Common Desktop Environment that comes with Motif does include an editor widget, although it is not available on all systems.

Motif provides a wide range of container widgets and assumes that the application will use them hierarchically to control layout. MFC, on the other hand, makes simpler assumptions and relies on a resource editor and user-controlled manual layout. MFC provides three basic types of containers that differ more in their application then in how they affect layout or decoration. The first is a *dialog bar control*; this represents a portion of a static window that will contain controls. The second, a *formview control*, is used when the items should be laid out in a separate window, say in a dialog box. The third is a *property page* that contains the controls for a property sheet such as that in Figure 9-9. All these containers require the user to provide the absolute location of each contained control. This is where a smart resource editor becomes very helpful.

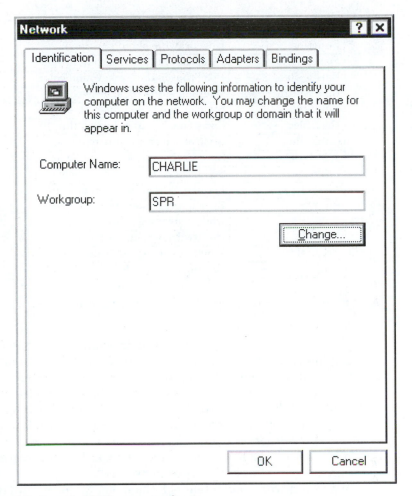

Figure 9-9 Sample MFC property sheet.

GRAPHICAL OUTPUT

While many applications can be written using only standard user-interface components, others such as the bouncing balls example involve drawing on the display. This is done using a variety of primitives, each with a variety of parameters. The primitives enable the programmer to draw the basic shapes that are the foundation of complex drawings. The parameters let the shapes be used in a wide variety of ways, colors, and styles. For example, a rectangle can be drawn as an outline, as a solid, in different colors, or with a fill pattern. A line can be drawn solid, dashed, in various widths, and with different styles of end and junction points.

Property	Description
Function	How drawing should be done.
Foreground	Pixel that is the foreground color.
Background	Pixel that is the background color.
LineWidth	Width of a line to be drawn.
LineStyle	Style of line (solid, dashed, etc.).
DashList	Size of dashes in a dashed line.
CapStyle	Style of the end points of a line.
JoinStyle	Style of the junction points where multiple lines connect.
FillStyle	Solid, tiled, or stippled — how to draw shapes.
Tile	Pixmap to be used when drawing a tiled shape.
Stipple	Bitmap to be used with foreground and background colors when drawing a stippled shape.
FillRule	How to draw complex polygons that overlap.
ArcMode	Whether arcs are pie-slices or chordal.
Font	Font to be used when drawing text.

Figure 9-10 Basic properties in an X11 graphics context.

The potentially large number of drawing parameters complicates the drawing interfaces provided by the graphical libraries. The interfaces must provide a mechanism for conveying these parameters to the library for each graphics call. This can be done in two ways. The first is to have each of the methods or routines take lots of parameters. This requires the programmer to be aware of all the parameters and makes each call to the graphics library more complex and error-prone. The alternative is to establish a context object for drawing as a repository for all the parameter settings. The user can change the settings in a given graphics context or can have multiple contexts with different settings. When a drawing operation is to be done, the user simply passes along a context in place of all the possible parameters.

X11/Motif and the Microsoft Foundation Classes both use a context in this way. The properties that the two hold differ somewhat but the concepts are the same. A **GC** object represents a *graphics context* in X11. It is independent of the window or pixmap into which the drawing will be done. It contains the properties shown in Figure 9-10, and provides calls for the user to access and set each of the properties.

In MFC, a **CDC** object is called a *device context*. It contains the basic properties shown in Figure 9-11. While many of these have equivalents in the X11 graphics context, there are some additions and the organization is different. Most basic drawing properties are encoded inside pens and brushes. A *pen* encodes the drawing properties for drawing lines while a *brush* encodes the properties for drawing shapes. This makes it relatively easy to switch styles for different lines or shapes in the same window. (Note that with X11, one typically creates separate graphics contexts to be used here rather than separate

Property	Description
Brush	Properties for drawing filled shapes.
Pattern	Pattern (bitmap) to be used for filled shapes.
Color	Color to be used for filled shapes.
Font	Font for drawing text.
Palette	Colormap for this region.
Pen	Properties for drawing lines.
Style	Line style (solid, dotted, dashed, etc.).
Width	Line width.
End cap	Style to be used at ends of a line.
Join	Style to be used when joining line segments.
Color	Color to be used when drawing lines.
Background Color	Background color for this window.
Background Mode	Whether background is opaque or transparent.
Polygon Fill Mode	Determines how to draw complex polygons.
ROP2	Function to use when drawing.
Stretch Bit Mode	Mode to use for stretched bit operations.
Text Color	Color for drawing text.
Map Mode	Determines how to translate application coordinates to screen coordinates.
Viewport, Window	Together these define the coordinate system for the region being drawn into.

Figure 9-11 Basic properties in a MFC device context.

brushes or pens. This is feasible since an X11 graphics context is a fairly light-weight object while a MFC device context is a fairly heavyweight object.)

While MFC device contexts and Motif graphics contexts contain similar properties, they also differ substantially. The principal difference is that a **CDC** object is associated with a window or off-screen bitmap, so that graphical operations are done using a member of the **CDC** object rather than with a function on the window that is passed a graphics context, as in Motif. While this introduces additional complexity in the object, it also offers flexibility and can simplify programming. In MFC, one has to pass around only a single device context, not a window and a separate graphics context. Moreover, a device context can be created for printing as well as for drawing, letting the same code that writes to the display be used to generate printed output.

Another difference between device and graphics contexts is that a MFC device context encodes a coordinate system while an X11 graphics context makes the user use the default pixel-based window coordinates. Encoding a coordinate system allows an application to address the window in whatever coordinate system is most natural. It makes it easy to do graphics applications in which the origin is at the lower left or even at the center of the window. Windows also lets the coordinate system be scaled arbitrarily, so that the window can be scaled automatically when it is resized. This scale can be measured in absolute terms rather than in pixels and thus can be used to make the output look the same no matter what size monitor it is displayed on.

Most of the properties these contexts provide are straightforward. The one that may not be is the function or raster-op (ROP). When a pixel is to be drawn onto the screen for any reason, it is actually combined logically with the current screen contents. The function property controls how this logical combination is done. The useful values here are to replace the screen with the source (GXcopy in Motif, R2_COPYPEN in MFC) and to xor the screen with the source (GXxor in Motif, R2_XORPEN in MFC). Xor is useful since it lets an object be undrawn or erased by drawing it a second time. Many other possibilities are available but of limited utility in a color system.

The basic shapes supported by both X11 and MFC include lines, rectangles, arcs, polygons, and text. Lines can be drawn individually or as a sequence of connected line segments. Rectangles and arcs are drawn aligned with the screen axis, either in outline form or as filled objects. Arcs are actually portions of ellipses specified by defining the rectangular box that would contain the ellipse. Arcs are specified by providing the start and end angle, and in X11 can be either chordal or pie-shaped. Polygons are filled or outlined regions defined by a sequence of end points. Both libraries support simple convex polygons as well as complex polygons that can contain intersecting edges.

Drawing text is more complex. Text is drawn using a font that specifies which bits are set and which are not. Bits that are set are drawn in the current foreground color. Bits that are not set are either ignored, letting what was originally on the screen remain, or are drawn in the current background color. Moreover, characters within a font have a variety of different properties that must be considered, such as the height and width of the character, the leading, and the space above and below the baseline and to the left and right of the character's origin.

The actual drawing calls and their various complexities are beyond the scope of this chapter. If drawing is to be done within an application, the programmer should become familiar with the vagaries of the underlying graphics library in addition to understanding the basic concepts outlined here.

SUMMARY

Applications with graphical user interfaces have a common structure. They typically contain an application class that gets control initially and sets up the overall application. They have a window class for each top-level window, either application windows or dialog boxes. They have a view class for each different display or view that can be placed in an application window. They have document classes that reflect the data the application maintains and eventually displays through the views.

Graphical applications also have an inverted control structure that can take some getting used to. The application does not have control all the time and calls the graphics library where appropriate; rather, the graphics library typically has control and calls the application. The application sets up all the windows and then calls the library main loop routine. The library then detects a variety of events, mainly caused by user actions, and passes them back to the application through callbacks.

X11/Motif and the Windows/Microsoft Foundation Classes both introduce a lot of new terminology and many additional complexities. They first require the programmer to understand the basic operation of the graphical display. This includes how pixels are used to represent color, how images are represented, and how text is displayed. Next they require the programmer to know the primitive user-interface components that each system provides, including the various widgets in the case of Motif and the different controls in the case of MFC. Finally, the programmer must understand how drawing is done in the two environments, grasping both the sets of primitives the systems provide and how they are used.

EXERCISES

9.1   Outline a top-level set of classes for a graphical tic-tac-toe program.

9.2   Enumerate the events and callbacks that might need to be dealt with in the bouncing balls application.

9.3   Describe how a graphical knight's-tour program would be implemented both from the user's point of view and from a description of the top-level classes.

9.4   Contrast the basic drawing models of X11 and Windows: which would you prefer to use for which applications?

9.5   What other widgets or controls do you think should be part of the various user-interface toolkits? Why?

9.6   Another way that graphical input and output is done is to use PostScript directly. While PostScript was originally designed for output only, it has been adapted for input both on the NeXT machines with OpenStep, by Sun in NeWS, and by Adobe in Display PostScript (available as an extension to X11). What are the advantages and disadvantages of using PostScript as compared to Motif or MFC?

9.7   One of the nice features of the Macintosh is that the graphics model allows windows to span multiple screens even when the capabilities of the different screens differ. Suppose such a feature were to be implemented in either Motif or Windows. What changes would have to be made to the drawing model and the graphics calls?

Chapter 10

Designing Graphical Applications

Designing a good user interface takes a lot more than understanding the concepts behind graphical applications. In this chapter we go over the basic steps involved in such a design, continuing with the bouncing balls example described in the previous chapter.

User-interface design starts with a comprehensive sketch of what the interface should look like. This is translated into a set of basic classes to support the interface. The interactors from the sketch and the overall structure of the interface lead to the basic set of methods that these interface classes must implement. Additional methods and classes are then introduced to support drawing the view windows and managing dialog boxes.

We next detail how a graphical application is implemented in stages. This gives the programmer the satisfaction of having a working system early, allows easier testing and debugging, and lets the user interface be evaluated early in the development process so that it can be changed as necessary.

SKETCHING THE INTERFACE

A user-interface design starts with sketches that show the form of the various windows and dialogs, all the interactors, and what happens in drawing areas. They should be as comprehensive as possible so as to be used as a basis for program design and implementation.

One usually starts by drawing an overview of what the application will look like, as done for the bouncing balls program in Figure 10-1. This overview can be a single diagram for a simple application, as here, or can consist of multiple diagrams forming a storyboard that illustrates different states of the interface. For example, a game application might have a start-up screen, a view of the game being played, and a display of the high scores when the game is over.

The sketch in Figure 10-1 shows that we want a top-level window consisting of a menu bar with three menus and a drawing area to display balls of dif-

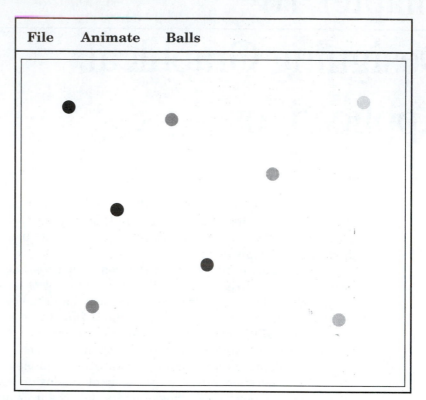

Figure 10-1 Top-level sketch of the bouncing balls example.

ferent colors. The drawing area is enclosed in a frame that separates it more clearly from the rest of the window. To be useful, this sketch should be augmented with a textual description that indicates the purpose of each component and what happens within them. Here the annotation would note that the drawing area is an animated view of the balls moving around.

The top-level diagram should also be augmented with graphical descriptions to provide the necessary details. In this case, we need to specify the contents of the three menus, as shown in Figure 10-2. This should be accompanied with annotations that describe what happens when each of the buttons is selected, as in Figure 10-3. In addition, when mouse or keyboard input is to be accepted, the annotations should describe the possible inputs and the resultant actions, as in Figure 10-4.

The button actions describe dialog boxes. One is needed to display information about the program in response to the About button. A second is needed to select the file to open and a third to specify the file for a Save As request. Additional dialog boxes are needed to let the user specify the number of balls, the maximum speed of new balls, and other ball properties. The first three of these should be standard dialog boxes that are either predefined or prescribed

File
About ...
Open ...
Save
Save As ...
Quit

Animate
Go
Pause
Restart

Balls
Set Number ...
Set Speed ...
Set Properties ...

Figure 10-2 Proposed menu buttons for bouncing balls.

Button	Description
About ...	Provide a brief description of what this program does in a dialog box.
Open ...	Let the user specify a file containing the animation parameters and load those parameters.
Save	Save the current parameters in the current file. Equivalent to Save As if no current file is known.
Save As ...	Let the user specify a file and then save the animation parameters in that file.
Quit	Exit the program.
Go	Start or restart the animation. The animation does not start until this is selected the first time.
Pause	Temporarily stop the animation. The Go button lets it continue.
Restart	Restart the animation from scratch using any new parameter settings.
Set Number ...	Display the dialog box that lets the user set the number of balls in the animation.
Set Speed ...	Display the dialog box that lets the user specify the maximum velocity of any new balls that are created.
Set Properties ...	Display the dialog box that lets the user to specify various properties of any new balls that are created.

Figure 10-3 Descriptions of the buttons for the bounce example.

by the underlying library. The latter three, however, are specific to this application and sketches of them should be included in the user-interface specification. (In a more sophisticated application, additional dialog boxes would be required for potential error conditions, and these too would be included at this stage.)

Figure 10-5 shows sketches of these three dialog boxes, which are designed using the basic components of the underlying graphics library. The first two boxes have a label indicating the box's purpose and a labeled slider to let the user change the value. The first slider handles integer values while the second

Input Event	Description
Key "r"	Restart the animation.
Key "n"	Go to next frame.
Left Mouse Button	Add one ball to the animation with current settings.
Middle Mouse Button	Remove one ball from the animation.
Right Mouse Button	Restart the animation.

Figure 10-4 Input descriptions for the bouncing balls example.

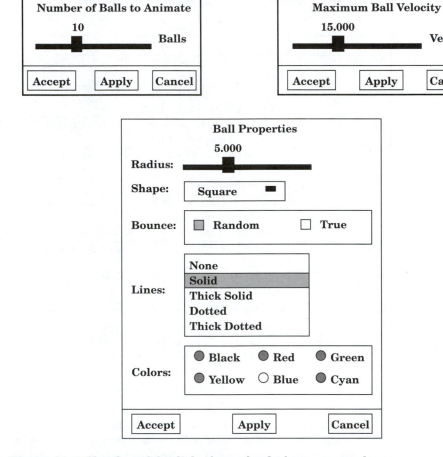

Figure 10-5 Sketches of the dialog boxes for the bounce example.

handles real values. Both boxes also contain the standard buttons to apply the new settings to the application, cancel and remove the dialog box, and accept and remove the dialog box.

The third dialog box contains a number of components. At the top is a label for the title. Below this is a slider for the ball radius, and below this is an option button that lists the various possible shapes and shows the current one. Then comes a radio box containing two push-buttons that let the user set whether the velocity after the bounce is random or the negative of the incoming velocity; in this radio box only one of the buttons can be selected at a time. The selector for the line style, just below the bounce-type radio box, lets the user choose one of the possible line types using a list component. The list component as drawn shows only one item selected, hence implying that only one item can be selected. If we wanted to allow multiple selections in the list, the sketch would show that. The final component in the dialog box lets the user select the set of colors. Here we use a radio box with buttons that let multiple items be selected simultaneously; this is indicated in the sketch both by showing multiple items as selected and by using circle buttons, not squares.

The proposed dialog boxes and the rest of the interface were designed to illustrate a range of different user-interface components, not to be an example of an ideal interface. Many factors come into play in designing a good user interface, as discussed in the next chapter. One of the most important of these is consistency. The interface should be consistent with standard applications on the underlying platform. This implied that our top-level view should have a menu bar on top and a display window below. The dialog boxes should also be consistent with the standard ones on the system. This implied that the `Accept`, `Apply` and `Cancel` buttons should be put along the bottom of each dialog. Consistency should also control how the user interacts with the various dialogs.

Consistency must go beyond interface standards to prevail within the application itself. For example, there should be a single, consistent means for inputting numeric data. Here we have chosen sliders throughout. Similarly, there should be a consistent approach to inputting selections. The properties dialog box violates this by using an option button, a list component, and radio boxes to input different selection items. A better approach would be to use option buttons for shape, bounce, and line style, all of which require a single selection. Color, because it requires multiple selections, could be done differently, but should be handled in a similar vein. (The interface here was designed as it is to illustrate the use of different widget types, hence these problems.)

This type of analysis should be applied to the complete sketched-out interface at this point. User interfaces are notoriously difficult to visualize without using them. However, because much of the program is devoted to the interface, they are also quite difficult to change once coded. The designer should check that the interface looks balanced, that all the buttons have logical names and are at logical positions, and that the interface is consistent with other applications on the target system and with itself. With a complex interface, the designer should create one or more storyboards illustrating how to use the interface for common tasks. The purpose here is to ensure that the interface is logical to use and that common operations can be done easily.

Another approach to such an evaluation is to prototype the user interface using appropriate high-level tools. There are several user-interface builders for Motif/X11 such as Sun's `Visu`, and most Windows programming environments support resource-based interface construction. These tools let the programmer see what the user interface will look like and even interact with the interface in some simple ways. We strongly recommend:

> **Evaluate the user interface before building it.**

USER-INTERFACE CLASSES

Once the complete interface is sketched out, annotated, and evaluated, we are ready to translate the interface design into a program design. This process has two parts. The first involves defining the classes inherent in the user interface, the second involves defining the appropriate methods for those classes.

The basic program structure of a graphical application implies a basic set of classes to handle the user interface. These include:

- A class for the application itself. For the bouncing balls example, this is the class **BounceApp**.

- A class for each top-level window that the application will provide. Most applications only have one top-level window. The **BounceWindow** class serves this purpose in the bouncing balls example.

- A class for each type of application-defined display that the system will provide. These correspond to the views to be provided by the interface. In the bouncing balls example, there is only one view, the window with the balls, represented by the class **BounceView**.

- A class for each type of data that can be observed through a view class. This class serves as an interface between the application data and the user-interface data. It is often combined either with the view class if there can only be a single view, or with a top-level class that describes the underlying data. In the bouncing balls example, the class **Bounce-Manager** is used both to handle this interface and as the actual data repository for the application.

- A class for each nontrivial interactor the user interface will provide. Dialog boxes are examples of such interactors. They require the user to define the contents and layout of the display and to handle intermediate and final callbacks as the user interacts with the dialog. In the bouncing balls example the meta-class **BounceDialog** provides a common framework for the other dialogs. The actual dialog boxes classes are **Bounce-**

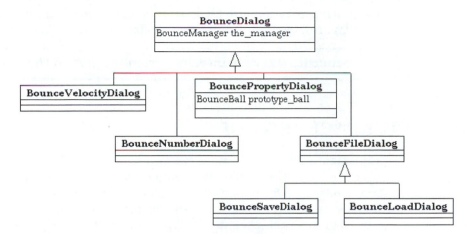

Figure 10-6 Classes used for bouncing balls dialog boxes.

NumberDialog, BounceVelocityDialog, BouncePropertyDialog, BounceAbout-Dialog, BounceSaveDialog, and **BounceLoadDialog**.

The other interactors in the proposed interface are the menu bar and its corresponding buttons and the keyboard and mouse interaction with the view window. If the menu bar required complex interactions, for example if it were user-configurable or if its buttons changed as the application changed state, then it would make sense to create a separate class for it. However, in a simple application such as the bouncing balls program, it is easiest to view this as a function of the **BounceWindow** class. Similarly, if the mouse and keyboard interaction were complex, it too could involve a separate class. Here, since both are simple, they are implemented within the **BounceView** class.

The new classes introduced above are shown in the second-level class diagram of Figure 10-6. We use a class hierarchy to hold common information. The **BounceDialog** class contains a reference to the manager class so that any dialog interactions can access and change the underlying application data. The **BouncePropertyDialog** class has a reference to the prototype ball for similar reasons. A common superclass, **BounceFileDialog**, was also created for the two file dialogs to handle their common processing.

Note that this set of classes does not include any of the classes for handling application data, the document classes cited in the previous chapter. This reflects the separation between the user interface and domain layers of the application. The document class **BounceManager** and its associated class **BounceBall** are needed as part of the program but we want to separate these from the user interface as much as possible both to simplify the overall system and to let the user interface evolve independently of the underlying application. Such separation also facilitates the use of graphical user-interface generators and related tools if they are available. Because of this we recommend:

> **Separate the user interface from the rest of the application.**

USER-INTERFACE METHODS

Implementing a user interface has two stages. The first stage sets up the user interface. Here the application defines each of the windows using the appropriate user-interface components, sets the properties of the components to describe how and where they should be drawn, and defines any callbacks related to these components. All this is generally done before anything is actually drawn on the screen or the main event loop is called. The second implementation stage involves handling callbacks for the initial drawing of the various views and components as well as all user interaction.

To implement the first stage, we need to add a setup method to each of the user-interface classes. This can be combined with the constructor in the actual implementation if it is simple, but should be done separately in most cases. Such separation lets virtual methods be used if appropriate and keeps the constructor simple, separating the concerns of creating the underlying object from defining its drawing properties.

Setup is generally done hierarchically. Thus the main program calls setup on the application class; the application class then calls setup on the window class; the window class calls setup for all of its interactors and for each of the view classes it supports; the view classes call setup for any of their interactors; and each interactor class calls setup for any secondary interactors. All setup methods should be similar. A method should first define any local user-interface components that accompany the class, including setting parameters for these components and defining their callbacks. Next it should define other callbacks such as time-outs; finally it should call the setup method for each of the classes at the next level of the hierarchy.

To implement the second stage, we need to add a method to the application class that invokes the graphics library event loop and add methods to handle each of the possible callbacks. We also need to define the methods these callbacks will use to change the state or behavior of the system.

The class diagram of Figure 10-7 shows the result for the bouncing balls program. The class **BounceApp** has two methods, one to set up the application and one to enter the main event loop. The class **BounceWindow** has a setup method, a callback method to handle the timer for animation, and a callback method for each menu button. The class **BounceView**, managing the display area, has a setup method, a callback to handle a drawing request, a callback to handle the window being resized, and callbacks for each of the input events to be processed. Finally, the virtual class **BounceDialog** has been augmented

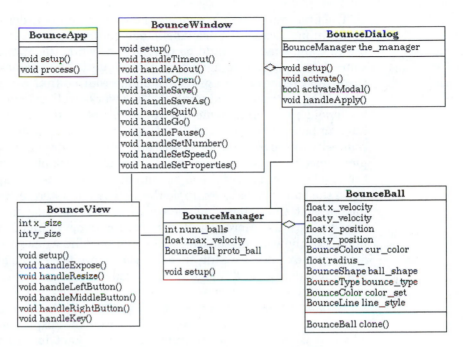

Figure 10-7 Class diagram showing user-interface methods.

with a setup method, a method to apply the changes specified to the application when the dialog is accepted, and two methods to display the dialog box.

The two dialog-box display methods differ in the ways in which the user can interact with the corresponding dialog box. The `activate` method is used when the dialog box should be displayed as an adjunct to the application and lets the user set values while the application continues to run and the user continues to interact with this and other parts of the system. All but the file dialogs use this method. This lets users have both the number dialog and property dialog boxes visible and allows them to interact with either. The file dialogs are *modal* and use the `activateModal` method. When one of these is displayed, the user must complete the interaction with this dialog box before interacting with any other component of the system.

MANAGING THE DRAWING

The above classes and methods handle setting up and managing the basic interface. What remains to be done is to design the implementation of the various views. In the bouncing balls example, this means describing the drawing area in which the balls will be displayed and animated.

The first issue in implementing the view windows is deciding when to draw them. In most cases the drawing is done either upon an expose event indicating that the window should be refreshed or when the application detects that some data has been changed by a user request. The simplest way to deal with these dual requests is to provide a single routine that redraws the whole display using the current data values. This works well as long as drawing is done fast enough that an incremental update is not needed and the data that might have to be accessed is guaranteed to be in a stable state whenever a refresh request can occur. If either of these is not true, drawing becomes more complex, since the view manager must then keep track of the state of the data on the display in order to refresh or compute an incremental update.

In the bouncing balls example the view is animated rather than static. This means that the underlying data changes in response to user requests and time-out events. Moreover, for smooth-looking animation, an incremental update of the balls on the display should be done whenever possible. Thus, to manage the drawing within this application we need to be able both to redraw the whole display and to update the display by moving each ball from its previous location to a new one.

To handle these dual requests, we need to maintain, for each ball, information about whether it is currently drawn on the display and the location at which it is drawn. Such information can be kept in two ways. In a simple application such as the one here, it is easiest to keep it within the ball structure itself. In a more complex system, it would make sense to simplify the underlying data structure by keeping all such drawing information in a separate structure that is either linked to the ball or maintained separately by the view window.

We will use this extra information associated with each ball to implement both draw requests. To update a ball's position, we undraw it at its current position and then draw it at its new position. To simplify this process and not have to worry about overlapping balls, we draw a ball by xor-ing it onto the display and undraw it by xor-ing it again at the same location. (Recall that A xor B xor A = B.) In this way undrawing can be handled by the drawing routine. The flag indicating whether the ball is drawn is set when the ball is drawn and unset when it is undrawn. If the flag is not set, then the undraw routine does nothing.

To implement a complete refresh, we first clear the window to the background color (white) and mark each ball as undrawn; then we draw each ball. This approach is necessary since we can make no assumptions regarding the state of the display when we get a expose event: it may be partially obscured, completely invisible, or fully visible. The drawing state of each individual ball thus cannot be determined. Clearing the screen lets us set the state of each ball to a known value.

To simplify the drawing process further, we can combine the update of the ball positions with the drawing. The standard approach to update is to loop through all the balls updating their positions, and then loop through them all

```
BounceManager::nextFrame()
{
    Foreach Ball b
        b->undraw();          // undraw at current position
        b->update();          // compute new position
        b->draw();            // draw at new position
    }
}
```

Figure 10-8 Psuedocode for updating ball positions.

again and redraw them on the display. Because our application is simple, we can combine these two into one loop, as in Figure 10-8, and thus avoid having to store the previous position of each ball. Note that for a more complex application, it is probably better to separate the drawing and the update for logical simplicity than to worry about the extra overhead of maintaining the old drawing information.

The next design issue to consider is how to combine the data to be displayed with the view window in which the display should appear. One approach here is to put the view in charge of drawing the display. Here the view simply requests data from the document and puts up the display. This approach works if the information to be displayed is quite simple, say a string or simple set of items, and the document is not structured. However, in most cases this approach overcomplicates the design by making the view class too dependent on the document class, since the view class must know the structure of the document and all the information that is relevant to the display.

A better approach is to have the document display itself through a drawing context. A drawing context is a new class created by the view as a mediator between the view and the data. It holds any information required from the view to do the drawing. It provides high-level methods that the document or data class can call to create the output, thus encapsulating the information needed from the document for drawing. In addition, it is responsible for doing the low-level drawing. For example, in the bouncing balls application, when the view is to draw a ball, it actually passes the **BounceBall** method `draw` a drawing-context object. The ball object can then tell the context object its shape, color, and other properties, and then tell it to draw at the appropriate location. Note that the structure and contents of the document (in this case the set of balls) are hidden from both the view and the drawing context: the context provides a high-level graphics abstraction to the document, hiding the low-level graphical details.

In a simple application, the view object itself can act as the context. However, it is generally better to create a new drawing context class and to use an object of this class. This provides a separation of the view class into managing the view and all the details involved in low-level drawing and makes it easier to change drawing packages or to port from one system to another. In the bouncing balls example, we add the **BounceDrawContext** class with methods to set the line style, color, and shape, to draw the current shape at a given location with a given size, and to clear the window.

Using a separate drawing context can also facilitate the implementation of multiple views. Here an abstract drawing-context object is defined with a generic interface that the document objects use for drawing. Each different type of view is represented by a separate drawing context class that is a subclass of the generic class. This means that the document classes need know and support only a single drawing interface for all the views. Moreover, new views can be added and existing views modified with minimal change to the rest of the applications.

Figure 10-9 shows the updated design for bouncing balls embodying most of the design decisions discussed above. The markUndraw method of **Bounce-Ball**, indicating that the ball is not currently drawn, is called when the window is cleared for redraw. The nextFrame, getSize, and redraw methods in **Bounce-View** process the various events the view window needs to handle. For example, the expose callback invokes getSize and nextFrame when the window is first created and invokes redraw at any other time, while the resize callback calls getSize and redraw. The redraw and nextFrame methods invoke the corresponding methods in the manager with the addition of the context and the boundaries as needed.

MANAGING THE DIALOG BOXES

Dialog boxes are a convenient way for a graphical application to input a set of related parameters: they provide an organized grouping of user-interface components with which the user can interact. Such interaction is done either modally, when the dialog box essentially takes over the application, or non-modally, when dialog-box input can occur at any time during the run of the application. In either case, a dialog box must be able to set itself up, display itself, handle interactions, and propagate the input back into the application.

The most convenient way to implement dialog boxes within an application is to view each dialog box as a class, as previously outlined, and to create a common superclass for these classes that provides any common functionality and ties the dialog boxes to the application. To facilitate such a tie-in the bouncing balls example, the superclass **BounceDialog** contains a reference to the **BounceManager** object, as shown in Figure 10-6. It also contains other common elements that depend on the underlying implementation. In a Motif-based application, the superclass would contain the dialog widget; in a MFC-based application, it would either contain a reference to a **CDialog** widget or would itself be a subclass of **CDialog**.

A dialog box can be set up in a variety of ways. In MFC, this is typically done by creating an appropriate resource file using a resource editor that lets

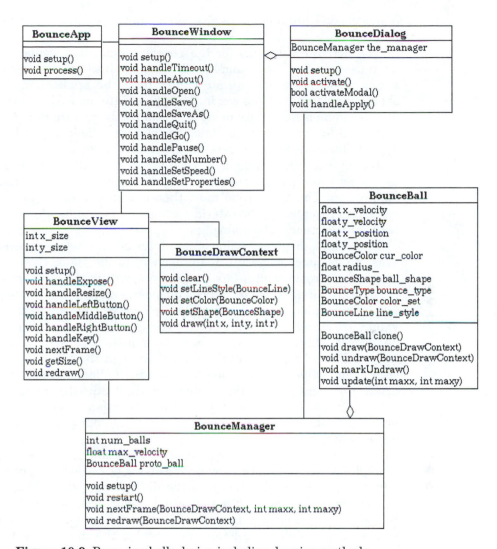

Figure 10-9 Bouncing balls design including drawing methods.

you see the dialog box as you construct it. A similar technique can be used with Motif using the user-interface language (UIL), though the tools that implement it are still quite hard to use and the results are often difficult to integrate into the application; thus most nontrivial Motif dialog boxes are still made using hand layout with a form widget. (Motif provides several standard dialog boxes to handle the simple cases in which a single value is being input or a simple message is being displayed.) The actual implementation of the dialog box should generally be done as part of the constructors for the individual dialog classes, although individual setup methods can be used if the dialog box is complex.

The activate callbacks for the generic dialog box display the dialog box upon user request. They should first set the values associated with the components by querying appropriate values from the application data, and then should display the dialog box in the appropriate mode. The former is handled by the common superclass using a virtual method, such as `setupValues`, that is defined by the individual dialog-box classes. The latter action is done with appropriate calls to the underlying graphics library.

Dialog interaction is the most complex part of dialog processing. In general, each user-interface component of the dialog box can make callbacks to the application. The application must then maintain and handle changes in the values represented by the interface components and handle the overall acceptance or rejection of the dialog box.

Each value displayed using a user-interface component needs to be stored. This can be done using explicit storage within the dialog class or, if values can be accessed from the interface components, within the components. The latter is generally preferable since the components store the value anyway and the result is simpler. Most dialog callbacks involve changes to the values. If the values are stored in the components, these callbacks involve no action and can be ignored. If the values are to be used immediately (without the user accepting the dialog box) or if multiple components in the dialog are related in that setting one value changes another, then the application needs to define appropriate handlers for the intermediate values. Such handlers should get the value from the component and use it to call action routines in the application and to set the values of other user-interface components of the display as appropriate.

The handlers that are almost always necessary are those to cancel, accept, or apply (accept without removing the dialog box) the dialog box. These can be handled by a general callback in the dialog superclass along with a virtual method implemented by the individual dialog classes. The top-level method removes the dialog box from the display if it is accepted or canceled and returns a flag indicating accept or cancel if the dialog box was modal. The method calls a virtual method such as `handleApply` if the dialog box is accepted or applied. This method, implemented for each individual dialog class, gets the values associated with the dialog components either from the components or from the class object and makes appropriate calls to application objects to effect the changes.

For the bouncing balls example, these considerations yield the design shown in Figure 10-10. The class **UIC** here represents a user-interface component. For Motif, this would be a widget or a C++ wrapper around a widget; for MFC, it would be an appropriate subclass of **CWindow**. We have also indicated a single callback method in **BounceDialog**, `dialogCallback`, that handles all dialog interaction. Whether or not this is feasible depends on the underlying

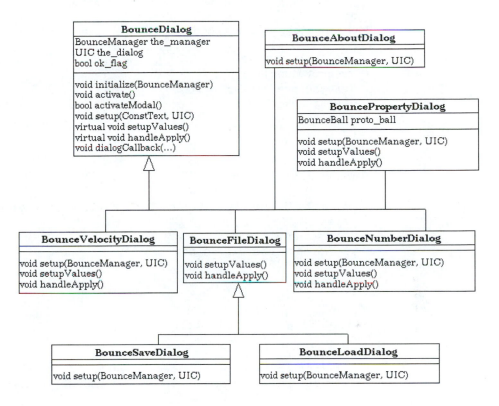

Figure 10-10 Design for managing bouncing balls dialog boxes.

graphics package and on the needs of the various dialog boxes. Also, the setup methods in all cases can be implemented using the various constructors.

The superclass methods in this case are relatively simple. Consider first the pseudocode for a modal dialog at the top of Figure 10-11. This routine assumes that the ok_flag is set to TRUE in the callback routine if the dialog box is accepted. The method for non-modal activation is similar, as seen in the middle of the figure. Here the if statement checks if the dialog has previously been activated and if so just pops it up on the display. Otherwise the dialog values are reset and the dialog is created.

The basic action of the callback method is shown at the bottom of Figure 10-11. The first conditional sets ok_flag if the dialog is modal. The second uses the virtual method handleApply to change the application data. The third removes the dialog box when required.

To see how the individual dialog boxes implement the virtual methods here, we consider the number dialog. Here we assume that two methods have been defined for **BounceManager**:

```
int BounceManager::getNumBalls() const
void BounceManager::setNumBalls(int)
```

```
Bool
BounceDialog::activateModal()
{
    ok_flag = FALSE
    setupValues()
    create the dialog modally
    return ok_flag
}


void
BounceDialog::activate()
{
    if (the dialog is activated) raise it on the display
    else
        setupValues()
        create the dialog non-modally
}


void
BounceDialog::dialogCallback(...)
{
    if (reason == ACCEPT) ok_flag = TRUE
    if (reason == ACCEPT || reason == APPLY) handleApply()
    if (reason == ACCEPT || reason == CANCEL) remove the dialog
}
```

Figure 10-11 Pseudocode for managing dialogs.

so that the dialog box can access and set the appropriate value. Then the set-upValues method and the handleApply method are implemented as shown in Figure 10-12. The final call in handleApply causes the manager actually to create or remove balls as needed.

The other dialog boxes are handled similarly. Both file dialogs are used to set the file name field of the manager and hence have common setupValues and handleApply methods.

IMPLEMENTING THE USER INTERFACE

A program with a graphical user interface is more complex than a non-graphical system. The user interface itself contributes to this complexity in various ways. At the same time, such applications give the programmer an opportunity for early feedback and gratification. The key to controlling the overall

```
void
BounceNumberDialog::setupValues()
{
    int n = the_manager->getNumBalls()
    assign n to the scale component of the dialog box
}


void
BounceNumberDialog::handleApply()
{
    int n = the value of the scale component of the dialog box
    ensure n is valid if this isn't done by the component
    the_manager->setNumBalls(n)
    the_manager->setup()
}
```

Figure 10-12 Pseudocode for number dialog methods.

complexity, achieving a high-quality interface, and gaining the potential benefits is to organize the implementation correctly.

Implementation Strategy

Graphical user interfaces themselves are complex and difficult to evaluate,
especially from a paper design; this can be seen in the large number of systems, both freeware and commercial, with poor user interfaces. One of the
goals of an implementation strategy should be to provide a framework in
which the user interface can be tested, evaluated, and changed early in the
development cycle, when such changes are still reasonably inexpensive and
easy. And because the user interface can affect how the rest of the application
should be implemented, the bulk of the interface should be understood as
early as possible.

The complexity of a graphical user interface is also reflected in the resultant code. In many applications, the code to manage the interface is a large
fraction (often 50% or more) of the overall system. Moreover, this code involves
implicit control flow through callbacks and possibly unanticipated ordering of
calls and events. Making this code work is a substantial part of the programming task. Thus one's overall implementation strategy should be geared to
ensuring that the user interface is well debugged and tested.

Testing a graphical user interface, however, is difficult. It is generally
impossible to create simple driver programs or input files to test the interface.
Instead, the programmer must actually interact with the interface in each
potential test. (Some commercial tools facilitate such testing, but they are not
generally available or widely used.) The overall implementation strategy

should facilitate interface testing by making the interface available early on to the programmer and others.

Taking all this into account, the best implementation strategy for a graphical application is first to build the user interface and then to develop the application around this interface. The initial user interface can be defined by implementing the setup methods in the various interface classes and providing dummy callbacks for all or most of the available actions. Such an implementation gives the programmer an application that exhibits the appropriate user interface, though it may have little functionality, and lets the programmer begin evaluating the aesthetics and overall feel of the interface. Moreover, it provides a simple framework in which the rest of the application can be tested, ensuring that the user interface is available to drive the testing of new code as it becomes available. Thus we recommend:

> **Develop graphical applications incrementally.**

In the bouncing balls example, one first constructs a very simple skeleton application. This implementation starts with the class **BounceApp** in which the setup and process methods could be readily coded. The implementation also includes an initial implementation of the class **BounceWindow**, providing a setup method with no subcomponents, and dummy routines to handle the various top-level callbacks such as the pull-down menu buttons. Most of these do nothing or print a diagnostic, but the Quit button is coded actually to exit the application. The final component of the implementation is a simple main program that creates a **BounceApp** object and then calls its setup and process methods. The result of this would be a program that creates a top-level window with the appropriate menu options. This program should actually be compiled and run at this point to offer the programmer a feel for the interface.

This program can then be extended by providing an initial implementation of the **BounceView** class, again including a setup method and dummy callbacks for keyboard and mouse interaction. This is integrated into the initial implementation by having the setup method of **BounceWindow** create or at least set up the appropriate view. Again the result is tested and the interface evaluated. Letting the programmer start with a simple working program and then incrementally add functionality not only provides a framework for testing the added functionality, but also offers the programmer the significant gratification of having a system that actually runs and does something on the display.

The next incremental step in the implementation is to add a basic **Bounce-Manager** class along with a **BounceBall** class. The manager-class implementation provides facilities for creating and managing the balls, including updating them. The drawing functionality, however, is omitted, and is integrated into the working skeleton by adding the appropriate setup calls to create and initialize the manager. The resultant application can then be tested.

Once a core implementation has been achieved, the programmer should proceed by implementing the various callbacks, doing a few at a time so that the result can be tested and modified as needed. As the callbacks are added, further functionality in the view, draw context, and document classes may need to be written and, moreover, all existing classes should be retested.

The key callbacks in the bouncing balls application involve starting and stopping the animation and handling time-out events. These should be added first to get a sense of how the application and the interface work. The callback for the *Go* button would request time-out events and a time-out callback handler would be created to call the `nextFrame` method of **BounceView**, which would in turn call the `nextFrame` method of **BounceManager**. The resultant application can be tested to ensure that the balls move, using either print statements or the debugger.

After this version of the system works, it is time to add the code for drawing balls. This is done by implementing the **BounceDrawContext** class and adding the appropriate calls to create it and use it for drawing and undrawing balls and for clearing the display. Once this code is tested, the programmer has a basic view of the overall system. The program would show the balls in action and would let the programmer modify parameters such as the default speed, ball size, or animation interval. This is enough to test the non-interface code in the application and get a feel for the overall program interface.

The remaining callbacks should then be added in the order of their importance and complexity. The simplest callbacks to implement involve mouse and button input. The left and middle buttons change the number of balls. Here we would add two methods, `getNumBalls` and `setNumBalls`, to the class **BounceManager**. The callback handlers here would use these to change the number of balls and then call `BounceManager::setup` to effect the change. The callback handlers for the right button and the key "R" simply call the `restart` method of **BounceManager**, while the callback handler for the key "N" calls the `nextFrame` method of the class. The resultant implementation can be tested to see what happens as new balls are added or removed.

The next step in the implementation is to add the dialog boxes one at a time. We can start with the class **BounceNumberDialog** since we already have a method to change the number of balls. Here we implement both the generic **BounceDialog** class and the specific **BounceNumberDialog** implementation and test the result. Once this is done, we continue with the remaining dialogs that are invoked directly from the menus. Here we add methods to **BounceManager** and **BounceBall** to handle the callbacks. Finally, we implement code to save and restore the bounce parameters along with the save and load dialog boxes to provide the last bit of specified functionality.

The complete code for the bouncing balls application for UNIX/Motif and for Windows/MFC is available from the web site for this text (`http://www.cs.brown.edu/people/spr/designbook`).

SUMMARY

Several steps are involved in designing an application with a graphical user interface, including:

- Start by sketching the interface. Both individual and storyboard pictures of the interface in action are helpful in understanding what the interface will look like and how it will operate.

- Continue by enumerating all the potential user actions and their effects on the system. This includes all the buttons as well as any keyboard or mouse input the system will accept. Determine what input is meaningless as well as what is meaningful.

- Expand this by enumerating any other events that the system should deal with, such as time-outs or file-based notifications.

- Evaluate the interface for both appearance and usability.

- Develop a set of top-level classes reflecting the application-window-view-document breakdown outlined in the previous chapter. Include classes for each of the proposed dialog boxes in the interface. Attempt to keep the user interface as separate as possible from the rest of the application.

- Add callbacks for each of the user actions and system events to the appropriate classes in the design.

- Add methods to handle the actual drawing of the view to the appropriate classes. Add further classes, for example a drawing-context class, as needed.

- Add the methods needed to maintain and manage the various dialog boxes both to the window class and to the dialog box classes.

The interface should be implemented incrementally. A basic core system that displays the interface but does no actions should be implemented first. Then the various callbacks, drawing methods, and dialog boxes can be added one or a few at a time. This allows the system to be tested incrementally, and lets the programmer ensure that the interface is appropriate and easy to use. The actual details of the implementation vary depending on the framework being used and the tools available to assist the programmer.

EXERCISES

10.1 Design and evaluate a user interface for the knight's-tour application.

10.2 Describe the classes that would be required in a graphical knight's-tour program. Show how the user interface is separated from the remainder of the application. Include descriptions of all callbacks and the methods needed to implement them.

10.3 Extend the bouncing balls program so that balls leave finite tails as they move.

10.4 Extend the bouncing balls program so that balls bounce off each other and change properties when they do so.

10.5 Implement a graphical tic-tac-toe program in which the computer plays against the user.

10.6 Implement a graphical version of the eight-queens problem in Exercise 2.2.

10.7 The Logo language was originally designed for introducing elementary school children to computers. It is a simple language that features a graphical interface. Design and implement an environment for running Logo programs. At the minimum, your environment should handle parsing and interpreting Logo code, a drawing area to show Logo output, and an appropriate user interface for loading and running programs.

10.8 Design and implement a program for designing patchwork quilts. The program should allow the user to specify a square pattern (showing the design and colors to be used) and should then show what the resultant quilt will look like.

10.9 Design and implement a program that plays pool. The program should allow balls to be positioned on the table and should provide some means for the user to indicate how the cue ball is to be aimed and shot. It should provide a dynamic graphical view of the pool table and simulate the physics of the pool table as much as possible. The program should do scoring and support both one- and two-person games.

Chapter 11

User-Interface Design

The utility of real applications depends strongly on the quality of the interface. A good user interface can make an otherwise mediocre program popular; a poor one can make even the best program fail. As indicated in previous chapters, designing a graphical user interface is a complex and difficult task. In this chapter we give a set of principles, culled from experience and the literature, that should guide the designer toward a better interface.

HUMAN FACTORS

Distinguishing a great user interface from a poor one is easy. Distinguishing a good user interface from a slightly better one is much more difficult. Understanding what makes a good interface involves understanding how the user interacts with the system and the system with the user. This, in turn, requires us to understand how people use computer software.

Human factors is the study of how people use and react to systems in general. Also called *ergonomics* or *human engineering*, it covers a broad range of issues in a broad range of systems. Chairs are ergonomically designed to make their users more comfortable and productive; keyboards are designed to minimize repetitive stress injuries; VCRs are designed to be used by children and to be hopelessly confusing to adults. Computer software, our primary concern here, can be designed to make the user want to use a given program. It can also be designed to ensure that the user will do anything possible to avoid using the program.

Studying the human factors of computer software involves addressing both its input and its output. Input considerations indicate how much the user must learn to use the system, how much work the user must do to achieve a given goal, and how prone to error the system is. Output considerations tell us how good the system looks, how well the user can understand what it is doing, and whether the user can understand how to use it from what it displays.

A software designer must understand human factors in order to understand the basic principles of user-interface design. Human factors tells the software designer what works in an interface and what doesn't. It also indicates why some things work better than others and suggests reasonable alternatives when user-interface problems arise. In general, human factors provide the knowledge base for the design and evaluation of user interfaces.

Human factors in computer software has been an issue for most of its history. Originally concentrating on the complexity and logic of command-line interfaces, today it is more concerned with the graphical presentation and the different ways the user can interact with the application. The guidelines for a good user interface that have been developed over time are based on experience with many different systems, user reactions, experimental studies of what works and what doesn't, and the judgment of experts in psychology, industrial and graphic design, art, and other related fields.

The basic tenet of human factors in user-interface design is to work from the user's point of view. With the power and flexibility of today's computers and software, it is much easier to adapt the software to the user than to make the user adapt to the software. Software should be designed with the user in mind from day zero. Satisfying the user's needs should be the primary goal of the software designer. All user-interface design decisions should revolve around what is best for the user. Hence:

> **Put the user first.**

USER-INTERFACE PROBLEMS

It is not surprising that the reasons user interfaces fail lie mainly in situations that are difficult or toilsome for the user. A good understanding of how to design a friendly user interface starts with understanding what should not be done. We thus begin by considering some of the problems with current user interfaces.

Lack of Conventions

Today's users have become accustomed to the convention that all programs on a machine operate in a similar fashion, so that a user who knows how to use one program can use another without too much effort. This has been one of the keys to the Macintosh's success: almost all its applications follow a simple set of conventions.

Programs that do not follow standard conventions are more difficult to use. On a Windows box, the interfaces provided by Windows 3.X are quite different from those provided by Windows 95. On a UNIX box, the problem is even worse: user-interface standards were slow in coming to UNIX so that today there are multiple standards. A UNIX user on a Sun workstation, for example, must be prepared to use Motif-style interfaces (*FrameMaker*), Openlook interfaces (*calendar manager*), and windows-style interfaces (*Netscape*). Moving among these and coping with all the different conventions is both difficult and confusing.

The lack of conventions can also occur within an application. Applications typically have different states and different modes the user can enter, and when these use different conventions, the user is sure to get confused. For example, in Windows, icons and buttons often look alike. However, icons require a double click to activate while buttons want only a single click. The lack of consistency leads one to double-click on buttons, typically invoking multiple instances of what is wanted.

Another area in which conventions have generally been lacking is in text editing. Each user has his or her favorite among the multitude of text editors available, generally finding it difficult to use any other editor. However, text editing is frequently necessary within applications, whether in user input from a shell or in a text widget in a dialog box. Users expect the same conventions here as in their favorite editor, and often make errors or become confused when the local editing conventions differ.

Overly Complex Displays

A growing problem with today's interfaces is the complexity of their displays. As applications become more powerful and acquire more and more options, programmers have attempted to make the various options more convenient to use by placing more and more icons and buttons on the screen. The default layout of Microsoft *Word* for Windows shown in Figure 11-1, has over 50 icon buttons and over 150 menu items, while Adobe *FrameMaker* includes about 20 widget buttons and 120 menu items. Some CAD/CAM programs have hundreds of displayed buttons. The presence of too many windows also makes for clutter. *FrameMaker*, for example, typically involves a combination of four or five different windows for editing just one document, while it is not uncommon to have ten or more windows open in Microsoft's *Visual Studio* or Sun's *Workshop* in order to debug a system.

Complex interfaces are not necessarily bad. Many of these programs have complex interfaces because the tasks they perform are complex. However, when the interface contains too many buttons or too many windows, users are often at a loss to find the one relevant to a particular task, especially if they are at all unfamiliar with the system. This is typically aggravated by the small size and abstraction of the icons mandated by placing lots of buttons in a small screen space. An interface that puts the user first should provide the necessary functionality with a minimum of clutter, enabling the user to see what is happening, readily locate any relevant information in the display, and find and activate commands as simply as possible.

Over-complex and disorganized menus induce a related problem. The user typically wants to find an option or command with a minimum of effort and searching. Menus with lots of different options make this difficult. Menus in which the names are misleading or the organization inappropriate only make

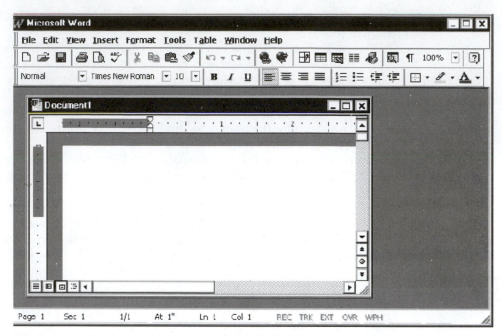

Figure 11-1 Default display for Microsoft Word.

things worse. It is almost impossible, for example, to figure out how to delete an item from one's bookmark list in *Netscape*. Moreover, the Go menu in both *Netscape* and *Internet Explorer* does not have a button or option to go to a specific site. (It's on the File menu.)

A similar problem arises when arcane keyboard sequences are used to enter commands. While the existence of hundreds of different escape or control character sequences can help the sophisticated user, it can also make the system quite daunting, not to mention confusing and error-prone.

Lack of Elegance

A more difficult problem to pin down in a user interface is a lack of technical elegance. This is most often felt when the application fails to do what one might reasonably expect it to do: the user simply feels it is doing something "the wrong way." For example, *FrameMaker* provides frames that float to the top of the next page or column, but floating tables can only float in place. In order to make a table float to the top of a page, the user must embed it in a frame and float the frame appropriately — a bothersome solution and far from elegant. Another example comes in selecting colors. Until its most recent version, *FrameMaker* forced one to define a new color by setting values either for red, green and blue; for cyan, magenta, yellow and black; or for hue, light and saturation, even though what the user usually wanted was to define a color by name.

Lack of elegance occurs for a variety of reasons. The programmer may not anticipate correctly how the software will be used and does not accommodate what end up being common situations. The programmer also may not understand what the user wants. In the case of colors, the original programmers may have assumed sophisticated users who would want to define colors very precisely, while in actuality, many users didn't understand any of the color models and just wanted to make something brown. Alternatively, the programmer might decide that implementing something "correctly" is too difficult with the current program design and thus put the burden on the user, rather than putting the user first and redesigning the application.

Intolerance to Error

Users are not perfect and computers generally believe in garbage in, garbage out; thus users occasionally do something unexpected or incorrect and the program responds accordingly. One of the worst aspects of many user interfaces is that they do exactly what the user tells them to and do not provide a way to correct mistakes.

Systems that put the user first must be able to deal with error in a user-friendly manner. Error here includes both user mistakes and internal errors such as a full disk. Reasonable error processing means not letting users do something stupid, or at least double-checking with the user before doing so, letting users recover gracefully from their mistakes, and not letting users lose work if at all possible.

Error-handling facilities, both good and bad, are best seen in editors, since these are where users spend most of their time and where error handling is most crucial. Most editors these days make frequent automatic backups of users' work for use in case of a system or editor crash. Most editors have some sort of undo facility. A one-level undo, as *FrameMaker* offers, for example, is useful but not always helpful. Fairly often one mistakenly double-clicks with the middle mouse button rather than the left. While the intent here was to select a word, the effect is to insert the contents of the cut buffer into the document twice. A single-level undo does not let the user recover from the damage so wrought. Much better is a multilevel or even infinite undo that lets the user revert over a large number of mistakes.

Bad Documentation

A final problem with user interfaces is second-rate documentation. This increases the difficulty of understanding how to use the application effectively and only leads to more problems with incorrect input, confusing layouts and buttons, and complex key sequences. A user interface is complete only when it is fully and accurately documented.

Documentation of the interface can take a variety of forms. It can include manuals, both off-line and on-line, explaining the purpose of each command and giving examples of how and when to use them. It can include on-line help information to give rapid answers to problems or questions. It can also include accurate and meaningful error messages indicating not only what went wrong but also how to fix it, and helpful labels on the menus and buttons.

Documentation must be geared to the user, not the programmer. Several types of documentation may be appropriate for a given interface. One type should give the user an overview of the application, how it is meant to be used, and what it can and can't do. This type generally takes the form of a tutorial or user's manual. Another type provides detailed and complete information on the behavior of each command under all possible circumstances, noting potential errors that might arise and their reasons. This is useful when the user has specific or detailed questions or when an error arises that the user does not understand, and is generally done in a reference manual. On-line documentation can include both types of manuals suitably cross-referenced, and should also include likely output messages describing what the system is doing and any errors that arise. Care should be taken to phrase these messages from the user's point of view, not the program's: a message such as *Error 123e56 occurred*" does not help the user in the least.

DESIGN GUIDELINES

Knowing about the pitfalls in user-interface design is the first step in avoiding them in a new interface. A second step involves following a set of design guidelines or principles. In this section we consider a set of such criteria.

Common Sense

The first guideline is that the interface should follow common sense. This means that the interface should interact with users in natural ways that meet their expectations. This is sometimes called the "principle of least astonishment": the interface should surprise the user as little as possible.

The prototype common-sense interface was included by Xerox Palo Alto Research Center (PARC) in many of its software systems. This facility, called *DWIM* for "do what I mean," attempted to determine what the user was trying to do when an error occurred and then to correct the input to achieve the desired result, for example by fixing spelling errors. This approach is a good idea in principle, but is hard to implement well in practice, especially in a general setting such as most interfaces provide. A current approach to this is found in Microsoft *Office '97*: the help facility keeps track of what the user is doing and then either suggests better ways of accomplishing the task or points the user to relevant on-line manual pages.

It is unreasonable to expect anything this sophisticated in a simple application. In designing a simple user interface, however, various things can make the interface meet the users' expectations. These include ensuring that commands do the logical thing, that command and menu names are well defined and proper for their context, and that anything users try to do, whether clicking on a box or attempting to manipulate the display directly, does what they would naturally expect. Another way to look at this is that the program should converse with the user: it should tell her, in a meaningful way, what it is doing, and she should tell it what it should be doing. Finally, clear and meaningful status and error messages from the application will help the user better understand the application and how it works.

Consistency

A second design guideline the interface designer should strive for is consistency. An application should be consistent both with the standards of its operating environment and with itself.

Consistency among the application and other applications is achieved by understanding and following the existing user-interface standards for the underlying machine. This means using the standard menus and windowing in a standard way, using standard menu and button names and locations, using standard dialog boxes, and so forth. It means understanding the basic principles these applications follow and then using them in your interface.

Consistency within an application is probably more difficult to achieve. Here consistency means doing things in the same way throughout the application. Thus colors should always have the same meanings, menus should be organized in a single way and displayed consistently, popup menus should pop up at a consistent location relative to the current pointer, and function keys and key sequences should have common meanings in all aspects of the application. Consistency implies that common commands can be invoked at any time, even in the middle of doing something else. More than anything else, it means that the program offers the user a consistent look and feel.

One way to achieve consistency while still keeping the interface relatively simple is through the use of *generic commands*: commands that can be applied to a variety of different objects to achieve a variety of different results. *FrameMaker* and other editors, for example, provide generic `Cut`, `Copy` and `Paste` commands that work on text, graphic objects, figures, and tables. The file interface provided by the Macintosh or Windows has a generic command to "open" a file that can be used to display the file's contents, to create a new viewer for a directory, or to run an application, all depending on the type of item selected.

While consistency is good and relatively easy to check, one should not carry it too far. Consistency should be constrained by common sense and by doing what the user expects. The Macintosh file interface is a clear example of a logical but inconsistent interface. Here dragging a file icon from one folder to another location is interpreted as a command to move the file, placing it in the new location and removing it from its original location, and is used to move files to the trash can to delete them. However, consider what happens when you move a file to a printer icon to be printed. Consistency would dictate that the file be printed and removed from the system, but this is not what the user would want or expect under most circumstances. Instead, moving the file to a printer icon is handled as common sense would prefer: it is viewed as just copying the file, with the original file remaining where it was.

Feedback

One of the easiest ways an interface can help the user feel more comfortable is through feedback. The application should keep the user informed of what it is doing. Users typically need to know if the actions they requested were accepted by the system. They need to understand what the system is doing if it does not respond immediately. They need to understand what the system expects and what it doesn't. Essentially, they want to converse with the system and they want the system to hold up its end of the conversation.

The application gives various sorts of feedback. *Display feedback* involves echoing and tracking the user's commands and movements. This includes ensuring that the pointer moves immediately (not difficult these days, but a serious problem ten years ago with slower machines), echoing typed characters immediately, showing graphics as they are resized or moved, and generally updating the display after some change is made. In general, the system should have response times that meet user expectations. Psychological studies have shown that this means commands should respond to the user in less than one second and keyboard echoing should occur in less than one hundred milliseconds.

Sequential feedback involves walking the user through a sequence of commands and subcommands to get the information necessary for an appropriate action. Microsoft applications often do this nicely by using a sequence of dialog boxes with Next and Back buttons to illustrate that the user is making a sequence of decisions, as seen in Figure 11-2. These boxes have the added advantage of letting the user abort the process or go back to previous boxes at any point. The interface provided by *Macintax* and *TurboTax* for filling in tax information is similar.

Finally, in *functional feedback* the application tells the user what it is doing. In a direct manipulation environment this is done in the problem domain by showing the actual objects being manipulated. For example, in the Macintosh and Windows file browsers, the user moves the file icons around and their current positions reflect their current file-system locations. Functional feedback in the control domain gives the user information on what the program thinks it is doing. A control panel telling the current color or fill style

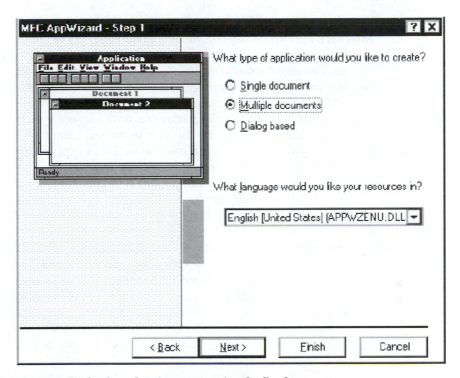

Figure 11-2 Dialog box showing sequencing feedback.

by showing the actual color or fill pattern provides such feedback. Other functional feedback can be done by displaying messages to the user or by giving the cursor different shapes and colors.

While feedback is generally beneficial, it can get in the way of the application and become annoying if not done correctly. Most feedback, unless it involves errors or requires immediate attention from the user, should be unobtrusive. No action should be required of the user to get or view the feedback, and the feedback should not obscure any portion of the display the user might need to see. The feedback should be easy to view but should not draw attention to itself, and should not require a substantial change in the user's current focus. The use of different cursor shapes to provide information, for example an hourglass or watch to say the program is busy, satisfies all of these criteria. A message window such as that in *Netscape* or *Internet Explorer* satisfies most of the criteria and can be quite effective as well.

Design for Error

Since many user interfaces fall short when dealing with user errors, it is only natural that one of the criteria for a good user interface is that it is designed to handle errors. This means both minimizing the chances the user will make mistakes and providing reasonable error recovery when the user does err.

The first rule an interface should follow is not to let users clobber themselves. The interface should not display, or at least should display as inactive, buttons that are not meaningful in the current context. Most UNIX, Windows, and Macintosh applications gray out currently inappropriate menu buttons to tell the user the command cannot currently be applied. The interface should also make dangerous actions difficult to accomplish or easy to undo. For example, most applications ask the user to confirm a quit action if the current file is not saved. Deleted files on the Macintosh and Windows are not actually deleted, but are moved to a temporary directory for later deletion, thereby letting the delete be easily undone. In general, any action that can result in loss of the user's work either should be easily undoable or should be confirmed with the user.

A second rule in designing for error is to avoid unexpected side effects. The program should do what the user asks, no more and no less. Printing a file should not delete the file, even if the user requests printing by "moving" the file icon to the printer icon. Saving within an editor should save the current file but should leave everything related to the user's current editing state alone. *FrameMaker*, for example, violates this last rule by having the save operation change the page currently being displayed if the current cursor is not on that page.

A third rule is to design the interface carefully to minimize potential errors. The system should make it difficult to misselect a menu item; barring this, it should be arranged so that if the user misses a common menu button and accidentally selects the one above or below it, nothing untoward happens. This can be accomplished by ordering the menu buttons suitably and inserting lines or spaces between critical buttons. Another way to minimize error is to ensure that command names are meaningful and unambiguous. Finally, as we noted, the system should ask for confirmation where appropriate.

However careful the designer is to reduce user error, errors will occur. The application must thus also be designed for error recovery. The first step here is to let mistakes be corrected readily through an undo facility. As noted, a multilevel undo is much better than a single-level undo, but anything is better than nothing. Another way to address user mistakes is to let commands be aborted. This is easy in sequential commands requiring one or more dialog boxes to obtain inputs: here the dialog box should provide a `Cancel` or `Abort` button to end the command but take no action. It is more difficult for commands that do not require user input. Long-running commands here, however, should let the user abort the command and return to a reasonable state. *Netscape* and *Internet Explorer*, for example, let the user stop or abort a download and go back to the previous page.

Another mechanism helpful in error recovery and beneficial in other ways as well is a history mechanism whereby the program records user commands as they are executed. This lets users understand how they got to a certain point, providing appropriate feedback. Such a mechanism can be used, as in the various UNIX shells, to let the user reexecute a previous command, possibly with slightly different arguments: users can go back to a previous command, edit it, and then reissue it. History mechanisms are also used in *emacs*, *FrameMaker*, and other editors to let the user capture a set of commands as a macro and then issue the whole command set by using a simple key or button sequence.

Types of Users

Systems typically need to handle several types of users. Users first attempting to use a system are considered novices: they are generally unfamiliar with the system, know none of the more detailed commands, and need to learn how to use the system effectively. As users become more familiar with the system, they become intermediate users whose primary concern is to make better and more effective use of the software. Eventually, they graduate to being experienced or expert users of the system for whom efficiency of use becomes a primary issue.

One of the goals of a user interface should be to accommodate users at all levels. It is a classic misconception that the primary goal of a user interface is to help the novice. While an interface that is good for the novice might draw people to try the system, novice users do not remain novices forever. If the interface cannot adapt to users' changing needs as they become more experienced, the system will fall out of favor and the interface will have failed.

To handle novice users, the interface should concentrate on simplicity and ease of learning. It should provide prompting and help facilities to lead the inexperienced user through complex interactions. Most facilities, at least in their simplest form, should be obvious and easy to use. The interface should hide as much system complexity as possible and its error messages should make sense and give suggestions to the user. It should attempt to minimize the amount of memorization needed to use the system. Most Macintosh applications, for example, have a standard, simple interface that lets the user do most operations using obvious menu buttons and mouse selection, while at the same time providing popup help information.

To satisfy intermediate users, the system should provide additional facilities to simplify its use and give access to more sophisticated features. Intermediate users want to minimize the amount of work necessary to use the system. This means avoiding hand motion between the keyboard and the mouse and avoiding excessive mouse movement. The system can help here through the use of keyboard accelerators and such facilities as automatic completion of file and command names. Again, most Macintosh applications attempt to provide this level of functionality as well, offering at least keyboard accelerators for most of the common menu commands.

Experienced users are most interested in efficiency of use of the system. Here the application interface can provide a tailorable interface to adapt the system to the user's needs. This can entail extensibility through either macros or a programming interface. For example, both *emacs* with its Lisp derivative and Microsoft *Word* with its scripting language provide simple macros and programmable extensions. Sophisticated users also like to tailor the interface to look and feel like other applications they know, in order to increase efficiency even more. Tailorability here can involve the ability to define keyboard mappings (as in *emacs*), the ability to define or customize buttons on the display (as in *Netscape* or *Internet Explorer*), and the ability to change presentation properties such as colors, fonts, and window layouts.

Evaluation

All these guidelines do the designer or programmer no good unless they are applied and the user interface is checked and double-checked. Evaluating a user-interface design is similar to evaluating a program design in being an ongoing process. Just as the programmer should always be attempting to improve the program design, the user-interface designer should be attempting to develop a better user interface. The user interface should be evaluated while it is still a paper design, with prototypes the designer and eventual users can play to get a feel for how it will look and react, and with the actual system once it is working.

While many things can be evaluated (for example, adherence to each of the design guidelines), most are difficult to measure. Some aspects that are easier to quantify, however, can serve as a basis for a more detailed evaluation or redesign. Two of these involve performance: the time it takes to learn how to use the interface and the speed at which the interface can be used for a standard set of common tasks. Both of these can be measured with either new or experienced users. A third, related item is how well the interface is retained over time; this can be measured in terms of how long a user takes to relearn the interface after being away from it for a while. A fourth quantitative measure is the error rate when using the interface, since errors can indicate that the interface is hard to understand, that it is not designed to minimize error, or even that users enjoy the system's error-recovery features so much that they just like to play.

Qualitative measures of the user interface are more difficult to evaluate, and the best that can be done is to obtain some sense of the users' subjective satisfaction with it. This can be done by a short interview with prospective users, by noting people's reactions to the interface while attempting to use it, or through a questionnaire asking people specific questions about what they liked and didn't like in the interface.

Evaluation, whether done by the designers and programmers involved with the project (who are typically biased because it is their interface and their code), by prospective users, or just by people off the street, should be used to get input on how to improve the interface. The overall goal here is not to cre-

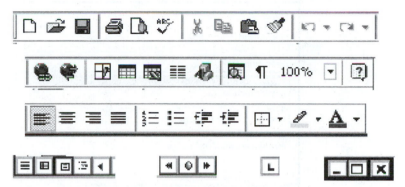

Figure 11-3 Some of the icons in Microsoft Word.

ate the best interface for the programmer, but rather to put the user first and create the interface that is best for the current and future users.

VISUAL GUIDELINES

The above guidelines for user-interface design concentrated on the ease of use of the interface. Another way to put the user first in interface design involves making the interface "look good." A good user interface must be comfortable to look at as well as to use. Being comfortable to look at involves both aesthetics and human psychology, which explains how people perceive what is being displayed and determines to a large extent what looks good and what doesn't. Extensive studies have been done in this area and visual guidelines have been derived that can be effectively applied to user-interface design. In this section we briefly discuss some of these guidelines.

Visual Clarity

The first visual property of a user interface is visual clarity. The meaning of a display should be readily apparent to the user. This applies at all levels, from simple icons to interactive widgets to the overall display.

At the lowest level, the user should be able easily to determine what an icon means, either a priori or after being told once or twice. When relatively few icons were used, this was not a significant problem. Today, however, more and more icons are being used, as seen in Figure 11-3, creating difficulties because the icons become smaller (to fit more on the display) and less descriptive. To alleviate this problem, software companies have resorted to providing popup help to describe an icon when the mouse stops on top of it.

Most users have become accustomed to standard widgets such as push buttons, radio buttons, scroll bars, text windows, and popup selectors. Here famil-

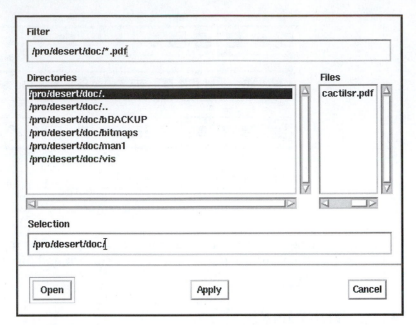

Figure 11-4 Motif dialog box for file selection.

iarity and the use of conventions help users quickly see what is meant. However, when presenting a new widget or a new application of an old widget, the interface designer should be careful to ensure that the use of the widget is obvious. For example, the standard Motif file selector shown in Figure 11-4 is not particularly intuitive to use. Normally an Apply button is clicked to use the selection without removing the dialog box. Here it applies the filter to the current directory. The actual selection, which the user would normally expect at the top, is at the bottom. Clicking on a directory changes only the filter, not the set of listed files; a double click is needed to do that.

The overall presentation of the system should also give a clear view of what is expected. The user should be able easily to ascertain from the overall display what each component of the system does. Standards and conventions, such as putting the menu bar at the top and scroll bars on the right and bottom, help. However, applications can still be confusing and care should be taken in designing an interface to make it as intuitive and natural as possible.

Any graphical presentation provided by the user interface should also be self-consistent. A number of psychological properties arising from how humans process visual information can be exploited to the benefit or the detriment of the display. These include similarity, proximity, closure, and continuity.

Two visual stimuli with a common property, such as a common color or shape, are perceived as being related or belonging together. This principle of *similarity* can be used effectively to relate items in different parts of the dis-

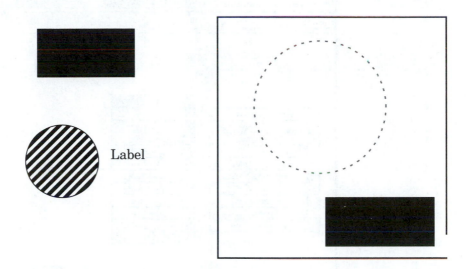

Figure 11-5 An illustration of visual principles.

play and remind the user that they go together. For example, the two solid boxes in Figure 11-5 appear to be related because of their similar visual presentation. Similarity can also confuse the user when similar shapes or colors are used but no relationship is intended.

Two visual stimuli close together on the display are also considered as related or belonging together. This is the principle of *proximity*. The label in Figure 11-5 appears to be associated with the hatched circle because of their proximity. As with similarity, this can be used to help or confuse the user.

If a stimulus almost encloses an area, it is seen as enclosing it. This is the principle of *closure*. The box in Figure 11-5 is perceived as a complete square even though a portion is missing. The related principle of *continuity* states that at line junctures, viewers see smoothly connected lines. Thus the dotted circle in Figure 11-5 is perceived as a real circle, even though it is only about half there.

In creating the visual display for an application the designer should take these principles into account, using similar shapes and colors only to imply a relationship, using proximity to associate items that should be associated (and similarly using distance to ensure that two unrelated items are not accidentally associated), and being careful to avoid illusions such as the complete circle or square where they are not intended.

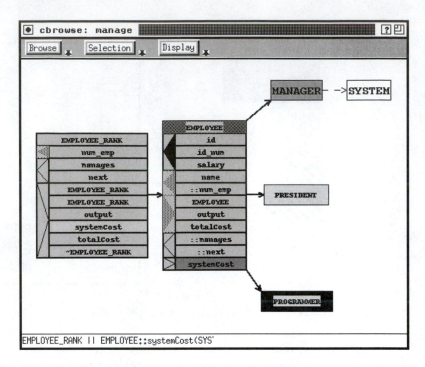

Figure 11-6 Class browser display showing visual codings.

Visual Codings

Colors, shapes, sizes, fonts, orientations, line styles and fill styles are examples of visual encodings that are perceived as relaying information about the objects being displayed. As we noted, objects displayed similarly are perceived as similar, while objects displayed differently are perceived as different.

This makes visual encodings a powerful mechanism for conveying information to the viewer. Figure 11-6 shows various visual encodings in a class browser we developed for the FIELD programming environment. Here color encodes the currently selected classes (light blue) and shows the current field and its relatives. The current field is shown in green, its actual definition location (since it is inherited) in pink, equivalent definitions from subclasses that do not redefine it in yellow, and any redefinitions in cyan. Thick lines show public inheritance and thin lines private, and dashed lines show friendship relations. A bar on the inheritance arrowhead indicates virtual inheritance. Additional line types could be used for call and client relationships between classes. Hatching around the class name indicates an abstract class, while a solid box indicates an unexpanded class hierarchy. The icons at the left of the class boxes are data fields if they point to the left, methods if they point to the right, or friend methods if they are rectangular. Their fill style indicates protection: solid for private, shaded for protected, and empty for public. An additional icon could be tacked onto each field to indicate the data or return type of that field, and another box could be inserted after the triangles to indicate field properties such as abstract, inline, pure, or virtual.

To use visual encodings effectively, one must use them consistently and logically and at the same time understand their limits. Color is the most accurate and generally powerful encoding mechanism. An application can use about ten colors simultaneously and have the user recognize them as encodings; more than ten colors begin to become confusing and hard to distinguish. Note, however, when using color, that six to eight percent of males are color-blind. Other properties are also useful but generally more limited. Object size or length can be used to distinguish about six different features. Four different intensities can be readily distinguished. Fifteen shapes and 24 angles can also be used with some accuracy, although the application of these are limited by context.

Visual encodings are also useful in attracting the user's attention. Here one must use a much smaller selection of encodings and use them more carefully. Studies have shown that to attract attention one wants to reduce the number of different encodings by about half. Additional encodings can also be used here: inverse video is often used to highlight a single selection, multiple fonts in a document make items stand out, and blinking at two to four hertz is sometimes effective, since the eye is attracted to things that change or move. Finally, audio, with soft sounds for positive feedback and harsher sounds for emergency conditions, can also be used to attract the user's attention.

While visual encodings are useful, they can also be misused or become overwhelming. Misuse occurs where information encodings convey information different from what the viewer might otherwise assume. Too many different types of encodings easily confuse the viewer. Here one should fall back on textual display and textual encodings, which are generally more flexible and easier to understand, even if they often take up more display space.

The problem with visual encodings to get attention is that of the boy who cried wolf: it is very easy to overuse such encodings so that users ignore them and concentrate on what they want to rather than on what the program wants them to. An effective application approach uses encodings to get attention when necessary but avoids their overuse.

Principles of Layout

Visual guidelines can also be applied to the overall layout of an application. Four design principles can be used effectively to create good-looking windows: balance, gridding, proportion, and consistency.

Window layouts look better when they are *balanced*. A layout in which all the menu bars are on one side or another tends to look unbalanced and uninviting. A display in which different features encircle the main display area can be much better. Consider the *FrameMaker* display in Figure 11-7. Here there are three rows of buttons on the top: the menu bar, the optional quick access

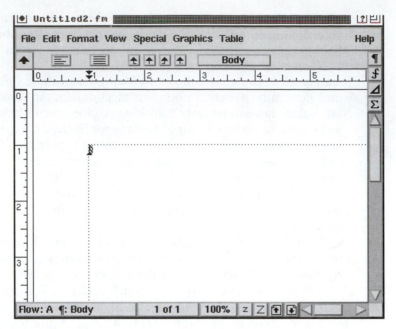

Figure 11-7 FrameMaker display showing a balanced layout.

bar, and the horizontal ruler. These are balanced by the icons at the bottom showing the current status and letting the user control page number, size, and position. Similarly, the scroll bar and icons on the right are balanced by the vertical ruler on the left. Placing menu options around the window makes the display look better.

The second layout principle is to use *gridding*, that is, to align display elements according to a grid. Items that are horizontally or vertically adjacent should be lined up accordingly. Consider the two examples in Figure 11-8. The left example, from Sun's *Workshop*, shows unaligned widgets (the default when using a Motif row-column widget). The right example shows aligned widgets in the corresponding view of the FIELD environment. The overall goal here is to make the windows look neat rather than helter-skelter.

A third design principle involves *proportion*. Some window sizes look better than others. A long, skinny window is generally long, skinny, and ugly. The best width-to-height ratios for windows are 1:1, 1:1.414, 1:1.618, and 1:2. (Recall that 1.414 is the square root of 2; 1.618 is the "golden ratio," the value of the continued fraction $1+1/(1+1/(1+1/(1+1/...$, which has been prominent in Western art since the Renaissance.) Other proportions generally less than 1:2 look okay, but the values given above are the most aesthetically pleasing.

The final layout principle is one we've harped on several times already, *consistency*. The layout of multiple windows, especially windows with similar purposes, should be consistent with one another. Moreover, the layout of windows

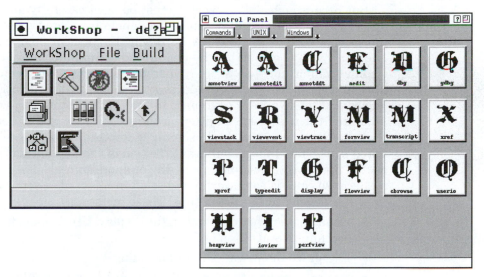

Figure 11-8 Examples of ungridded and gridded layouts.

in one application should be consistent with that in other applications the user will use. This is simplified these days by the adoption of user-interface standards for the different architectures.

Color

Color in an interface can do a lot of things. It is a powerful visual characteristic that can be a powerful contributor or a serious inhibitor in a user interface. Color can be soothing or striking to the eye. It can create an application (or a web page for that matter) that people feel comfortable looking at, or one that turns them off. Color can add accents to what would otherwise be an unpleasant display, attracting people to a program and making them want to use it. Color can evoke emotional reactions: red, green and yellow invoke cultural expectations based on their use in traffic lights, pastels are generally soothing, and certain colors (such as vomit green) are upsetting or disturbing.

Color can be used for visual coding. It can also be used to facilitate subtle discriminations in complex displays. The eye can discriminate about a million colors. Moreover, the mind can look at a display and isolate all items of a given color. Visual codings can use color effectively to emphasize the logical organization of information. Here the range of 10 discernible discrete values and the fact that color can easily be applied to a wide range of objects (including shapes, lines, and text) make it the most powerful visual coding technique. The same characteristics also make color one of the best ways to draw attention either to particular features of a display or to warnings and errors.

But because of color's power, it must be used carefully and conservatively. Too much color in a display can be overwhelming. Novices in the use of color displays often find this out the hard way. Early color computer applications and early web pages both exhibited an indiscriminate use of color that made them uncomfortable to look at. Inappropriately used colors can also make text unreadable. Try creating a window with red text on a blue background or with yellow text on a white background. In the first case the colors clash with each other and the text seems to jitter; in the second case there is so little contrast that the text is unreadable. Designing with color must also, as noted, be tempered by the fact that a significant fraction of the population (six to eight percent of males) is color-blind in one way or another.

Because color is so powerful and so often misused, a separate set of guidelines has developed for it over time. These include:

- Limit the number of colors on the display. Use at most four principal colors, and a total of ten or fewer.

- Recognize the power of color for coding.

- Use color coding to support the task at hand. It shouldn't be used superficially, nor should it be distracting.

- Put color coding under user control, since different users have different preferences. (This also provides a way to handle different types of color blindness.)

- Recognize the power for color for formatting and layout. Note that some of the balance of the *FrameMaker* display in Figure 11-7 comes from the use of color in the outline boxes.

- Be consistent in color coding.

- Be alert to common cultural expectations about color codes. For example, red typically means stop or alert, yellow go slow or caution, and green go or okay.

- Be alert to inappropriate color pairings.

- Use color changes to indicate status changes. Color changes are readily visible even if the user isn't looking directly at the changed area.

- Use color to achieve greater information density. Hue (the actual color) can be a powerful encoding function over a range of values.

Overall, the thing to remember is to minimize one's use of color, reserving it for those occasions where it is most appropriate and most powerful.

USER-INTERFACE MODELS

Putting the user first in user-interface design has several different aspects. We have already considered guidelines for creating more user-friendly and intuitive interfaces as well as guidelines to make the user interface comfortable to use and nice to look at. Another aspect of user-interface design is anticipating how the system will be used and either adapting the system to such use or providing the necessary clues so that the system is used as the programmer wants it to be.

When users work with a computer program they build *conceptual models* of how the program and its user interface work. They use these models to determine what to expect from various commands and to figure out how the system can and should be used. When they have a complex task, it is these models that they apply to break it down into smaller units that can actually be accomplished using the commands the system provides. It is these models through which they actually understand the system.

Programmers and user-interface designers also build models. The programmer's model encompasses the system design and indicates how the system actually works. The user-interface designer's model makes assumptions about how the user will view the system and how the system will be used. Many of the most egregious user-interfaces problems occur when the user's and the programmer's models of the system differ.

Consider drawing programs as an example. There are essentially two types of drawing programs, those that are bitmap-based, such as *MacPaint*, and those that are object-based, such as *MacDraw*. In the former the current picture is maintained as a bitmap and operations make changes to that bitmap. In the latter case, the current image is maintained as a set of objects and the current picture is actually obtained by drawing those objects in back-to-front order. If users assume that the program is an object editor, draw an object, overlay that object with other drawings and then want to delete the original object, they will be disappointed when the select and delete either don't work or do the wrong thing.

Most model mismatches are not as obvious as this, but they can be just as troublesome and painful to the user. Anyone designing a user interface should attempt to anticipate how different sets of users will approach the system and should attempt to understand the different models users might have for the system and its interface. This is quite difficult to do, and an alternative is to convey to the user the programmer's model of how the system works and should be used, so that the user builds a similar model in the first place.

This can be done in a variety of subtle and some not-so-subtle ways. The most obvious is through good manuals and on-line documentation describing how the system works and should be used. The only problem here is that many users just don't bother to read the documentation. Thus the programmer must resort to more subtle means, providing clues in the naming of buttons, the types of feedback the system provides, the error and prompting messages, the types and nature of the displays, and so on. The programmer should essentially attempt to guide users through the system by helping them learn the proper model for its use.

SUMMARY

Designing a high-quality user interface involves understanding how the user will perceive and use the resultant program. Human factors is the study of how people use and react to systems. The basic underlying principle coming out of these studies for user-interface design is to put the user first.

The importance of a good user interface and the difficulty of achieving one are both highlighted by the various problems in current interfaces. These include:

- Lack of conventions both within an application and among separate applications.
- Overly complex displays that are confusing and make it difficult to find buttons or items of interest.
- Lack of elegance, whether in the display or in how the user interface is used.
- Intolerance to errors made by the user or the underlying system.
- Documentation that is unreadable, incomprehensible, incomplete, or just inaccurate.

While building a high-quality interface is difficult, some guidelines can help. These include:

- Use common sense so that the interface does what the user expects.
- Be consistent throughout the interface and among applications.
- Give the user appropriate feedback.
- Design the interface to accommodate error.
- Design the interface simultaneously for all types of users, from novices who need to learn how to use the system to experts whose main concern is efficiency.
- Evaluate the resultant interface and improve it as needed.

These guidelines cover how the interface interacts with the user. Another set of guidelines can help make the interface look appealing and improve its presentations. These include:

- Use visual clarity so that the user understands intuitively what is being displayed.
- Use visual codings to convey information; avoid inadvertent visual codings. Be careful when using codings to draw attention to some aspect of the display.
- Create balanced layouts using aesthetically pleasing proportions.
- Use color sparingly and wisely.

Finally, we noted that a user interacts with a system by building a mental model of how it operates. Similarly, the programmer develops a user interface with a particular model of how the user will interact with the system. Where these two models coincide, the interface tends to work well; where they differ, the interface tends to fall apart. It is the responsibility of the programmer to anticipate and guide the user toward the proper conceptual model.

EXERCISES

11.1 Take a program with a graphical user interface and list the strengths and weaknesses of that interface.

11.2 Take a program with a graphical user interface. Rate it on the interface guidelines covered in this chapter, noting how well the application follows or obeys each guideline.

11.3 Take a program with a graphical user interface. Evaluate how good it looks on the screen, first using your own sense of aesthetics and then considering the visual criteria covered in the chapter.

11.4 Take a program with a graphical user interface and evaluate its user-interface aspects. Develop a list of suggestions on how to improve the interface. Take one of these suggestions and do a more complete evaluation. Estimate how much work it would take to make the change. Attempt to understand fully the consequences of the change on the remainder of the user interface and the application.

11.5 An often onerous task for programmers involves keeping on-line documentation up to date as the code evolves. Suppose you want to automate this task as much as possible. Design a user interface for such automation. (Don't worry about how the system will work — assume some magic occurs and concentrate on the interface to what you think such a system should do.) Evaluate your design by getting feedback from other programmers.

11.6 A clever idea developed by HP and Apollo and now available in part in Windows is the concept of compatible families of colors. Here the system predefines sets of compatible colors and the application gets all its colors from the user's choice of sets. Investigate this concept and indicate how it could be incorporated into user interfaces in either Windows or UNIX without putting too great a burden on applications wishing to use it.

11.7 Develop and evaluate a user-interface design for interior decorating. Your program should allow the user to define the size of the room and the location of windows, doors, closets, etc. It should then let the user put different pieces of furniture in the room and show what the result would look like.

Chapter 12

Creating Object Libraries

One of the primary motivations for object-oriented programming is to encourage and simplify code reuse. Reuse is important because it lets one produce higher-quality code inexpensively. Writing a program in which a significant portion of the code already exists is obviously easier. Moreover, code provided for reuse has generally been well tested and debugged, reducing the amount of debugging and testing needed in the application.

Objects are generally reused by defining classes that can be used in more than one application. In their simplest form, such classes are provided in a library implementing one or more object definitions that can be used directly by applications. Object-based reuse can also be accomplished with inheritance by defining new objects as specializations of previously defined ones. This lets new features be added without redoing the underlying implementation. In C++, reuse can also be accomplished using template classes, as we saw with the Standard Template Library.

In this chapter we look at how to integrate reuse into object-oriented design and implementation. We start by considering why reuse is both important and difficult. This gives us some guidelines for later design. Next we look at the design of reusable classes, and then create a template class and define an inherited template for our own interface to a standard library class. All this is done in the context of a simple example, an infinite-precision calculator.

REUSE AND OBJECTS

Object-oriented programming is widely viewed as reducing the cost of software development by making it possible to reuse existing software. Because objects are adaptable, self-contained entities, it should be feasible to use a set of objects developed for one application in another with little or no modification. Doing this in practice, however, is often difficult.

Implementing Reuse

Reusable objects can be incorporated into a new application in a variety of ways. The most obvious is the direct use of a set of objects defined for one application in other applications. Such objects would include interfaces to the operating system and other standard facilities. Here objects provide a convenient organization for what is essentially a library. Second, a set of predefined objects can be specialized through inheritance. Here the basic objects provide a core functionality that the new subclasses specialize for the particular application. Third, the reusable objects can be defined in a generic manner using templates, so that the new application can specialize the objects to its use by defining instances of the templates. This lets a much broader range of functionality be incorporated into the reusable library.

When reusable objects are available or anticipated, they can affect the approach taken toward object-oriented design. Once a set of reusable classes is available, it can be thought of as an extension to the language much like the standard C++ library (with strings, input/output streams, and a variety of data structure and algorithm templates). A program can often be designed more readily using such existing extensions.

Program design can also be done by defining reusable extensions. Here, in order to simplify a particular application, the programmer defines a set of extensions to the underlying language that become a new, higher-level application-specific language for writing the actual application. Such extensions can easily be designed for reuse, so that another application in the same domain can be written simply by using the new language. Another way to view such designs is in terms of a layered system: the application itself is the outer layer of the system, while the extensions, and the extensions on top of which they themselves are built, form the inner layers.

Both of these design architectures have been widely used for a long time. However, object-oriented programming and object-oriented design make them both easier to accomplish because the newly defined objects can easily be viewed as primitive types of the language. The programmer can use such objects as if they were primitives and have the class implementation in the library deal with all the details. This is especially true in C++: the library programmer can define appropriate constructors and destructors to create the object with default values or from other built-in types. The object can provide conversion operators to let the new type be used in lieu of other standard language types. It can provide a reasonable implementation of the copy constructor and assignment operator to permit for safe memory management as appropriate. And it can provide other standard operators, letting some classes be used as numbers and supporting control-like features such as iterators.

Why Reuse is Difficult

While object-oriented programming can facilitate code reuse, reusing code effectively is a difficult task requiring careful planning. The most obvious difficulty is finding the proper abstraction for reuse. This abstraction is reflected in the particular set of objects defined, the interactions of these objects with the application, and the interface that the objects provide.

One reason reuse is difficult is that the demands on objects designed for reuse can conflict. Reusable objects need to be quite general so they can span a wide range of applications. However, generality often implies a complex interface with lots of methods and an implementation that must handle large and unusual cases. This in turn leads to an implementation that is less efficient in terms of space or time than one specialized to a particular application. Moreover, the complexity inherent in such generality often makes the objects more difficult to debug, understand, and use. A second demand on reusable objects is that they must be easy to understand and use. This implies a simple interface rather than the full interface implied by generality. A good reusable design attempts to find a balance between generality and ease of use while achieving acceptable efficiency for almost all cases.

A second issue discouraging reuse is the poor quality of documentation for reusable objects. Accurate, up-to-date, readable documentation is essential to the whole process of reuse. The first requirement here is a good set of manuals or descriptions to help a new programmer understand how the classes are meant to be used and what they are good for. These should give a reference manual for the classes, detailing for each method its arguments, its return types, its exceptions, and exactly what it does. They should include examples of the most common class uses, with actual code that can be copied by the first-time user, and an overview giving the potential user a good feeling for where to look for the particular functionality needed. They should also document any limitations and restrictions on the use of the classes: what a class cannot do is often as important as what it can. Even the best documentation should be accompanied with easy-to-read, well-documented code that can be used as a last resort in determining if the reusable objects can serve a particular function.

A third problem involves using other programmers' objects in a manner consistent with the conventions and assumptions in a particular project. A new set of objects can easily violate the accepted naming or access conventions. The standard C++ library, for example, uses all-lower-case type names and method names with underscores, and introduces many objects that are not treated as pointers. The OpenInventor library, on the other hand, uses naming conventions much like the ones recommended in this book. Other libraries place demands on the user's object definitions. For example, the NIH class library requires any object that is to be placed in a container to inherit from a common superclass defined in the library. Defining a good set of reusable objects also involves attempting to minimize differences among conventions and making minimal external demands on the application.

A fourth problem in the development of reusable code is to some extent a political one. Reusable code generally takes longer to write, document, and debug than code specialized to a particular application. Few projects, whether student projects or industrial ones, have the extra time and manpower available for this effort when the immediate requirements of getting the system working as quickly and cheaply as possible get in the way. Programmers and companies need to realize the future benefits of reuse and allocate current resources to achieve them.

DESIGNING REUSABLE CLASSES

In order to talk about how reuse affects design, we consider implementing an infinite-precision calculator:

> You are to implement a simple calculator that maintains numbers to infinite precision. The calculator should support the standard arithmetic operators (+,-,*,/) and an output display with 10-digit accuracy. Input should be in post-fix form. Recall that "$a + b$" is denoted as "$a\ b\ +$" in postfix. The operator "=" prints its one argument and yields the original value, and the operator "@" clears the calculator.

Computers normally represent numbers by using a binary floating-point notation. The result is that numbers are rounded. For example, if one uses `calc-tool` on a Sun and enters (in scientific mode with nine-digit accuracy):

```
1 / 3 * 3 - 1
```

the result is `-9.956824445e-60` rather than the expected zero. The task in this problem is to implement a calculator providing complete accuracy without any round-off.

Infinite precision can be provided by storing the internal results as fractions so that no rounding is needed. It is clear that the result of adding, subtracting, multiplying or dividing two fractions is always a third fraction that can be computed exactly. Thus the above computation would be evaluated as

```
(1/1 / 3/1) = 1/3
(1/3 * 3/1) = 3/3 = 1/1
(1/1 - 1/1) = 0/1
```

The only place we have to round is in producing the output, and here we are supposed to output only a fixed number of digits of accuracy anyway.

Selecting Classes to Reuse

While we could implement a calculator of this type directly (since it is simple), we want to look at it in terms of reuse, asking ourselves what aspects of the eventual implementation can be generalized and extended to other problems. In this case, the obvious answer is the implementation of the data structure for fractional representations.

Identifying a class or set of classes with the potential for reuse is generally not as easy as it is here. For example, if one is implementing an application that requires two processes to communicate via sockets (see Chapter 14), the actual socket code can be either scattered throughout the application or encapsulated. Since sockets can be used in a wide variety of ways (for example

```
void
IPCalcMainInfo::process()
{
    IPCalcValue v, v1;

    while ((ch = next chararacter) != EOF) {
        if (ch is a digit)
            v = accumulate number
            push(v)
        else if (ch is a binary operator)
            v1 = pop();
            v = pop();
            v = v <op> v1
            push(v)
        else if (ch == '=')
            output top()
        else if (ch == '@')
            clear stack
    }
}
```

Figure 12-1 Pseudocode for the infinite-precision calculator.

as streams or for individual messages, with waits or with callbacks, statically or using dynamic connections), it is difficult to define a single reusable class for such functionality, or even an appropriate set of classes. Similarly, in graphical user interfaces, a lot of operations are to some extent common to a broad range of applications and should be encapsulated. Here, again, different applications approach the user interface in different ways and it is difficult to standardize on a single set of reusable classes containing enough functionality and at the same time offering the needed flexibility. In general, finding a candidate reusable class is difficult because it requires anticipating the class's full range of uses in future applications.

The class implementing the fraction data structure for the infinite-precision calculator is much simpler. The values we are talking about are to be treated as numbers and the operations on numbers are well understood and straightforward. Most applications that might want to use these fractions will want to use them as numbers, and the proposed calculator is a good exemplar of this.

To understand the immediate requirements for the fraction class, we look at the implementation of the calculator. We start by calling the fraction class **IPCalcValue** and the calculator class **IpCalcMainInfo**. We can then implement the calculator as a simple routine that maintains a stack, as in Figure 12-1. The whole calculator can then be implemented in a class that maintains the stack and provides an implementation of push, pop, and clear. The resultant header definitions are shown in Figure 12-2. Note that the calculator can be written

```
typedef   class IpCalcMainInfo * IpCalcMain;


class IpCalcMainInfo {
private:
   list<IpCalcValue> calc_stack;

public:
   IpCalcMainInfo();
   ~IpCalcMainInfo();

   void process();

private:
   void push(IpCalcValue);
   IpCalcValue pop();
   void clear();
};
```

Figure 12-2 Definitions for the infinite-precision calculator.

and tested without worrying about the implementation of the type **IPCalcValue** by simply defining it as floating-point:

```
typedef double IPCalcValue;
```

We later replace this typedef with one defining **IPCalcValue** as a new name for the fraction class.

Once the calculator is understood, we then proceed with the design of this reusable fraction class. We call the class **Rational** (since the fractions in question are actually rational numbers). The new name does not include the application prefix since it is designed to be used by other classes. We want to implement this class so that, when another application needs such precision in the future, we can reuse the class with little or no modification.

Defining a Reusable Class

The first problem in designing such a reusable class is specifying the proper interface. A relatively complete interface would include the methods in Figure 12-3. The first set of functions lets rationals be built from other **Rational** objects, integers, pairs of integers representing the numerator and denominator of the fraction, and floating-point values (where we take some approximation). The next set of methods provide the basic arithmetic operations, both in the form modifying the current **Rational** object (+=) and in the form returning a new **Rational** object.

```
class Rational {
public:
    Rational();                          // clear to 0 initially
    Rational(const Rational&);
    Rational(int);
    Rational(double);
    Rational(int,int);
    ~Rational();

    Rational operator +(const Rational&) const;
    Rational& operator += (const Rational&);
    Rational operator -(const Rational&) const;
    Rational& operator -= (const Rational&);
    Rational operator *(const Rational&) const;
    Rational& operator *= (const Rational&);
    Rational operator /(const Rational&) const;
    Rational& operator /= (const Rational&);
    Rational operator -() const;
    Rational& negate();

    Rational& operator =(const Rational&);

    int operator == (const Rational&) const;
    int operator <= (const Rational&) const;
    int operator >= (const Rational&) const;
    int operator != (const Rational&) const;
    int operator > (const Rational&) const;
    int operator < (const Rational&) const;
    int compare(const Rational&) const;

    double value() const;
    friend ostream& operator << (ostream&,const Rational&);

    Rational power(int);
    Rational& powerBy(int);
};
```

Figure 12-3 Proposed class for rational arithmetic.

The next method provides the assignment operator. Additional assignment operators could be given for integers and floating-point numbers, but here we let C++ interpret a statement of the form

```
    r = 5;
```

where r is a **Rational**, as a constructor call to build a temporary **Rational** using the integer value 5, an assignment of that temporary to r using the assignment operator, and finally a call to the destructor for r of the temporary. Defining additional assignment methods could improve the efficiency of this operation. (Note, however, that a good compiler should be able to inline most of this to yield an implementation of the statement as efficient as if the programmer had provided an explicit method.)

A similar situation arises if the application were to mix **Rational** objects with integer or floating-point values. The statement

```
r += 5;
```

would cause the compiler to build and destroy a **Rational** temporary in order to complete the addition. Again, efficiency and a desire not to depend on implicit C++ conversions might suggest expanding the class definition to include additional arithmetic methods such as

```
Rational& operator +=(int);
Rational operator +(int);
```

In addition, it would be nice to let the application use expressions of the form 5 + r. This can be done in three ways. The first would be to require the new methods:

```
friend operator + (int,const Rational&);
friend operator - (int,const Rational&);
friend operator * (int,const Rational&);
friend operator / (int,const Rational&);
friend operator + (double,const Rational&);
friend operator - (double,const Rational&);
friend operator / (double,const Rational&);
friend operator * (double,const Rational&);
```

These must be defined as friend functions since the class argument is second rather than first. As friend functions, they do not have a `this` pointer as an explicit first argument, but instead take the two listed arguments after appropriate conversions by the compiler.

A second implementation would force C++ to do the casting and conversions by just defining the functions:

```
friend operator +(const Rational&,const Rational&);
friend operator -(const Rational&,const Rational&);
friend operator *(const Rational&,const Rational&);
friend operator /(const Rational&,const Rational&);
```

in place of the original four methods. In theory this should work, but it could also lead to problems later on when the compiler has to disambiguate complex mixed-mode expressions. (Here, because we are not defining any conversion operators for the class **Rational**, these functions would be used only when one of the terms is a **Rational** and should yield no ambiguities. If the class is expanded, however, unintended ambiguities might suddenly arise and code that once worked would work no longer.) In general, because implicit conversions are difficult to anticipate and get correct, it is better to avoid them as much as possible. While this form has this drawback, it has the advantages that only these four functions need be defined and that they do not differ from the basic class operators that are not friends. This can reduce the amount of code to be written and make it clearer what is being called within an expression.

The third approach to these operators involves defining them as global functions outside of the class:

```
operator +(const Rational&,const Rational&);
operator -(const Rational&,const Rational&);
operator *(const Rational&,const Rational&);
operator /(const Rational&,const Rational&);
```

This is equivalent to defining these methods as friends except that the bodies cannot access the private or protected data or methods of the class **Rational**. Because the operators are actually associated with the class, it is probably better to define them as friends in the class definition than to define them only outside the class: this ensures that they are not overlooked by a programmer who wants to edit or use the class.

The next set of methods in the definition of the class **Rational** provides for comparisons of rationals. Again, multiple comparison functions might be desirable so that an object of class **Rational** can be compared directly to an integer (or floating-point) value without the compiler needing to construct and destruct a temporary value. The `compare` method returns -1, 0, or +1 and can be used to implement the various operators. While this method could be defined as private or protected, we include it in the public interface because it is often useful in avoiding multiple comparisons. (For example, the C library function `qsort` expects a function of this type as the comparator.)

Next we define the output operators. These let objects of class **Rational** be converted to floating-point values or be output directly to a **ostream**. These are followed by some additional methods an application might want to have on rational numbers, such as exponentiation. This should be viewed as an extensible set: further methods can easily be added to the definition.

This complete definition of the class **Rational** should be contrasted to what is actually required of the class in the infinite-precision calculator example. Here a definition such as that in Figure 12-4 would be sufficient. Note that we include both a copy constructor and a copy assignment operator in this definition; they are needed because we might want to use the class **Rational** as a structure rather than using pointers and allocating values.

Selecting the Level of Reuse

There are significant differences between these two class definitions. The larger definition has three times as many methods (more if you include the additional assignment, arithmetic, and comparison operators for integer and floating-point values). It is far more complex and would take much longer to implement and debug. On the other hand, the simpler class definition lacks a number of features that will probably be needed in a more general application.

```
class Rational {
public:
    Rational(int v = 0);
    Rational(const Rational&);
    ~Rational();

    Rational& operator =(const Rational&);

    Rational& operator +=(const Rational&);
    Rational& operator -=(const Rational&);
    Rational& operator *=(const Rational&);
    Rational& operator /=(const Rational&);

    friend ostream& operator << (ostream&,const Rational&);
};
```

Figure 12-4 Simple definition of the class Rational.

The proper design of a reusable class generally involves a compromise between a complete implementation that attempts to provide for all potential future uses and a simple implementation that merely satisfies current needs.

The first step in determining the proper reusable definition is to understand the future applications of the class. If the goal is to let future applications use rational numbers just as freely as integer or floating-point numbers, then an implementation closer to the complete definition would be called for. If future applications will make heavy use of rationals and will thus demand efficiency, then the additional methods for handling mixed types without creating temporaries are also desirable. On the other hand, if most of the anticipated applications in which rational numbers are needed will use them in a limited manner, a simpler definition is justified.

One of the concerns in choosing the proper level is that future additions to the class can break applications that worked with the old version of the class. For example, if we have the class **Rational** as shown in Figure 12-4 and add the constructor:

```
Rational(long);
```

then code such as:

```
Rational a = 3.0;
```

that compiled previously will now yield an overloading ambiguity. Other problems can arise if compiler overloading unexpectedly causes the new version of a function to be called with slightly different semantics or if new conversion operators are added to the class. In general, one should attempt to find the proper level in advance so that changes needed in the future do not affect previous applications.

For the simple calculator we are attempting to define, the trade-off is mainly one of additional methods that can be written easily but may not be needed. In more general cases, the trade-off is more complex, since the additional methods usually require additional internal fields and structure as well as a more complex implementation of the simpler methods that are actually used by the application. In our case, it would be relatively easy to implement a simpler class for the calculator and later just to add whatever methods are needed in future applications, provided we are careful in selecting the additions. In general, however, such additions can be quite complex, since they can involve changing a significant portion of the existing implementation or might best be done by changing the overall class interface.

Even in the present interface, some subtle points must be considered in achieving a proper balance. The first involves the difference between the arithmetic operators that work in place, such as +=, and those that generate new objects at each invocation, such as +. The former are easier to code and more efficient. They act like object methods, modifying values of the current object, require the user to start with a **Rational**, and create no ambiguities with overloading. However, they do put restrictions on the programmer using the class and essentially eliminate the use of **Rational** objects in expressions. The standard operators act more like functions than methods (this is why they can be defined as friends). They are less efficient, since the compiler must continually construct and destroy the temporary objects necessary to hold the return values. Doing this properly requires allowing mixed operands in which the rational is either the first or the second operand, and this complicates the definition and can easily induce the compiler to find ambiguities in resolving such expressions. However, this makes coding using the **Rational** class more convenient. In our case, since the class can easily be extended at a future time to include the standard operators, we define only the assignment forms in the initial implementation.

In order to make the new class **Rational** reusable, we should include at least enough of the basic methods that anything else can be implemented quite easily. Thus we include the compare method so that the various comparison operators can be added easily and so that comparisons can be done. Similarly, the value method should be defined since it is the only way to convert a rational number to a numeric value. In general we recommend:

> **Design a reusable class to handle all reasonable future requests.**

"Reasonable" here implies a proper balance between immediate requirements and future possibilities. As the above discussion indicates, this can be difficult and require considerable thought to get right.

The definition we actually provide for the class **Rational** is the one in Figure 12-5. Here we have used a type **RationalPart** to represent the values of

```
typedef long      RationalPart;

class Rational {

private:
   RationalPart _num;
   RationalPart _dem;

public:
   Rational(int v = 0);
   Rational(const Rational&);
   ~Rational();

   Rational& operator =(const Rational&);

   Rational& operator +=(const Rational&);
   Rational& operator -=(const Rational&);
   Rational& operator *=(const Rational&);
   Rational& operator /=(const Rational&);

   int compare(const Rational&) const;

   friend ostream& operator << (ostream&,const Rational&);

   double value() const;

protected:
   void normalize();
   static RationalPart gcd(RationalPart,RationalPart);
};
```

Figure 12-5 Class definition for rational numbers.

the numerator and denominator. While we defined it as a long, it could just as easily be defined as int or long long if desired. We have also defined two support methods. The first normalizes the value of the rational after an operation has occurred; this involves checking for zero and infinity as well as reducing the fraction to its lowest terms. The static function gcd finds the greatest common denominator for the normalize method. The implementation of the various methods of rational is straightforward. For example, Figure 12-6 shows the implementation of the += operator.

Given this implementation of **Rational**, we implement the overall calculator by defining its value type, **IPCalcValue**, to be the type **Rational**.

```
Rational&
Rational::operator += (const Rational& r)
{
    RationalPart d = _dem * r._dem;

    _num = _num * r._dem + _dem * r._num;
    _dem = d;

    normalize();

    return *this;
}
```

Figure 12-6 Implementation of rational operators.

REUSE THROUGH INHERITANCE

The above example illustrates how to create objects to be reused directly. Such objects are limited since the programmer must determine all potential applications and design the reusable object to handle them. They are also limited since any interactions between the library objects and the user's code must be implemented using callbacks and an associated callback structure. Using inheritance to facilitate reuse is an obvious way to avoid these two problems. This section describes some of the ways to use inheritance here. Further applications using inheritance with templates are considered later in this chapter.

Defining Inheritable Classes

One way to use inheritance is to let the user (or another library) extend the functionality of a library class by defining a new subclass of that class. Inheritance here should let the library define a basic class with the essential functionality. The user can then define the actual class with the functionality necessary to the application as a subclass of the library class.

While this seems simple, it often requires careful design of the original class. Consider, for example, what would happen if we want to define not a complete class for rational arithmetic but a basic class, as in Figure 12-4, and then let the programmer extend the class by using inheritance. Problems can arise if the two classes are not defined correctly. For example, the proposed simple definition for **Rational** includes multiple constructors. These may be essential to its operation but are not inherited directly by a subclass. A subclass would have to duplicate each of the necessary constructors by creating a subclass constructor with similar arguments. A class designed to be reused through inheritance should in general minimize the number of constructors it provides.

A second potential problem comes from having the superclass define an assignment operator. C++ normally defines a default assignment operator for a new subclass that correctly calls the superclass's operator. However, if the subclass redefines assignment for some reason, care must be taken that the superclass assignment operator is also invoked.

Another problem can arise if any methods in the base class return an instance of that class. Consider a base class that has a method returning the negative of the current value:

```
Rational negativeOf() const
```

If the application depends on having objects of the more complex rational sub-type, this operation cannot be used directly and would have to be redefined in the subtype. A class being designed for reuse through inheritance should not have methods returning new objects of its own type.

Overall, because of these difficulties, we recommend:

Define a class to be reused with inheritance in mind.

Inheritance for Callbacks

In "Inheritance for Callbacks" on page 123 we discussed why inheritance should be used for defining callbacks from one class to another. For a library class, this can be done in one of two ways. The first is a simple extension of the technique used previously: a class is added to the library just to handle call-backs. Programmers are expected to define their own classes as subclasses of this callback class and then pass instances of these classes to the class doing the callback.

An alternative implementation combines the callback class and the class doing the callback. Here programmers are expected to define their own classes by inheriting from the library class itself. The library class then includes virtual callback methods among its definitions. Programmers who want to receive a particular callback need only redefine the corresponding method in their subclass. The subclass here acts both as a specific instance of the library class and as the callback object for that class.

This alternative technique is used extensively in the Microsoft Foundation Class library (MFC) described in Chapter 9. For example, the class **CWnd** represents the basic functionality of a window or subwindow of the application. It has a variety of subclasses such as **CDialog** for dialog windows and **CButton** for button widgets or controls. Programmers needing to create a new dialog or button create their own class representing that element as a subclass of the appropriate window type. The generic **CWnd** class defines a large number of callback methods, such as `OnPaint` to repaint a portion of the window or `OnCommand` when a command is selected in the window. Some of these are handled directly by the library subclasses and some are passed to the application subclasses. The library subclasses also define their own callbacks as appropriate. For example, **CDialog** defines an `OnOK` callback invoked when the user accepts the dialog box. In either case, the application class can override the default action for any of the callbacks and provide its own handlers in order to extend the functionality.

MFC actually implements a second mechanism for using the user's class as a callback handler. It provides the concept of a message map, an internal structure mapping specific events detected by the underlying window to calls of arbitrary methods of the application's class. This provides a more general functionality, although its actual implementation involves uses of C++ that are not particularly type-safe or straightforward (in particular, it uses pointers to methods and casting). It provides a convenient interface and nicely extends the concept of callbacks to accommodate a wide variety of actions.

These two forms of inheritance for callbacks are useful under different conditions. Which one is used in an application depends on the wide range of factors cited above. An important point in choosing which to use is to ensure the overall simplicity of the application. Thus:

> **Use inheritance for callbacks consistently in an application.**

Application Frameworks

The Microsoft Foundation Class library is an instance of an *application framework*, a set of classes implementing a complete application that lets the programmer customize the application by specializing the classes. The classes provide everything needed to define a simple Windows application with standard functionality. Programmers create their own applications here by defining subclasses of the standard application, window, view and document classes. These subclasses define the specific functionality of the application and provide the callback methods needed to drive it.

Application frameworks have several advantages. They can easily hide much of the complexity of a library or package by providing common routines to manage such complexity, offering a simple interface, and providing reasonable default actions in most situations. They can ensure that applications follow a reasonable set of standards by making the use of such standards relatively easy and making applications that introduce their own standards much more difficult to implement. This is especially important in the user interface, where a consistent look and feel among applications benefits everyone. A third advantage is that an application framework generally simplifies the writing of applications, so that new applications can be written with minimum new code and maximum reused code.

Application frameworks do have disadvantages. They are applicable only in limited circumstances, in particular when a relatively large set of applications can share a common overall structure and significant base functionality. They are also very difficult to design and implement correctly. It is fairly easy in designing such a framework either to preclude some necessary application functionality or to make a wide range of applications more difficult to write rather than simpler. A framework in this case is more a restriction than a benefit, tending to limit the range and utility of applications rather than making them easier to write. The framework implementation must ensure that the user wants to use the framework and not continually find ways to avoid it. The classes all must be designed for inheritance, precluding some methods and limiting others, as noted above.

TEMPLATES

Library classes, whether inheritable or not, can go only so far in providing reusable functionality. Their main drawback is that they must be defined before the application is written and hence cannot be written to make effective use of the actual application types. For example, it is impossible to write a generic list class to let the programmer build a list of an arbitrary application type without using casting or defining a common supertype from which the application type must inherit. Templates provide a relatively clean way to include such functionality in a library, as illustrated in our discussion of the Standard Template Library (STL) in Chapter 7. In this section and the next we consider how to use templates in building new libraries. As noted in Chapter 7, templates are a complex feature of C++ and should be used with caution even by sophisticated programmers. Here we offer some guidelines and a methodology for creating usable templates. We note that the templates here are generally designed to be reused in a small, well-understood set of applications. Designing templates for a more generic situation is more difficult and should probably be left to the experts.

Let us go back to the infinite-precision calculator. Here we used intermediate type names to isolate the code from the implementation. In the calculator class we used the type **IPCalcValue** to separate the implementation from the type representing the value, while in the implementation of rational numbers we used the type **RationalPart** to isolate the code for maintaining rationals from the specific type representing the numerator and denominator. For example, the overall calculator, represented by the class **IpCalcMainInfo**, works with either of the settings:

```
typedef double      IPCalcValue;
typedef Rational    IPCalcValue;
```

and the type **Rational** works with any of the settings:

```
typedef int         RationalPart;
typedef long        RationalPart;
typedef long long   RationalPart;
```

What we have done in these cases is to parameterize the implementation with the inserted type. While this works in a single implementation, in order to add either of these classes to a class library, we would have to fix the selection and would lose the flexibility of changing the type parameter.

The solution here is to define these classes as templates, letting the application wanting to use the library select the proper type when it instantiates the template. For example, we could define the calculator as a template:

```
template<class IPCalcValue>
class IPCalcMainInfo {
    ...
};
```

and then simply instantiate it as:

```
typedef IPCalcMainInfo<Rational>  IPCaclRationalInfo;
typedef IPCalcRationalInfo *      IPCalcMain;
...
IPCalcMain cm = new IPCalcRationalInfo;
```

The result would be the same as initially defining **IPCalcValue** as **Rational** and compiling. However, using templates lets us also create an instance of the calculator using floating-point values without changing any of the calculator code or header files. It would even allow instances of both types of calculators to be combined in the same application.

Creating a Template

While templates can be used for a simple application such as the calculator, they are much more useful in more generic situations such as the rational number class. If we really want an infinite-precision calculator, we need to make it with rational numbers of arbitrary precision. Moving from `int` to `long` or to `long long` helps some, but none of these really provide infinite precision. What we need is a type supporting arbitrarily large integers. More importantly, different applications of rational numbers need different degrees of precision: some applications need a rational type with four-byte precision (`int`), some with eight-byte precision (`long long`), and some, such as our calculator, with arbitrary precision. In such a case, it makes sense to define the type **Rational** as a template.

In building a templated class, it is generally easier to define and debug that class without the hassle of templates. This is done by defining additional types to represent the type parameters, as we did with the type **RationalPart**. Once the implementation is complete and is thoroughly tested, it can be converted into an initial template by using a series of simple steps:

- First, the header and implementation files for rational numbers must be combined into a single file. This is necessary because when the template is instantiated, the application using it must instantiate all the methods for the particular type parameter. We do this by placing simple methods directly in the class definition and then simply creating a single file including the class definition and all the remaining method implementations.

- Next the class definition and each method definition outside the class is prefixed with a template line such as:

  ```
  template<class RationalPart>
  ```

  This locally defines the parameterized type, makes the class into a template, and defines each of the methods of the templated class as an appropriate template as well.

- Finally, each reference to **Rational** as a type name in the class and method definitions is replaced with the name of the templated type **Rational<RationalPart>**. Note that this includes neither the class label at the start of the class definition nor the constructor and destructor name, which are actually function names and not type names.

The resultant class definition, with the name **Rational** changed to **RationalT** to indicate a template and the parameter name **RationalPart** shortened to **Part**, is shown in Figure 12-7. Similarly, the code for one of the methods, operator +=, is shown in Figure 12-8.

Designing Template Classes

This simple conversion process, however, is generally not sufficient since it does not analyze or restrict how the type parameter is used in the templated class. The template resulting from the conversion will work, but is probably not the best or simplest template for the particular application. Various guidelines should be followed when doing the initial design and implementation of a class that will eventually be made into a template.

One of the most important criteria when defining a template is the set of assumptions or constraints placed on the type parameters. In order to allow as much flexibility as possible, this set should be as small as possible. We recommend:

> **Make minimal assumptions about template parameters.**

A good example of this is seen in the Standard Template Library. Here there are templates that require items to be sorted or that look for matching elements. While the standard UNIX sort function depends on a special comparison function returning -1, 0, or 1 to indicate whether the first argument is less than, equal to, or greater than the second, the templated functions provided by the Standard Template Library make do with a single method, operator <, that was probably defined for other reasons. This complicates the template code: all comparisons must be done using this operator, and checking whether two items A and B are equal requires checking that neither A < B nor B < A

```
template<class Part>
class RationalT {

private:
    Part _num;
    Part _dem;

public:
    RationalT(int v = 0);
    RationalT(const RationalT<Part>&);
    ~RationalT();

    RationalT<Part>& operator =(const RationalT<Part>&);

    RationalT<Part>& operator +=(const RationalT<Part>&);
    RationalT<Part>& operator -=(const RationalT<Part>&);
    RationalT<Part>& operator *=(const RationalT<Part>&);
    RationalT<Part>& operator /=(const RationalT<Part>&);

    int compare(const RationalT<Part>&) const;

    friend ostream& operator << (ostream&,const RationalT<Part>&);

    double value() const;

protected:
    void normalize();
    static Part gcd(Part,Part);
};
```

Figure 12-7 Template RationalT for rational numbers.

```
template<class Part>
RationalT<Part>&
RationalT<Part>::operator += (const RationalT<Part>& r)
{
    Part d = _dem * r._dem;

    _num = _num * r._dem + _dem * r._num;
    _dem = d;

    normalize();

    return *this;
}
```

Figure 12-8 Initial template for rational addition.

```
Part();
Part(int);
~Part();

Part& operator *=(const Part&);
Part& operator /=(const Part&);

Part operator *(const Part&) const;
Part operator +(const Part&) const;
Part operator -(const Part&) const;
Part operator %(const Part&) const;
Part operator -() const;

int operator == (int) const;
int operator < (int) const;
int operator > (int) const;

operator double() const;
```

Figure 12-9 Operations implied initially by Rational template.

holds. However, it makes using the templates with one's own classes much simpler.

In designing the class **Rational**, we did not take into account that we wanted to make a template from the class, and thus we did not consider what operations were required of the type parameter **RationalPart**. The result is that the proposed implementation uses at least the operations shown in Figure 12-9. This set is problematic for three reasons: its inconsistent and excessive use of arithmetic operators, its use of multiple comparison operators, and its use of a conversion operator.

The current implementation assumes that both the standard and assignment forms of the arithmetic operations are available on the type parameter. In particular, both forms of multiply are required, divide is required only in the assignment form, and addition, subtraction, and modulus are required only in the standard form. Where both forms are needed, as for multiply, this puts unnecessary requirements on the template parameter. Where inconsistent forms are required, it requires an unbalanced implementation of the parameter type. This also becomes a problem if the template is ever extended, since then the programmer must be careful to use only the assumed operations.

What we should have done when creating the initial class (and should still do as part of converting that class to the template) is to ensure that the set of operations is minimal and consistent. The programmer using our template should have to assume only that either the assignment form or the standard form of all five operators is required of the parameter type. This will simplify the definition and make it easier both to code candidate parameter types and to extend the template.

In order to resolve this problem, we convert everything to use only the assignment form of the operations on the type parameter. The assignment form, as noted in "Selecting the Level of Reuse" on page 307, is more efficient and somewhat easier to code for the template class. There are two problems here, however. The first is minor: the class **Rational** is more difficult to implement since a number of expressions must be broken down into the component operands with explicit temporaries. The second, more major problem is that the unary negation operator has no assignment form, so that in order to use the assignment form consistently we must avoid using unary negation. This can be done in general (since `-v` is the same as `0-v`), with some complexity. In our implementation, it is even easier, since unary negation is used only to change the sign when doing a comparison between two rationals and that function can be rewritten. Given all this, we opt here for the more efficient form and rewrite the template functions accordingly.

A second problem with the assumptions our code made on the type parameter is that the comparison operators used by the template are not consistent and too many of them are required. In the actual code, the comparisons compare a value of the type to zero. It would make more sense to do what the Standard Template Library does: require the parameter type to have a single comparison method. In this case the method:

```
int operator < (const Part&) const;
```

is sufficient, since the integer value zero can be converted to a **Part** value by using the defined constructor.

A third problem is more subtle and more difficult to avoid. The code for the **Rational** template must convert the rational value into a double-precision number so that it can be output or returned to the caller. In doing so it needs to convert the numerator and denominator into reals. The obvious way to do this is to assume the conversion operator

```
Part::operator double() const;
```

is defined (which it is implicitly for all the built-in integer types). However, once this is defined, C++ will use it freely. Thus if you define only the assignment form of the arithmetic operators and then write within one of the template's methods:

```
p = q + r;
```

where p, q, and r are all **Part** variables, C++ does not give an error but happily generates something equivalent to

```
p = (int) (((double) q) + ((double) r));
```

which is probably not what is desired and would produce subtle accuracy problems difficult for the programmer to track down. This problem can be obviated

```
Part();
Part(int);
~Part();

Part& operator *=(const Part&);
Part& operator /=(const Part&);
Part& operator +=(const Part&);
Part& operator -=(const Part&);
Part& operator %=(const Part&);

int operator < (const Part&) const;

operator double() const;
```

Figure 12-10 Assumptions made by the template Rational on the parameter type.

by taking care when coding the template functions to use only the assignment form.

An alternative is to handle it as the Standard Template Library handles comparison. Here the overall template would be extended with an additional class whose purpose is to convert an element of the parameter class to a double. This complicates the template and makes it more difficult to use, however, so we do not attempt it.

A third alternative is to define a new method for the class **Part** returning the real value. If we were to assume **Part** is always a class, this might be practical. However, since we want to let **Part** be a built-in type, we cannot do this. Thus, we will just have to be careful in our implementation of **Rational** and use only the assignment form of the various operators.

The resultant assumptions on the type **Part** made by the modified **Rational** template appear in Figure 12-10. These are simpler and more consistent and should make it easier to implement new types to be used with the template. The changes made to the template itself are substantial but still quite simple. We first changed the type of the parameters to the gcd method for efficiency:

```
static Part gcd(const Part&,const Part&);
```

This ensures that the parameter type need not be copied implicitly for any function call. Second, we converted all the functions to restrict themselves to the agreed-upon set of operators. Thus the operator += in Figure 12-8 was recoded as shown in Figure 12-11.

Now we can continue the implementation of the infinite-precision calculator by defining the class **BigInt,** which will be used as the parameter type to get arbitrary-precision rational numbers. We again foresee that such a type may have applications beyond our current use, so we attempt to encode it as a reusable class, adding methods much as for the class **Rational**. The actual definition, given in Figure 12-12, was designed to copy that of the class **Rational**. The only differences are the two additional operators at the bottom for use with

```
template<class Part>
RationalT<Part>&
RationalT<Part>::operator += (const RationalT<Part>& r)
{
    Part t,d;

    d = _dem;
    d *= r._dem;
    t = _dem;
    t *= r._num;
    _num *= r._dem;
    _num += t;
    _dem = d;

    normalize();

    return *this;
}
```

Figure 12-11 Implementation of the template for rational addition.

```
class BigInt {
public:
    BigInt(int = 0);
    BigInt(const BigInt&);
    ~BigInt();

    BigInt& operator =(const BigInt&);

    BigInt& operator *=(const BigInt&);
    BigInt& operator /=(const BigInt&);
    BigInt& operator +=(const BigInt&);
    BigInt& operator -=(const BigInt&);
    BigInt& operator %=(const BigInt&);

    int compare(const BigInt& v) const;

    double value() const;

    friend ostream& operator << (ostream&,const BigInt&);

    int operator < (const BigInt& v) const;
    operator double() const;
};
```

Figure 12-12 Definition of the class BigInt.

the **Rational** template, which will be implemented using the other operations (`operator <` using `compare` and `operator double` using `value`).

SPECIALIZING TEMPLATES

The class **BigInt** can be implemented in a number of ways. If we just want to test the templated implementation of the class **Rational** (along with the remains of the calculator), we could define a type compatible with **BigInt** that actually used `long` or `long long` integers, or even `long double` floating-point numbers restricted internally to be integers. We could also approximate it using a fixed array of integers to get the extended length. However, in this case we want actually to provide arbitrary precision and thus the class must represent integers of arbitrary length.

This is generally done using the same techniques as for mathematics. A standard number can be viewed as a list of digits in which the first digit represents the ones place, the next the tens place, the next the hundreds place, and so on. We represent a **BigInt** similarly, although here we use a base much larger than 10. The list of digits actually must be accessible from either end. When we implement addition, we start at the least significant part, add and check for carry, and then proceed to the next most significant part. However, when we divide, we start at the most significant part (as one normally does when doing long division). Thus we use a vector to represent the digits. (A deque or doubly linked list would work equally well.)

Since vectors are defined in the standard library as a templated type, it would make sense to use them directly, i.e. to have

```
typedef vector<int>    BigIntVector;
```

While this will work, it forces us to use method names that do not follow our naming conventions (i.e. the standard template uses names such as `push_back` where we would use `pushBack`). Moreover, objects defined using this template must be accessed directly using the "`.`" notation, rather than as pointers using the "`->`" notation we normally use. Finally, as noted in Chapter 7, the vector template class is not safe since the access operators do not do any bounds checking.

It is possible, however, to specialize the standard vector template so that the names and calling conventions follow our standard conventions and the result does error checking. We first define **BigIntVector** as an inherited class, as shown in Figure 12-13. The `pushBack` and `popBack` methods provide the necessary name mapping. The two definitions of `operator ->` let us use the list as if it were a pointer. This works because code of the form:

```
v->pushBack(4);
```

where v is a **BigIntVector,** is interpreted by the C++ compiler as

```
v.operator->()->pushBack(4);
```

```
class BigIntVector : public vector<int> {
public:
    BigIntVector();
    ~BigIntVector();

    void pushBack(int x)                    { push_back(x); }
    void popBack()                          { pop_back(); }

    BigIntVector * operator->()             { return this; }
    const BigIntVector * operator->() const { return this; }

    int operator[](int v)
        {   if (v < 0 || v >= size()) return 0;
            else return vector<int>::operator[](v);
        }
    const int operator[](int v) const
        {   if (v < 0 || v >= size()) return 0;
            else return vector<int>::operator[](v);
        }
};
```

Figure 12-13 Specialized vector class defined by using inheritance.

which is then equivalent to

```
(&v)->pushBack(4);
```

since `this` inside `operator ->` will be `(&v)`. Finally, this is the same as

```
v.pushBack(4);
```

The extra overhead added by the method call should be eliminated by a reasonable compiler through inlining the methods, and thus should not be of concern. Finally, the overloaded access operators do range checking.

To complete this definition consistently, we need to add other methods as well. Some lesser-used methods such as `max_size` also use the "wrong" naming convention and there are methods such as the constructors that are not inherited. A viable vector class of our own should include all routines and define a constructor to match each of the constructors of the base class.

This seems like a lot of work for a class that is used only within the class **BigInt** and is only a small part of the application. In addition, the redefinition should be done consistently; i.e. if the application uses vector (or list or map or set) anywhere else in the application, these classes too should be defined to have similar method names. Rather than adding all these classes each time we want to use a template, it is easier to define a reusable specialized template offering the desired functionality. Here we note:

> **Use templates to specialize other templates reusably.**

```
template<class T>
class Vector : public vector<T> {
public:
    Vector()                                            { }
    Vector(int sz,const T& v = T())  : vector<T>(sz,v) { }

    void pushBack(const T& x)              { push_back(x); }
    void popBack()                         { pop_back(); }
    int maxSize() const                    { return max_size(); }

    Vector<T> * operator->()               { return this; }
    const Vector<T> * operator->() const   { return this; }

    T operator[](int v)
        {   if (v < 0 || v >= size()) return T();
            else return vector<T>::operator[](v);
        }
    const T operator[](int v) const
        {   if (v < 0 || v >= size()) return T();
            else return vector<int>::operator[](v);
        }
};
```

Figure 12-14 Templated specialization of the vector class.

To do this, we convert the **BigIntVector** class into a template class **Vector** using the procedures we used to convert **Rational** to the template **RationalT**. The result is shown in Figure 12-14. Then we could define the integer vector class we need using the declaration:

```
typedef Vector<int>    BigIntVector;
```

Creating a templated specialization as part of a class library also lets one easily extend the class. A number of potential methods are missing from the Standard Template Library: for example, it would be nice to have pushFront and popFront methods for vectors or an indexing method for lists, even if their implementations are not particularly efficient. It would also be convenient to have a sort method for vectors (as we do for lists). These are all easy to implement and could be added to the specialized template.

Note that in creating a specialized template, we should strive for generality. The class **BigIntVector** might seem a logical place to put some of the processing methods needed to implement arbitrary-precision integers. For example, there could be a method to add or subtract a second **BigIntVector** from the current one, to manage carries, etc. Such a method is specific to this implementation and should not be included in the generic template. If we want a type that provides these, we should use inheritance, as in Figure 12-15.

```
class BigIntVector : public Vector<int> {
public:
...
    void add(const BigIntVector&);
    void sub(const BigIntVector&);
...
};
```

Figure 12-15 Extending the templated specialization.

SUMMARY

One of the principal benefits claimed for object-oriented programming and object-oriented design is the ability to create reusable software. Experience has taught us, however, that such reusability is difficult to achieve without some extra steps.

Reusability can be achieved in various ways. First, individual classes can be designed to be used in multiple applications. This requires identifying classes that may be reusable before a design is completed, and then redefining them in a general but consistent manner so they are easier to understand and incorporate into multiple applications. This requires the designer to try to anticipate how the class might be reused.

A second approach is to take advantage of inheritance. Here one must define the base class carefully so it can be inherited safely by various applications. The key is to identify and isolate those aspects of the class that will change from one application to another. A related issue involves combining multiple classes into a complete framework that can be reused.

A third approach covered in this chapter is to use templates for reuse, as done in the Standard Template Library for basic data structures and a small set of algorithms. We note that a working class can be translated into a template fairly mechanically if the class is carefully defined so that the type dependencies are minimal. We also showed how to transform existing templates into specialized templates to extend or clarify their operations for reuse. Note that templates are complex and quite difficult to get right, and we don't necessarily recommend them for most instances of reuse.

EXERCISES

12.1 Implement the class **BigInt**.

12.2 Take a program you have written recently and identify a portion of it that could be reused. Provide examples of other applications that could exploit equivalent functionality. Define an interface for the class or classes that could be reused.

12.3 Design a reusable finite-state automaton class (or set of classes). The class should allow the application to define states and transitions and should accommodate actions on the transitions. Think of applications that might use the class. Evaluate your design in terms of the simplicity of the interface and how easy it is to reuse in these applications. Once the design is complete, implement the design and use the class in an example program.

12.4 In Chapter 7 we used topological sort to find the correct order for a set of dependencies. Topological sort is not a standard function or template in the STL. How would you define it so it could be used in conjunction with the STL and reused in other applications?

12.5 Define a template that modifies the standard template list class to use our naming conventions and to have additional operators for finding and setting the nth element. Implement and test the template.

12.6 Design and implement a library for manipulating images. The library should allow the user to load an image from a variety of different formats and should then provide operations on that image including clipping, blurring, enlarging, shrinking, rotating, and storing. Write a driver program to test out your library class.

12.7 Design and implement a library for doing matrix arithmetic. The library should support a matrix type and should provide the common matrix operations including multiplication, addition, inversion, and scaling (multiplication by a constant). What additional operations would be appropriate?

12.8 Develop a library class for manipulating sounds. The library should support a sound class, providing input and output as well as a reasonable set of audio operations, including volume adjustment and mixing. The library should also provide conversions between different audio formats.

Chapter 13

Design Patterns

The difference between a good designer and a poor designer is experience. Most good designers have designed a variety of different programs and have lots of experience in what does and doesn't work. Good designers can look at a problem and "see" the right solution almost immediately, usually by relating the new problem to problems they have handled previously.

One of the trends over the past few years has been to attempt to formalize this experience-based knowledge and make it readily available to others. The codification is done in terms of *patterns* of the form: "if your problem has these characteristics, then try a solution that looks something like this."

Such patterns can be developed at various levels. At the lowest level, code patterns tell you how to build a loop of a certain type, how to use an iterator, how to implement a simple binary search. At the other end, architectural patterns attempt to provide a high-level view of the overall construction of a software system. Examples here include using pipes and filters as in the UNIX shell, or doing an object-oriented breakdown of functionality. In between these two are patterns detailing middle-level design techniques. In an object-oriented environment, these describe how to implement various functionalities using classes and methods. These techniques, currently termed *design patterns*, are the focus of this chapter.

The next section of this chapter describes what we mean by a design pattern and how to represent it. After this we look briefly at a variety of different patterns, many of which we have already encountered in previous discussions.

WHAT IS A DESIGN PATTERN?

A *design pattern* is a way to put together a small set of classes and methods to solve a problem in object-oriented design. Such patterns are often more elegant or more efficient ways of solving a problem than one might otherwise think of. They offer implementation suggestions that have been used and tested in a variety of situations. They give the designer ideas and methodologies that can turn a failing design into a working one. Finally, they are a high-level means of documenting or describing a design, one that facilitates understanding among programmers without having to go into detail.

A design pattern is a potential solution to a general design problem. As such, a description of a pattern involves a definition of both the problem and the potential solution. The problem statement, specifying what the problem is and when it might arise and giving examples, is probably the most important part of this description. One of the principal difficulties beginning designers have with patterns is to treat them as solutions in search of a problem and apply them in inappropriate places.

The solution for a design pattern involves a set of classes and some of the methods and data fields of those classes. Generally the solution addresses the problem through the interaction of multiple classes using the methods and private data of the classes. A design pattern provides a skeletal implementation of these classes, focusing solely on the features needed for this interaction.

There are several ways of providing such a design pattern description. One is to use a class diagram to show the classes, their appropriate methods and data, and the relationships among them. This, however, illustrates only one part of the pattern. It does not, for example, show the pattern-related code within the methods. An alternative description is to show the code that both declares the various classes and implements the methods, using appropriate comments or pseudocode to indicate where to insert code specific to the particular problem at hand. Yet another alternative is to provide an informal natural-language description of the solution with a number of examples.

The best description combines these three techniques. The description should contain a class relationship diagram to indicate quickly to the reader the classes, methods and data comprising the solution. It should contain code fragments to show how the various methods should be implemented, or what they should do if they are problem-specific. And it should contain a natural-language description to lead the reader through the diagram and code and illustrate the range of problems for which the pattern is a solution.

This technical description of the solution is incomplete unless accompanied by a discussion of the costs and benefits of the potential solution for the given problem. This discussion should help the programmer decide if the given pattern is actually appropriate for the specific problem at hand, should point out algorithmic and performance issues in the use of the pattern, and should suggest alternative solutions.

It is important to remember that design patterns typically address general problems arising in a range of applications. A design pattern can be thought of as a reusable portion of a system design. Abstracting a design pattern from a program and defining it so as to be reusable is hard. It incurs all the difficulties mentioned with respect to reusable code in the previous chapter. Moreover, it must be done with little or no support from the programming language. Using design patterns is also like using reusable code: designers must be aware of the pattern's strengths and weaknesses and how it will fit into the particular application. They must also be willing to modify the overall design to fit a pattern better and must justify the modification and its cost.

```
typedef class PinDrawInfo *            PinDraw;
typedef class PinCallbackInfo *        PinCallback;
typedef class PinTimeOutInfo *         PinTimeOut;
typedef class PinComponentInfo *       PinComponent;
typedef class PinBallInfo *            PinBall;

enum PinKey;
enum PinSide;
```

Figure 13-1 Basic types defined by the pinball support library.

To have a concrete framework for considering a variety of different patterns, we consider a C++ library designed to support a simple pinball program. The library lets an application create various types of objects such as bumpers, lights, or flippers and place them on a board. It draws the board, does the gravity computations involved in updating the ball's position, and checks for collisions. It also provides support for time-based events and sounds.

The basic classes supported by the library are shown in Figure 13-1. **Pin-Draw** provides a top-level interface to support drawing and playing the game. It provides methods to start and stop animation, play audio, display messages, and update the score. It also uses a user-created instance of **PinCallbackInfo** to call the application from the library to compute all events occurring at the next time step. **PinTimeOutInfo** is used to define time-out events and serves as its own callback structure. The application is expected to define instances of this type with an appropriate callback handler. **PinComponent** objects represent the range of different items that can be placed on the pinball board. These are arranged in a class hierarchy that is invisible to the application. **PinBall** represents the ball object. **PinBallInfo** is actually a subclass of **PinComponentInfo** with additional methods to let the application set and query the position and velocity of the ball.

In the following sections we take a quick look at a broad range of patterns, loosely organized by the overall function. We start with patterns aimed at building objects and then look at patterns that use delegation among objects for different effects. Finally, we look at organizational patterns used to structure an application, provide different control flows, or implement particular algorithms.

These discussions of different patterns should give the reader a sense of where patterns might be applied and what the potential solutions might look like. Several of the design patterns are related to techniques we have analyzed earlier in the text and are included here to show how design techniques can be generalized and made reusable. Other patterns are new and the discussion here is intended to be a starting point for investigating other design problems. In either case, a complete description of any of the design patterns, with a detailed problem statement, solution, and trade-off discussion, is beyond the scope of this text, and the reader should refer to a more comprehensive treatment.[1] We use the pattern names in Gamma et al.'s *Design Patterns* text.

FACTORY PATTERNS

Central to most object-oriented designs is the definition of class interfaces. A good design separates the interface of a class from its implementation so that other classes do not depend on the actual class implementation. As noted in "Interface Inheritance" on page 115, one convenient way to do this is to define an interface class to represent an abstract object of the given type. The interface class contains mainly pure virtual methods used by external classes to obtain the desired behavior. The implementation of the interface class involves one or more local classes that inherit from the interface and define the virtual methods.

The principal drawback of this approach (and of using interfaces in languages such as Java that support them directly) is that the interface provides no constructor for the concrete classes and hence there is no obvious way of creating an instance of these classes. The various factory or creational patterns provide solutions to specific instances of this general problem. We start by looking at the standard solution we used on page 115, creating a factory class to instantiate the concrete objects. This is an instance of a design pattern called a *Builder*.

Builder

A factory class is a separate class, typically named after the interface class, containing one or more methods each of which returns an instance of a concrete class implementing the interface. In the example considered in Chapter 5, we were working on differentiating and simplifying; here the expressions were represented as trees and we defined an abstract interface for an arbitrary expression tree node, **DeriveExprInfo**, with three methods, `print`, `differentiate`, and `simplify`. The implementation of the trees involved a class hierarchy that included eight different types of tree nodes. The factory class, **DeriveExprFactoryInfo**, then provided eight different creation methods each of which simply created an instance of one of the types of tree nodes. For

---

1. Most of the patterns in this book can be found in *Design Patterns: Elements of Reusable Object-Oriented Software* by Erich Gamma, Richard Helm, Ralph Johnson, and John Vlissides, Addison-Wesley, 1996. Other current books include *Design Patterns for Object-Oriented Software Development* by Wolfgang Pree, Addison-Wesley, 1995, and *Pattern-Oriented Software Architecture: A System of Patterns* by Frank Buschmann, Regine Meunier, Hans Rohnert, Peter Sommerlad, and Michael Stal, John Wiley and Sons, 1996.

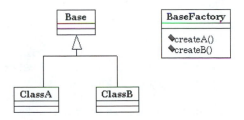

Figure 13-2 Generic diagram for Builder pattern.

example, the method `createConstant` created a new object of type **DeriveExprConst**. More importantly, the relationship of the method the user sees, `createConstant`, and the internal class this method returns is defined only in the factory class implementation. The implementation could be changed, for example, to support multiple types of constants or to merge constants with variables other than the one being differentiated against, without affecting any classes that use **DeriveExpr** and **DeriveExprFactory**.

An alternative way to describe a factory class is to use a diagram such as Figure 13-2. This diagram shows a generic instance of a factory class for a simple hierarchy and the relationship between the factory name and the name of the base class. It shows that the factory class has methods for creating each of the leaf objects of the base class. In essence, the diagram is a minimal description of what is involved in creating a factory class.

A complete description of this way to create concrete classes while only exposing the abstract interface would typically include examples such as we provided, a diagrammatic description, a more detailed discussion of the diagram and what it represents, and a discussion on using factory classes.

Some of the uses are not obvious. As we will see with other patterns, factory classes offer considerable flexibility in addressing the problem they are designed to meet. Here a standard set of parameters is often required for all the items being created. The pinball library supports a variety of different graphical objects whose application interface is shown in Figure 13-3. The implementation of the objects, however, is hidden from the application by using the factory class **PinComponentFactoryImpl** shown in part in Figure 13-4. The constructor for each of the component types takes the drawing window as one of its parameters so it can add itself to that window. Instead of having to pass this parameter to each creation function in the factory, we create a separate factory for each window and store the window in the factory object. Then this stored window is passed to the constructors.

This pinball-component factory also illustrates the flexibility inherent in using factories. It provides a generic `create` method that takes an **istream** as input, parses the text coming from the input stream to determine the appropriate type of object, and then calls the constructor for the appropriate class. The parameters for these constructors can be handled in one of two ways.

```
class PinComponentInfo {
public:
   virtual ~PinComponentInfo()                                    { }
   virtual void changeColors(PinColor,PinColor,PinColor) = 0;
   virtual void changeState(PinState) = 0;
   virtual void changeElasticity(PinCoord) = 0;
   virtual PinBoolean intersect(PinBall,PinSide) = 0;
   virtual PinBoolean bounce(PinBall,PinSide = PIN_SIDE_DEFAULT,
      PinCoord addforce1 = 0,PinSide s1 = PIN_SIDE_DEFAULT,
      PinCoord addforce2 = 0,PinSide s2 = PIN_SIDE_DEFAULT,
      PinCoord addforce3 = 0,PinSide s3 = PIN_SIDE_DEFAULT) = 0;
   virtual PinSide intersectInfo(PinBall,PinSide,PinCoord& xi,
      PinCoord& yi,PinCoord& xv,PinCoord& yv) = 0;
};


class PinBallInfo : virtual public PinComponentInfo {
public:
   virtual void changePosition(PinCoord,PinCoord) = 0;
   virtual void changeVelocity(PinCoord,PinCoord) = 0;
   virtual void cyclesPerSecond(PinCoord) = 0;
   virtual void setGravity(PinCoord) = 0;
   virtual void update() = 0;
   virtual PinBoolean bounceBall(PinCoord x,PinCoord y,
      PinCoord elasticity,PinCoord minforce,PinCoord add) = 0;
   virtual PinCoord xPosition() const = 0;
   virtual PinCoord yPosition() const = 0;
   virtual PinCoord xVelocity() const = 0;
   virtual PinCoord yVelocity() const = 0;
   virtual PinCoord radius() const = 0;
   virtual PinCoord cyclesPerSecond() const = 0;
};
```

Figure 13-3 Pinball component interfaces.

Either the routine parsing of the input text can also parse the parameters or
the various classes being defined can provide an alternate constructor taking
an **istream**. This constructor would then parse the parameters for the particular class from the input stream. The advantage of the latter strategy is that it
hides information. The advantage of the former is that common code for handling similar sets of parameters can be factored out easily and error checking
can be done before any object is constructed.

Abstract Factory

A second pattern with factory classes uses multiple factories to create different categories of objects. The pinball library currently supports 3D objects and

```
class PinComponentFactoryImpl : public PinComponentFactoryInfo {
protected:
    PinWindow draw_window;

public:
    PinComponentFactoryImpl(PinWindow);
    ~PinComponentFactoryImpl();

    virtual PinBall createBall(PinCoord x,PinCoord y,PinCoord sz);

    virtual PinComponent create(istream&);
    virtual PinComponent createWall(int npts,
                    PinCoord *,PinCoord *,PinCoord,PinCoord);
    virtual PinComponent createFloorTarget(PinCoord x,PinCoord,
                    PinCoord sz);
    virtual PinComponent createLight(PinCoord x,PinCoord y,
                    PinCoord sz);
};
```

Figure 13-4 Part of the PinComponent factory class definition.

3D drawing. On machines without appropriate graphics acceleration, both 2D and 3D displays of the game might be useful. Since the main function of the different objects is to draw themselves appropriately, this might best be implemented by defining a second hierarchy of objects, so that there would be one for 2D display and one for 3D display. The best way to support both sets would then be to provide two different factory classes. Here the top-level include file would define an abstract factory class, **PinComponentFactoryInfo**, and not its implementation. Internally, there would be two subclasses to this class, **PinComponentFactory3dImpl** for the 3D items and **PinComponentFactory2dImpl** if 2D display was desired. The application would get one or the other depending on its machine type, and would not otherwise need to know the difference.

An abstract class with multiple implementations has potential uses whenever the types of objects in a whole hierarchy might need to be changed. For example, a drawing program can use the same code to create a diagram that can then either be displayed or printed. It is also useful for portability: for example, different factories can be provided for different operating systems or different windowing packages.

Flyweight

Another pattern involving factory classes is useful when an application is to implement shared objects. Returning to the differentiation example, suppose we want to minimize the number of copies of an expression-tree node so that, for example, there is only one node for the variable X, one for the constant 1, and so on, no matter how many times these nodes actually appear in expression trees. Then the factory class could maintain a hash table or other appropriate structure to record what objects currently exist. When a creation request occurs, the class first looks in the hash table to see if the object already exists and returns a pointer to it if so. Otherwise, it creates a new object, adds it to the hash table, and then returns a pointer to it.

This pattern has a variety of applications. It can implement unique identifiers such as Lisp atoms, which allow a one-to-one mapping between names and entities, or let strings be used as identifiers. For example, one of our applications lets properties be assigned to objects using a common routine,

```
setProperty(PropertyName,PropertyValue);
```

where the name indicates which property to set and the value depends on the type. Because this is a common operation, it needs to be efficient, and continual string comparisons between the given property name and the set of valid properties for a particular object will not work. Here we implement a type **PropertyId** and a corresponding factory. The factory takes a string and returns either a new **PropertyId** object or one previously defined for the name. This is done quickly by using a hash table. Since **PropertyId** objects are unique, we can use them directly to determine which property to set.

This pattern is also useful when a system needs to create many similar objects. The classic example is a text processor that creates an object for each character of text. While a document will have lots of characters, the number of different characters (even including all the different allowable formats) is relatively small. Here each character gets its own heavyweight object with pointers to the proper font, style, size, and drawing properties. Each text position in the document gets a lightweight (or flyweight) object that just points to the appropriate character object.

Singleton

Another factory pattern is used when there should be only one object of a given class. The first time the factory is called here, it creates the object and stores a pointer to it; any later calls just return the stored pointer. This is useful, for example, for actually defining factory classes. Typically, there is only one factory class in an application. However, the application might prefer not to store a pointer to the factory object and just to request a new one each time. Rather than continually allocating (and remembering when to free) different factories, a unique object factory can be used here.

Singleton objects are also a class-oriented way to define global variables in an application. Here a class contains one or more global variables and provides a static factory method that returns a pointer to a singleton instance of the class. When the factory is first called, it creates the object and initializes the global storage; any later calls simply return a pointer to the created object. Other methods of the class then allow the application to set and access the global storage. This approach to global storage is typically safer and more object-oriented than explicitly defining such storage.

Factory Method

In many of the above cases, the factory class pattern can be implemented without actually creating a factory class. Here the particular factory class is merged with an existing class so that the factory's methods become methods of the existing class. In the pinball example, we wanted a single component factory object, and hence we needed to create a factory to create such an object. Rather than creating a new class for this purpose, we simply added the corresponding method to the **PinDrawInfo** class:

```
PinComponentFactory getComponentFactory() const;
```

in effect merging the two classes. Merging a factory class with an existing class is generally appropriate when the flexibility of a separate class is not necessary, when there is an obvious candidate class to merge with, and when the creation methods are relatively few.

One advantage of merging the creation method into a class is to allow the creation method to be inherited, thus letting an application create parallel hierarchies. Suppose, for example, that in a drawing program with a variety of drawing objects we want to create a manipulator to resize the objects. Here we assume that there are multiple manipulator types to handle different types of resizing, since resizing a line is substantially different from resizing a rectangle. The generic drawing object in this case can provide a virtual factory method to create the manipulator. Then each subobject would redefine this method to create the appropriate type of manipulator.

Prototype

A final factory pattern does not use factory classes at all: it uses prototype objects and clones them, as we did **BounceBall** objects in the bouncing balls example of Chapter 9. Here the application creates a prototype instance of an item and, when a new item is needed, it simply asks this prototype to clone itself into a new object. This approach lets the default parameters for a new object of the given type be stored in the prototype. Another situation in which a prototype-based approach to creating objects is useful arises in an editor where different types of objects can be created. For example, the bouncing balls program could let the user choose among a set of different balls using a palette. Here a prototype of each ball on the palette is created and the program keeps a pointer to the one currently selected. When a new ball is needed, the ball currently pointed to is simply cloned.

DELEGATING RESPONSIBILITY

In Chapter 5 we discussed a wide range of uses for inheritance. Inheritance is convenient in object-oriented programming because it provides a way to separate and reuse functionality between and among different classes. While inheritance offers many capabilities, it also has its drawbacks, primary among which is its lack of flexibility. The inheritance hierarchy must be fixed and defined in the source file; it cannot be determined dynamically. All the parents of the existing class must be visible and accessible. There can be multiple candidates for inheritance, but multiple inheritance is unavailable in some languages or is available but much too complex in others (such as C++). Finally, inheritance implies that the implementations are part of the resultant object.

In discussing when and where to use inheritance, we noted that delegation is often an alternative. Delegation involves passing responsibility from one object to another. It is a powerful mechanism that, with a bit of overhead and work on the programmer's part, can do everything inheritance can with more flexibility. Most dynamic object-oriented languages, such as Unger's *Self*, have delegation built into the language and use it exclusively in place of inheritance.

Delegation in C++ is more complex because there is no language support: it must be implemented explicitly by the programmer. This means that the object doing the delegation must maintain a pointer to the object to which it is delegating. Then, it must explicitly code each operation being delegated to call the appropriate method or methods on the pointed-to object.

Exactly when and how to use delegation depends on the particular problem to be solved. Design patterns describing the various uses of delegation then provide guidelines and alternatives to help programmers to the best design for the problem at hand. In this section we look briefly at these patterns.

Adaptor

The most obvious use for delegation arises when the functionality desired in a class is already defined in another object. If that functionality involves behavior, then, as we have mentioned, it is best to implement it not through inheritance but through delegation.

To illustrate this, we again consider the pinball library. In implementing the library we define an internal class, **PinWindowInfo**, to support the drawing window that actually provides the pinball-specific functionality required of a Motif drawing-area widget. In this case, we do not want **PinWindowInfo** to inherit from the class implementation of the drawing area widget for a variety of reasons. First, the widget class is essentially private. It is implemented in a separate library we do not control and our implementation cannot make assumptions about how the class is used. Second, the functionality of the pinball window class includes a considerable number of additional behaviors beyond those of the basic drawing area, among them maintaining other widgets to display the score and messages, controlling the various dialog boxes, and command processing. Third, most of the Motif class functionality is used either privately or not at all by the pinball class; it is not exported as one would expect with inheritance. Finally, we want to ensure that the pinball window class is independent of the underlying implementation so that the code originally written for UNIX and Motif can be readily ported to Windows and MFC.

In the actual implementation, **PinWindowInfo** uses delegation. When an object of this class is constructed, a set of widgets is created including a shell; a form widget for laying out the components; two label widgets, one for the score and one for the current message; and the drawing-area widget for doing the actual drawing. Any drawing request from the application to **PinWindow-Info** is then implemented by calling the appropriate methods on objects representing the drawing-area widget.

This approach ensures that the windowing and drawing behavior supported by **PinWindowInfo** is contained in its method implementations and is not directly available outside this class. It allows **PinWindowInfo** to provide an abstraction for drawing oriented to the particular task at hand rather than the underlying display implementation. It ensures that the rest of the application uses only the limited drawing methods **PinWindowInfo** provides rather than the more powerful and much less portable methods of the widget classes. It facilitates porting the drawing library to other platforms, since only the one class must be changed. Finally, it ensures that the interface to the **PinWindow-Info** class seen by the rest of the application is as simple as possible.

Bridge

Delegation is also used as an alternative to inheritance in separating an interface from its implementation. Consider the declaration of **PinDrawInfo** from the pinball library header file shown in Figure 13-5. This declaration provides a set of methods but no information on how they are implemented. However, it does not use inheritance. Instead, it defines a class type, **PinDrawDataInfo**, that is not otherwise mentioned in the header file and is the internal type that actually implements the **PinDrawInfo** class.

Implementing **PinDrawInfo** itself is straightforward. The constructor simply creates an instance of **PinDrawDataInfo** to be used for delegation; the destructor deletes the instance. Each of the methods is defined to invoke the corresponding method of this delegated object. For example, the method `playAudio` is:

```
void
PinDrawInfo::playAudio(PinSound a,PinBoolean r)
{ _data->playAudio(a,r); }
```

PinDrawInfo is one type of *wrapper class*, a class completely containing or wrapping the interface of a second class. Because access to the internal class must go through the wrapper, this is called a bridge pattern. In **PinDrawInfo**,

```
class PinDrawInfo {
private:
    class PinDrawDataInfo * _data;

public:
    PinDrawInfo(int& argc,const char ** argv);
    ~PinDrawInfo();

    PinComponentFactory getComponentFactory() const;

    void setCallback(PinCallback);// Set the callback for user
    void setCycleTime(PinTime);   // Set the time between cycles

    void startGame();             // Start playing the game
    void stopGame();              // Pause the game

    void playAudio(PinSound,PinBoolean repeat = 0);
    void changeScore(PinScore);
    void displayInfo(PinString,PinTime fortime = 0);

    void defineKeyMap(int key,PinKey);

    void mainLoop();
    void cleanUp();                   // call before exit

    PinDrawDataInfo * data() const;// for internal use only
};
```

Figure 13-5 Declaration of the PinDrawInfo.

there is a one-to-one correspondence between the wrapper object and the object it is wrapping. This type of correspondence is easy to manage because the constructors and destructors of the wrapper can be used directly to build or destroy the internal object.

Wrappers can also be used when this correspondence does not hold. A simple wrapper class without a one-to-one correspondence can be thought of as a pointer and is sometimes called a *pointer class*. Such a class typically has a single data field containing a pointer to the item being wrapped. Copying or assigning the wrapper class is equivalent to copying or assigning this pointer. Defining operator -> for the wrapper lets it be treated exactly as if it were a pointer. The advantage of using a wrapper instead of a pointer is that the wrapper can define additional methods to provide an external interface, as the **PinDrawInfo** wrapper does. Moreover, because the functionality of the pointer is now enclosed in a class, that pointer can now automatically handle things like checking for an undefined or unset pointer, data sharing, and reference counting.

The advantage of wrapper classes over inheritance is that wrappers require neither a factory class (either they automatically construct a new object when the constructor is called or they offer a natural location for defining a factory method) nor virtual methods. They also provide more flexibility, since it is easy to offer multiple wrapper classes for the same underlying object with different functionality. Moreover, the methods provided by the internal class can be changed without changing the wrapper declaration or the classes that use the wrapper, simply by changing how the wrapper's methods are implemented. The disadvantages of wrappers are that their methods must be invoked with the "." notation, that the user must implement the methods explicitly, and that certain operations like `new` and `delete` must be implemented using methods. Our preference is to use the built-in facilities of the language and thus to use inheritance rather than wrappers. A more important consideration is to maintain consistency throughout an interface: that is, use either inheritance or wrappers throughout, but not both.

Decorator

Another problem in which delegation is useful arises when some behavior of an object can change significantly over the course of an application. With delegation one can change the behavior of an object dynamically at run time simply by changing the object that is pointed to. A system can use this to adapt to users' preferences without being recompiled. It can also be used in situations in which objects must effectively change class. For example, some components in the pinball library have multiple states. A popup barrier can either be down or up, and how the ball intersects and bounces off it and how it is drawn are all affected by its current state. This can be implemented by putting `if` statements (or `switch` statements if there are more than two states) in each of the component's methods to handle the different cases. A better approach, however, is to have the barrier object delegate its intersection and drawing functionality to a third object and to simply change the delegation pointer when the object changes state. This use of delegation to adorn an object with different behaviors at different times is an example of a decorator design pattern.

Facade

The problems to which we have applied delegation so far all have one object delegating responsibilities or behaviors to another object through a single pointer. In other problems one must consider a generalization of delegation in which the wrapper object contains multiple pointers and implements its methods by using some combination of them.

Multiple delegation like this usually arises in complex, multilevel designs that require information hiding. Here one top-level object is used to encapsulate the interfaces of multiple second-level objects. The underlying objects can be thought of as a subsystem and the top-level object as the portal that allows the rest of the application access to that subsystem. The use of a single top-level object simplifies the interface to the subsystem and ensures that the rest of the application does not need to know the underlying details of its implementation. This increases the isolation among components, making it easier, for example, for different programmers to implement different subsystems. We see examples of this in "Design By Subsystem" on page 429. This use of a single class to provide an interface to a coherent set of implementation classes is an instance of a facade design pattern.

We already noted in the pinball program that the class **PinDrawInfo** is used as a wrapper to an internal class **PinDrawDataInfo**. In actuality, the class **PinDrawDataInfo** is a facade with multiple delegation. The pinball library is responsible for a variety of tasks. Representing objects and handling collisions is done by the **PinComponentInfo** hierarchy. Managing an arbitrary set of time-outs and their associated actions is done by the class **PinTimeOutList**. Letting the front end select and define input keys and then processing user input is done by the class **PinKeyMapInfo**. Interacting with Motif and OpenGL is done with the class **PinWindowInfo**. Providing audio output for background and immediate sounds is done in the class **PinAudioInfo**.

Except for the root class of the **PinComponentInfo** hierarchy, none of these classes is exposed to the front end of the pinball system. Instead, whatever interaction the front end needs with these various back-end classes is done through the facade class **PinDrawDataInfo**. For example, to play a bell sound, the front end calls

```
PinDrawInfo::playAudio("bell");
```

which serves as a bridge to

```
PinDrawDataInfo::playAudio("bell");
```

This function in turn delegates, with its body looking like

```
void
PinDrawDataInfo::playAudio(PinSound audiofile, PinBoolean repeat)
{
    if (pin_audio == NULL) pin_audio = new PinAudioInfo;

    pin_audio->playAudio(audiofile, repeat);
}
```

Calls for managing time-outs, window management, and key mapping are all handled similarly.

Proxy

Another problem in which wrappers and delegation can be appropriate arises when the underlying objects might not exist. An application might want to use objects that are not immediately available to it under various circumstances, including implementing persistence and remote objects.

Consider a system that supports persistent objects through an object database. Here objects have a lifetime extending beyond any particular run of a program. Any object created or modified by the application is stored in a database when the application exits; the next time the application starts up, the objects are loaded from the database. To be effective, such systems should not load all the objects from the database immediately, but instead load them as they are needed. However, when an object is loaded from the database, it often contains references to other objects, some of which have not yet been loaded. This is typically handled by replacing normal pointers to these objects with intelligent wrappers or proxies. When such a wrapper is accessed, it first checks if the underlying object has been loaded from the database. If not, the wrapper accesses the database to load it and sets up new proxies for any new objects it points to. Once the wrapper ensures the object is loaded, it does the appropriate pointer access. This use of a wrapper object as a proxy is an instance of the proxy design pattern.

Another increasingly common use of proxy objects occurs in a distributed or client-server application. Here an application is divided into multiple processes, some of which run as servers, potentially handling multiple users simultaneously, while others run as clients, generating requests to the server. In an object-oriented world, one can think of such applications in object terms, with some objects being maintained by the clients and others being shared and maintained by the servers. In order to simplify coding such applications, one can code the clients so that they can treat the server objects as if they were actual objects in the client application. This is done by creating proxy objects or wrappers for the server objects. These proxies implement all the external methods required by the client from the server object and delegate the implementation of these methods to the server. The difference here from a standard wrapper is that the proxy objects do not simply invoke the underlying method. Instead, they create a message that is sent over the network to the server process, wait while the server process receives and processes that request, and then read the reply sent back over the net and translate it into a return value to pass back to the original caller. A more detailed explanation of such remote objects is given in "Remote Objects" on page 368.

While coding such proxies can be rather complex, today's environments attempt to automate their implementation as much as possible. Both DCOM under Windows and CORBA under UNIX have programs to take a description of the methods the server objects should provide and generate an appropriate proxy class.

CONTROL PATTERNS

So far we have considered a variety of different patterns dealing first with problems involving object creation and then with problems involving behaviors obtained through object interaction. These are the patterns of broadest applicability. In this and the next section we look at some patterns that arise less frequently but are still useful. The problems these patterns address are a bit more difficult to characterize. They concern somewhat complex control or structural situations that are often difficult to handle but have relatively standard solutions with broad applicability.

Composite

We first consider problems arising when a logical grouping or composite of application objects can be treated as a single application object, for example treating a group of shapes as a single shape. Such applications typically involve drawing or graphical editing. The underlying applications here have an abstract class representing a generic drawing object. A composite design pattern addresses the need for group objects by defining a subtype of this abstract type to represent the group. This subtype contains a list of the group elements that has pointers to objects of the abstract type and hence can contain other groups as well as primitive objects. It implements the various generic operations of the abstract type by iterating through its list of components and calling the corresponding operation on each subcomponent.

Hierarchies of objects requiring composites are not restricted to drawing applications. Another instance where they arise involves trees that reflect language constructs such as expressions. The symbolic differentiation example of Chapter 5 used the abstract class **DeriveExprInfo** to represent an expression tree that could either be a leaf node or a subtree. Subtrees in this case consisted of an operator and one or two additional subtrees that could again be leaf nodes or other subtrees. The abstract class defined methods such as `print` that the non-leaf nodes then implement by calling print on their components.

Interpreter

The use of tree objects to represent expressions is a specific instance of the more general situation in which a tree of objects represents the syntactic structure of a language. This is done by parsing the language into an intermediate tree form reflecting the grammar of the language. While the specific details of this are beyond the scope of this text, we consider expression trees similar to those used in the symbolic differentiation example to clarify the basic principles.

While trees are a natural representation for grammar-based languages, it is sometimes not clear how to use them. The interpreter pattern shows how to use the tree representation directly to implement the language. Here implementing the language generally means evaluating it, but can just as easily refer to code generation, printing, or some other related use. The interpreter design pattern handles these uses by defining an abstract method for the tree to perform the desired operation. This method is then implemented for each node type to do whatever local interpretation is required for that node type.

This is best illustrated with an example. Consider a calculator program in which the user types in an expression and the program then prints the resultant value. One way to implement such a program is first to parse the input expression and build an expression tree similar to those we built for symbolic differentiation. Interpreting the expression tree in this case would mean evaluating it. A generic method, `evaluate`, would be defined for the abstract class representing the tree. Then each type of node of the tree would provide an implementation of this method. A leaf node would return its constant value or, if symbols are allowed, would look up the symbol name in the symbol table and return the corresponding value. An operator node would first get the value of its subtrees by calling the `evaluate` method on them, and then build the resultant value according to the type of operator it represented. The result calculated at the root would be the value of the input expression.

Programs dealing primarily with textual input generally define a command language to let the user enter commands and their corresponding arguments. This language is generally easy to parse and is an excellent candidate for a tree representation that can then be interpreted as above.

Command

The problems that come up when dealing with command languages in today's applications, however, often require more sophistication than a simple interpreter pattern can provide. Most modern systems have gotten away from textual input and instead allow a mixture of mouse, menu, button, and keyboard input. Moreover, a mark of a good user interface today is the ability to manipulate commands. One almost ubiquitous example of this is the UNDO button that makes the application undo the effect of the most recent command. In better user interfaces, an UNDO command can be used for many commands and can be mixed with a REDO button to execute the command that was just undone. Another, less common instance involves command macros. Editors such as *emacs* or Microsoft *Word* let the user create keystroke macros consisting of a sequence of commands; the commands in the macro can then all be executed with a simple keystroke.

In order to create an application that can handle command undo, macros, or any other feature in which the user manipulates commands, one must make commands concrete. The command design pattern lets one create objects to represent the different commands by defining a class hierarchy to reflect the various commands. For example, a simple editor might include the command classes shown in Figure 13-6.

```
            EditCommandInfo
        EditCommandBuffer
            EditCommandCut
            EditCommandPaste
            EditCommandcopy
        EditCommandMove
            EditCommandUp
            EditCommandDown
            EditCommandLeft
            EditCommandRight
            EditCommandTop
            EditCommandNextLine
        EditCommandTyping
            EditCommandKey
            EditCommandTab
            EditCommandReturn
```

Figure 13-6 Parts of an object hierarchy for editor commands.

Implementing a system in which classes are used to represent commands is fairly straightforward. The user interface merely handles creating command objects and passing them off to a central interpreter. It is not responsible for taking any actions. The central interpreter maintains a list of the current commands for undo or for embedding in a macro. After it has stored the command appropriately, it invokes a do method on the command object to actually execute the command. Each command is thus responsible for all its interaction with the system.

It is often useful in this case to add other methods besides do to each command. For example, an easy way to provide an undo facility is to have each command offer an undo method as well. Here the command stores the information needed for undo when the do method is called. Other useful additions are input and output methods to let the command be saved in a file and later reloaded, thus supporting savable macros. The output methods can also be used to provide a user-readable log of the session.

Iterator

There are several problems in which the programmer must organize the algorithms and control flow of an application but the standard programming constructs of the implementation language do not seem appropriate or adequate. A very convenient solution in these cases is to use objects to represent pieces of the program.

A clear instance of this strategy occurs when the application must iterate over a complex data structure. While somewhat messy-looking loops can step through a linked list, iterating over a hash table, over binary tree nodes in a given range, or over some more complex user structure can involve considerable code and complexity. A solution that simplifies this task involves representing iterators with objects. Iterator objects are used extensively by the Standard Template Library. Each type of composite object in the library provides an iterator to access the elements of the composite in order.

Iteration objects have a broad range of applications. If a program creates a collection object of any sort and some part of the application will need to access an identifiable subset of the elements of this collection, it is a good idea to provide such access through an application-defined iterator class. Using a new class here lets the programmer restrict how the iterator is used and how access to the individual elements is obtained. It also provides a convenient hook for adding operators that are relevant to the iterator itself.

Iterators can be implemented in two different ways. The Standard Template Library uses iterators as an adjunct to the collection class. Here operations involving a position in the class are passed both the iterator and the class. For example, to erase a list element at the position indicated by an iterator, one uses the method

```
void list<T>::erase(list<T>::iterator);
```

The alternative implementation is for the iterator to keep track of the list it is iterating over. Here operations affecting the list can be done using only the iterator. For example, the Rogue Wave template library list iterators provide the corresponding deletion operation without any reference to the actual list object:

```
Boolean RWTValSlistIterator<T>::remove();
```

The two methods also differ in their basic loop constructs. With the Standard Template Library, the list must be referred as well:

```
Iterator iter;
for (iter = list->begin(); iter != list->end(); ++iter) ...
```

while for Rogue Wave, only the iterator needs to be considered:

```
Iterator iter(list);
for(iter.reset(); ++iter; ) ...
```

Both approaches have their advantages and disadvantages. The most important reason to decide which to use, however, should be to achieve consistency in how iterators are used throughout the application.

Strategy

A second problem in which objects are useful as control structures concerns complex algorithms that may be subject to change or uncertainty. Many applications require such an algorithm. Rather than making the overall design and hence the whole application dependent on a particular algorithm, it is preferable to encapsulate the algorithm in an object. This approach to design using algorithm classes is an important one first introduced in Chapter 2, where the class **KnightHeuristicInfo** was used for the heuristics involved in selecting the next move.

Algorithm classes are useful in many situations. The most obvious type of situation is analogous to the heuristics in the knight's-tour problem. In these situations the application needs some task to be done for which the methodology or algorithm is not well defined. Creating an algorithm class here isolates the rest of the application from the eventual decisions about the implementation. It also lets different implementations of the task be tried to determine which best suits the task at hand.

Another situation in which algorithm objects are useful occurs when a program might want to use one of several different approaches simultaneously. Graph layout is such a problem. There are a lot of algorithms for laying out a graph, all with their own strengths and weaknesses; no one algorithm works well for all graphs. It is often desirable to let the user try different algorithms to achieve the most aesthetically pleasing layout. Making the layout algorithm into an abstract class here lets a variety of different approaches be tried and lets the program easily switch from one approach to another.

A third situation in which algorithm classes are useful occurs when the designer can isolate an algorithm or programming task that might change as the program evolves. Isolating the task in a separate class simplifies such changes since the change and its effects are restricted to the new class and do not involve a large portion of the application. For example, a word processor might be equipped initially with a simple spelling checker. The programmer, anticipating that this will need to become more sophisticated in the future (say to include grammar checking or additional languages), isolates the checker in a separate class to ensure such evolution is relatively simple.

Template

Some of the problems in which algorithm objects are useful are more complex than the above examples. Here, while the overall algorithm stays the same, some of the algorithmic details vary depending on the situation in which the algorithm is used and the data on which it is used. Here the algorithm actually defines a generic template for the solution. Objects and the programming language are then used to specialize the template for each particular use.

There are three approaches to such specialization. The first is to use templates directly. This is what the Standard Template Library does to define a range of different algorithms that can be tailored by the application. For example, it defines a sort algorithm using the template

```
template <class Iter,class Compare>
void sort(Iter first,Iter last,Compare comp);
```

Here the programmer defines an instance of the template by calling sort with appropriate iterators and a comparison object, as in Figure 13-7. The sort template here is parameterized in two ways. First, the type of iterator determines

```
typedef vector<int>          IntVector;
typedef IntVector::iterator  IntVectorIter;

class IntCompare {
public:
    operator ()(int a,int b)       { return a < b; }
};

void
test(int ct)
{
    IntVector v;
    int i;

    for (i = 0; i < ct; ++i) v.push_back(rand());

    sort(v.begin(),v.end(),IntCompare());

    for (i = 0; i < ct; ++i) cout << v[i] << endl;
}
```

Figure 13-7 Using the standard library sort template.

the type of item to be sorted. In this case the iterator needs to be a random-access iterator, meaning that the underlying type must allow an index operation; in this case, we use a vector.

The second parameterization is the type of comparison to be done. The Standard Template Library expects this to be an object function, i.e. an object with operator () defined for two elements of the base type. Here it interprets it as a comparison (<) function that determines the sort order. The parameter in the sort call, IntCompare(), creates a temporary object of this type. This use of sort allows arbitrary comparison operations of varying sophistication by simply using different objects in the call. For example, to allow a complex sort on multiple fields with multiple sort directions and sort types, the compare object would have data fields describing the fields and sort types and would implement the comparison accordingly.

The use of an external object to assist an algorithm, as in the sort, shows the second approach to parameterization and is a good general technique that does not require templates. A typical approach to such parameterization uses callbacks and callback objects (as described in "Inheritance for Callbacks" on page 123). The pinball library, for example, provides the main loop for a pinball game. The basic algorithm for the main loop is to do any logical actions required by the game logic, update the current ball position, and check the current timers. However, the library does not know what the game logic is. The algorithm thus provides an abstract callback object of type **PinCallbackInfo** that is invoked at the proper time to handle the game logic.

The third technique for parameterizing an algorithm is to use inheritance. Here a general algorithm is implemented in the superclass. Where this algorithm needs to take specialized actions, it defines a virtual method that can be used either to define different actions for different elements of the hierarchy or to provide a generic algorithm in a library that can be specialized by the user through inheritance.

In the pinball example, we use such specialization to define the algorithm for intersection. There are two top-level methods to handle intersections between the ball and an arbitrary component, as shown in Figure 13-8. The first, `intersect`, just checks if the ball is touching the given component. The second, `bounce`, checks if the ball is touching the component and, if so, causes the ball to bounce off that component, possibly with an extra force that depends on the side of the component it hits. The generic algorithms in this case handle the tests that are independent of the individual component types. The `intersect` method first uses the bounding box of the component to make a quick intersection check. If this succeeds, it calls the virtual method `inter-sectInfo`, which determines if the ball actually intersects the component and, if so, provides the point of intersection (xi, yi), the velocity of the ball orthogonal to the component (xv, yv), and the side of the component the ball is hitting. The routine uses the latter value to determine if intersection actually occurs. The `bounce` routine is more sophisticated: after checking for intersection in the same way, it then uses the values returned by the `intersectInfo` method to change the velocity of the ball using the method `bounceBall`.

Visitor

Templated algorithm objects allow slightly different methods to be applied to different members of a class hierarchy. This is done frequently, since it is one of the primary reasons for creating a hierarchy in the first place. However, it is sometimes not convenient or practical to expand the class definitions for all the elements of the hierarchy every time some new operation needs to be defined. The classes may already be too large or, more commonly, the class hierarchy is defined in one portion of the system and the need to use the hierarchy occurs in another. In these cases, it is desirable to separate the hierarchy from the new methods that will use it.

This type of separation can be done using a visitor design pattern. Here an abstract type, **Visitor**, is defined outside of the hierarchy to implement abstract operations. For each subclass in the hierarchy, the **Visitor** class defines a virtual method to implement the abstract operation for that subclass. Each subclass in the hierarchy is augmented with a single virtual method, `accept(Visitor)`, that calls the corresponding member of the **Visitor** class. The visitor pattern thus works by translating a virtual call to

```
object->Subclass::accept(Visitor v);
```

into a call to

```
PinBoolean
PinRootComponent::intersect(PinBall pb,PinSide wh)
{
    PinCoord xi,yi,xv,yv;
    PinSide ps;

    if (pb == NULL) return FALSE;
    if (!bounding_box->check(pb)) return FALSE;

    ps = intersectInfo(pb,wh,xi,yi,xv,yv);

    if (ps == PIN_SIDE_NONE) return FALSE;
    return TRUE;
}


PinBoolean
PinRootComponent::bounce(PinBall pb,PinSide ps,
        PinCoord force1,PinSide ps1,PinCoord force2,PinSide ps2,
        PinCoord force3,PinSide ps3)
{
    PinCoord xi,yi,xv,yv;
    PinBoolean fg = TRUE;

    if (pb == NULL) return FALSE;
    if (!bounding_box->check(pb)) return FALSE;

    ps = intersectInfo(pb,ps,xi,yi,xv,yv);
    if (ps == PIN_SIDE_NONE) return FALSE;
    if (ps == PIN_SIDE_TOP) return TRUE;

    if (ps1 == PIN_SIDE_DEFAULT || (ps&ps1) != 0)
        fg = pb->bounceBall(xv,yv,_elasticity,min_force,force1);
    else if (ps2 == PIN_SIDE_DEFAULT || (ps&ps2) != 0)
        fg = pb->bounceBall(xv,yv,_elasticity,min_force,force2);
    else if (ps3 == PIN_SIDE_DEFAULT || (ps&ps3) != 0)
        fg = pb->bounceBall(xv,yv,_elasticity,min_force,force3);

    return fg;
}
```

Figure 13-8 Intersection methods for pinball components.

```
v->visitSubclass(SubClass object);
```

A new operation can then be added to the hierarchy by defining a subtype of **Visitor** and defining the appropriate methods to implement the given operation for the different subtypes. The operation is invoked by creating an appropriate object of the operation subclass and then calling accept on the object to be operated on with this new object as the parameter. The method in turn invokes the method of the operation corresponding to the type of node and passes the actual subclass object. This lets the new visitor object actually implement the operations differently for different elements of the hierarchy.

While this sounds complex, it is really rather simple. An example will make it clearer. A primary use of visitor patterns is to support multiple operations over complex, multi-class data structures such as expressions or parse trees. Consider the simple expression trees we constructed in Chapter 5, and suppose we want to separate our previous design into reusable components by separating the expression parser from the code that does printing, differentiation, and simplification.

To achieve such isolation, we use a visitor object to support arbitrary operations on the expression trees. This requires several changes. The top of Figure 13-9 shows the new definitions of **DeriveExprInfo** without the `differentiate`, `print`, or `simplify` methods and their support methods but with a virtual `accept` method added. The middle of the figure shows the corresponding definition of the abstract visitor class. Note that this class includes methods for each of the creatable subtypes of **DeriveExprInfo** and that these methods are each passed an actual pointer to the particular subclass type. Given the definitions of the visitor class, the methods for the various subclasses look like the example at the bottom of the figure.

The final step in building a visitor pattern is to use the visitor class. Here we define a subclass of **DeriveVisitorInfo** and then define the implementation of the operation to be performed for each of the methods. The top of Figure 13-10 shows the definition of the visitor class for printing. Note that the class is used to contain the argument (the stream to print to) so that it need not be passed in each call. The bottom of the figure shows the implementation of the print operation for the add class. Note here the recursive calls to visit the various subtrees.

ALGORITHMIC PATTERNS

The visitor pattern is actually a combination of control and an algorithm, since it provides a structure for dealing with additional methods as well as the code techniques required to utilize that structure. There are a number of additional patterns that are more algorithmic in nature. These tend to be needed to handle situations in which objects are used to simplify what might otherwise be considered a purely procedural task.

Mediator

One such situation arises when multiple objects have complex patterns of interaction. Rather than allowing the objects to interact directly, a cleaner and

```
typedef class DeriveVisitorInfo *          DeriveVisitor;

class DeriveExprInfo {
protected:
    DeriveExprInfo()                                  { }
public:
    virtual ~DeriveExprInfo()                         { }
    virtual void accept(DeriveVisitor)        { }
    virtual DeriveExpr clone(DeriveExpr * = NULL) const = 0;
};



class DeriveVisitorInfo {
protected:
    DeriveVisitorInfo()                                  { }
public:
    virtual ~DeriveVisitorInfo()                         { }

    void visitConst(DeriveExprConst *)               { }
    void visitVar(DeriveExprVar *)                   { }
    void visitAdd(DeriveExprAdd *)                   { }
    void visitSub(DeriveExprSub *)                   { }
    void visitMul(DeriveExprMul *)                   { }
    void visitDiv(DeriveExprDiv *)                   { }
    void visitExp(DeriveExprExp *)                   { }
    void visitUnaryMinus(DeriveExprUnaryMinus *) { }
    void visitPatVar(DeriveExprPatVar *)             { }
};



void
DeriveExprConst::accept(DeriveVisitor v) { v->visitConst(this); }
```

Figure 13-9 Definitions for implementing expression tree visitor.

more flexible solution can often be obtained by introducing a new object to control the interaction. This occurs naturally in defining dialog boxes, as we saw
in Chapter 10. The dialog-box object serves here as a controller or mediator for
the various widgets of the dialog box. The different widgets handle their own
local interaction, but the overall dialog-box interaction, including relationships among the widgets and interactions between the widgets and the application, is handled by the dialog controller. For example, the dialog controller
may use the value of one field to set or update other fields, as in a set of radio
buttons where only one should be set at a time, or a numeric slider with a separate text widget.

```
class DerivePrintVisitorInfo {
private:
    ostream& out_stream;
protected:
    DerivePrintVisitorInfo(ostream&);
public:
    void visitConst(DeriveExprConst *);
    void visitVar(DeriveExprVar *);
    void visitAdd(DeriveExprAdd *);
    void visitSub(DeriveExprSub *);
    void visitMul(DeriveExprMul *);
    void visitDiv(DeriveExprDiv *);
    void visitExp(DeriveExprExp *);
    void visitUnaryMinus(DeriveExprUnaryMinus *);
};


void
DerivePrintVisitorInfo::visitAdd(DeriveExprAdd * a)
{
    out_stream << "(";
    a->lhs_expr->accept(this);
    out_stream << "+";
    a->rhs_expr->accept(this);
    out_stream << ")";
}
```

Figure 13-10 Examples of visitor pattern implementations.

Memento

Another problem that can arise in a variety of applications involves the need to save and restore the state of an object. For example, we have already discussed the use of command objects to represent commands so as to implement an undo facility. However, implementing the undo method for a command requires preserving portions of the previous state of the system. While this can be done by duplicating the original objects, the amount of work involved (especially if the objects represent a complex structure) and the need for book-keeping can make this a difficult task.

An easier approach is to create another object that can be used to save or restore the state of any objects whose contents might later be needed to implement the undo. This memento object can be more compact than the original object since it needs only enough information to create a new object equivalent to the original. It can also be a single object representing a complete set of objects. The implementation of such a memento pattern requires that the original object have a method to create such a memento and that the memento class provide a method to recreate the original object.

A variant of this technique can also be used to save and restore objects on disk, as with serialization in Java. Here the memento is not an actual object but instead is represented as a string of characters or a record in a data file. Each object needing to be stored must again provide two methods, one to create the memento and one to restore from it. However, in this case the methods take an **ostream** or **istream** object as the location to record or retrieve their information, rather than creating another object.

Observer

One final problem in modern applications involves coordinating the actions of a diverse set of objects. While the mediator pattern is designed to handle a fixed set of interacting objects, there are times when the objects needing to interact are not known to one another. For example, a spreadsheet program might give the user both spreadsheet and graphical views of the data. What graphical views are displayed at any one time is up to the user and cannot be known in advance. However, if graphical views are displayed, then these views should be updated whenever the spreadsheet changes.

An observer class is one solution to this type of problem. Here, a class is created to handle interactions between the spreadsheet and other views. The class provides a method to be called by the spreadsheet to indicate that something had changed, and also a method a view could call to register the fact that it was interested in changes. The observer object keeps a list of currently active views and, when told by the spreadsheet that a change has occurred, it invokes appropriate callback methods for the currently registered views.

This approach is often called a *publish-subscribe* methodology: the spreadsheet is publishing, in that it is telling everyone something has changed, and the various views are subscribing through the observer so that they receive instances of the spreadsheet's publication. The approach is easily adapted to multiple subscribers and multiple publishers. It can also be generalized to work with clients in separate processes using messages.

SUMMARY

Design patterns are a valuable tool for the designer. They provide tested and workable solutions to common problems and lead a design in a direction that will most probably be correct and effective.

A design pattern describes how to assemble a small set of classes and methods to solve a problem. In order to use the full potential of design patterns, the designer must understand them fully. The most crucial part of their description, the problem, is often overlooked. Each design pattern is a solution to a particular problem. Unless the designer understands exactly what that problem is, the pattern either will not be applied where it should be or, possibly worse, will be applied where it shouldn't be.

The various patterns can be divided into three categories. Those in the first category, factory patterns, are used for different problems involving creating new objects without directly calling the object's constructor. These patterns include:

- *Builder*: using a simple factory class.
- *Abstract factory*: using multiple factory classes for a common set of objects.
- *Flyweight*: constructing shared objects.
- *Singleton*: providing a global variable using a factory class.
- *Factory method*: putting the factory inside another class.
- *Prototype*: creating new objects by cloning.

A second category of patterns involves coordinating objects by using delegation. These patterns include:

- *Adaptor*: using delegation to provide functionality in one object that is already available in another.
- *Bridge*: treating a class as if it were a pointer to separate an implementation from an interface.
- *Decorator*: using delegation to obtain behavior.
- *Facade*: combining groups of related objects into subsystems with a common front end.
- *Proxy*: using delegation to provide placeholders to remote objects.

The final category of patterns deals with control. The first three of these are used for structuring control in an application, the next four provide control constructs of various types, and the remainder offer more specialized functionality. These are:

- *Composite*: using objects to achieve groupings.
- *Interpreter*: interpreting a meta-language.
- *Command*: organizing commands for easy undo/redo.
- *Iterator*: stepping through a composite structure.
- *Strategy*: using an object to represent an algorithm.
- *Template*: dividing a algorithm into fixed and variable portions.
- *Visitor*: providing indirect methods on a class hierarchy.
- *Mediator*: using an object to control the interaction of other objects.
- *Memento*: providing a way of saving and restoring an object's state.
- *Observer*: implementing a publish-subscribe framework.

EXERCISES

13.1 Take a program you have written and attempt to identify the patterns used in it.

13.2 For each pattern in the set of delegation patterns, find a particular problem, either in one of your programs or in some anticipated task, to which it is applicable. Justify the pattern's applicability.

13.3 Repeat the above exercise for the various factory, control, and algorithmic patterns.

13.4 Identify all the patterns used in the solution to the knight's-tour problem shown in Appendix B.

13.5 Do a top-level design of the orrery program described in "Object-Oriented Design" on page 6, paying particular attention to patterns. Make a list of the patterns used and the problems they solved.

13.6 Implement the symbolic differentiation program using visitors, as outlined in "Visitor" on page 348.

13.7 Design a program to handle filling out forms. The program should support the definition of arbitrary forms containing text, graphics, and boxes that need to be filled in. Each box to be filled in should have associated information designating what it should look like and a range of legal values. The program should provide the user with a on-screen image of the form and should allow the user to enter values in each of the boxes. Appropriate checks should be made as the values are entered. The output should include an image of the completed form as well as a listing of the fields and their values in a computer-readable form.

Chapter 14
Multiple-Process Programming

Most programs used to be written as single systems needing little if any communication with other programs except through files or an occasional database system. As computers have become more powerful, programs larger and more complex, and computer networks more pervasive, this has changed. Today, most complex systems, from word processors to databases to the computers that run aircraft, are made up of multiple programs communicating with one another. Many applications now run over the Internet or use "client-server" computing. Companies such as Microsoft and Sun as well as computer pundits are hailing a new world in which programming involves hooking up independent components. All this means that today's programmers must learn to survive in a multiple-process world.

Writing a system using multiple communicating processes running on the same or different machines has several advantages. It can make the individual components easier to write since the components themselves are simpler than the overall system. It can be used to isolate faults and make the system more fault-tolerant. It lets one define large-scale reusable components and thereby can encourage extensive reuse. It can provide a clean division of labor when multiple programmers are working on a project. It can make project evolution easier through the addition or substitution of high-level components rather than a low-level rewrite of the overall code.

There are also clear disadvantages to the multiple-process approach to programming. The most obvious is that multiple communicating processes can increase system complexity by orders of magnitude. The patterns of communication among the components, which used to be simple procedure calls, are now time-dependent, possibly error-prone, asynchronous messages. Understanding and debugging timing and synchronization issues in a multiprocess system can more than soak up the savings achieved by dividing a problem into processes in the first place.

A variation on multiple-process programming is multithreaded programming. Here multiple threads of control exist within a single address space, effectively using multiple processors for a single application. This means that the different threads all share the same easily accessible data, and thus have less need to communicate through messages or some related mechanism. But this also means that the programmer must ensure that the different threads do not interfere with one another by attempting to manipulate the same data simultaneously. The attention to synchronization issues this requires can easily make multithreaded programs very complex. Moreover, the need for synchronization can counteract the benefits of multiple threads, often making programs run slower rather than faster.

In this chapter we begin to look at how to construct workable multiple-process programs. We start with an overview of simple interprocess communication mechanisms. Then we look at sockets, the most commonly used communications mechanism today. We illustrate how to program with sockets and show how they can be used in an object-oriented manner to facilitate structured communication among processes. We next relate this to the current evolving approaches involving distributed objects such as CORBA under UNIX or ActiveX under Windows. Finally, we give an extended discussion of multithreaded programming and synchronization issues.

INTERPROCESS COMMUNICATION

Most programs need to communicate with the outside world and with other programs. In our day-to-day programming experiences we see compilers passing data to loaders and debuggers. We see airline reservation systems in which individual computers need to communicate with a central database and with one another. We see fly-by-wire airplanes whose computers interpret information from sensors and must rapidly communicate the state of the airplane to other computers that decide how to fly, which then communicate with yet other computers that actually manipulate the control surfaces that keep the plane in the air.

As these simple examples illustrate, there are a variety of ways of doing multiple-process programming, each of which involves some sort of interprocess communication mechanism. To illustrate these mechanisms and to provide a framework for understanding design issues in multiple-process programming, we again consider an example problem:

> You are to write a "chat" program. This is a program to let an arbitrary number of users on the same local Internet talk to each other electronically. Each user should be able to type messages that are then broadcast to all other users. Users will be able to view a transcript of all messages sent since they entered the session. The transcript should indicate when users enter and leave the session.

This problem, while simple, has many of the elements found in more complex systems. In involves a central mechanism for gathering messages and redistributing them to all interested users. It requires two-way communication between the individual users and this central mechanism: users provide new messages to be broadcast, and the controller sends messages from different users. Finally, it involves asynchrony since messages from different users can be input at the same time and messages can be sent to the user while the user is entering a new message.

Later in this chapter we sketch the design and implementation of this program. At this point we concentrate on the communication between the user portion and the central mechanism.

Files

The simplest way to share information among applications is to use files: one application writes information to a file and other applications read it. This is the mechanism used by the compiler to save information for later use by the loader and the debugger. It could also be used for our chat problem.

Here we use a central file to represent the current transcript. A client application periodically checks to see if the file length has changed. If so, it reads from wherever it left off to the end of the file, updates its display and continues. When the user writes a message, it is simply appended to the end of the file.

This solution requires a bit more effort to make it actually work. First, the file must be accessible to all users. Within a local Internet, assuming a distributed file system, this may not be a problem. However, if the application has to deal with machines that do not share a common file system, this approach would not be feasible. Second, the solution has many sites of potential failure. It must ensure, for example, that two users cannot write to the file simultaneously and that users read from the file only when messages have been completely written. This requires some coordination and cooperation among the users through a locking mechanism. Here either a system file-locking mechanism or a separate lock file would be used to ensure that only one user has write access to the file at a time and that, when a user has write access, no one can read it. Getting such a mechanism correct can be tricky.

The solution is also problematic in that it is "busy": all the users must actively look at the file periodically to see if it has changed. This means that all the processes must be active and consuming resources on the individual machines. Where the system is small, as here, and the poll can occur at relatively coarse granularity (seconds), this should not be a problem. But under many other circumstances, this approach would be too costly.

Shared Memory

A second approach to sharing information would be to use *shared memory*. Here a segment of memory is shared among the different users, so that the same block of memory is accessible (possibly at different addresses) from multiple processes. Whatever one process writes into the memory is immediately visible to the other processes sharing the memory. Here, when a user sends a message, the program does not write it to a file but simply appends it to the string in shared memory. A relative pointer or offset is used to keep track of the current "end" of the messages in memory, and users keep track of the last address they looked at in memory.

This solution has much in common with files. The different systems need to poll to check if memory has changed and they need to synchronize with each other so that only one writes to memory at a time and so that no system reads from memory while another is trying to write. The mechanisms for this type of synchronization are typically included in systems that provide shared memory, so implementing such locks should be relatively easy.

Shared memory has both advantages and disadvantages when compared to files. Its obvious advantage is that it can be significantly faster. Looking at data in memory is several orders of magnitude faster than looking at the same data on disk. There are, however, two primary disadvantages. The first is that while the file system is designed so that files can grow arbitrarily, memory is typically preallocated so that the amount of shared memory the program can allocate must be fixed. This would probably force one to treat the shared memory segment as a circular buffer, thereby complicating the coding of the various clients. The other problem is more serious. Few current operating systems or environments provide shared memory across the network. Processes can share memory only if they are running within the same machine, which severely limits the use of a program such as chat.

Messaging

Shared memory and files require operating-system support to provide a common data space accessible from multiple machines, whether as a distributed shared file system or as distributed memory. A more general approach that works with different architectures and different machines and can extend beyond the immediate network is to use messages to communicate between processes.

Messages have several advantages for interprocess communication. First, they work over a broad range of applications. They can be used for both tightly coupled applications with low-overhead, high-performance messages (such as modern supercomputers) and for systems that work over the whole Internet. Second, they can easily be implemented without polling and with little or no synchronization. The application can treat the reception of a message as an event to be handled by the main event loop, just like an event from the user interface manager. The program does not have to check continually if things have changed or new information is available. Moreover, the application is guaranteed to process only one event at a time. A third advantage is that messages are flexible. They can be used directly to send information between applications. Alternatively, they can be used to support remote procedure calls where one application uses messages effectively to invoke routines in another application. In an object-oriented application, this can be extended to support remote objects, where one application invokes methods on objects in other applications. The final advantage of messaging is that it is conceptually simple to design, providing a natural and intuitive basis for a multiple-process system.

SOCKETS

The standard interprocess message interface is based on sockets. A *socket* is a file connecting two processes. What is written by one process into the socket can be read by the other. This lets the processes communicate directly in any way they choose and provides a basic foundation for a number of different communications protocols.

Sockets have several features beyond simply letting one process write and the other read. First, they provide two-way communication channels: either process holding the socket can write so that the other process can read. This is useful for acknowledgments, for replying to requests in client-server processes, and for two-way communication in peer-to-peer processes.

Second, sockets provide both reliable communication and faster (but not necessarily reliable) messaging. Messages sent over a network can be lost or can take different routes and thus arrive at the receiver in a different order from that in which they were sent. *Datagram sockets* provide a raw interface that makes no guarantees about delivery or delivery order. These are useful where speed is most important and the application can afford to lose occasional messages. For example, a game server may continually send out state information to various front ends. A front end can afford to miss one or more messages, since future messages will provide the new state anyway. Most applications, however, expect reliable communication, and this is achieved by *stream sockets*. Stream sockets provide an operating-system layer on top of datagrams to reorder and resend messages to guarantee that the information put out by the sender is received in full and in the order sent. Unless an unusual situation demands otherwise, we strongly recommend that only stream sockets be used.

In addition to providing various forms of bidirectional point-to-point communication, sockets can also let multiple clients connect to a single server. A server that deals with multiple clients must eventually establish a separate socket connection to each client. It must keep track of which clients are active and which clients requested what services. It also must let new clients connect to the server. The server does all this by creating a socket that acts as a portal. When a client wants to establish communication with the server, it creates a new socket and connects it to this common portal socket. At this point the server is informed and can establish a point-to-point socket link with the client's socket.

In order to code up our chat program or any other multiple-process application, we need to understand how to use sockets, especially in client-server

```
typedef class SimpleSocketInfo *SimpleSocket;

class SimpleSocketInfo {
public:
   SimpleSocketInfo();
   virtual ~SimpleSocketInfo();

   bool create();                        // create a socket
   void close();                         // close the socket

   bool bind();                      // bind socket to local port
   bool getSockName(char *,int&);// return socket name
   bool enableNonblocking(bool); // enable/disable blocking
   bool listen(int n = 5);          // let socket listen
   bool accept(SimpleSocket);    // connection for new socket
   bool connect(char *,int);     // client connect to server

   int send(const void * buf,int bln);  // send a message
   int receive(void * buf,int bln);     // receive a message

public:
   virtual void onAccept();   // accept available on the socket
   virtual void onClose();    // other end closed the socket
   virtual void onConnect();  // connection ready on this socket
   virtual void onReceive();  // socket has data to read
   virtual void onSend();     // socket ready to send
};
```

Figure 14-1 Basic SimpleSocket interface class.

computing. This provides a firm foundation for understanding messaging and hence the use of remote objects. The remainder of this section attempts to provide such an understanding by considering the interface of a simple class-based socket implementation.

A Simple Socket Interface

The sample **SimpleSocket** class shown in Figure 14-1 is based on the Microsoft Foundation Class library class **CAsyncSocket**.[1] The class provides five callback methods (the virtual methods at the bottom of the definition) invoked when events occur on the socket, and is used by an application through inheritance. For each use of sockets, an application should define a subclass of **SimpleSocketInfo** to provide appropriate actions for these callbacks.

---

1. An implementation of this class for UNIX is available from the web site for this book, http://www.cs.brown.edu/people/spr/designbook.

To understand this interface, we consider how it is used in client-server computing. We start with socket creation. Constructing a **SimpleSockeInfo** object merely sets up a placeholder for a socket; the actual socket is created with the `create` method. This creates one end of a socket that exists only within the current process. The group of methods in the definition starting with `bind` is then used to connect this socket to another process.

A server process wanting clients to attach to it must do the following to set up its portal socket:

1. Create a new socket with the `create` method.

2. Use the `bind` method to assign a name to that socket. Sockets are generally identified by the host name or Internet address (IP number) of the machine on which they are created and by a port number. Binding in general lets the application either specify a port or, given a port number of zero, have the system assign a port. In either case, the `getSockName` method ascertains the host name and port number actually assigned.

3. Use the `listen` method to indicate that the socket will accept connections. The parameter to `listen` indicates not the number of connections but rather the number of pending connections that can accumulate before connections are automatically refused. The default value is generally sufficient here.

At this point the portal socket is ready for potential clients. However, in order to use the socket to connect to the server, these clients need to know the new socket's name (host address and port number). Several techniques can be used to provide this information. The simplest is just to use a fixed port number and host machine. This requires, however, that the server always run on the given machine, and while this is acceptable if the server process is small or if a machine can be dedicated to the task, it is not a good idea in general. A simple variant in some cases is to fix the port number but have the user, in starting up a new client, indicate the machine the server is on.

A more general approach requires that the server communicate the connection address to the client in some way. The simplest way to do this is to use a distributed file system. Here the server writes the address into a known file in the file system. A client simply reads the address from that file and uses it to establish its connection. This works, however, only when the clients and server are on a local network with a common file system. If they are not, a more general approach is needed. The most general approach is to use another process as an address book. This process can reside on a fixed machine at a fixed port number, since it is relatively small and uses few resources. Here the server, when it comes up, registers the address of the connection with the address-book process. As clients start up, they communicate with the address-book process to request the address of the current server.

Once the socket is set up and its name is available, the server uses the standard user-interface event loop to wait for events. When a client attempts to connect to the socket, the `onAccept` method is called as a callback routine. Then:

4. Within the server's redefinition of the `onAccept` method, it should construct a new object of an appropriate subclass of **SimpleSocketInfo**, but should not call its `create` method. A pointer to this object should be passed to the `accept` method of the server's socket. This actually creates the passed socket as the server's end of the original client's socket. At this point the server can communicate with the client using the new socket object.

Socket communication can be either blocking or nonblocking. With blocking communication, a read from a socket blocks or waits until data is available. Similarly, a write waits if the local buffer for the socket is full. With nonblocking communication, both reads where no data is available and writes with a full buffer return immediately with an appropriate status. Nonblocking sockets offer the application more flexibility and ensure that one client cannot bring the whole system to a halt. They do so, however, with a large increase in complexity because nonblocking sockets require the application to handle both input and output buffering internally. Getting such an implementation correct is quite difficult. We thus recommend that you use blocking communication if you are developing your own socket code, and use nonblocking sockets only if such code is available and debugged and then only in a server. In any case:

5. If nonblocking communications are desired, the server should use the `enableBlocking` call to disable blocking.

The client end of a client-server connection is set up in a different but somewhat simpler manner. After the client has determined the address of the server's socket using one of the methods discussed above, it must:

1. Use the `create` method to create a new socket.
2. Use the `connect` method to establish a connection with the server. This method is passed the address of the server's socket in the form of a host name and a port number.
3. Wait for the `onConnect` method to be called before using the socket. This is invoked automatically when the connection is completed.
4. If nonblocking communication is desired, use the `enableBlocking` call at this point. Clients especially should not use this mode, since the benefits of having the client be nonblocking are few and the added complexity is significant.

At this point, both the client and the server can send and receive information over the established connection. The `send` and `receive` calls provided by the **SimpleSocketInfo** interface are used just as read and write calls would be for this purpose. Note that the server should use the **SimpleSocketInfo** objects created using the value returned by `accept` only to do the actual communication. The original server socket is used only to establish connections.

Processes normally send messages synchronously, i.e. send a message in response to a user action or a time-out event. However, messages sent by remote processes can arrive at any time. The **SimpleSocketInfo** interface ties messages to the normal window interface event loop. When a message arrives, the interface is called by the event loop and then invokes the virtual method onReceive as a callback to tell the application that data is available. At this point the application should use receive to read the data.

The onSend callback in the interface is used less frequently, never if the socket is used in the normal blocking mode. Sockets have a finite internal buffer size. If a write attempts to send more information than can fit into the buffer, it succeeds only partially or not at all. In this case the application must buffer the remainder of the write until there is space in the internal buffer. The socket interface provides this callback to tell the application when such space is available.

Finally, when either process is finished communicating, it can use the close method to disconnect from the socket. The process on the other end of the socket is then notified by having its onClose method called. At this point it should close its end of the socket and take appropriate action.

MESSAGING

Sockets provide a generic interface to support interprocess communication. This interface is fairly low-level, however, and most applications must build one or more layers on top of sockets to provide a simple and understandable interface between processes. The simplest such interface involves sending messages back and forth.

In a message interface, sockets are used to send discrete messages between processes. Each process provides a callback to be invoked when a message arrives. These callbacks are tied to the main event loop, so that messages are handled cleanly and within the normal mode of processing. In effect, a message from another process can be treated much as an event from the user interface.

Such messages can be used as the basis for a client-server system. Here one specifies the syntax and meaning of any message clients can send to the server and any messages the server might send to the client. Each message is typically embodied in a pair of methods, one that encodes it in either the client or the server and one that decodes it on the other side. Both the client and the server then treat incoming messages as events requiring appropriate actions. A more modern and generally cleaner approach when using object-oriented design is to use messages and messaging as a basis for remote objects.

Whether using messages directly or as a support mechanism for remote objects, a generic interface is usually desirable. In the remainder of this section we define a simple such interface using an inheritable C++ class. In doing

```
        typedef class ConnectInfo *   Connect;

        class ConnectInfo {
        private:
           ConnectSocket conn_socket;

        public:
           ConnectInfo();
           virtual ~ConnectInfo();

           int openServer(const char * file);
           int openClient(const char * file);
           int openAccept(Connect);
           void close();

           void sendMessage(int len,const void * msg);
           void sendMessage(const char * msg)
              { sendMessage(strlen(msg)+1,(void *) msg); }

        public:
           virtual void acceptCallback(ConnectAcceptId);
           virtual void closeCallback();
           virtual void messageCallback(int len,void * msg);
        };
```

Figure 14-2 A connection interface for message passing.

so we demonstrate how to keep a messaging interface simple and how to implement it on top of sockets. The example provides a detailed discussion of the proposed interface and also illustrates the use of sockets. Note that a more complex implementation of this interface could use nonblocking sockets without any change to applications wishing to use the interface.

A Messaging Class Interface

Using sockets to send messages is straightforward. A message is sent in two parts, the first containing the length of the message and the second containing the message itself. The recipient reads the size of the message and then the message itself. The added complexity of sending the length first is needed since otherwise the recipient would not know when a message was complete and might only read part of this message or might read multiple messages as a single one. Implementing messages is quite simple when sockets are blocking.

Because sockets are commonly used for messaging, we want to define a generic, reusable interface class for message passing and implement this class using sockets. A simple such interface, featuring the class **ConnectInfo**, is shown in Figure 14-2. The interface is designed to be used as either a server or a client. It uses a file in the file system to communicate the address of the server socket to the clients and provides callbacks for processing messages.

To use this interface, an application defines different subclasses of the **ConnectInfo** class. One subclass, defined in the server, acts as the master socket, letting clients attach to the message connection. This subclass must redefine the `acceptCallback` method. A second subclass is created by the server to act as the server's end of the actual message connection to a client. This subclass should redefine the `messageCallback` method to handle incoming messages and the `closeCallback` method to handle client termination. The client application creates its own subclass to handle its end of the connection to the sever. This subclass must redefine `messageCallback` to handle messages from the server and `closeCallback` to handle unexpected server termination.

A server uses the interface by first constructing a **ConnectInfo** object of the first subtype and then calling its `openServer` method, passing it the name of a well-known file in a distributed file system. This creates a new socket and does the appropriate `bind` and `listen` calls. It then gets the address of the socket and writes it to the given file. When a client connects to the socket, the `acceptCallback` method is invoked. This method constructs a new **ConnectInfo** object of the appropriate subclass to handle the client connection and calls the new object's `openAccept` method to attach the object to the socket resulting from the connection.

A client uses the interface by constructing a **ConnectInfo** object of the appropriate subclass and calling its `openClient` method using the same file name. This creates the underlying socket and connects it to the server. Both the client and the server can then send messages using the `sendMessage` method. Messages are viewed by the interface as byte streams so that arbitrary messages can be passed (binary or ASCII). When a message is received, the interface invokes the appropriate object's `messageCallback` method from the main event loop of the application.

Implementing Messaging Using Sockets

The implementation of the **ConnectInfo** interface starts by defining its own type of socket, as shown in Figure 14-3. This class provides a data member to store a pointer to the **ConnectInfo** class for handling callbacks. It also gives definitions for the three callback functions, `onAccept`, `onClose`, and `onReceive`. Representative code for these is shown in Figure 14-4. The first simply invokes the `acceptCallback` method on the connection object. The second invokes the `closeCallback` on the connection object and then closes the connection. The third reads first the message length and then the message body, and then calls the `messageCallback` method of the connection class.

The implementation of the **ConnectInfo** class follows the outline indicated for using sockets. The constructor creates a new **ConnectSocket** object; the destructor closes the socket and deletes it. The three open methods are more interesting and are shown in Figure 14-5. The first sets up the server's master

```
typedef class ConnectSocketInfo * ConnectSocket;
typedef long                       ConnectMsgLen;

class ConnectSocketInfo : public SimpleSocketInfo {

private:
    Connect for_connect;

public:
    ConnectSocketInfo(Connect);
    ~ConnectSocketInfo();

private:
    void onAccept();
    void onClose();
    void onReceive();
};
```

Figure 14-3 SimpleSocket subclass for the Connect interface.

socket. It first calls `create` to define the socket, then `bind` to assign it a name, `listen` to enable it to receive connections, and `getSockName` to get the name, which is then written to the passed file. The second reads the host name and port number from the passed file, calls `create` to define the socket, and then uses the `connect` method to associate the socket to that port. The third simply calls the `accept` method on the underlying socket.

The other methods are again simple. The `close` method calls `close` on the underlying socket and the `sendMessage` method calls the `send` method of the socket twice, first to send the length in four bytes and second to send the actual message.

REMOTE OBJECTS

Messages, while they represent an abstraction above sockets, are still relatively low-level. To write the chat application described previously using messages would require us to come up with the set of messages to be sent from the client to the server and the set to be sent from the server to the client. We would have to determine the form and contents of these messages. Then we would add calls to send the messages at the appropriate points and define message-callback handlers for both the server and the client to decode the incoming message and take appropriate action.

```
void
ConnectSocketInfo::onAccept()
{
    for_connect->acceptCallback();
}


void
ConnectSocketInfo::onClose()
{
    for_connect->closeCallback();
    for_connect->close();
}


void
ConnectSocketInfo::onReceive()
{
    ConnectMsgLen len;
    Integer i;
    Character buf[1024];

    i = receive(&len,sizeof(ConnectMsgLen));
    if (i <= 0) return;
    i = receive(buf,len);

    for_connect->messageCallback(len,buf);
}
```

Figure 14-4 The callback methods for the connection socket.

Basic Concepts

This approach, while conceptually simple enough, requires a good degree of coordination. Since there is a central callback method for incoming messages, all messages must be encoded so that they can easily be distinguished from one another. Moreover, because the messages can have arbitrary contents, reasonable and consistent coding conventions must be adopted so that they can be assembled and decoded in common ways. This keeps the system from getting too complex.

This need to coordinate and define messages consistently and extensibly across all aspects of a system is the reason that messages themselves are generally used not directly, but instead to support higher-level primitives. The simplest primitive operation for which messages are used is to support *remote procedure call*. Here the client application effectively calls procedures in the server. What really happens is that each remote procedure exists in both the client and the server. The code in the client simply takes the arguments and

```
int
ConnectInfo::openServer(const char * file)
{
    char host[1024];
    int port;

    if (!conn_socket->create()) return false;
    if (!conn_socket->bind()) return false;
    if (!conn_socket->listen()) return false;
    if (!conn_socket->getSockName(sn)) return false;

    ofstream ofs(file);
    if (!ofs) return false;
    ofs << host << " " << port << endl;
    ofs.close();

    return true;
}


int
ConnectInfo::openClient(const char * file)
{
    ifstream ifs(file);
    char host[1024];
    int port;

    if (!ifs) return false;
    ifs >> host >> port;
    if (ifs.fail()) return false;
    ifs.close();

    if (!conn_socket->create()) return false;
    if (!conn_socket->connect(host,port)) {
        conn_socket->close();
        return false;
     }

    return true;
}


int
ConnectInfo::openAccept(Connect c)
{
    return conn_socket->accept(c->conn_socket);
}
```

Figure 14-5 Open methods for the connection interface.

uses them to construct a standardized message indicating the routine to call and the values of the arguments to that routine. It uses a message interface to send this to the server. The message callback routine in the server decodes the information on what routine to call, uses information about this routine to decode the arguments, and then calls the routine. If the call has a return value, it is sent back in a separate message.

While remote procedure calls seem to involve a lot of work in packing and unpacking the arguments and do restrict somewhat the types of values that can be used as parameters (pointers to structures in the client are useless in the server), they can be automated. Most systems supporting remote procedure calls provide a package that takes a set of procedure declarations and automatically generates both the client routines and the decoding routine for the server.

Remote procedure calls are best suited for a framework in which procedure calls are the basic means by which packages interact. This is true in procedural programs, but not generally true of object-oriented programming. The basic unit of interaction in an object-oriented program is the object. Objects exist, have data representing their state, and have methods representing actions. In an object-oriented framework, it makes sense not to use remote procedure call but to build a framework to support *remote objects*, objects existing in one process that are accessible from another.

Ideally, an application should be able to use remote objects just as it uses local objects: it should be able to create them, access their data, and invoke their methods with arbitrary arguments. While it is possible to go to this extreme, it is simpler and more consistent to restrict remote objects in various ways. First, remote objects should be defined via *interface classes*. An interface class contains only methods and does not define the implementation of the methods. Since it cannot be created directly, a factory class is generally provided. The advantage of an interface class here is that the class hierarchy can be used in the implementation. The client can be given a concrete class inheriting from the interface and implementing all the methods using messages or remote procedure calls to the server. The server can provide its own concrete class to receive the messages, do the actual work, and then return any result using a separate message.

A second restriction common in defining remote objects is that the arguments to all the remote methods must be understandable by both client and server. In a remote procedure call, this generally limits the arguments to simple data types (integers, reals, strings) or structures made up of simple data types; i.e. no pointers are allowed. If remote objects are handled correctly, this can be augmented to let the methods have arguments referring to arbitrary remote objects.

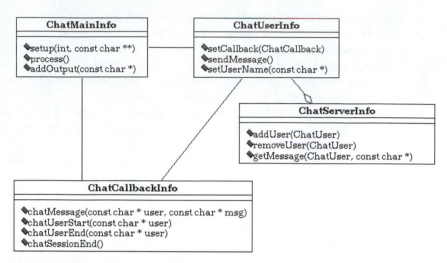

Figure 14-6 Top-level classes for the chat program.

Designing with Remote Objects

Designing with remote objects is similar to designing with standard objects. The difference is that at some point in the design process some classes are designated as remote and their objects are assigned to different processes. Given this, we can start to design an implementation of the chat program. A general design without considering multiple processes requires the classes in Figure 14-6. These include:

- **ChatMainInfo**: This class handles the user interface as well as startup and overall control for each user. The setup method initializes and reads arguments, the process method sets up the windows and enters the main event loop, and the addOutput method adds a line to the transcript.

- **ChatUserInfo**: This class represents the workings for a single user. Its methods support setting the user name and specifying a callback as well as handling input lines created by the user.

- **ChatServerInfo**: This class represents the server. It provides methods to add and remove users as well as accepting a message from each user. It invokes the appropriate user callback routines as required for all active users whenever a user is added or removed or a message is sent.

- **ChatCallbackInfo**: This class acts as a callback handler for a particular user. The methods here, called by the server, call the appropriate routines in **ChatMainInfo** to add to the transcript or close the session.

The only unusual thing about this design is the use of a callback class to interface between the server and the user. An alternative design might add the callback methods directly to the **ChatUserInfo** class, as done with the **SimpleSocketInfo** and **ConnectInfo** classes discussed earlier in this chapter. In these cases the callbacks were implemented using inheritance. For example, in order to use sockets, an application had to inherit from **SimpleSocketInfo** to create its own socket class with the properly defined callbacks. Using inheritance in this way reduces the total number of classes in the interface and hence achieves a degree of simplicity. It has the drawback that the methods of **SimpleSocketInfo** cannot construct a new socket since they cannot know the actual socket type. This meant that the code for accepting a connection had to use callbacks actually to build a socket object of the appropriate subtype and use it in a call to `accept`. If a callback object had been used here instead, the socket could have been created directly by the support code, provided that the user did not plan to subclass **SimpleSocket** for some other reason.

Our socket class was based on the Microsoft Foundation Classes **CAsyncSocket** class. Adding callback classes to MFC in general would almost double the total number of classes and make this library much more complex than it is already. Moreover, a library such as MFC should strive for consistency in order to provide the simplest possible interface. Since some classes in the library, particularly those for the user interface, were designed to be specialized by the user through inheritance, it makes sense to use such inheritance for defining callbacks for all its classes. By effectively merging the callback into the base class, Microsoft has reduced the overall complexity of the library at the cost of some special application semantics, as with socket `accept`. This is a design trade-off for building object-oriented libraries in which the whole library, its potential applications, and how it might be used are all taken into account.

With the chat program, however, we are trying for simplicity only within the application. We are also trying to design a system that can be divided and implemented using distributed objects. When objects are distributed, they are accessible from multiple processes but actually only exist in one process. This means that objects of the remote class cannot be subclassed by the client application. Moreover, all communication with the remote object should be one-way: methods on the remote object should be invoked, but the implementation of these methods should use only objects and methods available in the server. These two consequences imply that separate callback objects should be used in remote computing. Here the callback object can be a remote object within the client referring to the actual object that exists in the server. When the server object needs to invoke a callback, the roles are reversed and it simply invokes a method on the remote callback object.

Now we can separate our simple chat design into a client portion and a server portion. The obvious splitting point is the **ChatUserInfo** class. The server process or chat controller will consist of the **ChatServer** object along with **ChatUserInfo** and **ChatCallbackInfo** objects for each connected client. The client process or chat program will consist of the **ChatMainInfo** object, a local instance of **ChatUserInfo** referring to the remote object in the server, and a **ChatCallbackInfo**

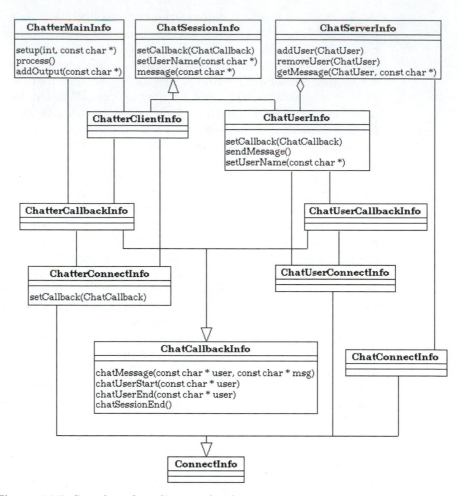

Figure 14-7 Complete class diagram for chat program.

object. In addition, there will be a connection object in the client, a master connection in the server, and a connection in the server for each user. All these will be subclasses of **ConnectInfo**. To separate the packages, we call the front end *chatter* and the back end *chat*. The resultant class diagram is shown in Figure 14-7.

This diagram at first glance is too complex. However, it is actually two diagrams in one, both of which are highly symmetric. The left side of the diagram shows the four classes of the client code, **ChatterMainInfo**, **ChatterClientInfo**, **ChatterCallbackInfo**, and **ChatterConnectInfo**. The right side of the diagram portrays the server code containing equivalents to these four classes, **ChatServerInfo**, **ChatUserInfo**, **ChatUserCallbackInfo**, and **ChatUserConnectInfo** respectively, and the additional master connection class, **ChatConnectInfo**. The classes in the middle, **ChatSessionInfo** and **ChatCallbackInfo**, are the abstract superclasses that the client and server have in common. The library class **ConnectInfo** is included merely to indicate how the message connections are used by the client and server.

The client design uses a single **ChatterMainInfo** object to manage the user interface and the system startup. The **ChatterClientInfo** and **ChatterCallbackInfo** objects created by the main object provide the two directions of communication with the server: **ChatterClientInfo** is used for communicating information to the server and **ChatterCallbackInfo** is used when the server needs to send information back to the client.

The server design uses a single **ChatServerInfo** object as the controller and manager of the set of currently active users. Each active user is assigned a **ChatUserInfo** object that is the server's side of **ChatSessionInfo** and handles requests from the client associated with the user. The user object gets a handle to the local copy of the callback object that actually exists in the client and uses it to communicate messages from the server to the client. Finally, the **ChatUserConnectInfo** and **ChatConnectInfo** classes represent the physical connection for the particular user and for the master end of the socket respectively.

Implementing Remote Objects

To show how to implement remote objects, we consider the implementation of the chat program according to the above design. We start with the server.

The chat server is controlled by a single **ChatServerInfo** object whose declaration is given in Figure 14-8. The constructor for this class just initializes the variables; the destructor deletes the server connection; the main routine, `process`, creates and opens the server connection and then calls the window system event loop. The actual processing is done by the `addUser`, `removeUser` and `getMessage` methods, as shown in Figure 14-9. The first two respectively add and remove a user from the list of active users maintained by the server. The `removeUser` method also checks if this is the last user connected to the server and causes the server to exit if so. It is important in designing a server to have a well-defined termination condition. All three of the methods loop through the set of all active users and use the appropriate callbacks to send messages back to the client windows.

Figure 14-10 shows the definition of the **ChatUserInfo** class. Its implementation is straightforward. The constructor saves the pointer to the server, creates the slave end of a new connection, sets the user name to unknown, and creates a callback object. The class is assumed to own the connection and the callback object, so the destructor frees both of these. The `setUserName` method saves the user name and then calls the server to add this user. The user is added only after its name is registered, so that other users receive the proper name when they are told a new user has been added to the session. The `message` method simply calls the corresponding routine in the server.

```
typedef class ChatServerInfo *          ChatServer;
typedef class ChatUserInfo *            ChatUser;
typedef class ChatConnectInfo *         ChatConnect;
typedef class ChatUserCallbackInfo * ChatUserCallback;
typedef list<ChatUser>                  ChatUserList;
typedef ChatUserList::iterator          ChatUserListIter;


class ChatServerInfo {
private:
    ChatConnect server_connect;
    ChatUserList active_list;

public:
    ChatServerInfo(int,const char**);
    ~ChatServerInfo();

    void process();

    void addUser(ChatUser);
    void removeUser(ChatUser);
    void getMessage(ChatUser,ConstText msg);

    Connect masterConnect() const;
};
```

Figure 14-8 The chat-server controller class.

Note that the **ChatUserInfo** class does not provide a setCallback method. Here we have taken a shortcut by assuming that the message socket between the client and server is only used for one object in each direction and hence that all messages coming in on the socket are for the **ChatUserInfo** class, while all messages going out on the socket from the server are for the corresponding callback class. In a more complex example, where the same message socket is used for multiple objects, we would need to specify the object to which the message is directed in addition to the message's contents. In this case, the server would use the setCallback call to store the identity of the callback object to be used for later messaging.

The **ChatUserConnectInfo** class is used for both sides of this client-server communication. The class itself acts as a standard message connection that includes its own definition of the closeCallback and messageCallback methods. The first of these simply deletes the affected user, letting the destructor remove it. Removing the user, as we saw in the implementation of removeUser for **ChatServerInfo**, then informs other active users and terminates the server if this was the last user. The messageCallback method actually decodes the message and invokes the corresponding routines of the **ChatUserInfo** object.

```
void
ChatServerInfo::addUser(ChatUser cu)
{
    ChatUserListIter uli;

    for (uli=active_list.begin(); uli!=active_list.end(); ++uli) {
        (*uli)->callback()->chatUserStart(cu->name());
      }

    active_list.push_back(cu);
}


void
ChatServerInfo::removeUser(ChatUser cu)
{
    ChatUserListIter uli;

    active_list.remove(cu);
    if (active_list.empty()) exit(0);

    for (uli=active_list.begin(); uli!=active_list.end(); ++uli) {
        (*uli)->callback()->chatUserEnd(cu->name());
      }
}


void
ChatServerInfo::getMessage(ChatUser cu,ConstText msg)
{
    ChatUserListIter uli;

    for (uli=active_list.begin(); uli!=active_list.end(); ++uli) {
        (*uli)->callback()->chatMessage(cu->name(),msg);
      }
}
```

Figure 14-9 Handling user interactions in the server.

For simplicity and ease of debugging, we decided to make all the messages for the chat program strings. This is a good idea in general, especially when a program is being developed. The messages for chat have the form:

```
<type> <argument1>
```

or

```
<type> <argument1> <argument2>
```

where <type> is a single character denoting the type of message. The actual messages handled by `messageCallback` from the user are:

```
class ChatUserInfo : public ChatSessionInfo {

private:
    ChatServer for_server;
    ChatUserCallback user_callback;
    ChatUserConnect user_connect;
    StdString user_name;

public:
    ChatUserInfo(ChatServer);
    ~ChatUserInfo();

    void setUserName(const char * id);
    ConstText name() const            { return user_name.c_str(); }
    ChatUserCallback callback() const { return user_callback; }

    void message(const char * message);
};
```

Figure 14-10 The server end of the chat-session class.

```
void
ChatUserConnectInfo::messageCallback(int len,void * msg)
{
    Text tmsg = (Text) msg;
    ChatMsgType mtype = tmsg[0];
    Text mbody = &tmsg[2];

    switch (mtype) {
       case CHAT_MSG_SET_USER :
           for_user->setUserName(mbody);
           break;
       case CHAT_MSG_CLIENT :
           for_user->message(mbody);
           break;
       default :
           break;
    }
}
```

Figure 14-11 Callback routine for message decoding in the server.

```
U <name>                    // setUserName(name)
C <text>                    // message(text)
```

The decoding routine is shown in Figure 14-11. Again, in a more complex environment this routine would have to decode the message to find the object to which the message is directed, find that object, and then invoke the corresponding method on the object. In this case, since only one object can be

```
void
ChatUserCallbackInfo::chatMessage(const char * u,const char * m)
{
    Character buf[10240];
    ostrstream ost(buf,10240);

    ost << CHAT_MSG_SERVER << " " << u << CHAT_MSG_SEPARATOR <<
        m << ends;

    user_connect->sendMessage(buf);
}
```

Figure 14-12 Remote handler that encodes a callback message.

involved, the callback simply extracts the argument and calls the known object.

The other class involved in the server is the remote end of the callback class. This class creates the messages that are eventually decoded by the client and translated into calls on the actual callback object. The messages sent here include:

```
S <user> <message>          // chatMesage(user,message)
N <user>                    // chatUserStart(user)
R <user>                    // chatUserEnd(user)
```

Note that the `chatSessionEnd` method of the callback is actually invoked by the appropriate callback if the corresponding connection is closed. The actual coding of these is straightforward, as can be seen from Figure 14-12.

The client program *chatter* contains similar routines for encoding and decoding messages. The remote implementation of the client's chat session is managed by the class **ChatterClientInfo** in Figure 14-13. The `setUserName` and `message` methods act like the callback methods of the server in that they simply create a string representation of the call and send it along to the socket. Note that this class and its parallel in the server, **ChatUserInfo**, are both implementations of the abstract class **ChatSessionInfo**. This is the essence of a remote object design.

The class constructor in Figure 14-14 is more interesting. The constructor needs to establish the connection with the server and tell it there is a new user. The code first attempts to establish the connection using the `openClient` call with the file containing the server socket address. This fails, however, if no server is currently running. To handle this case, the constructor checks for failure and attempts to start the server as a background process if the connection was not established. Then it tries to connect to the server again, attempting to allow enough time for the server to come up.

There are several problems with this implementation. The first is that it is subject to a *race condition*, a timing problem occurring when two or more processes simultaneously attempt to get control of a resource. In this case, if no server is running and two chatter clients start up at the same time, both will

```
typedef class ChatterMainInfo *      ChatterMain;
typedef class ChatterClientInfo *    ChatterClient;
typedef class ChatterConnectInfo *   ChatterConnect;
typedef class ChatterCallbackInfo *  ChatterCallback;


class ChatterClientInfo : public ChatSessionInfo {
private:
    ChatterConnect comm_connect;
    ChatCallback user_callback;

public:
    ChatterClientInfo();
    ~ChatterClientInfo();

    void setCallback(ChatCallback cb);
    void setUserName(const char * id);
    void message(const char * msg);

public:
    ChatCallback callback() const     { return user_callback; }
};
```

Figure 14-13 The client end of the chat session.

start servers and the file containing the socket address of the first one will be overwritten by the second. The result will be that the first client is left talking to a server no one else can communicate with, and is not connected to the second client. Such conditions are not uncommon in dealing with multiple processes and are one of the many reasons why multiple-process programming is more difficult than single-process programming.

The solution to this problem lies in the implementation of the **ConnectInfo** class. The openServer call here must ensure that no other server is currently running before the call can succeed. This can be handled in various ways. The simplest is to use the file-locking capabilities of the operating system. Here the server attempts to lock a file (which can be the file containing the socket address) when it starts up. If the file is already locked, some other server must be running and the open attempt fails. Since the operating system guarantees that only one process can get a file lock, this approach ensures that only one server can run. Note that care must be taken to ensure the file lock disappears when the server exits.

Another problem with the **ChatterClientInfo** constructor does not arise in our simple example but would in a more complex environment in which the communications channel is used for multiple objects. Here opening the channel is not sufficient to create a new object. The constructor code must first check if a channel to the particular server had already been opened for some other

```
ChatterClientInfo::ChatterClientInfo()
{
    Integer i;

    user_callback = NULL;
    comm_connect = new ChatterConnectInfo();

    if (comm_connect->openClient(CHAT_SERVER_FILE)) return;

    Character buf[1024];
    ostrstream ost(buf,1024);

    ost << CHAT_SERVER_NAME << " &" << ends;
    system(buf);

    for (i = 0; i < 10; ++i) {
        if (comm_connect->openClient(CHAT_SERVER_FILE)) break;
        sleep(1);
    }
    if (i >= 10) {
        cerr << "CHAT: can't connect to server" << endl;
        exit(1);
    }
}
```

Figure 14-14 Constructor for creating a new remote connection.

object, and must open the channel and possibly create the server only if not. Then the code must send a message requesting that a new remote object of the appropriate type be created; finally, the client must get a handle to this new remote object.

Obtaining a handle to a remote object requires the cooperation of the server process. For the callback object created in the chatter program, the handle is passed to the remote process in a call using the session object. For the session object itself, there is no other object to call to get the appropriate handle. The solution typically used here is to create a third remote class, **ChatSessionFactoryInfo**, to take requests to create a new remote session object and return the handle to it. The factory object is itself a remote object implemented in the chat server. Then the constructor for **ChatterClientInfo** simply calls the appropriate method on this object to obtain the remote session handle.

But this is not a real solution to the problem. In order to call the remote factory, the client needs the handle of the remote factory object. We could establish a factory-factory object, but then the same problem arises. The solution here is to assign some object a permanent handle or name known by both client and server. This name can either be known a priori by the two processes or can be stored in a generally accessible global registry from which the two processes can look it up based on a unique string name.

Figure 14-15 User interface for the chat program.

The only other difficult component of the chatter front end is the user interface. The running version of the interface shown in Figure 14-15 consists of a frame widget enclosing a form widget that allows the arbitrary layout of its components. Within the form are, at the top, a scrolled text display window to handle the session transcript, a text-input window to let the user enter new message lines, and a Quit button. The code to support the interface has a set-upWindows method that defines all of these widgets, callbacks for handling the Quit button and the input region, and a routine to add lines to the transcript. This latter routine is used by the implementation of the class **ChatterCallback-Info** to create different messages for each of the callbacks it receives and add them to the transcript. The implementation of this class and the rest of the chat interface follows the lines of the server and is fairly straightforward.

ActiveX and CORBA

The code required to support general remote objects is quite complex. It must go beyond our simple chat program and message-based connect interface to provide buffered connections, ways of identifying and finding servers, ways of naming objects, a central registry or repository of well-known objects, and the encoding and decoding of a broad range of arguments for the methods of remote objects. Much of this code, however, either is the same for all programs (i.e., could be made part of a library) or can be generated fairly mechanically given a specification of the objects and methods that are to be remote. Thus several systems exist to support remote objects.

The principal mechanism on Windows systems goes by various names. The basic common object model, called the Component Object Model (COM), provides for multiple objects that can be shared by processes in the same machine. Distributed COM (DCOM) builds a distributed layer on top of this, letting objects be shared across the network. ActiveX (formerly OLE for Object Linking and Embedding) builds a higher-level protocol on top of DCOM to provide application-level support, for example, letting a word-processor application embed a spreadsheet from another application within its document.

A similar but older and less widely used mechanism exists on UNIX systems, the Common Object Request Broker Architecture (CORBA) model. CORBA supports basic network-wide remote objects and a common repository for the addresses of well-known objects, as well as a variety of services such as transactions.

While neither of these is difficult to use, they each have their own idiosyncrasies and rather steep learning curves. Understanding the basic principles of remote objects and how they are implemented is helpful (and sometimes necessary) in understanding these systems, and we have therefore shown here how to build remote objects basically from scratch. However, in building a real application, one should use one of these standard mechanisms rather than replicating the large amount of work these mechanisms represent.

MULTIPLE THREADS OF CONTROL

Multiple-process programming gives the application some degree of parallelism and lets multiple actions be accomplished simultaneously. In the chat program, for example, multiple clients can all be interacting with their user interfaces, say typing in a new message, at the same time. Multiple-process programming, however, introduces a lot of overhead and has its limits. The time to call a method on a remote object is typically four to six orders of magnitude greater than the time to call a local method. Moreover, in a client-server model, while multiple clients can be doing things in parallel, the server can process only one action at a time.

Multithreaded programming, in which a single process can have multiple threads of control, addresses these issues. A *thread of control* here represents an abstract processor executing in the application. Threads typically have their own program counter, register set, and stack, and execute independently. If one thread has to wait for input or output, the others can still continue. Individual threads can be readily created and destroyed.

Multithreaded programming has two principal applications. The first is to let individual applications exploit machines with multiple processors by using multiple threads to speed up its computations. Using multiple threads in this way is typically difficult. Programmers must learn how to reformulate the underlying algorithms so they can be parallelized. The amount of communication needed among the different threads must be minimized so that the resultant overhead does not overwhelm the potential benefits. Finally, the programmer must be quite aware of the underlying thread implementation, since it quite often affects performance in poorly understood ways. Because of these difficulties, using multiple threads to achieve higher performance is beyond the scope of this text.

The other application of multithreaded programming is as a simple framework in which a single application can perform multiple actions simultaneously. Such a framework is most often used in servers with multiple clients to process requests from different clients at the same time. This allows the server to provide rapid response to all clients, to be fair to all clients, and to be robust in the face of client errors.

One problem with the simple, single-threaded implementation of the chat server described in the previous section is that it can process only one message from one client at a time. For the chat server, where processing a message takes very little computation or time, this is not a major problem. If, however, the server were a database system or some other complex process, processing a client request could take considerable time and resources. It would be neither equitable nor desirable for other clients of the server to wait for the server to finish the first client's request before beginning to handle theirs. Using multiple threads of control here lets the server process each incoming request separately and thereby offer fair and rapid response to each client.

A second problem with the simple implementation of the previous section is that it will hang if a client decides to stop processing messages. When processing a message, the server sends the new message to each client using blocking sockets. If any of the clients stops reading from its socket (because it is stopped, the network is down, or its machine crashed), then the server essentially halts and no further processing is done until the client either closes its socket or starts reading again. This could be mitigated somewhat by using nonblocking sockets, but even so problems will remain. Using multiple threads lets each client be allocated a thread so that the bad behavior of one client does not affect any others.

While multiple threads of control solve these problems, they do not necessarily enhance the performance of the application. Considerable overhead and programming complexity are required to maintain and synchronize multiple threads. In general, because of the difficulties in implementing, understanding, and debugging multiple threads, they should be used only when absolutely necessary for doing multiple tasks simultaneously.

Designing for Multiple Threads of Control

There are several approaches to incorporating multiple threads into a server. One is to create a new thread of control for each incoming request. This provides the most parallelism in dealing with requests, but raises a number of problems. The first is that a high level of synchronization among the threads is needed to ensure that no two commands interfere with each other. A second is that it does not solve the problem of a single client hanging the system. If a client's socket is nonresponsive, then each of the multiple input requests hangs while attempting to write to that socket. To get around this, each input message would have to spawn separate threads to write to each of the clients, making the overall system even more complex and confusing.

A compromise between this model with maximal parallelism and the previous model of using a single thread for everything is to provide one thread of control for each client. Here a new thread of control is started when a client is created that is responsible for dealing with all requests from that client as well as handling all output back to that client. This approach does not let a single client initiate multiple requests in parallel and take full advantage of the server, but does ensure some fairness among the clients and isolates the server from the failure of a single client.

Another possible approach is to provide parallelism that is not tied to individual clients. Here a fixed number of threads are assigned to handle incoming message requests. When a request comes in, it is assigned to a thread if one is available and queued for future processing if not. This approach, while more complex than creating new threads for each incoming request, can provide a more reliable server, since it can ensure that the server does not become overburdened by processing more requests than it should at any one time. Moreover, by letting the different threads handle requests of different priority, this approach can ensure that high-priority or simple requests are handled quickly even if lower-priority requests requiring substantial processing time exist.

All these approaches and their variants are appropriate under different circumstances. The designer of a server must consider how it is going to be used, the amount of processing required for each incoming request, the likelihood and mode of client failures, and the degree of parallelism desirable or achievable. This analysis can then be used to determine the appropriate model for a given application. For the chat server, all the requests can be handled quickly and the main reason for using multiple threads is to isolate the server from

```
class SimpleThread {
public:
    SimpleThread();
    ~SimpleThread();

    bool createThread(bool suspended = 0, int stacksize = 0);

    int getThreadPriority();
    bool setThreadPriority(int);

    int suspendThread();
    int resumeThread();

public:
    virtual int run();
};
```

Figure 14-16 A simple thread class.

the vagaries of the clients. Here, the one-thread-per-client approach makes the most sense.

Using one thread per client in the chat server changes how it operates. Each thread will be responsible for handling both incoming and outgoing messages for its client. Here the server maintains for each client a queue of tasks to be performed. The thread for the client takes tasks off the queue and processes them one by one. These tasks include input tasks, such as adding a user or sending a messages to other clients, and output tasks, such as conveying a messing from some other client to the client supported by the thread. The server code has to be modified to use the task queues. For example, when a message arrives, the server does not process it directly but simply adds a corresponding task to the appropriate queue. Similarly, a message is broadcast to all clients by adding a corresponding task to each client's queue.

The thread itself should be implemented in an object-oriented fashion. Most operating systems provide a library interface to threads, and it is best to build a class-oriented approach on top of this. Figure 14-16 shows a simple thread class, **SimpleThread**, modeled on the Microsoft Foundation Class **CWinThread**. Like much of MFC, this class is designed to be inherited and redefined by the application. In this case a thread is created using the `createThread` method. Creation is done here rather than in the constructor to provide additional flexibility to subclasses. This ensures, for example, that the subclass is completely initialized and ready for callbacks before the new thread begins execution. Threads can either be running or suspended. The first parameter to `createThread` controls its starting state, while the `suspendThread` and `resumeThread` let the state be changed dynamically. The two priority calls control the priority of the thread within the process: higher-priority threads are run in preference to lower-priority ones.

When the `createThread` method of a **SimpleThread** object is executed, a new thread is created and the virtual `run` method of the thread object is executed. This method should contain the code to be executed by the thread and must be redefined by the application-thread subclass for the thread to be at all useful.

Synchronization Mechanisms

In order for multiple threads to work correctly, the different threads have to cooperate with one another. It would not work, for example, to have one thread attempt to put a task on a queue at the same time another thread is taking a task off the same queue: the result would be either a mangled queue or a request that was processed twice or not at all. Moreover, a thread taking tasks off a queue and processing them will occasionally find the queue empty and should go to sleep until a task is put on the queue. Here the thread adding the task to the queue needs to wake up the sleeping thread in order to get that task processed.

A variety of synchronization mechanisms can provide these types of cooperation among the threads. One of the simplest conceptually is a *mutex*, a mechanism used to ensure that only one thread at a time executes a piece of code. The code that is so protected is called a *critical section* and the overall process is called *mutual exclusion* (hence the term *mutex*). Before executing the critical section, a thread *locks* the mutex and when it is done it *unlocks* it. The system ensures that only one thread at a time can lock the mutex, so that the mutex can ensure that only one thread at a time executes the critical code. Any thread attempting to lock a mutex that is already locked blocks (halts temporarily) until the mutex is unlocked by its current holder. Note that the critical section here need not be contiguous code: it is generally a set of distributed code fragments with a common purpose, such as maintaining a queue or some other data structure that may be accessed by multiple threads simultaneously.

In the chat example, assuming that we create a thread for each client, two data structures are accessed by multiple threads. The first is the set of task queues. Each of these should be accessed by one thread to find the next task and by other threads to add to that thread's queue. The second global data structure is the list of active users maintained by the server. The different client threads need to access this list either to add or remove their client or to loop through all clients to send an appropriate message.

A second synchronization mechanism is needed to wake the client thread when something is added to the queue. Here we use a *semaphore*. A semaphore is similar to a mutex except that it is counter-based. A thread locks a semaphore by attempting to decrement its counter. As long as the counter starts above zero, it is decremented and the thread is allowed to proceed. If the counter is zero, the thread blocks. Unlocking a semaphore increments its counter, letting a blocked thread continue. In the case of the queue, we use a semaphore to count the number of tasks on the queue. Whenever a thread

```
class SimpleMutex {
public:
    SimpleMutex(int on = 0);
    ~SimpleMutex();

    bool lock();
    bool unlock();
};


class SimpleSemaphore {
public:
    SimpleSemaphore(unsigned int count = 0);
    ~SimpleSemaphore();

    bool lock();
    bool unlock();
};
```

Figure 14-17 Mutex and semaphore class interfaces.

places a task on the queue, it unlocks the semaphore. Before the thread processing the queue takes a task off the queue, it attempts to lock the semaphore. If a task is waiting, the semaphore's counter is greater than zero and the processing task can continue. If the queue is empty, the counter is zero and the processing task blocks until something is later added.

Simple class definitions for mutex and semaphore objects are shown in Figure 14-17. Both of these are modeled after their MFC counterpart (**Simple-Mutex** after **CMutex** and **SimpleSemaphore** after **CSemaphore**). Their interfaces are quite simple. The constructor creates and initializes the construct, letting the mutex be set initially on or off and letting the counter of the semaphore be set as desired. Both provide `lock` and `unlock` calls, with the lock call blocking the thread when appropriate.

A variety of other synchronization mechanisms can be constructed from semaphores where necessary and are provided as primitives in some systems. For example, a *reader-writer lock* deals with the common situation where it is okay for multiple threads to read a data structure simultaneously, but only one thread should modify the structure and it should do this only if no one is currently reading it. Here the readers do not block each other but do block a thread attempting to write. Moreover, a writer blocks all readers. In the chat server, the list of active users is generally only read, not modified. More parallelism can be obtained in the server if a reader-writer lock is used here instead of a mutex.

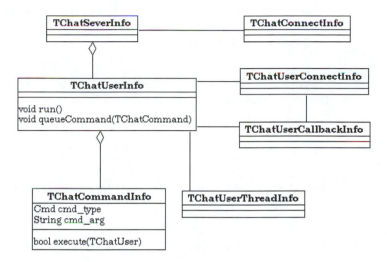

Figure 14-18 Class diagram for threaded chat server.

Multithreading the Chat Server

A multithreaded chat server can be derived from the original chat server without too much difficulty. The overall design of the server is augmented with two additional classes, one to represent the thread that will execute for each user and one to represent a task that can be queued for that thread. The actual task queue is maintained as a list of the task objects. A simplified class diagram for the revised server with these two classes is given in Figure 14-18. The methods shown here are those that must be added to handle multiple threading. Note that we have changed all the class names to use the prefix TChat (for threaded chat) rather than Chat.

The basic idea behind this design is to maintain a queue of tasks for each user, including both requests coming in from the user and requests to send messages to the user coming from other threads. The queue is maintained as part of the **TChatUserInfo** structure. Tasks here are represented by the **TChatCommandInfo** class, which indicates the type of command and an optional argument. If the set of commands and arguments had been nontrivial, this class would have been implemented as a class hierarchy following the command design pattern described in Chapter 13. However, because the commands are simple and the range of arguments is small, the overhead of creating six additional classes outweighs the complexity of an execute method that must deal with six different cases.

The actual processing of the task queue is done within the **TChatUserInfo** class by the run method, which is invoked by the corresponding method of the **TChatUserThreadInfo** class, which is a subclass of **SimpleThread**. It would have been possible just to make **TChatUserInfo** a subclass of **SimpleThread**, but this

```
class TChatUserThreadInfo : public SimpleThread {
private:
    TChatUser for_user;

public:
    TChatUserThreadInfo(TChatUser usr);
    ~TChatUserThreadInfo();

    int run();
};


TChatUserThreadInfo::TChatUserThreadInfo(TChatUser u)
{ for_user = u; }


TChatUserThreadInfo::~TChatUserThreadInfo()              { }


int
TChatUserThreadInfo::run()
{
    for_user->run();
    return 0;
}
```

Figure 14-19 Declaration and implementation of the thread class for the chat server.

would have entailed using multiple inheritance and would have limited the flexibility of the system for future evolution. In general, it is better to create separate classes for entities such as threads, sockets, or connections that represent self-contained units but must be specialized for a particular application than to merge these classes with other application functionality. This separation lets the library class change over time without necessitating major changes in the application. It also facilitates portability by not tying the rest of the application to a particular library class. Finally, programmers generally find that as a system evolves and becomes more complex, the underlying entity and the application functionality will need to be separated in any case.

Given all this, the implementation of the user thread class is trivial, as shown in Figure 14-19. The implementation of the command class is also straightforward, but a little more complex. Figure 14-20 shows the declaration of the class and the implementation of its execute method. The command class holds the command type and argument, which are set by the constructor. The execute method uses the passed-in **TChatUser** to invoke an appropriate method either on the user or on its callback object. It returns false if the user has closed the connection and is completed. EXIT was added as a command

```
struct TChatCommandInfo {

public:
    enum Cmd { SET_USER,MSG_FROM,MSG_TO,USER_START,USER_END,EXIT };

private:
    Cmd cmd_type;
    StdString cmd_arg;

public:
    TChatCommandInfo(Cmd,ConstText = NULL);
    ~TChatCommandInfo();

    bool execute(TChatUser user);            // return false to exit
};


bool
TChatCommandInfo::execute(TChatUser usr)
{
    bool fg = true;
    ConstText a = cmd_arg.c_str();

    switch (cmd_type) {
       case SET_USER :
           usr->setUserName(a); break;
       case MSG_FROM :
           usr->message(a); break;
       case MSG_TO :
           usr->callback()->chatMessage(usr->name(),a); break;
       case USER_START :
           usr->callback()->chatUserStart(usr->name()); break;
       case USER_END :
           usr->callback()->chatUserEnd(usr->name()); break;
       case EXIT :
           fg = false; break;
    }
    return fg;
}
```

Figure 14-20 Implementation of the command class.

here since we no longer want to delete the user as soon as the socket is closed, but might instead want to process pending commands sending messages to other users first.

The command structure is used by the run method inside of **TChatUserInfo**. This method, shown in Figure 14-21, utilizes both a semaphore and a mutex, both of which are created as data members when the class is created. The

```
void
TChatUserInfo::run()
{
    TChatCommand cmd;

    for ( ; ; ) {
        queue_sema.lock();                    // wait for a message

        queue_mutex.lock();                   // to get item off queue
        cmd = command_queue.front();
        command_queue.pop_front();
        queue_mutex.unlock();

        if (!cmd->execute(this)) break;

        delete cmd;
    }

    for_server->removeUser(this);
    delete this;
}


void
TChatUserInfo::queueCommand(TChatCommand cmd)
{
    queue_mutex.lock();                  // to put item on queue
    command_queue.push_back(cmd);
    queue_mutex.unlock();

    queue_sema.unlock();        // to let command be processed
}
```

Figure 14-21 The run method for each user.

semaphore is used to wait for a pending message while the mutex is used to ensure the integrity of the queue. The corresponding method to add a command to the queue is also given in Figure 14-21. It too uses the mutex while modifying the command queue. It unlocks the semaphore after adding an event to the queue to let the run thread continue if it was waiting for something to do.

The other changes needed in the chat server to complete multithreading included creating and initializing the user thread when the **TChatUserInfo** object is created, protecting the list of active users in the server, and modifying the server and message-decoding methods to queue commands rather than doing the actual processing. The latter two changes can be seen in the modified addUser method shown in Figure 14-22. Here we use a mutex to protect

```
void
TChatServerInfo::addUser(TChatUser cu)
{
    TChatUserListIter uli;
    TChatCommand cmd;

    server_mutex.lock();

    for (uli = active_list.begin();
            uli != active_list.end();
            ++uli) {
        cmd = new TChatCommandInfo(TChatCommandInfo::USER_START);
        (*uli)->queueCommand(cmd);
      }

    active_list.push_back(cu);

    server_mutex.unlock();
}
```

Figure 14-22 The addUser method for the threaded chat server.

the list of users. Moreover, instead of sending the "new user" message directly to all users, we build a command for each user and simply queue that command for the particular user.

SUMMARY

New applications require programs to deal with multiple users or multiple activities simultaneously. Often the easiest way to do this is to design the system in terms of separate processes or separate threads. Moreover, as today's systems become larger and more complex and need to deal with multiple users simultaneously, it is often easier to design and build them using multiple processes. In all these cases, the various processes or threads must communicate and synchronize with one another, issues coming under the rubric of interprocess communication.

The actual communication among processes can be done in a number of ways. In the text we summarized the use of files, shared memory, and sockets. Additional communications mechanisms include pipes (which are essentially one-way sockets) and mailboxes. Each of these mechanisms has its advantages and disadvantages. However, today sockets seem to be the predominant form of interprocess communication when a combination of timeliness, widely distributed processes, and high bandwidth is required.

Sockets are most often used to send messages back and forth: that is, communication between the client and the server is viewed in terms of discrete units. Messages form a convenient substrate for implementing multiple-process applications. Moreover, as we demonstrated with the **Connect** class, it is relatively easy to implement a message framework on top of sockets.

In an object-oriented world, messages can be treated much like method calls. Thus the easiest way to design a multiple-process object-oriented application is to view the system in terms of remote objects, objects that actually exist in one process but can be called from the other. In this case messages are used to effect method calls in the other process. While remote objects can be used directly, as illustrated in the chat example, there is growing support for them in such frameworks as ActiveX and CORBA.

In a client-server framework, the server often needs to handle multiple tasks simultaneously. One relatively simple way of coding this is to use multiple threads of control. Multithreaded programming is complicated by the need to ensure that the various threads do not interfere with one another and are synchronized correctly. A variety of synchronization methods exist, including mutexes and semaphores as well as read-write locks and monitors.

Multiple-process and multithreaded programming should be used only when needed and when they simplify the implementation of the target system. Both introduce additional complexities that must be balanced against the simplification in design and potential increase in performance they offer. In particular, remember that both multiple-process and multithreaded systems are generally much more difficult to test and debug than simple single-process, single-threaded programs.

EXERCISES

14.1 Implement a chat program that uses only files for interprocess communication.

14.2 Design a multiuser 3D tic-tac-toe (using a 4×4×4 board) program.

14.3 If you have access to a multiprocessor machine, see if you can use multiple threads of control to improve performance. You could write a multithreaded and single-threaded version of any of the following easy tasks and see which runs faster:
a) Write a program to multiply two large matrices.
b) Write a program to sort a large array.

14.4 Implement a version of the bouncing balls program described in Chapters 9 and 10 using multiple threads, allocating one thread to each ball.

14.5 Design an orrery program (as described in Chapter 1) using remote objects to represent the planets. Note that this is not a natural representation and hence the design is going to be a bit convoluted. It will, however, demonstrate a lot about setting up remote objects.

14.6 Design a reusable application framework for multiple-player game programs. The framework should support servers, clients, and a central process to act as an address book for multiple servers. It should not make any assumptions about the game being played, and should allow the client and server to send arbitrary messages back and forth. Discuss the design trade-offs that must be made.

14.7 Design a whiteboard system that supports multiple users editing the same document. The system can support text (in outline form), graphics, or some combination of the two.

14.8 Design and implement a system that monitors a game of chess. The program should allow the two players to connect to it and then it should provide each user with a chess board. Each user should be able to input a move when it is his or her turn. The program should check that all moves are legal and should maintain the timers for the two players. It should also record the moves of the game. Options include showing the players' pieces under attack, showing the legal moves, allowing players to use their display to try different move sequences, and showing standard moves from a book on chess openings.

14.9 Another old-time computer game is pong: two players each control a paddle and bounce a ball back and forth, attempting to make it miss the other user's paddle. This is relatively simple to implement if a single display is being used. What problems might you run into in attempting to implement it as a distributed system? How might you address these problems?

Chapter 15

Software Engineering

So far we have talked in terms of one programmer designing an already specified system. Software development in real life is seldom like this. Software is typically developed by programmers for customers who do not know precisely what they want. Programmers must understand the customer's needs and then define exactly what the software should do before they can do any actual design. Software development is also typically done by teams of programmers, ranging from a small group of two to four people to a large team involving hundreds of people. Testing and deployment of software is also a major effort, often done by yet another group. Moreover, most of the effort put into a software system, especially a successful one, is spent fixing bugs and adding new features once the system has been "completed," rather than on the system's initial development.

The study of software development, from a crude need on the part of a customer, through design and coding of a software system, and on through the ever-continuing process of fixing and improving the software, is called *software engineering*. This field has as its goal making software development simpler and the resultant software better. This chapter provides a brief overview of software engineering, describing the terminology and basic ideas developed by researchers and practitioners over the past thirty years. We first consider the problems that led to the field in the first place, proceed to describe the various phases of software development, and finally discuss the ways in which these parts can be put together.

THE FOUNDATIONS OF SOFTWARE ENGINEERING

In the early days of computers, software was often ignored. In the 1950s, system development concentrated on the hardware, since software contributed only about 20% of the overall system cost. Software was typically small (as were the machines) and hand-coded in assembly language to make the most efficient use of the machine possible. By the mid-1980s, however, the hardware-software ratio had inverted and software accounted for 80% of the system cost. Today, with inexpensive machines and personal computers already on people's desks, software is even more dominant, making up 95-100% of the cost of a system.

Software takes an increasing share of the system cost not only because hardware has gotten cheaper, but also because software has gotten larger. A large software system in the past was thousands of lines of code. Today's systems are generally millions of lines long. As software grows, its cost and complexity grow faster. Just as writing a thousand-line program is more than ten times as difficult as writing a hundred-line one, writing a million-line program is much more than ten times as difficult as writing one with one hundred thousand lines. The techniques used in developing small-scale systems do not scale up, and new techniques and methodologies are required.

The Problems of Software

The result of the software explosion has been a set of now-predictable problems. Software has become notorious for these difficulties and whole industries have arisen to alleviate them. Some of the problems, no doubt familiar to the reader, include:

- *Software is late.* Software is often advertised as available on a given date and then is delayed by months or even years. No company is really immune to this, and numerous examples can be found from such well-known manufacturers as Microsoft, Sun, and IBM.

- *Software is expensive.* Companies must estimate how much it will cost to develop a piece of software. These estimates are notoriously low: software always costs more than the original estimate, often by factors of two or more. This comes in part from the personnel costs in software delays, but other factors come into play as well.

- *Software doesn't do what it is supposed to.* Systems are hyped as solving all one's ills and never do. Even well specified, narrowly targeted systems often do not meet the expectations of the potential users.

- *Software is unmaintainable.* Software maintenance entails fixing bugs and evolving the software to meet new user or system demands. Complex systems tend to be extensible up to a certain point, after which either they completely fall apart or programmers refuse to touch them for fear they will do so. The standard solution is to rewrite the ancient software completely rather than attempting to modify it.

- *Software is not understandable.* This should be taken in two ways. We have been emphasizing the importance of making software readable by others because most software written today can be understood only by its author, and then only within a few months of writing it. This, of course, contributes to making software difficult to maintain. Another way of viewing this is that the documentation accompanying the code, which is essential and should be considered part of the software, is rarely helpful, often unreadable, sometimes nonexistent, and at times just plain wrong. Both design documentation and user documentation must be kept up to date and accurate, and should also be organized so as to present the necessary information in a usable form.

- *Software is unreliable.* Bugs, bugs, bugs. Anyone who has used software is aware of bugs. We are told to save often in the editor, to avoid this or that feature, and we know that our program or machine freezes or crashes periodically. Today's software is so complex and so poorly understood that it can't help but have some problems. Moreover, testing methods are rarely adequate; indeed, many companies resort to letting the user do the testing.

- *Software is inefficient.* Efficiency can be measured in various dimensions — run time, user-interaction time, memory utilization, and disk utilization. Each time we get a new version of a complex piece of software we need to upgrade our machine to run it, since while the old version might have been designed to run on a smaller machine, the new one does not run well enough to be used there.

- *Software is too complex.* This can again be taken at two levels. The inherent complexity of today's systems, requiring coding and maintaining millions of lines of code, leads to many of the problems above. In addition, the interfaces today's systems offer the user have grown in complexity to the point that few people understand all the available features and the extra buttons and widgets only get in the way. (Much the same can be said of C++.)

It is because of these problems that people look for better approaches to producing better software. The studies, experiments, approaches and methodologies developed here and their validation in real-life programming are the heart of software engineering.

Software Engineering

Software engineering has been defined by several authors as the use of engineering principles to obtain high-quality software. Engineering principles include the use of both knowledge and skills in an organized and practical manner. High-quality software has many aspects, most of which involve avoiding the above set of problems.

The first foundation for software engineering is a good working knowledge of computer science theory and practice. The theoretical background involves knowing how and when to use data structures, understanding a broad range of useful algorithms, knowing how to develop new algorithms where necessary, and understanding what problems can be solved and what can't. The practical knowledge includes a good understanding of the workings of the hardware as well as thorough knowledge of the available programming languages and tools. It also involves understanding a multitude of approaches to design such as the design patterns discussed in Chapter 13.

This knowledge is typically accumulated over time through course work, readings, and practical experience in the design, development and maintenance of systems. Good programmers are like good teachers, always striving to broaden their horizons and learn more. The best programmers and designers have a good background and can remember and apply to a new situation everything they have seen previously.

In addition to knowledge, good software engineering (and good engineering in general) requires a number of skills the programmer should develop, including inventiveness, judgment, communication, and objectivity. Inventiveness is needed to put together solutions to new problems as they arise. It can be overdone, but programming is problem solving to a large extent, and understanding how to solve problems has an important role. Good judgment comes into play in deciding among competing solutions, in tracking down bugs, in determining what features can and cannot be added to a system, and even in figuring out what system to build in the first place. It comes with experience and knowledge, but must also be exercised and kept fresh.

Communication skills, both oral and written, are often underemphasized in training programmers. Programmers today rarely work alone. Most work in groups, and senior programmers typically find themselves leading teams of programmers. As teams grow larger, more time is typically spent in meetings and in interacting with the other programmers than in doing the actual coding. In all these circumstances, the ability to get one's point across and to understand what others are saying is an essential part of the job. Written communication is equally important: one's design descriptions must be readable so that others can understand them later, and documentation on how the system can and should be used is equally essential.

The final thing a programmer needs is a questioning attitude. Early on we indicated that design is an evolving process, that one should always ask oneself how a design can be improved. The same is true of the code, the user interface, and most other facets of the system. A questioning attitude is also essential in reviewing your own and others' code and designs. A technique that has evolved for improving software is reviewing the design and code as early in the development process as possible. During such reviews, one questions if the design will work under all circumstances and attempts to figure out how to break it. A questioning attitude also comes into play in testing and debugging. Testing involves finding ways to make the program fail and asks how this can be done. Debugging involves asking the related question: if the program failed in this way, what was the cause?

Asking questions in the programming process is all the more difficult because programmers are put in the situation of criticizing themselves. Looking for a better design involves assuming that your own design is not the best; finding problems in code requires assuming that your code may be wrong, that you may have made a mistake. What programmers are told to strive for here is the ability to question oneself without being critical. Such an egoless attitude takes a lot of practice and self-confidence, but it does tend to make better programmers.

Software Quality

The quality of a piece of software, what software engineering is designed to achieve, is assessed in a variety of ways. Unfortunately, all these assessments are imprecise and the best one can do is to estimate the quality of the software from a variety of hard-to-measure values.

The most obvious measure of quality is whether the software does what it is supposed to. Here one would like to take the definition of the problem the software was meant to address and see if it actually solves that problem. This is called determining the *correctness* of the software; the process of doing this is called *verification* because one is attempting to verify or prove the software does what it should. Verification, however, is generally impossible since the statement of what the software is supposed to do is usually imprecise and does not cover all the cases. Moreover, proving anything about something as complex as a piece of software is impractical at best and generally intractable.

A better measure of the utility of the software is whether it meets the user's needs. This is called *validation*. Validation is typically the result of a long testing process in which the testers and the eventual users of a system try it out to see how well it meets their actual needs. Validation is a much more tractable problem than verification. However, it does not necessarily prove that the software actually works or that it works for all cases or under all circumstances. Like testing, it is an incomplete process.

The problem with validation is that it can overlook aspects of the *reliability* of the software. Reliability is a measure of the number of bugs remaining in the software. It is probably the best quantitative measure of software quality; it is the only such measure proven to have a strong correlation with the software's overall perceived quality. Moreover, since bugs are generally the aspect of the software most irksome to the user, their elimination can only help to make the software better.

Software bugs can be mere nuisances or major problems. The *robustness* of a software system is a measure of how it reacts in the presence of errors, whether the user's, its own, or the underlying machine's. A robust system recovers gracefully from errors, generally displaying a message and indicating how to undo any damage or to accomplish what was actually meant. A system that is not robust will crash, lose the user's work, or display some other undesirable behavior in the face of an error.

Another measure of quality is the *performance* of the system. Performance can be viewed along a variety of dimensions. Some of these involve the utilization of machine resources such as processing time or memory and disk space; others involve the performance of the user interface and whether it meets user expectations (see Chapter 11). In measuring system performance, one must take into account what the system is supposed to do and measure performance relative to the minimum required for these tasks.

User perception of a program affects quality in ways other than performance. An increasingly important criterion for software quality is the quality of the user interface, generally measured by how easy it is to use. A *user-friendly* interface is easy to use both for novices and experts and provides the necessary information in the best manner possible. Assessing the quality of a user interface involves all the human-factors criteria discussed in Chapter 11.

Two other measures of software quality concern the system's evolution over time. The first, *portability*, has to do with how easy it is to move the system from one platform to another. This could be as extreme as moving from UNIX to Windows or as simple as moving from one release of an operating system to another. Portable software is generally more adaptable and easier to evolve. The second measure, *extensibility,* is more difficult to pin down; it concerns how easy it is to add new features to the software or to adapt it to different applications. While this is often difficult to determine, it does become one of the most important criteria for a long-lived system.

Software Management

As software has gotten larger and teams of programmers must be coordinated to build a system, software engineering has come to include many of the tasks typically associated with management. These include organizing people, devising an overall process for software development, and estimating costs.

When people started to work on software in teams, they soon discovered that team programming offered diminishing returns. The amount of code generated by one programmer decreased as more programmers were added to a team. Some studies showed that with a team of five, each programmer's productivity went down by 20%, while a team of ten yielded a 40% decrease in productivity. My own experience with student teams suggests that once a team reaches a critical size of around five, little further work is accomplished by adding more programmers.

This phenomenon was called the "mythical man-month" by Fred Brooks.[1] The cost of software is typically measured in terms of the amount of work required for its development. In most industries, software included, this is calculated by multiplying the number of people working on a project by the time, in months or years, that each person works. Thus, if four people work on a given project for six months each, the project is said to require twenty-four person-months (or man-months in the standard terminology). The fact that programmers become decreasingly productive as teams get larger makes this

---

1. See Frederick P. Brooks, Jr., *The Mythical Man-Month: Essays on Software Engineering*, Addison-Wesley, 1995, for more information. (This is the second edition, the first edition actually dates back to 1975.)

measure inappropriate for software: two people working on a project for ten months generally produce more and better code than ten people working on the same project for two months.

The productivity loss with increasing numbers of programmers is due primarily to the increased communication costs. One way to minimize these costs and thereby maximize productivity is to concentrate on organizational methods for software teams. These techniques look for an organizational structure for the team that minimizes the number of people each programmer needs to communicate with, generally by employing some sort of managerial hierarchy. This goal is often undercut by the independent nature of many programmers and the complex interdependencies in most software systems.

Another approach to increasing productivity is to design the application to be easy for multiple programmers to work on. This involves breaking the program into isolated components and developing well-defined interfaces between them. If components are independent except for well-defined interfaces, then in principle each component can be written and tested independently by different programmers and the pieces will fit together quite readily. In practice, this is often not the case, since interfaces change and are not always well-understood even if well-defined. However, a good design goes a long way toward simplifying the work of a programmer team.

This initial breakdown into separate interfaces is one place where object-oriented design really shines. An object-based design allows the definition of sophisticated yet simple-to-understand interfaces. The power of objects lets the interfaces be organized and presented in a way that is natural for the given problem. Object methods generally require fewer parameters and are easier to understand than a corresponding procedural design. Also, because objects are generally self-contained, each object definition is a natural basis for dividing the problem into independent subproblems. We address issues in designing larger systems more fully in the next chapter.

Other management issues arise in developing a programming process that determines what is done where and by whom. This includes the documentation required at each stage, how testing is to be done, coding conventions, as well as design and code reviews. Many companies doing software development have a book describing their programming process (even if it's not always followed) that they expect incoming programmers to adopt. We address some of the process issues further in discussing the various programming stages later in this chapter.

A final management issue addressed by software engineering is estimating the cost of a software project. Cost here can be the monetary cost or just the amount of time necessary to write a program. Cost estimation is important at all levels. Companies need it to determine whether or not to build a given system and what resources should be devoted to its construction. Professors need it to determine how long a given assignment should take or how complex an assignment can be for a given amount of time. Students need it to determine when to start their assignments.

There are a variety of techniques for cost estimation. The more complex involve building a detailed model of the software system that includes information on the complexity and interactions of each component. This approach requires both a good understanding of the system to be written and accurate modeling parameters. It is sometimes useful in industry but not that useful to students. The most widely used approach to cost estimation remains expert judgment, i.e. asking someone who has built a lot of systems (preferably similar ones) to evaluate the requirements, complexity, environment, etc., and make an educated guess at the amount of time involved. My own personal approach is to make such an estimate and then multiply it by four.

Other approaches to cost estimation exist. Some involve using a top-down or bottom-up breakdown of the software to divide the cost estimate into smaller, more tractable pieces, and then putting the result back together. Others, including most student projects, use Parkinson's Law; i.e. the time needed to complete a software project increases up to the maximum time available. In industry, another approach is cost-to-win. Here, in bidding on a contract to write a software system, one determines the cost level necessary to win the contract and estimates that, regardless of what the actual cost may be. All told, however, as one gets more experience with writing systems, one tends to get better at estimating the amount of effort involved. Our advice here, especially to students, is always to start software development as soon as possible since it always takes longer than you expect.

THE PHASES OF SOFTWARE ENGINEERING

Software development has a lot in common with other engineering problems. In the engineering domain, developing a solution to a given problem, whether building a bridge or making an electronic component, involves a sequence of interconnected steps. The steps or phases occur in software development as well.

The first step is formulating the problem. Here the goal is to understand the nature and general requirements of the problem. In building a bridge, this means understanding the load the bridge must carry, the approximate locations where it can be built, the height requirements, and so on. In software development it typically means understanding the problem from the user's perspective and is called *requirements analysis*.

The second step involves defining the problem precisely once it is understood. Here one would specify the site for the bridge, its size, and a general outline of the type of bridge to be built. In software development this step is called *specifications* and involves developing a precise statement of exactly what the program will do, often even to the point of writing user manuals and other such documentation for the prospective system.

The third stage of development is detailing the solution to the problem. In building a bridge this would mean determining the exact configuration, computing the size of the cables and beams, and developing the complete blueprints for the bridge. In software development, this is the design process we have been talking about throughout this text. *Top-level design* involves developing an outline to the problem solution while *detailed design* involves specifying all the details needed so the design can be handed off to a programmer.

The next stage of development, *implementation*, corresponds to the actual building of the bridge or the actual coding of the program. If the design was done correctly and in enough detail, this should be the easiest stage (at least conceptually).

The final stage of development, *maintenance*, starts once the solution has been built. For a bridge it means continually repainting, repaving, and making any other repairs necessary. For software it involves fixing bugs, adding new features, and adapting the software to new architectures as needed.

In the remainder of this section, we consider these phases in more detail from a software point of view. To illustrate these phases, we introduce the problem we discuss here and in the next chapter:

> One of the oldest computer games (it was created at MIT in 1962 and I was playing it at Dartmouth in 1970) is Spacewar, where two (or more) spaceships are flying around a 2D universe consisting of one or more suns. The suns have gravity and the ships have thrusters (forward or forward and reverse) and the ability to rotate left and right. They can also shoot unguided, unpropelled missiles that decay after a given time. The object is to shoot the other player(s).

> Your job is to program an updated version of this game. Your implementation should handle multiple users playing on separate machines. You might also consider a 3D universe rather than a 2D one. (Note that one current invocation of Spacewar is the network game *netrek*.)

Requirements Analysis

The first step in software development is to understand the problem from the user's perspective. The developer should understand exactly what the program needs to accomplish and how it fits into the user's current or proposed environment.

This step is generally accomplished by interacting with the prospective users by written questionnaires, formal interviews, talking to the potential users, or even working alongside them until the problem and how the solution will fit in are well understood. The important point here is to undertake the process with an open mind, not with a solution already in hand. The idea is to determine what the actual problem is so as to find the proper solution, not to take a solution and fit it to the problem. Note that if you are building a system for yourself, this step simply involves introspection.

Once the problem is understood, the developer's next step is to put together a list of requirements the eventual solution must meet. These requirements determine the outlines of the "best" solution to the problem. (Note that the best solution in some cases isn't even a program.) This process is generally done in two stages. The first involves gathering as many requirements as possible. Here the developer uses the interaction with potential users to construct "wish lists" of solution features that should be as broad and inclusive as possible. The second step is to merge and then prioritize this combined list. The outcome here should be a list of the features required in the solution and a second list of optional features, with some indication of their desirability.

Determining the mandatory requirements and assigning priorities to the others is a nontrivial process. Ideally, it should be addressed in conjunction with the eventual users of the system, determining what their actual and perceived needs are and how the proposed system can best meet these needs. This is often done through questionnaires asking potential users to rate various items in order of importance. One should also determine the aspects of the system most crucial to its intended purpose and the aspects needed for its acceptance or commercial success.

The requirements should not be limited to the technical aspects of the solution. They should also include such items as the target architecture and environment, current systems with which the new program should interact, limitations on resources such as memory or disk, display requirements, user interface requirements, and so forth. Figure 15-1 organizes some of the requirements for the Spacewar program as either mandatory or optional. A further refinement might assign actual priorities to the optional requirements.

The result of all this should be a good understanding of the problem without any need to define an actual solution. The developer should understand, after requirements analysis, whether a particular solution will be acceptable to the user and, of two different proposed solutions, which will better suit the user's needs.

Specifications

The second step in software development is to restate the requirements from the programmer's point of view. The object of this stage is to produce a document detailing exactly what the eventual system should do. The new document, a specification for the eventual software system, is then a sound basis for actually designing and building the system.

Specifications concentrate on what the program does rather than how it does it. During this development stage, the programmer is attempting to outline the software system so that it can ultimately be designed. This is generally done in four steps: building a model of the system, defining the system inputs and outputs, defining the actions of the system for those inputs and outputs, and finally detailing other information pertinent to the design and eventual coding of the system.

Mandatory requirements:

1) Multiple players should be able to connect to or disconnect from the game at the start of each round. Players each have their own display.

2) Each player has a unique ship.

3) The game is divided into rounds.
   a) At the start of a round the players are given an initial position and velocity by the system. The position and velocity should be safe (i.e. not inside or directed toward a star).
   b) Each player gets a fixed number of missiles per round.
   c) Missiles time out after going about half the size of the screen.
   d) If an active missile hits a ship, both explode and the player whose ship was hit is out of the round.
   e) If a missile hits another missile, both explode.
   f) A round ends when either only one player remains or when all remaining players are out of missiles. The end can come only when no bullets are on the screen.
   g) A player "wins" a round by being the last player remaining.

4) Players should be able to control their ship from either the mouse or the keyboard.

5) Ships should have main thrusters as well as rotation thrusters.
   a) Main thrust is cumulative; i.e. the thrusters accelerate or decelerate the ship, not start it or stop it.
   b) Rotation is on/off. When a rotation thruster is on, the ship rotates. As soon as it is turned off, the ship stops rotating.

6) The program should run on Sun workstations.

Optional requirements:

7) The game can be in 2D or 3D.

8) Main thrusters can be forward only or forward and reverse.

9) Keep track of each person's score, i.e. the number of times he or she has won.

10) The system should port to NT.

11) The NT and Sun versions should be interoperable.

Figure 15-1 Sample requirements for the Spacewar program.

The first step is to construct a model of what the system will do. This is generally done using a combination of text and diagrams. The most relevant diagrams are data-flow diagrams detailing not how the system will work but rather what data comes into the system, what transforms are applied to that data, and what data comes out of the system.

Consider the Spacewar program. The system must read and interpret user input and translate this input into internal commands. These commands are sent to a central controller that maintains the state of the game and sends commands back to a display package to display this state. In addition, the cen-

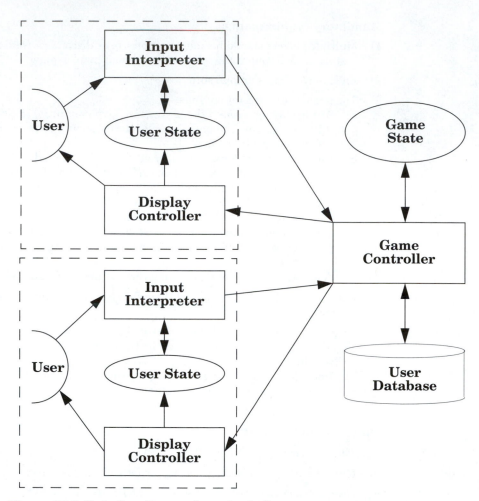

Figure 15-2 Data-flow diagram for a simple Spacewar program.

tral controller maintains a database of users to keep track of their wins. This information can later be provided to the display controller when a round is over. Finally, the display controller needs to interact with the input processor so that only currently relevant inputs are processed.

This simple structure is reflected in the data-flow diagram of Figure 15-2. There are several different types of nodes here. The semicircles on the left represent the users of the program; these are actors that can generate inputs and outputs as needed. The rectangular boxes represent actions; these take data in, process it, and then generate other data out, and are typically labeled with a description of what they do. Arrows between the users and the boxes or between different boxes represent the flow of data, typically commands or messages, between the actions. The elliptical boxes represent local data repositories, which are data structures maintained only while the program is running. The action box connected to such a data node can either store or retrieve data from the data structure. The cylindrical box at the bottom right is a more permanent data repository that is typically saved between system runs and can even be a full-fledged database system shared among multiple users. Finally, the dotted lines group components together to form units.

The diagram shows that commands flow from the user to the input interpreter, which uses information from the local or user state to determine what is legal and eventually to send the next move or other information to the game controller. The game controller processes these requests from multiple users, using the temporary repository reflecting the state of the game and the permanent repository of user information. The result of this processing is sent back to each user's display controller, which in turn updates the user's display and modifies the local state information. The dotted boxes indicate the grouping of components for each user in case additional users are allowed.

A data-flow diagram like this, annotated to describe what each of the nodes and arrows is responsible for, is a starting point for a more complete specification. It contains the outlines of a model describing what the eventual software will do. This model must be fleshed out with details of the system's inputs and outputs and the processing the system will perform.

There are no standard forms for data-flow diagrams. (Actually, there are quite a few different ones, but many standards do not make a "standard.") The format we use here represents a simplified consensus approach and illustrates the different types of notes and relationships typically included within such a diagram. Programmers should generally adopt a particular convention and use it consistently.

An alternative approach here is to create an object-oriented specification in which one uses objects to describe the problem rather than a data-flow diagram. The two approaches are closely related, since the elements of the data-flow diagram are often essentially objects. However, there are differences in emphasis that are important for inexperienced designers. Specifications should define the problem, not its solution. When using objects, one is immediately tempted to think in terms of the solution, especially if one will be using an object-oriented design. This essentially bypasses the specifications stage and generally yields less well-thought out and hence poorer designs. Using a separate notation here helps distinguish the two phases and lets the designer concentrate on the problem rather than the solution.

Once the programmer has completed a diagrammatic model of the system, the next step is to detail the inputs and outputs. The idea here is to describe the user interface so that it can be easily implemented. If the user interface is graphical, this should include the interface sketches discussed in Chapter 10. If the interface is textual, it should include a grammar describing all the commands. In any case, all buttons and commands available to the user should be noted along with their appropriate meaning and corresponding actions. The

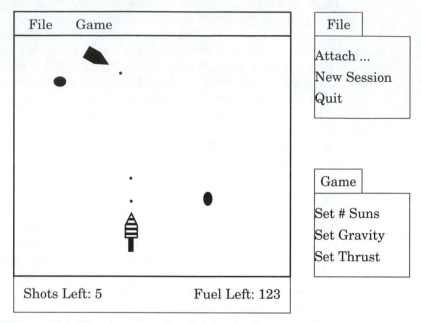

Figure 15-3 User-interface sketches for the Spacewar program.

output views, both standard and resulting from the different inputs, should also be detailed.

For the Spacewar program, the user-interface specification might show sketches of the interface, as in Figure 15-3, accompanied by a description of how users control their spaceships showing which keys are used and how the mouse buttons work. It would also include sketches of other screens and dialog boxes. In Spacewar, dialog boxes are needed for creating a new session (to name the session so others can attach to it), for attaching to a session, and for displaying the current scores list at the end of a game.

Describing the processing performed by the action boxes of the model is the third step in a specification process. This description should be precise and detailed enough that a software designer can understand the overall system well enough to evaluate alternative designs. It should include information about both normal and error processing. Here information would be given about how the positions of the stars are determined; how gravity, spaceship motion, and missile motion are computed; how close missiles must be to explode, what happens when an explosion occurs; what happens if two ships collide or if a ship collides with a star; and so on.

In saying what the program should do, it is often useful to talk about the different states the system can be in. This can be done graphically with a state-transition diagram such as that in Figure 15-4. Such a diagram should

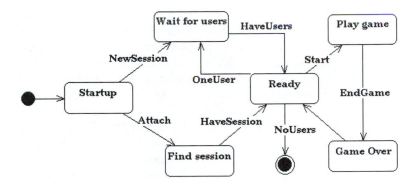

Figure 15-4 State-transition diagram for Spacewar game logic.

again be accompanied by appropriate annotations and a natural-language description to make it comprehensible.

Figure 15-4 shows the top-level logic of the program. The black dot indicates a starting point, the rounded rectangles indicate states and the arcs indicate transitions between the states. The diagram indicates that when the program starts, the user is given the option of starting a new session or attaching to an existing one. If a new session is started, the system waits for another user to attach before starting a game. If attach is selected, the user is prompted to select a session. Once attached, the program can be in one of three states. The ready state exists before the game actually starts; no input is allowed here. Once the game starts, the play state takes over. Here the user can control the spaceship, fire missiles, etc. Finally, once the system detects that a round has ended, the program enters the game-over state in which the winner is declared, high scores are displayed, and the system waits for each user to be ready to go again before reentering the ready state. An additional detail indicated in the diagram is that the system checks whether multiple users are still attached when in the ready state: if only this user remains, the game reenters the wait state, and if no user remains, the game exits. The black dot with a circle around it indicates an exit state.

State-transition diagrams such as this one are part of the Unified Modeling Language (UML) described in Chapter 6. A number of different formats exist for such diagrams and, as long as the programmer is consistent, all of them are acceptable. However, since we are using UML for other design diagrams, it makes sense to use the UML notation for these diagrams as well.

The final step in the specification process is to provide any additional information that might be relevant to the designer. This could include the architectures the system should run on, size limitations, other programs the system should interact with or look like, how the system should handle users connecting or disconnecting, the deadline for the system, and how many programmers will work on it.

The details of the specification can be given in forms ranging from informal comments to formal mathematics. The more mathematical approach, called *formal specifications* or *formal methods*, generally involves using set theory in a programmer-friendly notation to state precisely what the system should do. While such specifications can be helpful for some problems, they are very difficult to do correctly, especially for large interactive systems, and their use is beyond the scope of this text.

The most practical form for larger specifications centers around an outline. The outline details the major components of the system as described in the model and divides each component into major pieces as appropriate. At the lowest level of the outline is a series of short and precise natural-language paragraphs providing the necessary information about some particular aspect of the component. This form can be used as well for simpler specifications to ensure completeness, but in the simpler cases it is often easier just to use diagrams and a natural-language definition, without the formality of an outline. Figure 15-5 shows excerpts from a sample specification for the Spacewar program.

Design

The specifications serve as a prelude to the overall design process. Design, as noted throughout this text, involves analyzing, developing and detailing an appropriate solution to the problem defined by the specification process. It is a process of exploration in which the developer looks at various solutions, determines which solution is best, and then details that solution. It is also a hierarchical process in which the problem is broken down into tractable units.

Designing a moderate-sized software system, especially one involving multiple programmers, is typically more complex than the simple designs discussed so far. However, many of the techniques we have introduced and emphasized were specifically designed to handle the more general case.

The design process works by breaking the system into a small set of components that interact with each other in fixed ways. In a large software system, these components are typically developed by separate programmers or even separate teams of programmers. As such, it is essential that the function and interfaces to each of the components be well defined. This lets the components be developed with minimal interaction with the other components, thereby minimizing communications costs during development. It also provides a basis for testing the individual components. When a component is itself complicated, a good understanding of its function and interface provides the starting point for the second-level design of that component.

The first step in designing a large-scale system, *top-level design*, involves doing such a breakdown and developing the interfaces as the top level. The purpose of this step is solely to understand the function of each component and to specify the interfaces to that functionality. In an object-oriented design, these interfaces are defined as a small set of top-level classes along with their

Game Startup

1) When the program starts, the user is asked to choose whether to begin a new session or attach to an existing one.
   a) An appropriate dialog box should be provided.
   b) Cancel here should cause the system to exit.
   c) The dialog should provide a list of active sessions to attach to.
   d) The dialog should let the user name a new session.

2) Sessions exist as long as at least one user is attached. When all users have quit or detached, the session should disappear.

3) (Optional) Users should be able to detach from a session and attach to another session without quitting.

Game Control

1) Each spaceship maintains a current velocity, position, and orientation.
   a) When the main thruster is on, it provides a constant acceleration in the direction of the current orientation.
   b) The rotation thrusters changes the orientation by a fixed amount at each interval. It should take 5-10 seconds to rotate 360 degrees.
   c) Stars have gravity that provides additional acceleration.

2) Missiles are fired from the front of a spaceship.
   a) Missiles have the spaceship's current velocity plus an additional constant velocity in the direction of the spaceship's orientation.
   b) Missiles do not accelerate but are affected by gravity.
   c) A missile should explode if it gets within one missile diameter of another missile, the outside of a spaceship, or a star.
   d) A missile should last for about half the display when the spaceship is moving at average velocity.

3) Stars have a fixed position on the display.
   a) This can be predetermined or optionally assigned at random for each game.
   b) The number of stars should be settable by the players.

4) The game continues until either at most one player remains or until all players remaining are out of missiles.
   a) The game does not end if missiles are active.
   b) Once an end condition has been determined, there should be a delay (about 5 seconds) before the game ends.

Figure 15-5 Sample specifications for the Spacewar program.

public interfaces. In the next chapter we consider different techniques and conventions for creating effective designs for larger software projects.

Interface-centric design is generally repeated until the problem becomes small enough for an individual programmer to understand. It is at this point that implementation details in the form of helper classes, data members, and method pseudocode are typically provided. This is called the *detailed design*. While the top-level design is generally done by a committee of designers or an expert who can understand the overall system, the detailed design is generally done by the programmer who will eventually implement the corresponding code. The use of objects and interfaces ensures that the rest of the system is isolated from the low-level design decisions made here. Moreover, as we noted, programmers are generally more productive when they work alone, and a compartmentalized solution encourages this.

Coding

As we have seen, translating a detailed design into working code should be straightforward. While many little details must be worked out here, the hard part has already been done.

Coding should not be neglected. The emphasis here for a large software system should be on many of the techniques we have stressed throughout the text. Making a large system work and be maintainable over time requires programmers to adhere strictly to a set of programming conventions. This is generally reflected in naming conventions, stylistic conventions about such issues as indentation and the choice of variable names, and coding conventions such as the order of commonly grouped parameters.

Another emphasis should be on defensive programming. The hardest part of coding a large system involves integrating into a single working unit the pieces of the system written by different programmers. One of the main difficulties here is that bugs arising in the combination are difficult to attribute to any one piece. Defensive programming helps to find these bugs early on and isolate problems more quickly.

Testing

Once code is written, it needs to be tested, as discussed in some detail in "Testing" on page 216. Here we noted that testing is the process of finding errors in the code and that a successful test is one that actually finds an error. Programmers taking this negative approach to testing are more likely to find the problems in their code early and fix them while they are easy to fix. In that section we also covered various approaches to testing, emphasizing low-level testing of individual functions or classes.

Testing of a large system generally is done in stages. First each individual component is tested, generally by the programmer who wrote the code. This *module testing* is generally done either one class at a time or with a small set of related classes. The programmer typically needs to define a *test-case driver*, a simple program to make the appropriate calls on the class being tested.

Once programmers have some confidence in their individual components, they can be put together and the result tested. Such *integration testing* continues until all the components are together. Integration testing generally follows the hierarchical breakdown of the overall system, with components at each level being tested before they are integrated. Integration testing is generally more difficult and time-consuming than module testing, first because the program being tested is more complex and second because it needs to check for mismatches between the components.

When the whole system is put together, *system testing* begins. This involves testing the overall functionality of the system and is generally done at first by the programmers involved. In a larger company, the final stages of system testing may be done by a separate group to avoid the problems arising when programmers test their own code.

The final stage of testing involves handing the program over to the people who requested the system in the first place and asking them to ascertain that the resultant system meets their needs. This *acceptance testing* often determines whether a program written on a contract basis is acceptable and whether the company writing the program will be paid or not. For student programs, it is used to grade the assignment.

Operation and Maintenance

The final stage of software development, and the one most often ignored by students and many programmers, occurs after the software has been accepted and is in operation in a community of users. While one wishes software would just keep going forever once it is released, this never really happens. Software, no matter how well written or well tested, will have bugs. The systems on which the software runs will change with new hardware or new operating systems. The demands made on the software will also evolve over time. As users become more familiar with the software, they will want additional features. Moreover, the problem the software was originally designed to handle is also likely to change and the software must adapt to such changes.

Maintaining a successful software system is generally the most costly and most time-consuming phase of software development. It is also a difficult, often thankless task that is not particularly liked by programmers. In many companies, maintenance is done by programmers other than those who wrote the initial code, often by new or less respected programmers. This only tends to make the situation worse.

Maintenance programming is hard because it involves understanding the whole system and the whole development process. Fixing a bug or adding a new feature to an existing system actually means going back and redesigning some aspect of the system. Typically, however, design information for an existing system is either nonexistent or out of date, and hence useless. The maintenance programmer must understand the complete program with little more than the code as a resource. Modifying or adding to the code in a large system is difficult because changes to one routine can have unintended and unforeseen side effects in some other routine. Moreover, for consistency, the maintenance programmer must adopt the style of the original programmer.

Making maintenance easier and less costly is one of the principal objectives of software engineering. Much of what can be done along these lines involves design and coding. As we have noted throughout the text, a variety of strategies such as keeping the code and design as simple as possible, defining strict interfaces, maintaining consistent naming and coding conventions, defensive programming, good and accurate commenting, and insuring code readability can all help to make maintenance a more tractable task. It is important, throughout the whole development process, to specify, design, and develop code that can be maintained and can easily meet new or evolving demands.

Testing must also be adapted to the maintenance process. Here one creates a collection of test cases. Each time the system is upgraded, all the test cases in the collection are used to check that the new version of the system does at least what previous versions did. Such *regression testing*, discussed in Chapter 8, is aimed at ensuring that the new system is an advance rather than a regression over the previous one. To make such testing effective, the programmer should attempt continually to add new test cases to the overall collection.

THE SOFTWARE DEVELOPMENT PROCESS

The various phases of software development described above are not done independently. One of the focuses of software engineering has been to determine how to put these different phases together in an overall software development process. The actual connections among the phases and the formalization of a process based on them have evolved as developers explore different alternatives and as software systems become more complex.

The Waterfall Model

The simplest model of the software development process is to view its stages as successors to one another, as shown in Figure 15-6. Here software development proceeds in clearly defined and distinct stages. The first step is to develop a set of requirements for the system to be built, which is written down, evaluated and then approved. Next, assuming these requirements are fixed, complete specifications for the system are developed and are again reviewed and accepted.

Once specifications are complete, the next step is to design the whole system. The top-level design is developed and the problem is broken down. Each of the subcomponents is designed as well and the design is completed for all components of the system down to the stage where their coding is obvious. Once the designs of all components are complete and have been reviewed and checked, coding begins and the whole system is coded according to the design. Once the system is coded, it is then tested, starting at the module level and moving up to system testing. Once testing is complete, the system is distributed and maintenance begins.

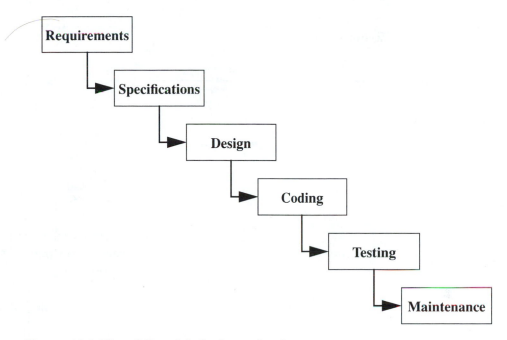

Figure 15-6 Waterfall model of software development.

This process is called the *waterfall model* of software development because the development stages proceed as a cascade, with the diagram of the phases looking a little like a waterfall. The model does allow some flexibility. For example, it should be possible to begin coding some sections of the program before completing the detailed design of everything else and it should be possible to begin module testing of components as they are coded. However, the general view here is that each phase of development is completed before the next is begun.

This model of software development has proven unrealistic for real systems. Information tends to flow not only from one phase of development to the next, but also from each phase back to its predecessor. When a system is being specified, developers often note new features that might be desirable or want to change the priorities of others in the requirements. When doing design, one often needs to change the specifications either to enhance the system or to handle what would otherwise be conflicting demands. When doing coding, one often finds that the design must be enhanced with additional methods or even at times changed to handle some unforeseen situation. When doing testing, one often must go back and change the code to accommodate bug fixes. Finally, maintenance involves new user requirements that should percolate down into new code.

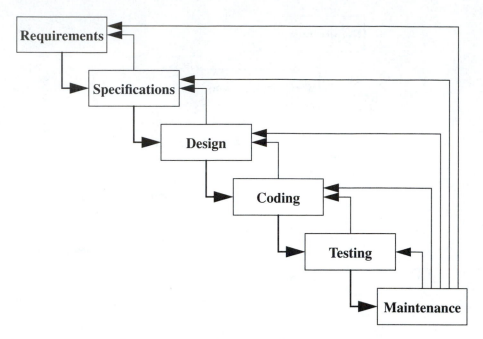

Figure 15-7 The feedback model of software development.

A more realistic model of software development takes these additional information flows into account, typically by augmenting the waterfall model with feedback paths as shown in Figure 15-7. The result is a *feedback model* of software development. Here the principal flow of information is still from one stage to the next. However, unlike the waterfall model, the feedback model lets information flow from any stage back to the previous stage and explicitly notes that maintenance changes can restart development at any stage.

Most software engineering today follows more or less along the lines of the feedback model. Requirements are generally gathered first and then the developers attempt to define the system to be built. As they begin to design the system, feedback from the design causes the specifications to be modified in various ways that are then put into the evolving design. Coding is typically not done until the portions to code have been designed, although coding of some sections and the detailed design of others often proceeds in parallel. Most module testing also occurs as the code is being written, while integration testing, of necessity, requires most of the code to be present. Testing often finds code errors requiring design changes (and sometimes even the specification if something was found to be too difficult or complex) and development then continues.

Prototypes and the Spiral Model

Both the waterfall and feedback models of software development assume that design can be done before coding begins. While this is generally the case, it can sometimes be better to code first and then design. The prime example of this is user-interface design. It is very difficult to design a good user interface on paper without being able to experiment with how the interface can be used, and one often develops a simple program for this purpose. There are other design decisions, too, whose impact or feasibility cannot be decided a priori. In these cases it is often useful to experiment with simple programs illustrating different design alternatives as a means of exploring the design space. This is especially true where a particular design decision can affect the overall success or failure of the eventual system.

The process of writing a simple program to explore the design space is called *prototyping* and the program itself is called a *prototype*. Prototyping is a viable strategy when the choice among different essential design alternatives is not clear, since it lets the developer experiment with the different alternatives and determine which is best. Putting up a prototype user interface gives the designer a sense of both what the user interface looks like and how it feels to interact with it. A user-interface prototype can even be shown to prospective users to get a feeling for how well it meets their needs.

It is generally desirable to build experimental prototypes as quickly as possible so that they can be evaluated more rapidly and take less time away from the overall design process. Because of this, prototypes are often made by using special systems or different programming languages. For example, user-interface prototypes can be developed rapidly by using a user-interface generator that lets the user select components and put them together graphically. Smalltalk and other interactive languages with extensive user-interface libraries are also used for this purpose.

The main drawback of prototypes is that they must be discarded after use. If they are developed by using a prototyping system or very high-level language, they are usually too inefficient for inclusion in a production program. If they were developed as quickly as possible in the target language, the quality of the code and documentation is generally quite poor and the result is not suitable for inclusion in a system that eventually must be fully debugged and maintained. Unless the programmer is willing to throw the prototype away after it has served its purpose (and to recode its functionality using proper design and implementation methods), prototyping is not a worthwhile alternative.

As systems and user interfaces have become more complex, more design issues have become potential targets for prototyping. Moreover, the development of large, complex systems involves a high degree of risk. A poor design decision at a critical point in the development can make the software unfixably slow or useless for its intended purpose. To take this into account and to

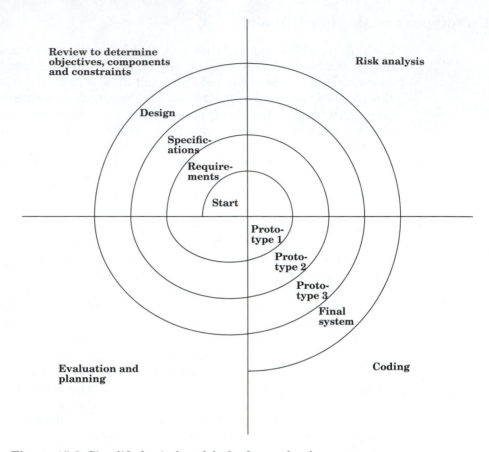

Figure 15-8 Simplified spiral model of software development.

decrease the cost of prototyping, an alternative model of software development has been proposed.

This *spiral model* of software development, shown in simplified form in Figure 15-8, assumes that successive prototypes of the system are built. One starts at the center by reviewing the problem to be solved. Then one does risk analysis to determine the most vulnerable or least understood parts of the proposed system, and these become the subject of the first prototype. The prototype is then tested and reviewed and the results of this analysis are used to derive a set of requirements for the eventual system. Using these desired requirements, a further risk analysis is done again to determine which parts of the system are the least understood or most vulnerable. A second prototype is built to analyze and understand these better. This prototype is again used, tested, and assessed to evaluate the different alternative designs, and from this analysis specifications for the eventual system are developed. These are then tested, after appropriate risk analysis to determine the most vulnerable portions, in a third prototype. The third prototype is then a fully operational model of the target system. It is again tested to find any weaknesses. From this analysis, a detailed design for the final system is developed and the final system is built using more traditional coding techniques to ensure code quality and maintainability. The last stage involves the normal testing process for this system.

This model can be varied in different ways. If prototypes are unsuccessful or indicate major problems, additional cycles and hence additional prototypes might be required. A third prototype might be used, for example, to experiment with different aspects of the specifications, and a fourth prototype would then represent the fully operational system. The various prototypes, and to some extent even the final system, need not be developed from scratch but can be built on top of their predecessors.

In general a prototype should be as focused as possible. It should provide the minimum functionality necessary to validate or check the design alternative for which it is being developed. This ensures that it can be developed as rapidly as possible and limits the temptation to use it as a production system. In the spiral model, the initial prototypes typically test a single design alternative that must be evaluated in order to understand better how the system should eventually be built. The final prototype is used to demonstrate that the whole system is feasible and actually meets the needs of the target users. In all cases, the prototypes are designed to be discarded, and only their designs and concepts are actually used in the final system.

The proper choice of a development model for a particular system depends on a variety of factors. The more complex and risky the system, the more one tends to use prototyping. If the system is relatively straightforward, for example if it duplicates and extends an existing system, then a design-oriented approach is preferred. If the prospective users aren't sure what they want, prototyping is an inexpensive way to experiment with different alternatives. If the user's requirements are well known in advance, the expense of building and discarding a prototype is probably excessive. In general, prototypes should be used when issues can be resolved only by experimenting with a real system and when the programmer is willing to throw away the prototype and all the work that went into it.

SUMMARY

Software engineering is the use of engineering principles to obtain high-quality software. It has been developed to help with the many problems arising in software development and in software itself. These problems primarily involve the excessive cost of developing and maintaining software and the low quality typical of most software systems.

Software engineering has multiple facets. It involves the proper training and use of programmers. It involves the development of appropriate techniques for defining what to build and how to build it. It involves the development of tools to aid the developer. It involves the use of appropriate management techniques and skills. Throughout all this, it puts an emphasis on developing and maintaining high-quality software.

Software development occurs in phases:

- *Requirements Analysis*: Here the programmer attempts to determine the user's needs and to outline the proposed system. The result is generally a user model and a prioritized list of features to be included in the proposed software.

- *Specifications*: Here the programmer determines precisely what software will be built. This includes a annotated system model, complete user-interface designs, and a prioritized list of the capabilities of the proposed software. The emphasis here is on what is to be built, not how it is to be done.

- *Design*: Here the programmer determines how the software will work. This involves both top-level design, where the overall framework for the system is constructed, and detailed design, where individual packages are specified.

- *Coding*: Here the detailed design is translated into code in the appropriate target language. This should be the easiest phase of software development.

- *Testing*: The code must then be tested. This is done at various levels, starting with module testing to check individual packages or classes, moving up to integration testing as the different packages are put together, and finally ending with system and acceptance testing in which the system is tested as a whole.

- *Operation and Maintenance*: Here the system is used, bugs are fixed, and changes are made to accommodate new user demands or a changing environment. In a successful system, this phase is typically the longest and most costly, often accounting for 80% or more of the overall software cost.

These phases can be organized in various ways. Ideally, they occur one after another, each one finishing before the next one starts; this is the waterfall model of software development. In practice, the knowledge gained in each phase makes one change decisions made in the previous stage. This leads to the more common and practical feedback model. A more recent strategy is to use prototyping to direct software development in order to minimize risk and produce higher-quality software. This is reflected in the spiral model.

EXERCISES

15.1   Write complete requirements for the Spacewar program.

15.2   Write the requirements for the orrery described in Chapter 1.

15.3   Write complete specifications for the Spacewar program.

15.4   Suppose you wanted to explore using computers in teaching introductory geology. Interview faculty and students in this area to determine what a suitable system should or could do and then draw up a full set of requirements for the system.

15.5   Computer systems are beginning to be equipped with software libraries for speech input and output. Suppose such a library is available. You want to develop a new product that would allow the use of speech in any application currently running on the machine (i.e., it should be able to speak error messages and prompts and simulate keyboard or mouse input based on speech commands). Draw up requirements and specifications for such a system.

15.6   Investigate and describe the software development process at some company in your area.

15.7   Draw up specifications for a system that allows the user to design and visualize a flower garden. The system should allow the specification of what should be planted when and where in a garden setting. Using a database of the growth characteristics of different plants (height and color based on time from planting), the system should show the user what the garden would look like at any point in time. The system should also provide a user-friendly front end to let the user design the garden.

15.8   Develop specifications for a system that simulates a car race. One part of the system should allow a user to design race tracks. The core of the system should support one or more users racing their cars around the predefined tracks.

15.9   Develop specifications for a system to do menu planning. As a first step you should do a requirements analysis to determine how people who cook at home might use a computer to help them with planning meals, shopping, adjusting recipes, etc. Then you should draw up complete specifications for a system to meet these requirements. Evaluate the specifications by presenting them to the potential users.

Chapter 16

Writing Larger Systems

As software systems get larger, the methods and techniques used to organize, develop, and implement them change. The problems surrounding the development of large software systems are inherently different from those of smaller systems. The solutions to these problems, the approaches necessary to ensure success, and the overall philosophy of software development have all evolved to deal with large-scale development.

Larger software systems are inherently more complex than smaller systems. This has several implications:

- Large software systems are more prone to failure than smaller ones. There are more places in the design and code where errors can creep in. Problems are more difficult to find and fix correctly. Testing, because of the sheer number of different options, alternatives, and program states, is much more difficult to do comprehensively. Design and implementation techniques must take into account and mitigate these problems.

- Large software systems require multiple programmers. Even the most productive programmers do not write much more than 50,000 lines of code a year. At this rate, a million-line system would take twenty years to write and would be out of date before it started working. Large systems must be designed and managed to let teams of programmers work on them.

- Large software systems are difficult to understand. The overall gestalt of how the system works is buried under multiple levels of detail and is typically invisible to the individual programmer. No one programmer can be expected to understand all aspects of the system. The system must be designed and developed in a compartmentalized manner on a need-to-know basis that minimizes the amount of detail any one person must learn.

In this chapter we look at some of the issues arising in the development of larger systems. The techniques we emphasize are applicable to at least moderate-sized systems of up to several hundreds of thousands of lines, and work well for smaller systems of tens of thousands of lines. Larger systems, with millions or tens of millions of lines of code, require more emphasis on management issues and additional design and coding techniques.

The chapter is broken into three main parts. We start with a brief overview of larger problems and how to get started, and then cover techniques for developing practical designs for larger systems. This is followed by a discussion of management issues for larger projects.

GETTING STARTED

The first steps in developing a large-scale project are much the same as for a small-scale project. However, the overall success of a large-scale project is much more dependent on doing a good job here than in a small-scale project. Errors in identifying the problem or its potential solution or errors at the top level of design will be magnified by the scale of the problem and can prove ruinous to the overall software effort.

Requirements Analysis and Specifications

The first step in undertaking a software project, then, is thoroughly to understand the problem and its potential solution. The methodologies for doing this were covered in "Requirements Analysis" on page 405 and "Specifications" on page 406. This understanding is gained in two phases. The first involves understanding the problem from the user's perspective. Here the developer must work closely with potential users to understand the needs the software system is planned to meet. This can involve interviewing users, distributing questionnaires, working with users to understand how things are currently done, and analyzing the problems of current techniques or systems.

The second phase in understanding the software system involves looking at the potential solution from the programmer's point of view. Here one attempts to detail exactly what the eventual system will do, describing the various interfaces it will provide as well as particulars on the actions it will perform. A multipronged approach is used to derive this specification. The principal technique is to develop a model of the proposed solution and then describe that model in detail. The model is typically based on data- and control-flow diagrams, as discussed in the previous chapter. The important point here is not how the system works, but what it does. These diagrams are augmented with detailed explanations of the function each box or arc performs.

The second part of the specifications includes a tentative design of the system's various user interfaces. This design can be described either through appropriate sketches or through a user-interface prototype that lets the designer and perhaps even potential users test whether the system will meet its requirements. In principle, the description should provide enough detail that a user manual could be written for the proposed system.

The final part of the specifications puts these two items together, along with any additional information such as system and portability requirements, to produce a specification document. This document is the foundation for the subsequent design and implementation of the software system. Just as in a building, it is the strength of this foundation that determines whether the system will stand up or collapse. Attempting to build a large system that is poorly defined or understood before one starts is a sure step toward failure.

In Chapter 15 we introduced a simple spacewar problem as an example for large-scale software development. We illustrated there how to develop requirements from the user's point of view and showed part of the result in Figure 15-1. Then we developed a system model, showing the data flow in Figure 15-2, user interfaces in Figure 15-3, and control flow in Figure 15-4. Samples from the overall specification were shown in Figure 15-5. We use this problem and these specifications as the starting point for our discussions here.

Design

An object-oriented design for a large system is developed in much the same way as for a small system. The differences are a much stronger emphasis on hierarchy in design, an emphasis on interfaces and interface definition, and a variety of techniques for selecting and organizing the implementation classes so as to minimize risk and make it easier for multiple programmers to work on the system simultaneously.

The design process starts by looking for candidate classes. This process is much the same as for a smaller program, except that the starting point here is the specifications document that completely describes the target system. The data-flow diagrams in this document provide one set of candidate classes, since each data element here can correspond to a class, as can each of the action boxes. The user-interface diagrams provide a second set of classes, with one top-level class corresponding to each interface and separate classes underneath this for each component of the interface. Another set of candidate classes can be derived from the textual specifications; if this is broken down into subsystems, there should be a class for each subsystem. A part-of-speech analysis of this specification text can produce more candidate classes. A final set of classes can be obtained by understanding the solution and how it works under one or more scenarios. These could be written either as part of the specification (say as the basis for the user-interface diagrams) or by the designer in order to understand the software better.

The difficulty with a large-scale system is that the number of potential classes is so enormous that it is impractical to list them all. The designer has to begin using hierarchy and eliminating classes from consideration even before the design begins. The initial goal here should be to develop 20 to 30 high-level classes from which the overall design of the system can evolve.

Figure 16-1 shows the initial set of candidate classes for the spacewar program. This set has been pruned from the overall set of classes we could have identified. For example, rather than listing all the different types of entities in the game such as spaceships, missiles, stars, and explosions, we include only

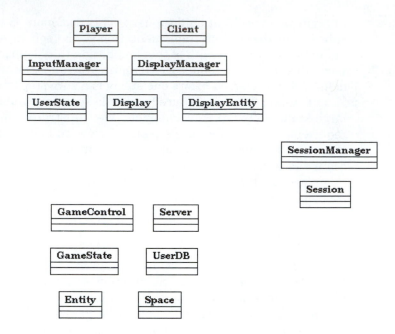

Figure 16-1 Candidate top-level objects for the spacewar program.

the candidate class **Entity**. We also exclude some obviously lower-level classes such as thrusters on the spaceship and gravity for doing computation.

The other thing we have done, as suggested in "Top-Level Design" on page 140, is to cluster the candidate classes. Here we formed three clusters. The top cluster contains information on each individual player. The **Player** class represents the player; the **Client** class represents a connection to the server. The **InputManager** and **DisplayManager** classes handle input from and output to the user respectively, and the **UserState** class represents information about the state of the game as seen by the user. Finally, the **Display** and **Dis-playEntity** classes represent the actual display and the items on the display.

The second cluster, at the bottom, represents information needed or used by the server. The **GameControl** class handles the game logic while the **GameState** class stores and manages the current state of the game. The **Server** class represents the connection between the server and each client and the **UserDB** class represents the database of information on how often each user has won a round. The **Entity** and **Space** classes represent information in the game state.

The final cluster has a class representing a session and another class for managing sessions in some way. These are needed to implement some of the connection logic brought out in Chapter 15.

The next step in small-scale object-oriented design would be to select a sub-set of these classes to represent the top-level design. Here we would select a set of five to 10 classes encompassing everything else in the design. These classes would then be characterized by defining their obvious data fields and interconnections as well as any top-level methods. We would proceed from there to provide pseudocode for these methods, introducing new methods and secondary classes as needed.

In large-scale design the approach is similar but much more compartmentalized. We first identify the set of top-level classes. In doing this, we look not for the most logical set but instead for the set that breaks the problem up into the most plausible set of independent pieces and maximizes our chances of building a successful system. Next we try to define the interfaces among these pieces without referring to the implementations underlying them. Once proper interfaces are designed, each component can be treated as an independent system on its own and can be designed and implemented using object-oriented techniques. All this is described in more detail in the next sections.

The essential idea in large-scale design is to break the program up into well-defined and independent components. This lets different programmers tackle each component without having to interact excessively with other programmers. Complete interfaces ensure each component is well defined and let the programmers work on their own component without needing to know the details of other components. A high degree of independence ensures that components can be implemented, tested, upgraded, and even replaced without adversely affecting the rest of the system.

Achieving such a design takes practice and understanding. Experienced designers can generally look at a problem, understand it, and then suggest a workable overall design, using their experience with similar systems and their understanding of what types of designs work and which ones don't. They also use methodologies that minimize potential problems and let the design be flexible enough to allow future changes.

DESIGN BY SUBSYSTEM

There are a variety of techniques for selecting and organizing the small set of top-level classes in a large-scale design. These techniques focus on providing independent components with well-defined interfaces and on ensuring that the system built from these components ultimately works.

The simplest technique is that outlined in the previous section. Here the designer identifies a set of candidate classes, clusters them, and then uses the clusters to select a small final set of top-level classes. While this technique is always helpful, it is not in general sufficient for most problems: the set of candidate classes is sometimes incomplete or wrong, the groupings are based on too little information, and the result is often not the best design. This approach is thus often augmented with other techniques.

One of the most powerful such techniques involves adding rather than removing classes. Here we apply a facade design pattern, as described in "Facade" on page 339, to create a new class to be a front end for a set of related classes. The top-level design can then use the facade class and ignore the classes it is a facade for.

This is an instance of *design by subsystem*. The facade class identifies a high-level component or subsystem of the overall program. It replaces a cluster of classes in the initial design with a single class and thereby simplifies the overall design. The actual classes represented by the facade can be defined at a lower level of detail and can be ignored at the top level of the design.

Thus design by subsystem offers advantages in terms of both simplicity and information hiding. It also lets the designer concentrate on the external interfaces needed by the set of classes the facade represents without having to worry about the interfaces among the implementations of these classes. Since these external interfaces both are the important details at the top level and are essential for getting the remainder of the system working, this generally leads to a better and easier-to-understand overall design.

Care must be taken in defining subsystems using facades: if the subsystem is not correctly identified, the overall design is generally more complex and weaker, not simpler and stronger. The essential element is choosing the right set of initial classes as the underlying subsystem. These classes should have a common purpose so that the facade class is cohesive: it should be possible to state the function of the facade class in a simple, non-compound clause. The grouped classes should also exhibit some coupling: most of the communication these classes do should be among themselves, not with other components of the system. This ensures that the facade is a gateway and not a hindrance to the eventual implementation. Finally, the classes should be chosen so that classes outside of the identified subsystem do not need detailed access to individual elements within the facade.

Subsystems that can be defined naturally will greatly simplify the design and generally lead to a better system. Thus we recommend:

Design a large system with subsystems in mind.

RISK-BASED DESIGN

Another technique useful in selecting a good set of top-level classes is to minimize the risk that the design may be bad or the system may fail. A large system has no "correct" design. Instead, there is a wide range of acceptable designs, some better than others. But while a number of designs will work, there is also a broad range of designs that will yield a marginal or nonfunctional system. A first step in the design process is to ensure that a system based on the design one is developing will work.

One way to do this is to identify the critical issues of the problem and design either for or around these. A novice designer has trouble identifying which aspects of the design are fundamental. A good starting point, however, is to determine the portions of a potential solution that seem to be the most difficult.

There are several ways of identifying the difficult issues in a system. One can start with the specifications as they are presented. While the specification model describes what the system does, it is not a big jump for the designer to attempt to determine how each of the actions described could be undertaken. Any actions whose potential implementation is not clear should be identified as potential problems. The designer should list the potential problems and then order them by difficulty.

Building a Design Model

While this is a starting point, it is unlikely to be sufficient to identify all the potential difficulties or even the most crucial ones. Many of the thorniest design problems arise because the implementations of several different actions are inconsistent with one another. Locating these problems is difficult. The best approach is actually to build a model of a potential solution using the set of candidate classes and go through the specifications to ensure that all actions can be done within the model. Where different actions conflict, one can either change the model and try again or just note the potential problem.

An initial design model can be most easily derived by starting with the data-flow diagram contained in the specifications, which shows the basic components and data structures. In an object-oriented implementation, both the components and data structures will be viewed as classes, so the diagram can readily be mapped into an object-oriented framework. Of course, the diagram should be augmented with any additional assumptions and should attempt to show object communication rather than simple data flow.

Figure 16-2, an initial design model for the spacewar program, shows boxes representing classes and arcs representing connections among them. Note that the connections here indicate that one class needs to interact with another — they are not the more constrained associations typical of a static structure diagram. If we ultimately accept this design, the relationships will be refined in a future step. This diagram breaks the design into three components. The first, represented by the five classes in the upper left, is the code for each user. The second, represented by the five classes in the upper right, is the server. The remaining component, the session manager, contains the two classes at the bottom.

An essential component of such a model is a description of how each component works. The **Player** class is the manager for the user code. It uses the **Client** class for all communication with the server or with the session manager at start-up. It creates a model of what should be displayed and the state of the game in the **UserState** class. The **InputManager** class uses this to determine

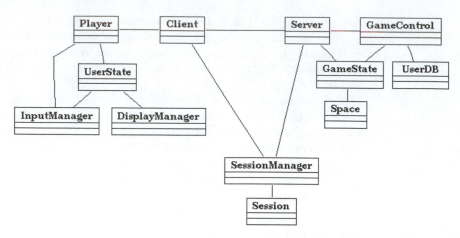

Figure 16-2 Design model for the spacewar program.

what inputs are valid before passing them onto the **Player** object to send to the server. The **DisplayManager** class reads the game state and continually puts up the corresponding display.

The server component is centered around the **GameControl** and **GameState** classes. The former manages the overall server, determining when to connect, who is playing, and when to start a game. The latter manages each actual game, keeping track of all the objects and their positions and using the **Space** class to store the objects. The **UserDB** class manages the set of users and their cumulative scores. Finally, the **Server** class manages all communication with the users and with the session manager.

The class design of the session manager itself is fairly simple. The **Session-Manager** class keeps track of currently active sessions and starts a new session when appropriate. The **Session** class represents a single session and the information about that session.

Identifying Difficult Problems

Once a design model is developed, the designer should ensure that each action in the specifications can be accomplished within the framework the model provides. Again, any actions difficult to describe within the framework should be added to the list of potential problems. Finally, the set of potential problems should be sorted by order of difficulty.

Several potential problems in the spacewar program can be identified by this process:

- How to convey the game state from the server to the client in a timely fashion. The client display must update at least 10 times per second for smooth animation. Can the server send the game state to the client this fast, can the server send several frames at once, or should the client handle some object movement?

- How to identify the active sessions when a new user wants to connect to the system. The session manager needs to know what is currently running; moreover, the client and server both need to talk to the session manager.

- How to achieve smooth animation on the client display. Should we use xor, as in the bouncing balls example? Should we use a fixed background display and just update the moving objects? Should we do double buffering? Or are overlay planes available for moving objects?

- When to update the display. Should the display be updated automatically to achieve a constant frame rate, or only when new information comes to the client from the server? In the former case, what assumptions can be made about moving objects? In the latter, should we assume a fixed delay between frames or should we update immediately?

Solving the Difficult Problems

Once the difficult problems are identified, the next step is to focus the design to solve or isolate those problems. For each problem, the designer should determine whether a solution in the current framework is possible. This can be done either analytically or, where necessary, by implementing a prototype to test possible alternatives.

Consider the first problem above. This is crucial to the overall program. If the server can't provide the information fast enough to the client, then we must restructure the solution completely so that the game is actually played independently at each client, with the server simply coordinating input and ensuring that the various clients remain consistent. This is a much more difficult design to implement, but it can be done. Here we could run a few experiments to determine the number of messages per second the server can send to the client to determine if a problem will arise. It turns out that hundreds of messages per second can be sent without putting too great a load on either the server or the client. Since this is much greater than the ten-message-per-second target, we should be okay. However, we will have to take care in designing the server to ensure that messages are sent frequently, and in designing the client to ensure that messages are read frequently.

Next consider the second problem. Determining the active sessions is not as easy as it sounds. Ideally we want to put the session manager in the client. If we use files to store the different server sockets' address, then we can go through whatever directory these are stored in and identify the different sessions, since each server corresponds to a session. However, if a server crashes or doesn't remove its address file, this solution will make spurious sessions be reported. This could be alleviated by having the server lock the file using system-wide locking and having the session manager in the client check to see if the file is locked. A little experimentation here shows that this almost works, but locks are not reliable and can still exist for an extra five or ten minutes if a server crashes.

The preferred alternative solution is to view the session manager as a separate process in the design. Both the server and the client connect to the session manager when they start up. The session manager keeps track of the servers currently connected and reports that information to the client when asked. It also detects when a server disappears through the loss of the connection and can update its database accordingly. Here, then, the solution has a strong effect on the eventual system design.

The third problem involves the best way to handle the display. Here we know that different solutions are possible and that at least one of the solutions will work. We may want to experiment with the different solutions to see what works best, but this is really an implementation detail and need not be considered at the top level of the design. What we want to do for problems like this is to ensure that the top-level design isolates the problem within a class. The display manager class should be the only class affected by the technique eventually used here. Moreover, the interface to this class should not reflect the solution but should be independent of it. Here we are using information hiding to isolate the potential problem from the rest of the design. Doing this lets us change the implementation of the display manager as needed without affecting the rest of the system.

The last problem again involves the display. The mechanism used to trigger updates will depend to some extent on how animation is done. It will also depend on how fast the server is and on aesthetics, which are difficult to determine without actually using the system. Our design should again isolate this decision within the display class so that the rest of the system is not affected. The one difficult aspect of this is giving a way to guess an interim position for an entity if no new information is obtained from the server. To avoid this, we assume that the server provides updates at least as fast as the frame rate, possibly faster. Otherwise, we would have to do linear interpolation within the display component itself, with each display entity keeping track of its current velocity (as the change of position between frames) and possibly its current acceleration (as the change of velocity between frames). Note that here we are changing the specifications by putting an additional constraint on one of the other components to ensure that the problem can be solved.

This approach of identifying and either solving or isolating the difficult problems attempts to reduce the risks in the solution. It provides a good starting point for the design, offering points to focus on and identifying classes and interface requirements. The spiral model of software development, introduced in "Prototypes and the Spiral Model" on page 419, formalizes this and incorporates it into industrial practice. For most moderate-sized systems, however, just identifying the potential problems and using them as the focus for the

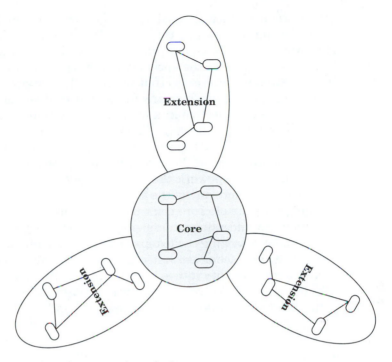

Figure 16-3 Core-plus-extensions design.

design model and the eventual design should be sufficient. Thus we recommend:

> **Design a system with the difficult problems and their solutions in mind.**

CORE-PLUS-EXTENSIONS DESIGN

Another technique for large-scale design focuses on organizing the system so that it consists of a small core and various extensions that plug into the core, as shown in Figure 16-3. This is called a *core-plus-extensions* design.

The core of a core-plus-extensions design is a small set of *interface classes*, classes that other components can see. They are publicly available, generally by being defined in public header files. There should be no more than 10 such classes. The core also includes whatever support classes are needed to implement these public classes, and represents the heart of the system, providing the basic functionality needed by all the other components.

The extensions are designed to plug into the core and interact with the rest of the system only through the interface classes of the core; they do not interact with one another. Extensions can give other extensions such basic services as input and output, but they do so through methods provided by the core. However, most extensions provide optional functionality that expands the basic system to meet the specifications better. Such functionalities are sometimes viewed as *features*, so that the core-plus-extensions approach boils down to a core system onto which any number of features can be grafted.

The primary objective in a core-plus-extensions design is to keep the core as small as possible, using the independent extensions for most of the system's actual functionality. All programmers on a project need to understand thoroughly the interface to the core, since all extensions must fit neatly and precisely into the framework the core provides. The core must be designed and implemented before any of the extensions.

A logically simple core consisting of a small set of classes is easy for programmers to understand completely. It provides more flexibility and a better interface for attaching the extensions, and it should be easier to design, implement, test, and debug so that it should be ready earlier. Putting most of the system's functionality into extensions makes the system inherently more flexible and easier to evolve. It also gives the various programmers more independence, leading to fewer misunderstandings and higher productivity.

Pros and Cons

The core-plus-extensions design methodology has several advantages:

- A basic working system is available early in the development cycle. This is good for the programmers psychologically since they have something tangible to show for their efforts. It is also good for the system since it can help programmers understand the strengths and weaknesses of the design and correct any flaws early on.

- Communications among programmers are minimized. Once the core of the system is written, programmers working on separate extensions need only minimal communication with other programmers, since extensions do not interact directly. This should enhance productivity in a multiple-person project. Also, the overall system is less dependent on any one programmer. If an extension is incomplete because a programmer was ill or incompetent, the other extensions and the rest of the system can still be developed and tested.

- The framework provides a good basis for testing. The core, as the most important part of the system, is generally tested first using drivers. It is then tested again and again as new extensions are added, thereby ensuring that the heart of the system is the part most tested. Extensions can be tested one at a time as they are added to the core.

- The overall system should be easy to extend and evolve. If the core is specified correctly, it should be simple to extend the system by adding new functionality, whether by replacing existing extensions or adding new ones. Porting to a new operating system or to new hardware can be done by upgrading the core.

These benefits, however, do not come without cost: the designer here must be aware of the problems and pitfalls associated with a core-plus-extensions design. These include:

- The success of the overall system is highly dependent on a well-designed and well-implemented core: this approach can only amplify problems in the design of the core.

- Changes to the core, especially its interfaces, can necessitate changes in a large part of the system. This can make evolving the core itself very difficult and means it is very important to get the design of the core right the first time.

- Attempting to bundle the core functionality of a system inside a small set of classes can be artificial: the resultant classes may not be cohesive and the methods they provide may be quite complex.

- The resultant implementation may not be as efficient or direct as with another design. Extensions may very well need to interact with one another. A core-plus-extensions design forces these interactions to go through the classes of the core, thus adding several unnecessary levels of indirection.

- Because extensions interact with each other, the system is also prone to the *feature interaction problem*: while each extension or feature is considered independent, they actually interact with one another through the core in weird and wondrous ways whose results are not always predictable. This problem has been particularly vexing in the digital telephone-switching systems in which new features interact to cause problems with existing features.

In general, however, the benefits of a core-plus-extensions approach outweigh the drawbacks if a core can be naturally defined. When a system is large enough to require a sizeable team of programmers, it is worthwhile to try to cast the design into this framework by identifying core classes and then forcing all the interactions among the non-core classes to go through the core.

Defining the Core

The difficult part in a core-plus-extensions approach is determining what is in the core. This requires a careful analysis of the communications among the proposed classes. It requires modifying the interaction paths to minimize the interaction among potential extensions. It also requires some analysis of how the system might evolve in the future so that the design of the initial core can take these changes into account.

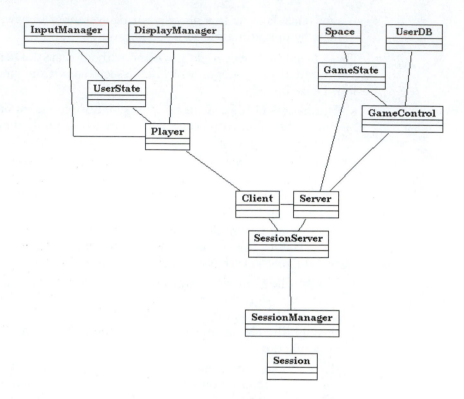

Figure 16-4 Core-plus-extensions overview of the spacewar program.

In designing a complex system, it is best to do a top-level system design with all the extensions and features one can possibly identify. This large design can then be pruned down to include only those features needed in the initial implementation. This approach tends to make the resultant system easier to modify and evolve, especially for previously identified functionality. This is helpful in a core-plus-extensions design where it is important to minimize the changes needed in the core as the system evolves.

While the spacewar program is a bit too simple to benefit greatly from a full core-plus-extensions approach, it can still serve as an example. At a trivial level, it already exhibits some of the characteristics of this approach. Because we have tacitly assumed that the client, server, and session manager are distinct entities, we can recast the design to use the communications classes as the core, as in Figure 16-4. Here the core is the three classes **Client**, **Server**, and **SessionServer**; the three extensions are the client program, the server program, and the session manager program. All interactions among these components must go through the core classes.

The design of the server for the game provides a more instructive example. Figure 16-5 shows a more detailed design for the spacewar server. Here we

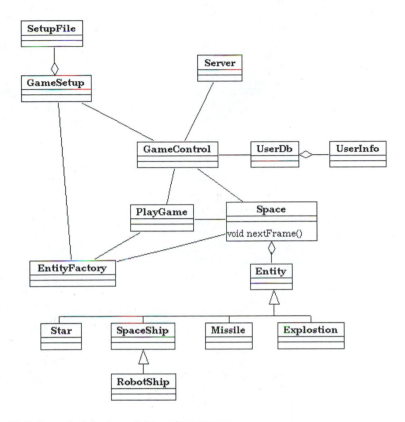

Figure 16-5 Detailed design of the spacewar server.

have added the entity hierarchy; a factory class for creating entities; a class for setting up a new game, possibly based on one or more setup files; a class to actually play the game; and classes containing the per-user information in the user database.

   We can do a core-plus-extensions version of this design by focusing on the communications paths and identifying the central system components. A first approximation to such a design focuses on the classes **GameControl**, **Space**, and **EntityFactory** as the core. These form five extensions, one for the entities, one for the user database, one for playing the game, one for setting up the game, and one for the server. While this is a viable design, it has the drawback that the entity factory probably should be associated with the entity extension, not with the core. To get around this, we can add a method to the **Space** class to serve as an entry to the factory. We thus recast this design in the core-plus-extensions form shown in Figure 16-6. Here the core is the two classes **Game-Control** and **Space** and the diagram shows that none of the five extensions communicates with anything other than the core.

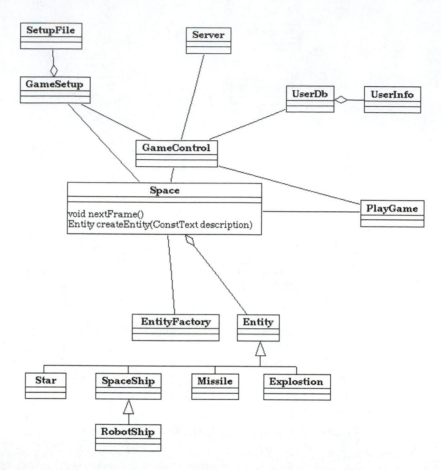

Figure 16-6 Core-plus-extensions version of spacewar server design.

One difficulty with this approach in this case is that the core must call the extensions; in particular, the game control module needs to invoke methods in the **GameSetup**, **Server**, **UserDb** and **PlayGame** classes. The best way to accomplish this is to view the calls from the core to the extensions as callbacks. The core should include a set of callback classes defining its interface to the extensions. These classes are designed to be inherited (as noted in "Inheritance for Callbacks" on page 123) and the callback methods are redefined by the extensions. The core can then be self-contained, making calls on the abstract callback objects as needed. Extensions can be plugged into the core by simply defining their implementation of the callback class.

Exactly how callbacks are used here depends on the situation. The easiest but least extensible approach is to define a separate callback class for each extension needing to be invoked from the core, so that there will be a single, well-defined object the core needs to use for each particular set of callbacks.

This simplifies both the core and the particular extension. It has the disadvantage, however, of forcing one to understand the extension fairly completely while developing the core: it is difficult to change the extension's interface or functionality or later to divide the extension into separate extensions. This approach should be used where an extension can be well defined early in the design process and the interface to that extension from the core is specialized and well understood.

An alternative is to use some sort of observer design pattern (see "Observer" on page 353). Here the core defines a generic callback interface for multiple extensions. For example, if the core maintains a data structure, it might provide a callback to inform arbitrary extensions whenever a portion of the structure changes. Alternatively, it might provide an interface to let extensions specify portions of the data structure they are interested in and then provide callbacks only when those portions change. This approach can support a wide range of different extensions using a single interface to the core. If it can be achieved, it can make developing both the core and the extensions easier and can yield a more robust and flexible system.

This alternative does, however, have its drawbacks. It is often difficult at best to identify the "right" generic callbacks in a given situation. A general mechanism like this can also be inefficient in having to do too much checking or making too many unnecessary callbacks, and can also lead to extensions that are over-complex or have unnatural designs. Still, where a generic callback facility can be identified, it is generally better to implement it in the core than to provide a set of more targeted interfaces.

INTERFACE DEFINITION

Once an object structure has been determined for the system, the next tasks are to separate the system into components and to define the interfaces between these components as precisely as possible. The number of components should be kept relatively small and the interfaces between them should be kept as simple as possible.

If a core-plus-extensions approach is used, the first relevant classes are the public classes of the core, including any abstract or callback classes representing functionality to be invoked in extensions from the core. In a more traditional approach, the relevant classes are those included in the top-level design. Note that the design of Figure 16-6 can be simplified into the traditional high-level design seen in Figure 16-7. Here we have changed the names for consistency with what follows: the standard prefix `Space` indicates the program; the class previously named **Space** is now **SpaceArena**, since "Space-Space" didn't sound good, and some of the other classes have shortened names as well.

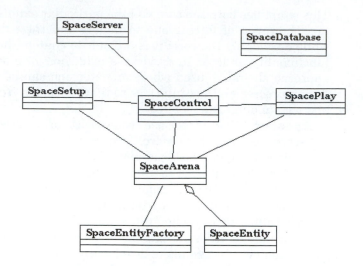

Figure 16-7 Top-level design of spacewar server.

Finding Initial Methods

In our previous designs we arrived at the set of methods by starting with a known method and adding methods as needed. This involved writing pseudocode for each method in turn to determine what information or functionality it needed from its or some other class. This approach is not feasible in a large-scale system, since it is important to determine the interface methods for the top-level design without having to fully specify how the components of this design actually work.

What is used here is an iterative approach. We first derive an initial set of interfaces by using high-level algorithms for the various components and intuition about what might be needed. Then, with this set of interfaces, the different components are designed in more detail. As these designs proceed, the interface is forced to change. Some components require additional information or functionality from the interface. Other components find it difficult to provide the desired functionality and propose instead to provide something close but not exact. Some of the interface functionality will be found to be superfluous. Negotiations among those responsible for the various components, moderated by those overseeing the whole project, then evolve the candidate interface into a stable and workable solution.

The first step in this process is to provide a good set of candidate interfaces. Here one looks at each class in turn and provides a detailed description of the class with respect to the overall design. From this description one can list the methods the class should provide as part of its interface. For example, the **SpaceControl** class could be described as:

The SpaceControl class is responsible for the overall control of the game. It takes control when the server starts and waits until a user is ready to play. It manages the set of currently active users, adding or removing from this set as needed. It also manages when to play a round. It uses the SpaceSetup class to set up a new round and then uses the SpacePlay class to play the round. When a round is over, it sets up for a new round. It also handles requests from the clients to display the high scores.

This description implies aspects of the **SpacePlay, SpaceSetup**, and **SpaceDatabase** classes that are discussed below. It also indicates that we must be more specific about the interface between the client and the server, probably indicating the possible messages in terms of methods of the **SpaceServer** object. Finally, since it indicates that this class is invoked when the server starts, we should add a method to it:

```
void play();
```

that is called by the main program and sets everything up.

The communication between the client and the server is embodied in the **SpaceServer** class. The calls from the client to the server, obtained from a detailed understanding of the client and the workings of the overall system, include:

```
void newClient(SpaceClient id,ConstText username);
void removeClient(SpaceClient id);
void readyToPlay(SpaceClient id);
```

These should correspond to methods in the **SpaceControl** class that are invoked by the **SpaceServer** object. Note that clients are identified by an item of type **SpaceClient** that might be an integer or a structure (we can defer this decision until the actual implementation). The server should also provide communication back to the client. Here the messages include:

```
void highScores(...);
void objectPositions(...);
```

where the first returns the set of high scores for possible display by the client and the second returns the current game state as a set of objects and their positions. These we place as methods of **SpaceServer**.

We can continue with the **SpacePlay** class, whose description might be:

The SpacePlay class is responsible for conducting a round of Spacewar. It assumes that the game has already been set up and that the SpaceArena class holds the proper entities at the proper locations. It cycles continually, possibly with some time delay (to cause the cycles to be at a constant time interval). In each cycle it uses the SpaceArena class methods to update the position of each object. It then must check for collisions among the objects, again using methods in the SpaceArena class. The SpacePlay class should check after each cycle whether the game is over (i.e. whether there is at most one ship left and no missiles). If an end of game is detected, it should set a timer for some number of seconds. When this time period elapses, it should determine if any ships are left in the system and, if so, should indicate that the corresponding player has won the round.

From this description we can define the one method needed in the abstract **SpacePlay** class:

```
virtual SpaceUser playRound(SpaceArena,SpaceServer);
```

This method returns the user who won the round (or NULL if there is no winner). Rather than assuming that the object knows of the arena object, we pass in the current **SpaceArena** object as a parameter. Similarly, we pass in the server object for it to call the objectPositions method as needed.

In addition, this description suggests the following methods for **SpaceArena**:

```
virtual void moveEntities();
virtual void handleCollisions();
virtual void reportPositions(SpaceServer);
virtual Boolean checkEndOfGame(SpaceUser&);
```

The last one here checks if there is at most one spaceship and no bullets currently active. If so, it returns TRUE; otherwise it returns FALSE. The parameter here is used to return the owner of the remaining ship.

A description of the **SpaceSetup** class might be:

The SpaceSetup class is responsible for setting up the game board for a new game. It does this by first clearing the SpaceArena and then using the factory method this class provides to create the necessary entities, including ships of varying kinds (one for each user) and possibly robot ships and stars. It can get the game information from a file or from a static game or can generate it randomly.

This implies an abstract interface with the method:

```
void setupRound(SpaceArena,Integer numuser,SpaceUser * users);
```

where the arena to set up is passed in as well as the number and names of the users. The description also requires at least two new methods for **SpaceArena**:

```
void clear();
SpaceEntity createEntity(ConstText);
```

The latter method is actually the sole responsibility of the **SpaceEntityFactory** class and should also be a method in that class.

A brief description of the **SpaceDatabase** class might include:

The SpaceDatabase class is responsible for maintaining the scores of all users of the system. When a round is over, the class should be told of all the participants and the winner. The class should also provide information about the people with the top scores so far.

This could be implemented by an interface offering the three methods:

```
SpaceUser findUser(ConstText name);
void recordRound(SpaceUser winner,Integer num,SpaceUser *);
Integer topScores(Integer max,SpaceUser *);
```

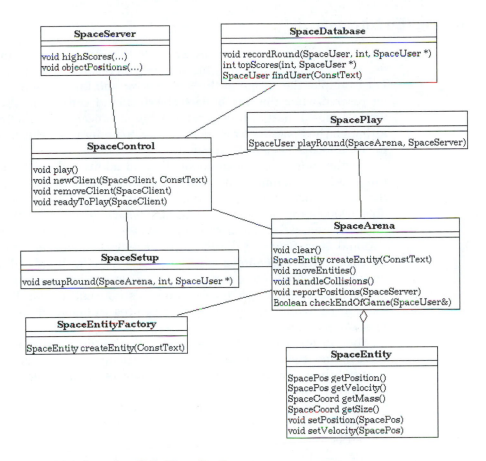

Figure 16-8 Interface definitions for the spacewar program.

where the scoring information is retained and thus returned within the **Space-User** class.

Finally, we consider the **SpaceArena** class. We know it must maintain the set of entities. It also must move the entities and check for collisions. This means it must be able to get the position, velocity, size, and mass of each of the entities; remove and add new entities (explosions); and change the position and velocity of the entities. We thus add the corresponding methods to the **SpaceEntity** class.

The result of all this can be seen in the initial interfaces in the static structure diagram in Figure 16-8. This interface is by no means complete: we still need to determine what the classes **SpaceUser** and **SpaceClient** contain and how they are accessed. We need to determine how the **SpaceControl** object gets handles to the other objects. We need to determine the contents of the high-Scores and objectPositions messages sent to the clients. Most importantly, we must evaluate the design to ensure it is both high-quality and workable.

Evolving the Interface

The next step in the design process is to take each class in turn and begin to design its implementation. This will help us resolve some of the design issues. For example, the design of the **SpaceServer** and **SpaceControl** classes will help us resolve what the **SpaceClient** object should consist of; the design of the **SpaceDatabase** class will help refine what is expected from a **SpaceUser** object, although the **SpaceServer** class may need to understand this as well to communicate information back to a client.

Furthermore, we will undoubtedly find additional methods needed in the interface. For example, the above description assumes that we can tell who the user is for a given spaceship, but that information is not currently available. Depending on how the **SpaceEntityFactory** and **SpaceEntity** classes are implemented, we may want to augment the `createEntity` method to take an optional **SpaceUser** and then augment the **SpaceEntity** class to return the current user. The **SpaceArena** class may also want to handle different types of entities separately. For example, it may want to compute gravity only between **Sun** objects and movable objects, and this information can be encoded in the mass or be available separately. The choices will depend on the design of the **SpaceArena** class.

The various classes are designed with the given interface in mind. They each define their own subclasses and their methods and data. Whatever changes they require in the interface must be resolved by the overall project team. While some changes, such as adding a data field to the entity to hold the corresponding user, are simple, others can be quite complex. Suppose, for example, that the designer of the **SpaceArena** class decides that each entity should be responsible for computing its own next position. Not only does this require additional methods in the interface, it also shifts a possibly significant part of the application burden to the **SpaceEntity** class, which might not be appreciated by the designers in charge of that class. Resolution of these conflicts requires both introspection by the designers and some arbitrators who have a good overall view of the project.

Finally, during the creation of the initial set of interfaces one must continually evaluate the design and be prepared to make it better. At this point, the goals of the design process are to ensure that one can achieve a working system, to minimize the inherent risks, and to make the remainder of design and implementation as simple as possible. To a large extent, this implies developing simple interface descriptions, and a reasonable question here is whether the proposed interfaces can be simplified in a meaningful way.

Because the interfaces drive the rest of the design and thus control the implementation, testing, and maintenance of the whole system, one must put great emphasis on this part of the development process. In essence:

> **A project lives or dies on its interfaces.**

OTHER DESIGN ISSUES

A number of other issues can become important in the design of a large, long-lived system. These issues are best understood and taken care of during system design even if their effects are not apparent until later in the development cycle.

Portability

The first such issue is portability. Portability can have multiple dimensions. Multiple platforms exist today, including Windows, UNIX, and the Macintosh. It might be desirable to have one's system work on all or some of these platforms. The effort involved in moving a system among these platforms can range from a small amount of work done only once for a variety of systems, to a huge amount of work for each system. The effort required is generally determined by whether or not the system was designed to be portable in the first place.

Portability is also an issue within a given platform. Programs written for Windows 3.1 can have difficulty running under Windows 98 or Windows NT. Programs written for SunOS 4.X on the Suns are generally not compatible with Solaris 2.X, even though both run on the same hardware and are considered UNIX. Operating systems and environments tend to change over time. While most strive to provide backward compatibility, this doesn't always happen and old programs often cannot take full advantage of any new features the system might provide.

Portability can also be an issue even with the same operating system on the same architecture, as the hardware options change. The most notable such change involves display architectures, although features such as the availability of a CD-ROM can also make a difference. A program designed solely for a black-and-white monitor is not going to look good on a color system. A program designed to make extensive use of 3D graphics is going to perform poorly on a system lacking the necessary support hardware. A program that can't take advantage of a large window will be frowned upon by users who have spent more to buy a large display.

In each of these cases, the difficulty of modifying the system to accommodate the new software or hardware is strongly dependent on how the system was originally designed. Better designs try to anticipate and then encapsulate potential portability issues. They try to arrange the system so that the changes needed to achieve portability are restricted to a small set of classes that can easily be replaced without affecting the rest of the system. This allows the programmer porting the software simply to rewrite or modify those classes while ignoring the bulk of the system.

For this type of simplification, one must try to anticipate how the system might be ported during its lifetime. Then, any functionality the designer thinks might change in the future should be encapsulated within a class so as to provide an abstract interface to that functionality.

Consider what one must do to let a program handle multiple operating systems, say UNIX and Windows. The key here is to define a set of classes representing an abstraction of the operating-system functionality needed by the program and to use these classes exclusively throughout. Then these classes can be implemented separately for each operating system. To some extent, C++ has already done this for you, since its standard I/O library provides operating-system-independent input and output calls (although even here file-name conventions may have to change from one system to the next). The **SimpleSocket** and **SimpleThread** classes we defined in Chapter 14 are other examples, encapsulating sockets and threads respectively. Other classes can be designed to handle other operating-system issues such as dates and times, shared memory, file names and permissions, and process execution.

A similar approach can be taken to support multiple display environments, whether these are display technologies on the same operating system or different approaches to windows in different operating systems. Here the system should be designed with an abstract interface to the display that has its own notion of windows, menus, dialogs and drawing commands. The remainder of the system is coded to this interface and then the interface itself is implemented separately for each different display environment. Some commercial systems provide this type of functionality in general terms. For many applications in which the display demands are not excessive, this design can even simplify the overall application. For example, a specialized interface can provide a method to draw a box of a certain style or to draw a menu given a simple tabular specification. For both of these, the interface might have to issue dozens of drawing commands to achieve the result, while, with the interface, the application itself has to issue only one method call.

Extensibility

This approach to portability can also be applied to other aspects of the design. Another issue arising in design is extensibility, the need eventually to add new features to a system. In general, any system that is used extensively will find new applications and users who want additional functionality. Moreover, in today's world of shrink-wrapped software, such new functionality must be added merely to remain competitive.

The best way to handle extensions is to try to anticipate in the initial design what or at least where changes might be needed in the future. When planning a system, one should plan it with all the possible bells and whistles imaginable. One can even do a top-level design incorporating all these extensions. The initial implementation, however, should then be simplified to include only what is necessary for the first version of the system. Designing a system larger than one needs to build makes any planned extensions much easier to add. If the extension is represented as a class with little or no initial functionality, adding it to the overall system can entail merely adding to or replacing the designated class.

Design can also help with unplanned extensions. Designing a larger system forces the designer to use more abstraction and to make the system more generic, and this makes it more amenable to extension. A good core-plus-extensions design, one where the core is correctly identified and makes it easy to plug in additional functionality, can also make adding unplanned extensions easier. In general, however, extensions anticipated during the design phase are much easier to add than ones that were not, and we recommend:

> **Design a system with all possible extensions in mind.**

This approach is taken to its logical conclusion by systems with a generic external interface to accept a wide range of plug-in extensions. Adobe *Photoshop*, for example, achieves much of its power and popularity by providing a standard interface to support arbitrary plug-ins. It is often difficult to identify such an all-purpose interface and even harder to define it to accommodate all possible extensions. However, if this approach can be used, it generally produces a much more powerful and flexible design that is easy to evolve.

Existing Frameworks

A third issue that can be handled by encapsulation in the design phase and can profoundly influence system design is the use of existing frameworks. Existing frameworks can arise in a variety of ways that must be anticipated throughout the design process.

Consider the design of a user interface. In developing a program for Windows, one wants its user interface to conform to the conventions and standards used by other Windows applications. Similarly, in developing for the Macintosh, one wants the application to look and act like a standard Macintosh application. This use of existing conventions affects the design and implementation of the user interface. It constrains the designer's options in setting up window formats and menus and might also make the designer add new options and buttons. Windows, for example, assumes a view and document model in which all applications can save and load their views from a file, in which files are typed, and in which the File menu offers the set of recently used files as options. The designer must take all this into account in developing both the user interface and the overall structure of the application.

Library packages are another example of the use of existing frameworks. The current C++ standard includes the template library we have described as well as many functions from the standard C library. These libraries, however, cover only some of the necessary functionality. A large application might want to use a library for 3D graphics, libraries for statistical computations, libraries for graph drawing, etc. The choice of such libraries can significantly affect the design of the system.

Consider, for example, an application that needs 3D graphics. Various libraries are available to accomplish this, each with its own strengths and weaknesses. OpenGL is a C-based library now available on a broad range of different platforms. OpenInventor, a C++ library built on top of OpenGL, offers much additional functionality and is generally easier to use; however, it is a bit slower, more geared to modeling than interactive applications, and is not freely available on all platforms. DirectX is a high-performance library directed toward game applications available only on the Windows platform. XGL is Sun's low-level library. The choice among these alternatives will affect the design and implementation of the application. For example, if OpenInventor is used, the application might be developed in part by subclassing from the OpenInventor classes. If the application will use OpenGL and have any type of animation, it must implement its own main drawing loop to refresh the screen.

If the application is not too complex, it might be possible to write a wrapper class embodying the 3D functionality the application uses, code the rest of the application so that it uses only this class, and then implement this class using any of the target packages. A more sophisticated use of 3D graphics, however, would probably make this difficult or impossible, since the definition and drawing would pervade the system. Here one must evaluate the different libraries early on, choose one, and then take the conventions and functionality of this library into account throughout the design.

Libraries are one type of functionality available to an application. Other functionality is available through separate systems and interfaces. For example, a database server is generally available on most platforms. This is a separate application to manage relational (or other) databases. Generally, the server provides an interface through which the application can send SQL-based commands to access or modify the database. (SQL is a standard high-level database query language.) If such a server is available, one can simplify the design and implementation of the overall system by using it rather than implementing one's own database system.

Just as with libraries, however, care must be taken in using an external system. Different systems have different interfaces, different functionalities, and different availabilities. Designers can commit to a single system and design for its features. Alternatively, they can attempt to find a common subset of features and restrict the design to using these, so that it would be possible to move from one external system to another. A third choice would be to use encapsulation to hide the external system with an interface class.

Finally, a new system is generally designed not in isolation, but to cooperate with existing tools and systems. This can be as simple as sharing files or as complex as actively communicating with existing systems. In the past few years a number of somewhat standard frameworks have evolved to support such communications, including DCOM and ActiveX under Windows and

CORBA and the Common Desktop Environment under UNIX. If a system must send commands to other systems or handle requests from other systems dynamically using one of these frameworks, then it must be designed to make this possible. This interoperation requirement will have an impact throughout the design process and must be taken into account early in design.

MANAGING A SOFTWARE PROJECT

As noted in the previous chapter, a significant part of software engineering concerns techniques and skills for managing a software project. While most of this work has been geared to large projects with tens or hundreds of software developers attempting to work together, some of it is applicable to smaller projects with ten or fewer programmers. In this section we briefly cover some of the issues arising in these smaller projects, with an emphasis on management techniques for student projects.

Personnel Management

The primary reason that programmers working as a team are not as productive as programmers working alone is the need for communication. Programmers all want to have input on the design, and they all need to convey their interfaces to those who need them. As the system is coded and the interfaces change, the programmers must understand and negotiate on the changes. As bugs are found, they need to be attributed to one or another programmer's components so that they can be found and fixed. Misunderstandings among programmers regarding functionality or interfaces must be resolved, and ideas for extensions or changes must be discussed.

The time spent on communication increases with the number of programmers involved. Moreover, once there are more than around four developers, design and organization are effectively being managed by committee, since most groups attempt to reach a consensus and spend a lot of time doing so. As the team size reaches ten or so, however, design by committee no longer yields a useful result, and the time spent in meetings and waiting for other programmers significantly reduces everyone's productivity. This is reflected in the number of potential communication paths among programmers. In a four-person project, there are only six combinations; in a ten-person project, there are forty-five paths, as illustrated at the top of Figure 16-9.

A common solution here is to create a personnel hierarchy. An organized *chief programmer team* or *programmer team* generally consists of a project manager or chief programmer, a project librarian, and a core of programmers. The communications paths here are only between the project manager and librarian and the rest of the programmers, as shown at the bottom of

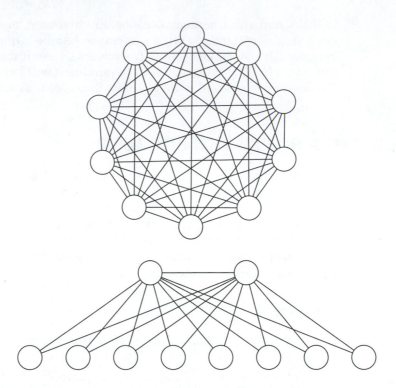

Figure 16-9 Communication paths in a ten-person project.

Figure 16-9. The programmers do not, in theory at least, need to communicate among themselves.

The programmer team is run as a benevolent dictatorship by the project manager. This provides a single focal point for design decisions and arbitrating among the different programmers when changes are required. It also lets one person define the overall program schedule, assign different programmers to work on the parts for which they are best suited, and ensure a better project.

The most experienced or most advanced programmer in the team is usually chosen as project manager. She is the one who must have a good overall understanding of the whole system. She must be able to assess the complexity of the different components so as to assign the proper personnel to that section and determine how long each section should take to get working. She is the one who assumes overall responsibility for the whole project. Whether the project manager does any actual coding depends on the size and complexity of the project. In a student project, the manager typically gets involved with some of the more important aspects of the system but has less code responsibility than the other programmers.

The project librarian acts as the repository of all the information about the system under development. He is in charge of maintaining system documentation and of ensuring that changes made to the design by one person are communicated to all the others. Any changes needed in an interface must be cleared by the project librarian: he ensures that the change is adequately documented, that appropriate changes are made to the design and specifications documents, and that the change is communicated to the remaining programmers. The librarian should be able to answer any questions on any aspect of the system by using the accumulated and maintained documentation. The librarian may or may not also do programming, again depending on the size and complexity of the project. If he has programming and design tasks, they are typically smaller to allow him time for his other duties.

The remainder of the programmer team, the programmers, are each given responsibility for one or more compartmented pieces of the system. They should design and code their portions so that they conform to the agreed-upon interface specifications. They should test their portions as much as possible before attempting to integrate them into the system. They should also be available to make prompt fixes to problems in their code as others start using it in the integrated system.

Good team programmers know how to fit into a group. They understand the costs involved in changing interfaces and the need for conformity to group standards and procedures. They provide input on proposed interfaces as needed, understand their component of the system, and attempt to make their interfaces both fair and functional. Most importantly, they code accurately and defensively and get their parts of the system done on time.

Design Management

The design of a larger software system is generally broken into two parts. The top-level design, where an overview and component breakdown of the system is achieved, is typically done by a few designers (possibly only one) who have a good overall understanding of the problem at hand and can evaluate potential solutions. The detailed design of each of the components is typically done by the programmer who is to implement that component. Along the way, both designs must be checked and be given room to evolve.

The best way to check a design is to present it to a team of critical reviewers whose job is to find the potential problems. This is called a *design review*. A typical design review starts when the designer hands out a complete design document to the reviewers in advance, so they can get a good overall sense of the design. At the actual review, the designer presents the design, emphasizing why critical design decisions were made, and then illustrates the design by showing how it will work under various circumstances that represent both normal operation and unusual conditions.

A successful design review identifies actual or potential problems with the design at an early stage, when they can be corrected easily and cheaply. The job of the panel of reviewers is thus to question the design, attempting to find such problems. They should identify possible alternatives and ask the presenter to justify the design presented in their light. They should attempt to bring up scenarios for which the design may fail. When the presenter gives a scenario, the reviewers should be thinking of "what if" questions to identify circumstances under which the design may fail. Finally, the reviewers should be attempting to determine if the design proposed is as simple as it can be.

The design review process is also a constructive one. As design problems are diagnosed, it is the task of both the presenter and the reviewers to identify potential solutions to these problems. Where the design is overly complex, simpler alternatives should be proposed and evaluated.

Design reviews are one critical component in managing the design aspects of a larger system. The other component is managing the interface specifications among the different programmers. This is typically the job of the project manager, often in conjunction with the project librarian, but can also be discussed in group meetings. As designs of the individual components are completed and reviewed, the interfaces these components provide or the interfaces they use often must be changed. When this happens, everyone involved with those interfaces must be notified of the change.

Managing the evolving interfaces is difficult because of the care necessary to maintain the overall integrity of the design. While one minor change probably will not hurt the design, a large number of such changes actually might. Changes tend to make the design more complex and to create additional dependencies among the components, and they also tend to create components that are no longer balanced. This can make future modifications and evolution of the system more difficult. It is the task of all the designers, and the project manager in particular, to evaluate the proposed interface changes in the light of the overall design and to propose alternatives where appropriate.

Code Management

Once the design has been completed, coding can begin. Managing the coding of a large project is probably more complex than managing the design. Code management requires developing an implementation plan, evaluating or reviewing code, ensuring that code meets project standards, and providing appropriate strategies for integration and system testing.

The first task here is to develop an implementation plan. This plan should designate who is in charge of each component and the deadline for its completion. The resultant schedule should take into account dependencies among the components so that a component can be tested and used when it is completed. For example, in a core-plus-extensions design, it is a good idea to complete the core before the extensions. This may involve putting the faster programmers on the core or splitting the core into subcomponents so that it can be developed by multiple programmers before they go off and work on the extension components for which they are responsible.

The best way of achieving a reasonable implementation plan is to identify *milestones*, dates by which a particular piece of functionality of the overall system must be achieved. For example, one might state: "By the last Thursday of this month, components A, B, and C will be tested individually and ready for integration into a base system." Such milestones, especially ones involving the whole or a substantial part of the team, provide incentives (in the form of achievements and peer pressure) for the different team members to get things done on time. They let the different programmers work at their own pace, taking their other commitments into account as necessary, and knowing when a task needs to be accomplished. They also provide the project manager with a whip of sorts to keep the team members in line and to identify how far behind the project might be. Because of this we recommend:

> **Use milestones to guide a project's implementation.**

The overall implementation plan should also take into account the unforeseen. Software development typically takes longer than one anticipates. This is especially true in a multiple-person project in which the actions of the different team members are somewhat independent. People will get sick, have outside commitments, or just sleep through meetings. Some parts of the system turn out to be more difficult than anticipated and some turn out to be easier (but try to get the programmers in charge of the latter to admit it). The operating system will crash or the hardware will be unavailable on a critical date. A reasonable schedule will try to take some of these factors into account by introducing some slack into the schedule and revising it as needed.

The second task in code management for a larger software system is to ensure consistency among the different designs and implementations. To some extent this involves developing and enforcing a common set of guidelines that are contained in comprehensive coding standards to be followed by all members of the team. The coding standards should cover code presentation including formatting and inline documentation conventions, naming conventions, as well as guidelines on parameter order, use of inheritance, callback methods, use of libraries, etc. A simple such set is shown in the course standards shown in Appendix A. The more the code developed by the different programmers can be made to look and feel the same, the easier it will be for them to read and understand others' code to facilitate debugging and testing, and the fewer problems there will be in integrating the different aspects.

One way to check this and to test code without a fully integrated system is to undertake selective *code reviews*. A code review is the implementation analog of a design review. Here the project manager selects one or more portions of the code that are complex enough or interrelated enough that problems are likely in the code or in how people use it. The programmers responsible for these portions then produce a set of handouts, generally the code listing along with the design information describing what the code should be doing, and distribute them to a panel of reviewers before the code review. In the actual code review, the programmer goes over the code in front of the reviewers, justifying why it is written as it is and demonstrating that it works. The reviewers' job, again as in a design review, is to find faults in the code so that they can be corrected early in the development process.

Code reviews can take two forms. The programmer can either simply go through the code line by line to ensure that all the reviewers understand the purpose of each line, or can take one or more scenarios and run the code on paper through those scenarios. In either case, it is the reviewers' job to identify other scenarios under which the code might fail and to indicate any potential problems with the code and ways in which it might be simplified. The review should also check that the programmer followed the coding standards adopted in the project and that other components needing to use or be used by the code integrate correctly.

Configuration Management

Another aspect of code management is managing the files of the project. This is the task of *configuration management*. There are two aspects to this task. *Version management* involves organizing, controlling, and sharing the source files among the programmers. *System modeling* entails directing how the source files are used to build the resultant system.

The first step in configuration management is to organize the project. This is generally done by identifying the various components of the overall project and putting them in a hierarchical structure. This is often represented first as a directory structure, with the top-level directory representing the project and its subdirectories representing the various components. Each subdirectory can be further subdivided either to separate source and binary files or to identify different subprojects. Note that for projects of the size we are addressing, one level of hierarchy is generally sufficient. The different directories provide a context for the corresponding component, supporting both version management and system modeling for that component.

Version management is supported by a variety of tools. The older tools, such as *sccs* and *rcs* on UNIX, assume that the single copy of the source is to be shared among the different programmers. Here a programmer *checks out* a source file, i.e. requests the right to be the current owner of that file so as to make changes to it. While this programmer has it checked out, no other user can modify it. When he or she is finished with the modifications, the file is *checked in* and other programmers can again access it. This works in small projects in which each component is almost the exclusive domain of a single programmer.

Newer version-management systems take a different approach in which each programmer has a full copy of the system to work on. Programmers can make changes to whatever files they want. When they go to commit or check in their changes, the system attempts to resolve any conflicts or asks the programmer to do so. This approach allows more cooperation among programmers, but also requires more coordination to avoid conflicts where two programmers make incompatible changes to the same piece of code.

Either form of version management accomplishes the primary purpose: letting multiple programmers work on a common set of files without stepping on each other's toes too often. Version management offers the developer other benefits as well. Version systems keep track of all past versions of the software, letting programmers easily go back to a working version if a set of changes they are trying does not work out. The systems support experimental development by letting multiple versions be developed in parallel. Finally, the systems support maintenance by letting the developer maintain a copy of the software as it was provided to the users so that user problems can be debugged.

Many tools support system modeling as well. In the UNIX environment, the common tool is a form of the *make* utility originally developed at Bell Laboratories. Here the system model is given as a text file listing the dependencies between the generated and source files and providing the necessary rules and commands for creating the generated files. *Make* lets the programmer define a variety of different targets in a single directory. It both supports the construction of arbitrary types of targets and lets the programmer define new commands such as "`make clean`" to remove all object files or "`make print`" to get an ordered listing of all the source files.

Modern environments try to integrate *make*-like facilities into the environment. Microsoft *Visual C++*, for example, uses the notion of a project that is targeted at building a single binary or library. The user merely tells the system (via a series of dialog boxes) what source files and libraries compose the project, and the environment then defines the appropriate system model for building the project.

System-modeling tools are very convenient because they provide a simple way of defining all the options and conventions that go into constructing a complex piece of software. They let the programmer easily change the compiler flags or libraries for a system. They also have the intelligence to recompile only those portions of the system that have been modified, allowing quicker turnaround on small changes.

Testing Management

The most complex and time-consuming part of a multiple person project is integrating the components written by separate programmers into a single working system. No matter how much work has been put into development, the individual pieces of the system will not fit together perfectly and bug-free. Finding and fixing the problems can become a frustrating and costly team effort: the cause of the problems is often difficult to pin down to one particular component, and (for a large project at least) the person whose code actually contains a particular bug is unlikely to be present to fix it when it arises.

The best way to deal with these problems is to avoid them as much as possible. This is where solid, well-understood interfaces, design reviews, code reviews, module testing, and all the other topics cited throughout this text come in. One of the more important aspects of group software, however, is defensive programming. The individual's goal during integration testing should be to prove that his or her code is not at fault when a problem arises. Programmers want to demonstrate that a problem, even if exhibited in their code, was actually caused by someone else. The easiest way to do this is to put lots of defensive code in those portions of the program dealing with the interfaces to other components. This was covered in depth in "Defensive Programming" on page 191, and has been emphasized throughout the text.

Defensive code should generally remain in the system even after it is completed. Such code will be very useful in tracking down errors that occur while the system is being used and in identifying problems as the system evolves. Using assertions is okay if the error is fatal and would cause a crash anyway, but the error message generated by an assertion is generally meaningless to the user. Print statements are usually worse: their output tends either to be a annoyance to the user or to be ignored. However, for an error condition that can easily be recovered from, they might be the preferred alternative. In general, however, exceptions give the best protection. They can return the system to a known state and possibly recover from whatever error caused the problem. At worst, they can trigger an automatic save and a clean abort so the user doesn't lose any work. Exceptions can also be easily changed to have different behaviors while the system is being tested (where they abort the system) than when the system is being used in production (where they provide error recovery and possibly send information about the error back to the developers).

Another helpful technique here is for programmers to maintain three versions of their components. The first version is the *working* version. This is the code the programmer is currently editing; it can change frequently and no other programmer is immediately dependent on it. The second version is the *experimental* version. When the programmer feels the working version is stable, i.e. is a clean build that incorporates the latest set of changes and has passed module testing, it can be upgraded to experimental. The experimental version is meant to be used by other programmers who need the component and contains code that should be better than before but has not been fully tested. As other components try to use it, it will become better tested and more stable.

When all the interested components have verified that an experimental version works for them, the version is upgraded to a *stable* version. The stable version is a non-changing implementation of the component. Other components are free to use it with the knowledge that the functionality there is stable and working, and that any bugs or features there will remain. This isolates them from the local changes to the module and from experimental changes that have not been completely tested.

This approach should be augmented with communications whereby all programmers are notified when new versions of components become available. It can also be synchronized by using milestones. For instance, a particular milestone might ensure that all components in experimental form have been bound together and passed some set of tests. When this occurs, all the experimental versions are converted into stable versions at one time and further development proceeds with the construction of new experimental versions.

Another approach to aid in system testing is to attempt to develop mini-versions of the system as milestones. Here one creates a very simple version of the system with only limited functionality early in the development cycle — a shell containing only the user interfaces, for example. This version of the system is then slowly augmented with additional functionality one step at a time. At each step, if the old system worked and the new one fails, the cause of the failure lies in the newly added code, either directly or indirectly (through using some feature of the previous code that hadn't been used before). Note that this approach not only aids testing but also gives the developers a sense of accomplishment in actually having a running system throughout most of the development process. This tends to increase programmer motivation and get the overall system completed more quickly.

While individual programmers are responsible for testing their own components, responsibility for system testing must lie with the whole team. To organize this, however, one of the team members, generally the project librarian, should be in charge of collecting and documenting system test cases. A set of standard test cases should check both the normal operations and error checking of the system, and these should be applied whenever a new version of the system is built. This is *regression testing,* as discussed in Chapter 8. When possible, it is often helpful to designate one person in the group as the "tester" whose job is to find successful test cases, i.e. those causing the system to fail. As noted, it is much easier to test other people's code or at least code in whose correctness one doesn't have a stake.

Documentation

Keeping a large project on time and organized depends, to a large extent, on documentation. Moreover, if the project is going to continue to be used and evolve, documentation will play a key role. Writing a software system involves not just writing the code but also writing all the documentation that goes along with the code. We thus note:

> **Without documentation, a system is incomplete and useless.**

System documentation serves a variety of purposes. During development, its most important use is as a reference for the programmers. Programmers should be able to look up details of an interface they need to use, browse through the available system libraries to find the method or classes required, understand what exactly is expected from their component, see why a certain feature is designed or implemented as it is from a specifications point of view, understand what the user wants out of the system, and know the current state of development and the current schedule. Once development is complete, documentation is even more important. Maintenance programmers need to know all the above information. In addition, since the maintainers are often a completely different set of programmers, they need information on the motivations and reasoning that went into the actual system design by the original developers.

In order to achieve these goals, the documentation must be accurate, complete, and up to date. If these criteria are not met, the documentation will be useless. If the documentation is not accurate, the programmers and developers learn it cannot be relied upon and resort to reading the appropriate code and header files instead. If the documentation is not complete, programmers either become frustrated with the missing information or simply do not use the undocumented features. If the documentation is not up to date, it will be considered inaccurate and again won't be used. Worse, it might be relied upon and cause misunderstandings and errors to be inserted into the system.

It is important therefore to maintain an up-to-date and complete repository of information about the system. This can be organized in a variety of ways, either electronically or in notebooks, and should contain at least the following information:

- *Requirements documents* stating what the users originally wanted. As additional input is obtained from the prospective users, these documents should be updated accordingly.

- *Specifications documents* describing the user interfaces and commands and what the system will do. As the requirements change or as the design imposes additional constraints or provides additional functionality, these should be updated.

- *User-interface documentation* defining the interfaces, how they look, and what they do. This can be derived originally from the specifications, but should be replaced with the design diagrams showing the user interface. This documentation should be updated as the user interface evolves, and should eventually be replaced by one or more user manuals for it.

- *Design documentation* describing the top-level design and providing a breakdown into components. This should include the top-level static structure diagram and its explanations as well as a detailed description of the purpose and function of each component. It should be kept current, with both the diagram and the descriptions changing as the system evolves.

- *Interface specifications* that precisely define the top-level interfaces provided by the components. These should provide both the syntax (the calling sequence with parameters and return types) and the semantics of both normal and error operation of all the public methods the various top-level components provide. Such documentation should be easy to access and search and must be kept up to date as the interfaces evolve.

- *Design documentation* for each component, showing the detailed design of that component. This includes static structure diagrams, descriptions, message-trace diagrams, and any other information generated by the individual programmers as they develop the various components. The individual programmers should maintain this documentation and keep it up to date.

- *Code documentation* contained in the source files detailing what the code actually does. Comments should be used wherever a reader might not immediately understand the function or workings of a particular piece of code. Assertions and suitably noted defensive checks should also be thought of as code documentation and should be broadly used. These are particularly valuable since they become part of the code and cannot get out of date.

- *Test-case documentation* describing the various system tests a new version of the system must pass before it can be accepted. This should include a description of each test case, how to run it, and what the expected output is. If the program can be tested mechanically (this is difficult for a program with a graphics interface), the test cases should be automated with an appropriate shell script or testing program. Otherwise, the documentation should be sufficient for someone to sit down with the system, run it according to directions, and check off the success or failure of each test case.

- *Current status and plans* describing the overall project. These should include all the project milestones, the expected start and end date for each top-level component, and a schedule showing when and how the various components will be integrated to form a working system. Ideally this should show a series of system versions, starting with a user-interface shell and ending with the completed system.

Another sort of information that can be helpful to both the individual programmers and the project manager is the time spent on the project by each programmer. This can be kept as time logs in which programmers log how much time they spend on what task each time they work on the system. These time logs help programmers see how to better use their time and let the manager more evenly distribute the workload of the overall development effort.

The overall responsibility for maintaining project documentation lies with the project librarian in conjunction with the rest of the project team. The librarian provides the means for organizing and accessing the documentation, but the actual documentation must be written and maintained by those most closely involved with the particular designs, interfaces, and code. Before accepting code to integrate into the rest of the system or letting a programmer install a new stable or experimental library, the librarian (with the assistance of the project manager) should insist on revised documentation to match the changes. Before code is written, the librarian should receive detailed design documentation from the programmer. Before an interface can be changed, the documentation for that change must be submitted and circulated to the affected programmers.

Finally, we emphasize once more that the code itself is a form of documentation. It is the source of last resort and the only thing guaranteed accurately to describe the actual workings of the system. Even when the documentation is complete and accurate, the code is still used to address fine details and must be understood on a line-by-line basis when making changes or debugging. As such, it is essential (as we have noted throughout this text) to:

> **Write your code to be read by others.**

CONCLUSION

The problems involved in designing large systems and the benefits of the various solutions can only be truly appreciated through experience. Similarly, the complexity and challenge of software design can only be understood by actually doing many designs for many different systems.

We have attempted to show how to go about building a software system. While we have concentrated on design, we have also covered both high-level issues of software engineering and a lot of low-level issues involving how the actual code gets written. However, even the best text is no substitute for experience. Many of the methods and strategies discussed here can be appreciated only after you have suffered through the consequences of not using them. Many of the statements about what works and what doesn't will not be compelling until you try different approaches and experience the results yourself.

Building a large software system is generally a valuable and rewarding experience. There is a thrill in demonstrating a system you or your team created that now performs some useful purpose and that other people might actually want to use. While the work can be great, the rewards are even greater. Thus:

> **Design and build a software system.**

SUMMARY

Software complexity tends to grow much faster than software size. Thus large software systems are much more difficult to design, implement, test, debug, and maintain than smaller systems.

The first step in building a large software system is to understand thoroughly what it is you want to build. This is where requirements and specifications, discussed primarily in the previous chapter, come into play. Once this is accomplished, design can proceed. In addition to the standard design techniques covered previously, we introduced four techniques aimed specifically at large-scale software development. These were:

- *Clustering*: Here the designer identifies a rich set of candidate classes and then forms clusters of these classes on the basis of the relationships among them. The clustering lets the designer remove classes from the candidate set and eventually settle on five to 10 top-level classes.

- *Design by subsystem*: Here the designer groups related classes together into subsystems, creating a single new class (a facade) as the interface to that subsystem.

- *Risk-based design*: Here the designer attacks a problem by identifying the difficulties that are potential risks to a successful system. Each of these problems is then either solved or isolated, leading to a less risky design that is more likely to work.

- *Core-plus-extensions design*: This design scheme organizes a large system so communication paths are minimized, it is easier for multiple programmers to interact, and the system is easier to change over time. A core set of classes is identified as the heart of the system. All other classes and subsystems are designed as extensions that communicate only with the core.

Other factors come into play in designing a large-scale system, including portability, extensibility, and interaction with existing systems and frameworks. These need to be understood as part of the specifications and taken into account throughout the design process.

These design techniques are generally applied to develop a top-level design for the proposed system. This design is then reflected in a set of interfaces defining how the various classes interact with one another. The key to a successful large-scale design is that its interfaces are well thought out, well developed, simple, and complete. A project lives or dies on its interfaces.

Finally, while a good design is necessary for a project, appropriate management techniques are required to convert the design successfully into an actual system. These include developing an appropriate personnel hierarchy; using design and code reviews to insure a workable and high-quality system; developing a project timetable with appropriate milestones; using appropriate tools for configuration management, coding, testing, and debugging; and, perhaps most important of all, documenting what is being done as it is done.

EXERCISES

16.1 Finish the top-level design for the spacewar program.

16.2 Suppose you have a four-person team to develop the spacewar program. Devise a timetable with milestones that assigns these people to components and specifies the order in which the components should be built. If you had six people, how would your plans change?

16.3 One of the best ways of learning about something is trying to develop a system to implement it. Suppose you are developing a program to facilitate defining, organizing, and accessing program documentation.
a) Draw up a list of requirements for such a system.
b) Draw up specifications for the requirements.
c) Draw up a top-level design meeting the specifications.

16.4 Design an XML browser that can read and display XML documents and follow links to other documents. Look into what libraries are available to build such a browser as part of the design process.

16.5 Implement the spacewar program designed in this chapter. What changes in the design were required during the implementation and testing of your system?

16.6 Fully design and implement the solar system example described in Chapter 1. Once the system is working, augment it with a graphical user interface. Be sure that the original system design can accommodate such an interface.

16.7 Design and implement the garden designer of Exercise 15.7.

16.8 Design and implement the race-car system of Exercise 15.8.

16.9 Design and implement the menu-planning system of Exercise 15.9.

Appendix A

Sample Coding Standards

This appendix contains the coding standards we use at Brown University in the introductory software engineering course on which this book is based. Note that this is only one set of standards and many others exist. The important thing isn't which set of conventions is better, but rather to have a standard and to use it consistently.

PURPOSE

CS 32 is a course about software engineering — a field in which the method used to develop the final product is as important as the product's functionality. This is why we require you to adhere to the coding standard presented here. The standards may at first seem irrelevant, but as your programs grow in length and complexity, and as you begin to work in teams, they will be valued companions. It is also important to remember that most software firms follow strict coding standards, and this is one of the many ways in which we simulate the real world as closely as possible.

Coding standards are an integral part of software engineering. Because of this, you are expected to conform to the CS 32 Coding Standards in your programming assignments. This will not only help your teaching assistants avoid migraines as they read (and grade!) your code, but will also give you good karma. If you ignore the coding standards, your code will be branded as "unacceptable" and you will be outcast from the CS 32 community at large (not to mention that your program won't pass). Adherence to the coding standards is of utmost importance, so read this document very carefully, and store it in a sacred place.

NAMING CONVENTIONS

One way to improve the readability of your code is to follow certain naming conventions that show what category an identifier is in. The examples that follow assume that your project is named "proj." The name of your project should appear whereever you see *proj*, **PROJ**, or **Proj** (in bold-italics). Please note that it is *not* necessary to use the full name of the project, if the name is long. For example, if your project's official title is "Ultra Duke-Nuke'em 4D," you can abbreviate this as UDN4, Ultra, or any other reasonable variant.

Files

As a software engineer, you should make your code as robust as possible and you should be able to reuse it without making many modifications. One way to do this is to break up your program into files. Thus each file will be specialized, and when you reuse your code in subsequent projects you can take only the pertinent code and leave the extra baggage behind. In addition to this, as a software engineer, you will be working in teams. As a result, you will often be using files written by someone else. In this situation it is especially important to follow certain conventions so that you can understand your partners' code quickly. In the following, *PKG* should be chosen to represent the class or group of classes defined in the file. **All file names should be lower-case**. This will help you in porting to systems that prohibit mixed-case file names, and will also help you distinguish your Makefile and README files from the rest of your code.

Organize your files into directories. This is not important in earlier assignments, but as the semester moves on (i.e. by the second project), the number of code files you use for a single assignment will be massive. Placing files in logically named directories and making them into libraries will help you survive.

File-naming conventions are as follows:

- PROJECT CODE FILE FOR CLASS (SET) PKG: *projpkg*.**cxx**

  Generally, you should have methods for only one of your classes in a class code file. Having more makes it difficult for you to locate appropriate code, difficult for teaching assistants to locate appropriate code, and difficult for us to not take off points from your assignment. We're sadists like that.

- PROJECT HEADER FILE FOR CLASS (SET) PKG   *projpkg*.**h**

  However, you're more than welcome to place multiple class declarations in one header file. This must, of course, be done within reason: for example, it may be appropriate for a class with two small subclasses. If you do this, you should name your file accordingly. Overall, however, your .cxx and .h files should probably match up — this increases the symmetry and overall beauty of your project.

- PROJECT HEADER FILES   *proj*.**h**

  These are declarations that all, or almost all, other files require for proper compilation. These files are for external consumption, so that other programmers can access your work. If you want to have project header files that are not for external consumption, you should name them *proj*_**local.h**. This does not mean you should always use globals — they're icky and should be avoided.

Types, Variables, and Constants

Another aspect of your code that needs to be standardized is the naming of your types, variables and constants. You should be able to tell at first glance if an identifier is a constant or a variable and whether it is a data member or a global, static, or local variable. We have come up with some conventions that let you differentiate easily.

- GENERAL TYPES   EXAMPLE: ***Proj*Boolean, *Proj*MyDataStruct**
  Type names start with the project name. They consist of mixed-case characters using an upper-case character to start a new word.

- CLASSES   EXAMPLE: ***Proj*MyClass**
  Class names are prefixed by the project name. Since they are essentially a programmer-defined type, they follow the same capitalization rules as general types. If you have a class hierarchy, the subclasses should have a common name prefix, as in ***Proj*Super*ClassA** and ***Proj*Super*ClassB**. Also any classes that are used as exceptions should end with the word Error, as in ***Proj*MyError**.

- METHODS   EXAMPLE: **myMemberFunction()**
  Methods start with a lower-case letter. New words in a method name start with a capital letter. Static methods are named in the same way as other methods.

- INSTANCE VARIABLES   EXAMPLES: **my_variable, myvar_**
  Instance variables start with a lower-case letter. New words are separated with the underscore character. One-word instance variables should have an underscore consistently at the beginning or the end. For one-word instance variables, we recommend putting the underscore at the end to help you distinguish them from the debugging symbols that are generated by most C++ compilers. Abbreviations and the use of plurals should be consistent throughout the application.

- CONSTANTS IN A CLASS   EXAMPLE: **MY_CONSTANT**
  Constants appearing in a class are all caps (the mark of a constant). Words are separated by an underscore.

- GLOBAL FUNCTIONS   EXAMPLE: ***PROJ*_myGlobalFunction()**
  A global function is one that is global to the entire project. Again, this follows the normal naming conventions for a function, except it is prefixed by the project name in caps and an underscore. Global functions should generally be avoided.

- GLOBAL VARIABLES   EXAMPLE: ***PROJ*__my_global_var**
  Global variables are those that are global to the entire project (similar to global functions). Therefore, we prefix them with the project name in caps and a DOUBLE underscore. Static class variables should generally be used in place of global variables.

  Special note: We have made the coding standard particularly ugly for global functions and global variables. This is because well-structured code should not have many of these at all.

- GLOBAL CONSTANTS   EXAMPLE: ***PROJ*_CONSTANT_VALUE**
  Global constants are prefixed by the project name in caps and underscore. Like class constants, they appear in all caps and use underscores to delineate the different words.

- FUNCTION LOCALS   EXAMPLE: **mylocalvariable**
  Variables local to specific functions should be entirely in lower-case and should contain no underscores. (If you find this format difficult to read, you may capitalize the first letter of each new word. However, this makes a function-local

variable look like a method name.) It is okay to name your loop counters with variable names such as i, j, k, and foo — please don't name them "loopCounter-One," since this says nothing and hurts your wrists.

Note that enumerated types have two parts. Consider:
>   enum *Proj*Boolean {*PROJ*_TRUE, *PROJ*_FALSE};

The first part (*Proj*Boolean) is a type declaration. On the other hand, *PROJ*_TRUE and *PROJ*_FALSE are constants. Enumerated types can be declared global or inside a class, depending on the context.

If you come across a case in which the naming conventions above do not apply directly, use your judgment to extrapolate from the existing standards, without violating the rules just explained. In the end, it is your job to make sure you and your teaching assistants can understand and follow your code. A gross misjudgment on your part can be tempered by an excellent explanation of why you did it in your README file.

COMMENTING CONVENTIONS

Block Comments

EXAMPLE:
```
/*************************************************************/
/*                                                         */
/*     block comment #1                                    */
/*                                                         */
/*************************************************************/
```

Block comments should be clearly separated from the rest of the code. This is the only style we allow. We have set up your accounts with three key bindings to help reduce the busywork of typing *'s. Note that the key bindings described here follow our block commenting style.

- FILE HEADER   M-p (meta key and "p")
  This creates a header with *name, account number, file, assignment* and *date* categories. All these need to be filled out and a brief description of the file should follow. *Note that these are created automatically upon opening a file for the first time, so you should rarely (if ever) need to use this hot key.*

- FUNCTION HEADER   M-h (meta key and "h")
  This creates a header with *function name, parameters, returns* and *effects* categories. Again, all these should be filled out and a brief description of the function should follow.

- CLASS HEADER   M-c (meta key and "c")
  This creates a header with a *class name* category. Type the name of the class here and follow it up with a detailed description of what the class models.

Note that when you use these key bindings you are put into *emacs* overwrite mode. You should just be able to type in the categories and the brief description without placing any of the comment identifiers (/* ... */) yourself. M-9 toggles you between C++ mode and overwrite mode.

Inline Comments

Contrary to popular opinion, inline comments are *vital* to the readability of your code. Commenting adds information to your code. It should add so much information that when you are working on a complicated routine, you can refer to your comments to figure out what you did just moments before. For this reason, you should **comment as you go**. Blindly writing code leads to headaches later, because you won't remember how it worked and you won't know how to locate the mistakes. Commenting while writing the code often helps you see what's missing or what's misplaced before you try executing your program.

There are three ways to use inline comments. First, you can comment individual lines. When you do this, the comments should appear at the end of the line. Use "// ..." and line them up appropriately. Remember, comments tell more about the code than the code itself: explain *why* you're doing it and *how* you're doing it. The following is an example of bad commenting:

```
counter++;                    // increment the counter
my_storage_object.init();     // init the storage
```

You can also use inline comments before a section of code that does something complicated, strange, or just plain frightening:

```
    // The following lines check to see if a Zonk has landed on a rounded
    // object, and if so, cause the Zonk to roll off it.
gridpiece = game_board -> getGridPiece( xlocation, ylocation );
if ( gridpiece -> getType() == INFOTRON_ZONK ) {
    lowerpiece = game_board -> getGridPiece( xlocation, ylocation + 1 );
    if ( lowerpiece -> isRounded() )
        // Try to roll the object, but don't worry if it actually rolled.
        // (That is, ignore the return value.)
      gridPiece -> roll( xlocation, ylocation );
}
```

You should use properly aligned inline comments for all of your variable declarations. This will help us determine how you should be using them, and will help you determine if you need them or not. (Seriously!)

Finally, inside your class declarations, it would be nice to add small comments before each method definition. As with the inline comments in the code segment presented above, you may wish to indent them for easier reading. For example:

```
class InfotronZonk : public InfotronRounded {
   public:
         // The constructor initializes the piece type and properties.
   InfotronZonk();

         // The destructor deletes subobjects, so be careful!
   ~InfotronZonk();

         // Call when you want the rounded piece to roll off of another piece.
         // Returns INFOTRON_TRUE if it rolled, false otherwise. You must
         // specify where the piece is on the board.
   InfotronBoolean roll( int xlocation, int ylocation );
   };
```

In the final analysis, your comments are primarily for your benefit — so make the most of them!

The Readme File

A "README" file should accompany each of your projects. This is a text file that explains the overall design of your project, including (but not limited to) class hierarchies, class interaction, and interesting algorithms. When presenting your design, you should discuss why you made the design choices you did. A teaching assistant should be able to explain and defend your design by only reading your README (without looking at your code). You should also discuss all known bugs, speculate about their cause, and explain how they could be fixed. Finally, you should include a description of any functionality that goes beyond the required specifications (i.e., all bells and whistles).

White Space

An important way of making your code easy to read is to space it out in a neat and orderly manner. Allow two blank lines between a block comment and the function it belongs to. Allow four to six lines at the end of a function before the next block comment. Separate logical chunks of code within a function with blank lines. Feel free to be liberal about this, but don't get carried away.

Order Does Matter

It is important that, within each file, you keep a consistent ordering of code components. It is up to you to determine the order that suits you, but pick one and stick to it. You should separate your program sections, i.e. includes, forward declarations, class declarations, etc., with block comments.

Within class declarations, certain other rules of order apply. You should usually keep your constructors and destructors together. It is often useful to keep your global, public, accessor, overloaded operators, and helper functions together within their own respective groups. However, the final grouping is up to you, and so long as it is logical and useful, you won't be marked down.

BREAKING UP YOUR CODE

Source and Header Files

Header Files (.h files) should contain class definitions, other type definitions (such as enums), constants, and function prototypes that are not private to the accompanying .cxx file. **Code Files (.cxx files)** should contain constants and function prototypes that *are* private to your implementation. Most function definitions (actual code) should be in your .cxx file. Inline functions should be in your .h files. We set up your accounts with a couple of spiffy-keen tricks to save you time. When you open a new file ending in .h or .cxx with Ctrl-x Ctrl-f, *emacs* automatically places a file header at the top of the file. If the file ends with a .h, *emacs* also inserts the necessary directives (see below). If the file ends with a .cxx, *emacs* inserts the #include directive (using the file's name, replacing the .cxx with a .h).

EXAMPLE:

- Constants representing error codes returned by your public functions to an outside caller should be in the .h file, since they are needed by someone using your package.
- Constants specifying fudge factors or widths of your widgets don't need to be public, and thus should be in your .cxx file.

Including a Header File Multiple Times

If you include the same header file in more than one place, the compiler will complain about multiple definitions. The `#ifndef` directive prevents this from happening. It tells the preprocessor to define a label if it has not been defined yet (this happens when the header file is first encountered by the compiler). The next time the preprocessor sees the header file (i.e., when the file is included elsewhere), the header label is already defined and the code up to the `#endif` directive is not declared again. You can see an example of this in the header file at the end of this document.

All header files must have the `#ifndef` construct, since they may be included more than once at some point. This happens especially frequently and unbeknownst to the user when dealing with C++ templates.

When naming the label, we take the file name and suffix it with "_USED." So in the example at the end, the label for a file named astspaceship.H is AST_SPACESHIP_USED.

Remember to use the `#endif` directive at the end of your header files. If you don't, you'll be a very unhappy person indeed.

Small Generic Functions

Any function that grows to be more than 50 lines long should probably be broken up into separate functions. Short functions are easier to understand and often need less commenting. If similar chunks of code appear multiple times in your code, you should probably write a function to handle that operation.

GLOSSARY

instance member — a variable of a class.

class code file — a .cxx file that contains the actual code for a class or set of classes whose interface is defined in a corresponding .h file.

class header file — a .h file that contains the declaration for a class or set of classes.

project header file — a .h file that contains public declarations needed by many files in the project.

project local header file — a .h file that contains private declarations needed by many files in the project.

external globals — globals declared in a different file.

global function — a function that does not belong to any class and may be accessed from other files.

type names — names of classes, typedefs, enums (not their constants, but their type, e.g. enum Boolean {FALSE, TRUE} — Boolean is the type, TRUE/FALSE are not).

file name — always means "insert a descriptive name here" without the project prefix.

CLOSING THOUGHTS

Once you get used to these standards, they will help you maintain your sanity when your programs get longer and when you must read other people's code. Therefore we strongly urge you to start using them today! **The coding standards presented here will help you write solid, cohesive, working code with a minimum of fuss; heed them well.**

Another important thought: sometimes you'll look at code that doesn't work and want desperately to fix it up. You'll know the problem and you'll see a possible hack to fix it. Resist the impulse. Analyze the problem from a detached and dispassionate point of view — that is, try to forget about the time you've spent writing the code. Most software projects require substantial rewrites before they ever hit the streets; it may at some point be necessary to rewrite a method, a class, a class hierarchy, or even an entire project in order to get the job done. Code is not sacred. It is better to rewrite code than to have the final product thrown away. **Know when your code is salvage-**

able, and remember that starting over sometimes ends up saving the entire project.

SAMPLE CODE

Header File Example

```
/**********************************************************************/
/*                                                                  */
/*      NAME: Wombat Man                                            */
/*      ACCT: cs032000                                              */
/*      FILE: astspaceship.H                                        */
/*      ASGN: #0 (asteroids game)                                   */
/*      DATE: 6/26/71                                               */
/*                                                                  */
/*      This is a sample header file.  The purpose of the code shown */
/*      here is to present the conventions in the context of a header */
/*      file.  This header file is not a complete file              */
/*                                                                  */
/**********************************************************************/


#infdef AST_SPACESHIP_USED
#define AST_SPACESHIP_USED


/**********************************************************************/
/*                                                                  */
/*      Type Declarations and Global Constants                      */
/*                                                                  */
/**********************************************************************/

enum AstShipActions {
   AST_TURN_LEFT,
   AST_TURN_RIGHT,
   AST_THRUST,
   AST_SHOOT
};




/**********************************************************************/
/*                                                                  */
/*      CLASS NAME: AstSpaceship                                    */
/*                                                                  */
/*      This class models the spaceship...                          */
/*                                                                  */
/**********************************************************************/

class AstSpaceship {                       // player flies this
```

```
public:
        // create the ship and its missiles
    AstSpaceship();

        // Destroy all captured ships
    ~AstSpaceship();

        // Changes the direction and informs others of the direction change
    void setDirection(AstShipDirection);

private:
        // Navigate the ship
    void moveShip();

private:
    AstShipActions action_;                 // what the ship will do this turn
    int direction_;                         // absolute direction ship is facing
}



#endif AST_SPACESHIP_USED

/* end of astspaceship.H */
```

Code File Example

```
/**************************************************************************/
/*                                                                        */
/*      NAME: Wombat Man                                                  */
/*      ACCT: cs032000                                                    */
/*      FILE: astspaceshp.cxx                                             */
/*      ASGN: #0 (asteroids game)                                         */
/*      DATE: 6/26/71                                                     */
/*                                                                        */
/**************************************************************************/

#include "astspaceship.h"

/**************************************************************************/
/*                                                                        */
/*      Local storage                                                     */
/*                                                                        */
/**************************************************************************/


static   int     AST__num_ships;                 // number of players in game



/**************************************************************************/
/*                                                                        */
```

```
/*      Function Name: AST_printStart                                */
/*      Effects: prints the welcome message for the game             */
/*                                                                   */
/*      This is a global function...                                 */
/*                                                                   */
/*********************************************************************/


void
AST_printStart()
{
   cerr << "Welcome to Asteroids...";          // This game is fun.
}




/*********************************************************************/
/*                                                                   */
/*      Function Name: AstSpaceship::moveShip                        */
/*      Effects: the specified action is carried out                 */
/*                                                                   */
/*      This is the function that moves the ship based on the        */
/*      action_ variable setting.  If it is set to AST_TURN_LEFT     */
/*      then the direction is affected by ...                        */
/*                                                                   */
/*********************************************************************/

void
AstSpaceship::moveShip()
{
   int temp;                                    // for new velocity

   if (action_ == AST_TURN_LEFT)
      direction_--;                             // turn left 90 degrees
}



/* End of astspaceship.cxx */
```

Appendix B
The Knight's-Tour Program

KNIGHT_LOCAL.H

```
/****************************************************************************/
/*                                                                        */
/*                knight_local.H                                          */
/*                                                                        */
/*      Local definitions for the knight's-tour problem                   */
/*                                                                        */
/*      Author: Steven P. Reiss, Brown University                         */
/*                                                                        */
/****************************************************************************/


#ifndef KNIGHT_LOCAL_USED
#define KNIGHT_LOCAL_USED


#include <iostream.h>
#include <iomanip.h>
#include <stdlib.h>



/****************************************************************************/
/*                                                                        */
/*      Local Type Definitions                                            */
/*                                                                        */
/****************************************************************************/


typedef int             Integer;
typedef char            Boolean;
typedef const char *    ConstText;
typedef char *          Text;
typedef char            Character;
typedef double          Float;



/****************************************************************************/
/*                                                                        */
/*      Parameters                                                        */
/*                                                                        */
/****************************************************************************/


const   Integer         DEFAULT_BOARD_SIZE = 8; // board size if not specified
const   Integer         MAX_MOVES = 8;          // max # moves from any square

const   Boolean         TRUE = 1;
const   Boolean         FALSE = 0;
```

```
/**************************************************************************/
/*                                                                      */
/*       Class Type Definitions                                         */
/*                                                                      */
/**************************************************************************/


typedef class KnightMainInfo *      KnightMain;      // Main pgm, I/O, controller
typedef class KnightBoardInfo *     KnightBoard;     // Holds squares, init tour
typedef class KnightSquareInfo *    KnightSquare;    // Single square, lcl search
typedef class KnightHeuristicInfo * KnightHeuristic; // Order moves; do heuristics
typedef class KnightSolutionInfo *  KnightSolution;  // Contain the solution



/**************************************************************************/
/*                                                                      */
/*       KnightMainInfo -- main program and controlling class           */
/*                                                                      */
/**************************************************************************/


class KnightMainInfo {

private:
   KnightBoard the_board;                            // board to compute tour over
   Integer board_size;                               // size of the board

public:
   KnightMainInfo();
   ~KnightMainInfo();

   void process(Integer argc,ConstText * argv);         // main loop

private:
   Integer getBoardSize(Integer argc,ConstText * argv); // input the board size

   void outputTour(const KnightSolution) const;         // output the tour
};



/**************************************************************************/
/*                                                                      */
/*       KnightBoardInfo -- container for the actual board              */
/*                                                                      */
/**************************************************************************/


class KnightBoardInfo {

private:
   Integer board_size;                                   // size of the board
```

```
   KnightSquare * the_squares;                          // sq[bd_size][bd_size]

public:
   KnightBoardInfo(Integer size);                       // setup the board squares
   ~KnightBoardInfo();

   KnightSquare findSquare(Integer row,Integer col); // find a given square

   KnightSolution findTour();                           // find complete tour
};




/**************************************************************************/
/*                                                                        */
/*      KnightSquareInfo -- keep track of moves and tour for a single square  */
/*                                                                        */
/**************************************************************************/


class KnightSquareInfo {

private:
   Integer row_number;                              // row index
   Integer column_number;                           // column index
   Integer num_moves;                               // number of legal moves
   KnightSquare legal_moves[MAX_MOVES];             // available moves

public:
   KnightSquareInfo();
   ~KnightSquareInfo();

   void setup(KnightBoard,Integer row,Integer col);    // find initial moves

   Integer numMoves() const;                        // count for heuristics

   Boolean findRestOfTour(KnightSolution);          // local path search
   void markUsed(KnightSquare);                     // remove legal move
   void markUnused(KnightSquare);                   // restore legal move
};




/**************************************************************************/
/*                                                                        */
/*      KnightHeuristicInfo -- order the moves to improve search time     */
/*                                                                        */
/**************************************************************************/


class KnightHeuristicInfo {

private:
   Integer num_moves;                                   // number of moves to consider
```

```cpp
      KnightSquare valid_squares[MAX_MOVES];       // squares for those moves
      Integer move_count[MAX_MOVES];               // move count for those squares
public:
      KnightHeuristicInfo(Integer movect,KnightSquare * squares);
      ~KnightHeuristicInfo();

      KnightSquare nextMove();                      // return next square or NULL
};



/****************************************************************************/
/*                                                                          */
/*      KnightSolutionInfo -- hold the resultant tour                       */
/*                                                                          */
/****************************************************************************/


class KnightSolutionInfo {

private:
      Integer board_size;                          // size of board for solution
      Integer num_moves;                           // size of current solution
      Integer * tour_index;                        // index[board_size][board_size]
public:
      KnightSolutionInfo(Integer bdsize);
      ~KnightSolutionInfo();

      void addMove(Integer row,Integer col);       // add next square to path
      void removeMove(Integer row,Integer col);    // remove last square from path

      Integer findIndex(Integer r,Integer c) const;// find index for given square
      Boolean isValid() const;                     // check if tour is complete
};


#endif

/* end of knight_local.H */
```

KNIGHT.CXX

```
/****************************************************************************/
/*                                                                        */
/*              knight.cxx                                                 */
/*                                                                        */
/*      Main program for knight's-tour problem                            */
/*                                                                        */
/****************************************************************************/


#include "knight_local.H"



/****************************************************************************/
/*                                                                        */
/*      main -- main entry for knight's tour                              */
/*                                                                        */
/****************************************************************************/


main(int argc,const char ** argv)
{
    KnightMain main = new KnightMainInfo;

    main->process(argc,argv);

    delete main;

    return 0;
}



/* end of knight.cxx */
```

KNIGHTMAIN.CXX

```cpp
/*************************************************************************/
/*                                                                     */
/*            knightmain.cxx                                           */
/*                                                                     */
/*      Implementation of the class KnightMainInfo                     */
/*                                                                     */
/*************************************************************************/

#include "knight_local.H"


/*************************************************************************/
/*                                                                     */
/*      KnightMainInfo constructors/destructors                        */
/*                                                                     */
/*************************************************************************/

KnightMainInfo::KnightMainInfo()
{
   the_board = NULL;
   board_size = DEFAULT_BOARD_SIZE;
}


KnightMainInfo::~KnightMainInfo()
{
   delete the_board;
}


/*************************************************************************/
/*                                                                     */
/*      KnightMainInfo::process -- main loop for knight's-tour problem  */
/*                                                                     */
/*************************************************************************/

void
KnightMainInfo::process(Integer argc,ConstText * argv)
{
   KnightSolution sol;

   board_size = getBoardSize(argc,argv);
   if (board_size <= 0) return;

   the_board = new KnightBoardInfo(board_size);

   if ((board_size & 1) != 0 || board_size <= 4) sol = NULL;
   else sol = the_board->findTour();

   outputTour(sol);
```

```
      if (sol != NULL) delete sol;
   }


/*******************************************************************************/
/*                                                                           */
/*        KnightMainInfo input methods                                       */
/*                                                                           */
/*******************************************************************************/

Integer
KnightMainInfo::getBoardSize(Integer argc,ConstText * argv)
{
   if (argc < 2) return DEFAULT_BOARD_SIZE;

   Integer sz = atoi(argv[1]);
   if (sz <= 0) return DEFAULT_BOARD_SIZE;

   return sz;
}



/*******************************************************************************/
/*                                                                           */
/*        KnightMainInfo output methods                                      */
/*                                                                           */
/*******************************************************************************/

void
KnightMainInfo::outputTour(const KnightSolution tour) const
{
   Integer r,c,i;

   if (tour == NULL || !tour->isValid()) {
      cout << "No valid tour found for " << board_size << " x " <<
         board_size << " board." << endl;
      return;
    }

   for (r = 0; r < board_size; ++r) {
      for (c = 0; c < board_size; ++c) {
         i = tour->findIndex(r,c);
         cout << setw(4) << i;
       }
      cout << endl;
    }
}


/* end of knightmain.cxx */
```

KNIGHTBOARD.CXX

```
/*****************************************************************************/
/*                                                                         */
/*              knightboard.cxx                                            */
/*                                                                         */
/*       Implementation of class KnightBoardInfo                           */
/*                                                                         */
/*****************************************************************************/


#include "knight_local.H"


/*****************************************************************************/
/*                                                                         */
/*       KnightBoardInfo constructors/destructors                          */
/*                                                                         */
/*****************************************************************************/


KnightBoardInfo::KnightBoardInfo(Integer size)
{
   Integer i,r,c;

   board_size = size;
   the_squares = new KnightSquare[size * size];

   for (i = 0; i < size*size; ++i) the_squares[i] = new KnightSquareInfo;

   for (r = 0; r < board_size; ++r) {
      for (c = 0; c < board_size; ++c) {
         findSquare(r,c)->setup(this,r,c);
       }
    }
}


KnightBoardInfo::~KnightBoardInfo()
{
   Integer i;

   for (i = 0; i < board_size * board_size; ++i) {
      if (the_squares[i] != NULL) delete the_squares[i];
    }

   delete [] the_squares;
}



/*****************************************************************************/
/*                                                                         */
```

```
/*      KnightBoardInfo methods to find a square by row and column    */
/*                                                                    */
/**********************************************************************/


KnightSquare
KnightBoardInfo::findSquare(Integer row,Integer col)
{
   if (row < 0 || row >= board_size) return NULL;
   if (col < 0 || col >= board_size) return NULL;

   return the_squares[row*board_size + col];
}




/**********************************************************************/
/*                                                                    */
/*      KnightBoardInfo methods to find a complete tour               */
/*                                                                    */
/**********************************************************************/


KnightSolution
KnightBoardInfo::findTour()
{
   KnightSolution sol = new KnightSolutionInfo(board_size);
   KnightSquare start = findSquare(1,2);
   KnightSquare sq0 = findSquare(0,0);

   start->markUsed(sq0);
   sq0->markUsed(start);

   start->findRestOfTour(sol);

   return sol;
}



/* end of knightboard.cxx */
```

KNIGHTSQUARE.CXX

```
/**************************************************************************/
/*                                                                      */
/*                knightsquare.cxx                                      */
/*                                                                      */
/*        Implementation of class KnightSquareInfo                      */
/*                                                                      */
/**************************************************************************/


#include "knight_local.H"


/**************************************************************************/
/*                                                                      */
/*        KnightSquareInfo constructors/destructors                     */
/*                                                                      */
/**************************************************************************/


KnightSquareInfo::KnightSquareInfo()
{
    row_number = -1;
    column_number = -1;
    num_moves = 0;
}



KnightSquareInfo::~KnightSquareInfo()
{ }



/**************************************************************************/
/*                                                                      */
/*        KnightSquareInfo::setup -- setup legal moves for a square     */
/*                                                                      */
/**************************************************************************/


void
KnightSquareInfo::setup(KnightBoard b,Integer r,Integer c)
{
    Integer i,j,k;
    KnightSquare sq;

    row_number = r;
    column_number = c;

    for (i = -2; i <= 2; ++i) {                    // generate all move combinations
        if (i == 0) continue;
```

```
        for (j = -1; j <= 1; j += 2) {
            k = (3 - abs(i)) * j;                    // in i and k
            sq = b->findSquare(r+i,c+k);
            if (sq != NULL) legal_moves[num_moves++] = sq;
        }
    }
}



/*****************************************************************************/
/*                                                                           */
/*      KnightSquareInfo::numMoves -- return current number of moves         */
/*                                                                           */
/*****************************************************************************/


Integer
KnightSquareInfo::numMoves() const                        { return num_moves; }


/*****************************************************************************/
/*                                                                           */
/*      KnightSquareInfo::findRestOfTour -- find path starting at this node  */
/*                                                                           */
/*****************************************************************************/


Boolean
KnightSquareInfo::findRestOfTour(KnightSolution sol)
{
    KnightSquare sq;
    KnightHeuristic heur;
    Integer i;

    sol->addMove(row_number,column_number);       // add this square to solution
    if (sol->isValid()) return TRUE;              // check if done

    for (i = 0; i < num_moves; ++i)               // remove moves to this square
        legal_moves[i]->markUsed(this);

    heur = new KnightHeuristicInfo(num_moves,legal_moves);
    while ((sq = heur->nextMove()) != NULL) {     // try each move in turn
        if (sq->findRestOfTour(sol)) return TRUE;
    }
    delete heur;

    for (i = 0; i < num_moves; ++i)               // restore moves to this square
        legal_moves[i]->markUnused(this);

    sol->removeMove(row_number,column_number);    // restore the board and fail

    return FALSE;
}
```

```
/*****************************************************************************/
/*                                                                         */
/*        KnightSquareInfo move marking methods                            */
/*                                                                         */
/*****************************************************************************/


void
KnightSquareInfo::markUsed(KnightSquare sq)
{
    Integer i,j;

    j = 0;
    for (i = 0; i < num_moves; ++i) {
        if (legal_moves[i] == sq) ++j;
        else if (j > 0) legal_moves[i-j] = legal_moves[i];
     }
    num_moves -= j;
}


void
KnightSquareInfo::markUnused(KnightSquare sq)
{
    legal_moves[num_moves++] = sq;
}



/* end of knightsquare.cxx */
```

KNIGHTHEURISTIC.CXX

```
/****************************************************************************/
/*                                                                        */
/*              knightheuristic.cxx                                       */
/*                                                                        */
/*        Implementation of class KnightHeuristicInfo                     */
/*                                                                        */
/****************************************************************************/


#include "knight_local.H"



/****************************************************************************/
/*                                                                        */
/*        KnightHeuristicInfo constructors/destructors                    */
/*                                                                        */
/****************************************************************************/


KnightHeuristicInfo::KnightHeuristicInfo(Integer ct,KnightSquare * sqs)
{
    Integer i;
    Integer numone = 0;
    Integer numzero = 0;

    num_moves = ct;
    for (i = 0; i < ct; ++i) {
      valid_squares[i] = sqs[i];
      move_count[i] = sqs[i]->numMoves();
      if (move_count[i] == 1) ++numone;
      if (move_count[i] == 0) ++numzero;
     }

    if (numzero > 1 || (numzero == 1 && ct > 1)) // check for unreachable squares
       num_moves = 0;
    else if (numone > 2) num_moves = 0;          // check  unreachable sequences
    else if (numone > 0) {                       // if single sequence, use only it
      for (i = 0; i < ct; ++i) {
         if (move_count[i] > 1) move_count[i] = MAX_MOVES+1;
       }
     }
}


KnightHeuristicInfo::~KnightHeuristicInfo()
{ }



/****************************************************************************/
```

```
/*                                                                    */
/*      KnightHeuristicInfo::nextMove -- return best move not yet tried   */
/*                                                                    */
/**********************************************************************/


KnightSquare
KnightHeuristicInfo::nextMove()
{
    Integer i,mv,ct;

    mv = -1;
    ct = MAX_MOVES+1;
    for (i = 0; i < num_moves; ++i) {
       if (move_count[i] < ct) {
          mv = i;
          ct = move_count[i];
       }
     }
    if (mv < 0) return NULL;

    move_count[mv] = MAX_MOVES+1;

    return valid_squares[mv];
}



/* end of knightheuristic.cxx */
```

KNIGHTSOLUTION.CXX

```
/****************************************************************************/
/*                                                                        */
/*              knightsolution.cxx                                        */
/*                                                                        */
/*        Implementation of class KnightSolutionInfo                      */
/*                                                                        */
/****************************************************************************/


#include "knight_local.H"


/****************************************************************************/
/*                                                                        */
/*        KnightSolutionInfo constructors/destructors                     */
/*                                                                        */
/****************************************************************************/


KnightSolutionInfo::KnightSolutionInfo(Integer sz)
{
   Integer i;

   board_size = sz;
   num_moves = 0;
   tour_index = new Integer[board_size * board_size];

   for (i = 0; i < board_size*board_size; ++i) tour_index[i] = -1;
}


KnightSolutionInfo::~KnightSolutionInfo()
{
   delete [] tour_index;
}




/****************************************************************************/
/*                                                                        */
/*        KnightSolutionInfo methods to add and remove moves from a tour  */
/*                                                                        */
/****************************************************************************/


void
KnightSolutionInfo::addMove(Integer r,Integer c)
{
   tour_index[r*board_size + c] = num_moves++;
}
```

```
void
KnightSolutionInfo::removeMove(Integer r,Integer c)
{
    tour_index[r*board_size + c] = -1;
    --num_moves;
}




/***************************************************************************/
/*                                                                       */
/*      KnightSolutionInfo methods for returning the solution            */
/*                                                                       */
/***************************************************************************/


Integer
KnightSolutionInfo::findIndex(Integer r,Integer c) const
{
    return tour_index[r*board_size + c];
}


Boolean
KnightSolutionInfo::isValid() const
{
    return num_moves == board_size * board_size;
}



/* end of knightsolution.cxx */
```

Appendix C
The Dependency Analyzer

DEPEND_LOCAL.H

```
/************************************************************************/
/*                                                                    */
/*               depend_local.H                                       */
/*                                                                    */
/*       Local class definitions for dependency analyzer              */
/*                                                                    */
/************************************************************************/


#ifndef DEPEND_LOCAL_ALREADY_DEFINED
#define DEPEND_LOCAL_ALREADY_DEFINED

#include <stdlib.h>
#include <ctype.h>
#include <iostream.h>

#include <bstring.h>
#include <list.h>
#include <map.h>
#include <vector.h>
#include <function.h>




/************************************************************************/
/*                                                                    */
/*       Parameter Definitions                                        */
/*                                                                    */
/************************************************************************/


const    int             MAX_LINE_LENGTH = 2048;




/************************************************************************/
/*                                                                    */
/*       Local Type Definitions                                       */
/*                                                                    */
/************************************************************************/


typedef const char *     ConstText;
typedef char             Character;
typedef int              Integer;
typedef string           String;
typedef bool             Boolean;




/************************************************************************/
```

```
/*                                                                          */
/*        Forward Definitions                                               */
/*                                                                          */
/**************************************************************************/


typedef class DependNodeInfo *                      DependNode;
typedef class DependNodeSetInfo *                   DependNodeSet;

typedef list<DependNode>                            DependNodeList;
typedef DependNodeList::iterator                    DependNodeListIter;

typedef map<String,DependNode,less<String> >        DependNodeTable;
typedef DependNodeTable::iterator                   DependNodeTableIter;




/**************************************************************************/
/*                                                                          */
/*        Class DependNodeVector -- dynamic vector of DependNodes            */
/*                                                                          */
/**************************************************************************/


typedef vector<DependNode>                          DependNodeVectorUnsafe;


class DependNodeVector : public DependNodeVectorUnsafe {
public:
   DependNodeVector()                               { }
   ~DependNodeVector()                              { }

   DependNode operator[](int v)
      { if (v < 0 || v >= size()) return NULL;
        else return DependNodeVectorUnsafe::operator[](v);
      }
   const DependNode operator[](int v) const
      { if (v < 0 || v >= size()) return NULL;
        else return DependNodeVectorUnsafe::operator[](v);
      }
};


typedef DependNodeVector::iterator                  DependNodeVectorIter;




/**************************************************************************/
/*                                                                          */
/*        Class DependNodeInfo -- node for a dependency                      */
/*                                                                          */
/**************************************************************************/
```

```
class DependNodeInfo {

private:
    String node_name;
    Integer num_link;
    DependNodeVector depend_on;

public:
    DependNodeInfo(String);
    ~DependNodeInfo();

    ConstText name() const;
    Integer numLink() const;

    void addLink(DependNode);
    Integer updateLinkCount(Integer by);

    DependNodeVectorIter links();
    DependNodeVectorIter linksEnd();
};


/******************************************************************************/
/*                                                                            */
/*      Class DependNodeSetInfo -- set of all nodes                           */
/*                                                                            */
/******************************************************************************/


class DependNodeSetInfo {

private:
    DependNodeTable node_table;

public:
    DependNodeSetInfo();
    ~DependNodeSetInfo();

    void readNodes(istream&);

    void topSort(ostream&);

private:
    DependNode findNode(String);
};


#endif

/* end of depend_local.H */
```

DEPENDMAIN.CXX

```
/*********************************************************************/
/*                                                                 */
/*              dependmain.cxx                                      */
/*                                                                 */
/*      Main program for dependency analyzer                       */
/*                                                                 */
/*********************************************************************/


#include "depend_local.H"

#include <fstream.h>


/*********************************************************************/
/*                                                                 */
/*      main -- main program                                       */
/*                                                                 */
/*********************************************************************/


main(int argc,const char ** argv)
{
   ConstText file = NULL;
   Integer i;

   for (i = 1; i < argc; ++i) {
      if (argv[i][0] == '-') {
         cerr << "DEPEND: Invalid option '" << argv[i] << "'" << endl;
         exit(1);
       }
      else if (file == NULL) {
         file = argv[i];
       }
      else {
         cerr << "DEPEND: Only one file can be specified" << endl;
         exit(2);
       }
    }

   DependNodeSet dns = new DependNodeSetInfo;

   if (file == NULL) dns->readNodes(cin);
   else {
      ifstream ifs(file);

      if (!ifs) {
         cerr << "DEPEND: Can't open input file '" << file << "'" << endl;
         exit(3);
       }
```

```
        dns->readNodes(ifs);
    }

    dns->topSort(cout);

    delete dns;

    return 0;
}




/* end of dependmain.cxx */
```

DEPENDNODE.CXX

```
/*****************************************************************************/
/*                                                                         */
/*                dependnode.cxx                                           */
/*                                                                         */
/*        Methods for dependency nodes                                     */
/*                                                                         */
/*****************************************************************************/


#include "depend_local.H"



/*****************************************************************************/
/*                                                                         */
/*        DependNodeInfo constructors/destructors                          */
/*                                                                         */
/*****************************************************************************/


DependNodeInfo::DependNodeInfo(String nm)
{
   node_name = nm;
   num_link = 0;
}



DependNodeInfo::~DependNodeInfo()                              { }



/*****************************************************************************/
/*                                                                         */
/*        DependNodeInfo access methods                                    */
/*                                                                         */
/*****************************************************************************/


ConstText
DependNodeInfo::name() const              { return node_name.data(); }


Integer
DependNodeInfo::numLink() const           { return num_link; }



/*****************************************************************************/
```

```
/*                                                                              */
/*          DependNodeInfo link management methods                              */
/*                                                                              */
/******************************************************************************/


void
DependNodeInfo::addLink(DependNode dn)
{
    depend_on.push_back(dn);
    dn->updateLinkCount(1);
}


Integer
DependNodeInfo::updateLinkCount(Integer by)
{
    num_link += by;
    return num_link;
}


DependNodeVectorIter
DependNodeInfo::links()                    { return depend_on.begin(); }


DependNodeVectorIter
DependNodeInfo::linksEnd()                 { return depend_on.end(); }



/* end of dependnode.cxx */
```

DEPENDNODESET.CXX

```
/*********************************************************************/
/*                                                                 */
/*              dependnodeset.C                                    */
/*                                                                 */
/*       Implementation of node sets                              */
/*                                                                 */
/*********************************************************************/


#include "depend_local.H"

#include <strstream.h>


/*********************************************************************/
/*                                                                 */
/*       DependNodeSetInfo constructors/destructors               */
/*                                                                 */
/*********************************************************************/


DependNodeSetInfo::DependNodeSetInfo()                          { }


DependNodeSetInfo::~DependNodeSetInfo()
{
   DependNodeTableIter titer;
   DependNode dn;

   for (titer = node_table.begin(); titer != node_table.end(); ++titer) {
      dn = (*titer).second;
      delete dn;
    }
}




/*********************************************************************/
/*                                                                 */
/*       DependNodeSetInfo file input methods                     */
/*                                                                 */
/*********************************************************************/


void
DependNodeSetInfo::readNodes(istream& inf)
{
   Character lbuf[MAX_LINE_LENGTH];
   String from,to;
   DependNode f,t;
```

```
        while (inf) {
            inf.getline(lbuf,MAX_LINE_LENGTH);
            if (inf.eof()) break;
            if (lbuf[0] == 0 || lbuf[0] == '#') continue;

            istrstream ist(lbuf,strlen(lbuf));
            ist >> from >> to;
            // if (ist.fail()) continue;           // string::<< sets this at eos
            findNode(from)->addLink(findNode(to));
        }
}




/*****************************************************************************/
/*                                                                         */
/*      DependNodeSetInfo hash table maintenance methods                   */
/*                                                                         */
/*****************************************************************************/


DependNode
DependNodeSetInfo::findNode(String nm)
{
    DependNode dn = node_table[nm];

    if (dn == NULL) {
        dn = new DependNodeInfo(nm);
        node_table[nm] = dn;
    }

    return dn;
}




/*****************************************************************************/
/*                                                                         */
/*      DependNodeSetInfo topological sort methods                         */
/*                                                                         */
/*****************************************************************************/


void
DependNodeSetInfo::topSort(ostream& ost)
{
    DependNodeList workqueue;
    DependNodeTableIter tbliter;
    DependNode dn,ldn;

    ost << "\nThe dependency order is:" << endl;

    for (tbliter = node_table.begin(); tbliter != node_table.end(); ++tbliter) {
        dn = (*tbliter).second;
```

```
            if (dn->numLink() == 0) workqueue.push_back(dn);
        }

    while (!workqueue.empty()) {
        dn = workqueue.front();
        workqueue.pop_front();
        ost << "\t" << dn->name() << endl;

        DependNodeVectorIter liter;
        DependNode ldn;

        for (liter = dn->links(); liter != dn->linksEnd(); liter++) {
            ldn = *liter;
            if (ldn->updateLinkCount(-1) == 0) workqueue.push_back(ldn);
        }
    }
}


/* end of dependnodeset.C */
```

Index